Community Economic Development
Building for
Social Change

Community Economic Development
Building for
Social Change

Edited by Eric Shragge
and Michael Toye

Cape Breton University Press
Sydney, Nova Scotia CANADA

NOVA SCOTIA
Tourism, Culture and Heritage

Cape Breton University Press recognizes the support of the Province of Nova Scotia through the Department of Tourism, Culture and Heritage. We are pleased to work in partnership with the Culture Division to develop and promote our cultural resources for all Nova Scotians.

Cover Design: Mike R. Hunter, Sydney Mines, NS
Layout: Gail Jones, Sydney, NS

Library and Archives Canada Cataloguing in Publication

Community economic development : building for social change / edited

by Eric Shragge and Michael Toye.

Includes bibliographical references and index.

ISBN 1-897009-07-0

1. Community development. I. Shragge, Eric, 1948-

II. Toye, Michael, 1971-

HC79.E44C625 2006   307.1'4   C2006-900021-2

Cape Breton University Press
PO Box 5300
Sydney, Nova Scotia B1P 6L2
Canada

Community Economic Development: Building for Social Change

Edited by Eric Shragge and Michael Toye

Contents

Eric Shragge and Michael Toye

Introduction: CED and Social Change

Community Economic Development (CED) emerged across Canada in the 1980s as a response to changes in the economy and role of government. Communities, particularly those dependent on large-scale industrial and primary production, had seen jobs vanish. Big government programs that aimed to support regional economic development had failed to generate employment and growth, particularly in rural and smaller communities. Unemployment and poverty were the consequences of these changes. Local organizations and coalitions searched for solutions to these difficult and at times desperate situations. Innovations and new practices were put in place based on the principle that small, local, decentralized approaches were both possible and necessary in the new context. Further, this new localism created possibilities for participatory democracy and citizen control of development. New organizations promoted the CED experience, looking for government recognition and support. Communities were ahead of governments in the development of this approach and, gradually, governments offered programs to support these initiatives. CED processes and organizations grew and expanded from coast to coast to coast. Along with them, a literature emerged that documented the numerous success stories, but much of it was either celebratory or descriptive; there was little in the way of critical discussion, analysis and debate. As we will argue, such an examination is now more important than ever. Without this critical examination and reflection, CED practice may become captured by the policies of the different levels of government looking for a place to shift programs for economic and social development that they used to provide. In doing so they will pull CED away from a vision of social change to one that is far more limited and constrained by state policy. CED organizations require autonomy and vision in order to push the agenda for social justice.

In 2004, Paul Martin responded to years of lobbying by the Chantier de l'économie sociale, a Quebec network of organizations involved in the social economy, and the Canadian CED Network (CCEDNet) and accorded both official recognition and financial support for social economy research and practice. At the 2004 CCEDNet conference in Trois-Rivières, opening night speeches by Quebec's Minister of Economic and Regional Development and Research and the Federal Minister of Industry announced support for the social economy. For the federal government, Lucienne Robillard stated that the $100 million promised in the recent government budget was a down payment for future developments in the social economy, as part of a new partnership with Ottawa. "We need to be collaborative," she emphasized. "We need joint ownership of this initiative. If this simply becomes an Ottawa-driven exercise it won't work."

In her speech, Eleni Bakopanos, Parliamentary Secretary to the Minister of Human Resources and Skills Development with special emphasis on Social Economy (who now reports to the Minister of Social Development) described businesses in the social economy as being in many ways just like any for-profit business: well-managed and subject to the discipline of the market place. She called on citizens to solve problems in their communities through innovative, community-owned social economy enterprises. She drew parallels between the social economy and the private sector and argued for "rigorous accountability" for its use of public resources.

So CED organizations, as developers of the social economy, are now government partners—part of the mainstream. While this can be seen as a victory for the CED/social economy movement, it also presents a new set of challenges and dangers. What is being won? Is it really more than just an extension of neoliberal ideas and agenda? The support by the federal government for the social economy may indeed create opportunities for local CED organizations to foster democratic and innovative practices as alternatives to mainstream capitalist development; however, leadership at both the local and national levels need be aware and cautious of the context within which this funding has been created and the related assumptions underpinning it. Having made major gains in practice and having built local capacities through innovation, CED now stands at an important crossroads. The question now is where CED as a practice and a movement will go from here. Will government recognition and support move it away from its vision of an alternative to mainstream values of economic and social development? Will it be able to sustain its democratic practices? CED practitioners have reached a point that requires critical reflection and analysis in order to move in a progressive direction that offers an alternative to the poverty and inequality produced by capitalist development. This book contributes to meeting this challenge. In this introduction, we examine the context of contemporary CED practice and the challenges it faces and then briefly present the content of the book.

Context

The context of CED practice has been shaped by a combination of globalization—the major force behind economic reorganization—and neoliberalism, the guiding ideology for social and economic policy formulation. Let's start with the question,

What is globalization? There is a huge literature on the subject and it's not for us to review it here; suffice to use it to draw on some basic concepts. "Globalization" has been used widely to describe profound changes in economic, political and social life. Atasoy provides a good starting point, arguing that globalization is nothing particularly new and grows out of colonization and imperialism.[1] It is about the underlying dynamics of capitalist economies to expand and conquer new markets. In acknowledging the continuities, however, one must note that important changes have taken place. Watkins supports the notion that globalization is the latest stage of capitalism and argues that there are multiple dimensions to it.[2] He includes economic or corporate globalization, which includes freer trade, unlimited mobility for capital and the "unceasing march of commodification and privatization of public space."[3] Technological globalization talks to the so-called wired world and the related restructuring of production, which include major changes in communication and contribute to the cultural globalization that is Americanization. Ideological globalization, the message of neoliberalism as a universal gospel, is supported by political globalization through organizations like the International Monetary Fund and the World Trade Organization that impose national priorities and policy directions, particularly on developing nations. Ultimately, these changes imply an increase of the power of corporations and the market to dominate social and economic development.

This is not to say that globalization is necessarily an imperial and exploitative process, but rather that the dominant form of globalization in the world today is neoliberal globalization. Globalization from below, social movements promoting fair trade and solidarity-based economies, are growing, but have yet to significantly shift mainstream discourse and action. Neoliberalism remains the cornerstone of globalization in national and provincial social and economic policies. Neoliberal ideology implies that markets should be open and, as far as possible, "…liberated from all forms of state interference, represent the optimal mechanism for economic development."[4] As a general framework of governments, it has impacts in many dimensions of local life. Jessop argues that there are several key features in this transformation. At the economic level, competitiveness and innovation become more important than full employment and planning. Social policy is subordinated to economic policy with downward pressures on working conditions. One related goal is to get people to become "enterprising subjects" and become less dependent on state welfare programs. Hence, an emphasis is placed on workfare and employability programs designed to get people from welfare to work, regardless of labour-market conditions. The importance of national governments is diminished, with greater emphasis placed on local, regional and supranational levels of government with new powers accorded to social partnerships with related processes of negotiation. Transitions have been seen in several key areas that affect the context of any kind of community-level work, especially transitions in immigration, work and the welfare state. The consequence of all of these changes is the general destabilization of daily life with particularly negative impacts on women and immigrant populations.[5]

We have witnessed a change in the nature of wage labour over the last twenty years. The "thirty glorious years" (1950-1980)—as it is referred to in the French literature—was perhaps the exceptional period in capitalist societies. The stability and relatively high levels of disposable income were traded off against monotonous working conditions. Consumption was the means and the reward of social integration in society, and this consumption was encouraged with jobs that were protected by relatively strong trade unions. The restructuring of the economy, linked to globalization, brought with it the loss of many blue-collar jobs, high levels of unemployment and difficulties for youth trying to enter the labour market as traditional working class avenues disappeared. Workers who were victims of job loss, faced with increased competition for the fewer remaining jobs and limits in income-support programs, have had to move downward in the market. Many who have lived through long-term unemployment have difficulties returning to work. Further, younger people in many low-income communities have never worked and, coupled with high rates of school dropouts, are not work-ready. In addition, there has been a growth of contingent work. This type of work includes "... those forms of employment involving atypical employment contracts, limited social benefits and statutory entitlements, job insecurity, low job tenure, low wages and high risks of ill health."[6] It is the fastest growing pattern of employment, and youth, women and immigrants tend to be absorbed into the labour market through these jobs. One consequence of these changes has been a simultaneous rise in the number of people participating in the labour market and an increase in poverty.

Neoliberalism and the Welfare State: From Social Rights to Personal Responsibility

The postwar welfare state, despite major differences in approaches such as universality and the level of benefits, did in practice guarantee an income for most people, and provided extensive services, often universally. Since the 1980s, we have witnessed that cutbacks of services and benefits as well as disengagement are part of the transition in social welfare. With these changes, policy has moved from one based on rights to one that emphasizes individual responsibility and reciprocity. McKeen and Porter argue that the new welfare state is characterized "... not by universality but by the selective targeting of benefits based on income."[7] These changes, they argue, are "... an increasingly punitive model; resulting in increased poverty, inequalities and hardship among certain groups; and the downloading of responsibility for meeting social needs to individuals and to the home."[8] Shields argues that as the state shrinks, "responsibility for 'welfare' is increasingly being downloaded onto the backs of individuals, families, and voluntary organizations."[9] Further, as part of this transformation and with the growth of contingent work, labour discipline is increasingly linked to the provision of social benefits. For example, Peck uses the concept of a "workfare regime" to describe an approach to social policy that prioritizes the linking of income support to labour market integration. He argues:

> ... functionally, workfarism implies an ascendancy of active labour-market inclusion over passive labour-market exclusion as workfarism seeks to push the poor into the labour market, or hold them in a persistently unstable state close to it, rather than sanctioning limited nonparticipation in wage labour in the way of welfare systems.[10]

Workfare has to be understood as an approach that means more than simply having to earn welfare benefits. It is a basic change in the income support system that makes an individual's right to income support dependent on some kind of work-related measure. Regardless of the conditions, the goal is to push people into work. As a consequence, recipients are encouraged to be part of the labour market, even if the job makes them worse off financially than they were while receiving social assistance. Employability and labour market participation, like in other countries, is a "contract of social assistance reciprocity" between the poor and the state.[11] Thus, poverty becomes associated with the personal shortcomings of the individual rather than being seen as a product of the social structure. Institutions and programs become necessary to make changes in these groups so that they can be successfully integrated into the economy either as flexible workers or as small-scale producers. These programs vary by the mixture of carrot-and-stick incentives and punishments, an ideology incorporating far more than the immediate administration of social benefits. It structures the expectations for those receiving social aid. It pushes recipients to a variety of institutions and organizations to seek programs that augment their benefits or maintain their eligibility.

We are not making the argument that all of the changes in the welfare state are linked to work, but this is an arena that is at the centre, and an example of how neoliberal inspired changes in policy act to put increased pressure on individuals to remedy their own situations. Families and the role of domestic labour—usually women—have taken on greater significance, as well as the pool of migrant labour, to fill gaps in provision. With the injection of the market into social provision through the privatization of services, personal income becomes the basis for accessing services, with a smaller residual sector designed for the poor. Because of these changes, the "community sector" has played a more significant role. For example, Shields points out that settlement programs for new immigrants and refugees, central to the integration process, are located in the non-profit sector. "Hence, a non-profit infrastructure has emerged in Canada that is vital to sustaining immigrant welfare."[12]

Another example of the interplay between government and the community in recent years is the growth and success of the social economy in Quebec. The Parti Québecois government supported the social economy, and it has grown to become an important component in local life. The social economy is broad and has many faces, including progressive organizations with radical agendas and popular educational tools. At the same time, however, it has had a propensity to create jobs in low-wage sectors.[13] In addition, many of the enterprises play a regulatory role for the unemployed and welfare recipients by becoming a safety valve—a means of training and absorbing surplus labour. CED in English Canada and in Aboriginal communities is heterogeneous, sharing little common practice. Practices range from programs training low-wage workers to participate in precarious jobs, to local neighbourhood projects designed to give citizens greater control of urban development.

The turn toward "community" is always contradictory; in virtually any community, alternative and opposition forces co-exist to varying degrees with forces that support neoliberal policies. The assumption that everyone in the community shares common interests can only be held by someone who has never been involved in a community. So even as the CED and social economy movements advance proposals for alternative approaches to development, the capacity to oppose ever-expanding neoliberalism must be maintained. Opposition is the only way for the poor, those marginalized by the fierce competition of neoliberal economies. They need to organize and build power in order to make demands to force new policies that will reduce these inequalities. Opposition is essential both for the well-being of all of those pushed under by the neoliberal juggernaut and for the future of the planet in broader ecological terms.

But the real possibility of CED and the social economy is in the proposal of alternatives that oppose the neoliberal agenda. Creating new forms of development that are democratic, ecological and that are engaged in critical analysis and related popular education, contributes to building a locally-based opposition movement. There are examples of these practices within CED and the social economy. However, behind a wide, all-inclusive definition, these practices are subsumed by service provision, small businesses and a range of other practices consistent with neoliberal policy directions. It is incumbent on the CED and social economy movement to develop a political definition of practice that is in opposition to neoliberal policy and will preserve its democratic, ecological and critical values. Without this, the power of government funding will increase the pressures of assimilation into the dominant system and gradually marginalize progressive practices. Local groups will have to push the radical oppositional agenda not only with funding policies, but also within the CED and social economy movement. Below are some of the specific challenges that, if answered, can move CED in a direction of positive social change.

CED and Social Change

CED is at a watershed. As discussed in this volume, practice has grown and organizations have proliferated, expanding in size and function. At the same time, CED and the social economy have received recognition from various levels of government. New opportunities are available, but what vision will drive these alternatives? The danger we are raising is that CED and related social enterprises may be used as an extension of government policy and become part of a redefined system of social provision, building a marginal entrepreneurial culture for the poor. This would not challenge the underlying causes of poverty and inequality or the way they are produced and reproduced by our economic system and related government policies. There will certainly be pressures to move CED and social-economy development in this direction. These will come from government funding policies, which is to be expected, but there is a danger that CED practitioners will support this direction out of pragmatism—accepting funding regardless of conditions attached to it—or out of a desire to make even the smallest positive change in their communities. In this book we are arguing for a broader vision; CED has to be part of a force for progressive social change.

It is important to name the values framework and the politics that motivate practice and acknowledge that there needs to be a critical examination of them. Not all CED and social economy practitioners work from the same framework nor do they necessarily share "progressive" social values. For example, some practice treats participants as clients without an analysis of the socio-political context. The fundamental question is how CED contributes to a process of progressive social change? What practices make a difference and how?

Below we present some of the challenges for CED. By examining practice in relation to them we can begin to construct a framework for CED that supports progressive social change. These challenges are key to understanding how CED is different from more mainstream economic development. They provide an implicit vision of what should be present in CED practice. At the same time, we have to acknowledge that these elements constitute huge challenges, particularly in a globalized and neoliberal world. Practice around these issues has to be understood as being in development, and might be strongest in organizations that are considered small and relatively weak in economic terms, but that have a focus on the social and a commitment to the mobilization and education of citizens.

The first challenge is the role that CED plays in relation to improving the material conditions and the living conditions of the participants and/or the wider community. One of the justifications of CED is that it contributes to poverty reduction. There is a danger that government will use this assertion to encourage CED instead of other programs such as income support. Levy's chapter discusses some of the policy issues in relation to this question. Defining the appropriate role for CED based on what it can achieve at the local level is fundamental. It is dangerous if CED practitioners believe that local work can be a substitute for national and provincial policies that provide income, housing and other basic services. Thus, defining the vision of CED with both its potential and its limits is an important first step in building a practice aimed at social change.

Moreover, CED can contribute to the reduction of inequality in a different way. Inequality of power because of class, gender, race, ability, age and so on are central features of our society. Power to make basic economic and political decisions is concentrated in fewer hands, and the role of citizen (read social actor) is to vote periodically. CED, like other forms of community organizing and development provides a place where people can gather, can organize and can build a collective voice in order to increase their power to negotiate. In other words, inequality is multi-dimensional and CED practice can support a process of collective action and power-building for those with little social or political power.

In order for this to happen, there have to be democratic practices associated with CED. Participatory democratic processes are deeply rooted in community development and organizing traditions. How are these expressed in CED organizations? One of the differences between CED and traditional economic development is who controls the process. Without active citizen involvement and power to shape decisions, CED will fall into the hands of technical experts, reproducing dominant models that value efficiency over democracy. Who participates and what are the mechanisms in place to broaden participatory processes? Does the CED organization and process encourage and support those who are the poorest and most marginal in that community? Do these practices contribute to the building of collective action and strengthen local collectivities? The implications of these questions are that, first and foremost, CED practitioners need to concentrate on the organizing dimension of practice. Doing this begins with processes but is based on ongoing social, economic and political learning.

CED processes and organizations have to be understood as places that offer learning opportunities. These are not always formal or structured, but they are rooted in the everyday experience of participation and engagement. Learning is a central process of building individual and collective capacity. Thus, knowledge is functional for organizational development and skill sharing to allow greater participation in all of its aspects. There is another dimension of learning that is often ignored as organizations work to maintain their daily activities: building critical consciousness and analysis. CED practice begins with situations generated by social inequality and injustice, and responds by creating alternatives that try, at least to some extent, to remedy the situation. To move beyond this, a process of analysis of the social forces that cause and perpetuate these problems has to be part of a CED agenda. Active critical discussion of both the specific policies that impact people locally and the wider social forces need to be included in this discussion. This implies that CED organizations position themselves in the wider debates and have an explicit political vision.

What is the vision of the organization and of CED practice more generally? From the chapters that follow we can see that there is a diversity of orientations and practice priorities. Much of it focuses on local work with either the neighbourhood and/or particular populations or groups given priority. Sometimes these overlap as people and place are considered together. One of the common features of CED, and community development in general, is that it views community as local. Working locally is prioritized as it should be, but critical analysis leads us to understand that the root of local problems and their broader solutions are not limited to the local. As we have argued above, there are wider social, economic and policy contexts that have a major impact on practice. The challenge is to move from the local to the global without neglecting local work. This is not always easy to do, however there are ways to begin the process. Building connections and alliances with other organizations and, more important for the global aspects, social movements is a first step. Common issues can be raised in the context of broader social mobilization. For example, some CED organizations help immigrants find work and integrate into the labour market, but at the same time many immigrants and refugees face problems because their prior education is not validated, or because they are "without status." In both cases social and political movements have challenged government policies on these questions. CED organizations should support these campaigns and actively participate in them. As this happens, CED practice becomes one that links daily programs at the local level to wider social and political struggles and begins to build a vision as part of a broader and deeper movement for social and economic justice.

Another aspect of the vision is the type of economic development undertaken. Can CED help build an alternative economy at the local level? Part of this is an understanding that community economic development implies choices about how goods and services are produced and under what conditions. Localizing and democratizing production and building links to other green or alternative efforts can contribute positively to economic change. That change should first start within CED organizations, consuming and producing resources in conjunction with others working toward a green alternative.

With the growing recognition of CED practice and the interest by government to fund it, there are real pressures exerted that can distort vision and move practice into directions that are pre-defined by those funding it. The underlying challenge, that in some cases is a precondition to responding to those already discussed, is the protection of the autonomy of CED organizations, so that they can through democratic practices determine local priorities and maintain their vision. The elements that contribute to building and protecting autonomy include an independent vision, active democratic processes and a diversified funding base. The vision of a CED organization needs to be understood by board, staff and community members, and periodically revisited and debated—a process which in and of itself helps to keep the organization in touch with its own direction and avoids drift related to funding. Active participatory democratic processes give the organization power because their mobilized public can act to protect and promote the interests of the organization. Finally, a diversified funding base increases autonomy and avoids what would otherwise amount to a sub-contracting relationship with a government agency. All of these factors are essential for creating the conditions for autonomous CED practice.

These challenges are by no means an exhaustive list, but represent some of the basic ones facing CED practitioners and organizations. The chapters that follow provide excellent insights into the many innovative ways these challenges are being addressed in a wide range of settings.

Content

The goal of this book is to describe and analyze CED practice, primarily in Canada, with a couple of examples from other countries. The chapters in this volume examine both the context of CED and its practices.

As an introductory chapter, Toye and Chaland begin this volume with a discussion of the evolution of definitions of CED and an overview of contemporary practice, profiling the diversity of the movement across Canada. The two chapters that follow form the theoretical part of the book.

Loxley and Lamb tackle the economic dimension of CED. They present basic economic ideas that are often the underpinnings of CED practice which will be useful to the many practitioners who do not have a background in economics and are not familiar with these concepts or have only an understanding of what seems implicit in CED practice. One of the challenges in the field is to articulate exactly what the practice means and what the ideas are that shape it. This chapter will contribute to that process.

Levy has written a major essay for this book that covers key elements forming the context for CED practice. Many CED initiatives began as responses to unemployment, and we have witnessed a transformation of wage labour over the past thirty years with many profound implications. Levy's chapter explores several features of this central question, including the changes in work itself, the changing role of the third sector in relation to work, the conditions of work in third-sector organizations and wider policy issues.

One of the weaknesses of CED literature in Canada is that CED is too rarely situated in wider political, economic and social contexts, and there is little critical discussion of its limits and challenges in those contexts. In order to broaden the debate and analysis, we have included the above two chapters, and most of the authors of the other chapters raise a variety of critical issues that challenge CED practice.

The other chapters are loosely presented in two categories, the first group of which is based upon geography. CED is a place-based strategy, reflecting the specific circumstances of different geographic regions. The variety of local traditions and approaches to different situations in these chapters provide powerful lessons and demonstrate the richness of practice in their diverse responses to specific cultural and social circumstances. In addition, these chapters bring different analytical and historical perspectives to each of the cases, including (from Canada) the institutionalization of CED organizations and practice in Montreal (Fontan, Hamel, Morin and Shragge), the challenges of facing de-industrialization in Cape Breton (Lotz and MacIntyre), the development of CED and the social economy by the Franco-Ontarian minority (Welch), and the role these practices play in preserving local identity. In addition, Wilder, Taliaferro, Jabbar-Bey and Sherif-Trask provide an historical overview and discussion of challenges facing CED organizations in the United States. This is particularly important because CED in the U.S. has a long history and has influenced the development of initiatives in Canada. Lyons, Majale and Chege examine CED and sustainable development issues in Kenya. This chapter not only allows readers in the North to appreciate challenges of developing countries, but it also provides insights into how CED can play a key role in that development. Lessons on partnerships are also provided.

Thematic chapters not only explore issues for CED practice, but also provide rich examples. Issues faced by Aboriginal communities are described and debated in chapters by Newhouse and Wutunee. These writers approach the questions in different ways, with Newhouse examining the impact of capitalist development on how Aboriginal communities develop their economies, and Wutunee exploring traditional values and presenting some successful case studies. The chapter on feminism and CED by Melanie Conn examines issues faced in using CED as a tool to support women and the contribution of feminism to building a progressive vision of CED practice. Church's chapter opens the question of disability and CED through the presentation of the experience of a film about alternative businesses organized by psychiatric survivors. These businesses, with their innovation and democratic participation, have provided an important model for CED practice.

Two areas that have not received enough attention within CED in Canada are housing and worker ownership. We have included these chapters to challenge practitioners to include these dimensions in their strategies. Hanley and Serge present an overview of housing policy and issues with an argument about why housing should be seen as a component of CED practice. Savory-Gordon and Broad use a case study of Algoma Steel in Sault Ste. Marie, Ontario, as an example of a worker-owned alternative to factory closures. Finally, Roseland's chapter makes the case for a new approach to sustainable community development, and describes its potential role in a variety of settings.

Collectively, these chapters demonstrate the scope of practice and some of the challenges and limits of CED practice. It is our hope that they, along with the reflections above, will help spur further critical discussion and debate that will strengthen CED as a force for progressive social change.

Notes

1. Atasoy, "Explaining Globalization," in *Global Shaping and its Alternatives*, 3-12.
2. Watkins, "Politics in Time and Space of Globalization," in *Changing Canada —Political Economy as Transformation*, 3-24.
3. Ibid., 5.
4. Brenner and Theodore, "Cities and Geographies of 'Actually Existing Neoliberalism,'" in *Spaces of Neoliberalism—Urban Restructuring in North America and Western Europe*, 2.
5. Jessop, "Liberalism, Neoliberalism, and Urban Governance: A State-Theoretical Perspective," in *Spaces of Neoliberalism*, 105-125.

6.   Fudge and Vosko, "Gender Paradoxes and Rise of Contingent Work: Towards a
       Transformative Political Economy of the Labour Market." In *Changing Canada*, 183.
7.   McKeen and Porter. "Politics and Transformation: Welfare State Restructuring in
       Canada," in *Changing Canada*, 109-134.
8.   Shields, "No Safe Haven: Markets, Welfare, and Migrants," CERIS working paper
       no. 22, iii.
9.   Ibid., iv.
10.   Peck, *Workfare States*, 12.
11.   Morel, *The Insertion Model or the Workfare Model? The Transformation of Social
       Assistance within Quebec and Canada*.
12.   Shields, v.
13.   See Levy in this book, and Deslauriers and Paquet, *Travailler dans le Communautaire*.

Bibliography

Atasoy, Y. "Explaining Globalization." In *Global Shaping and its Alternatives*, edited by Y.
       Atasoy and W. Carroll, 3-12. Bloomfield, CT: Kumarian Press, 2003.

Brenner, N. and N. Theodore. "Cities and Geographies of 'Actually Existing Neo-liberalism.'"
       In *Spaces of Neoliberalism—Urban Restructuring in North America and Western Europe*,
       edited by N. Brenner and N. Theodore, 2. Cambridge: Blackwell, 2002.

Deslauriers, J. P. with R. Paquet. *Travailler dans le Communautaire*. Quebec: Presses de
       l'Université du Québec, 2003.

Fudge, F. and L. Vosko. "Gender Paradoxes and Rise of Contingent Work: Towards a
       Transformative Political Economy of the Labour Market." In *Changing Canada—
       Political Economy as Transformation*, edited by W. Clement and L. Vosko, 183.
       Montreal and Kingston: McGill-Queen's University Press, 2003.

Jessop, B. "Liberalism, Neoliberalism, and Urban Governance: A State-Theoretical
       Perspective." In *Spaces of Neoliberalism—Urban Restructuring in North America and
       Western Europe*, edited by N. Brenner and N. Theodore, 105-125. Cambridge:
       Blackwell, 2002.

McKeen, W. and Porter, A. 2003. "Politics and Transformation: Welfare State Restructuring
       in Canada." In *Changing Canada-Political Economy as Transformation*, edited by W.
       Clement and L. Vosko, 109-34. McGill-Queen's University Press, Montreal and
       Kingston.

Morel, S. *The Insertion Model or the Workfare Model? The Transformation of Social
       Assistance within Quebec and Canada*. Policy Research, Status of Women Canada,
       2002.

Peck, J. *Workfare States*. New York: Guilford, 2001.

Shields, J. "No Safe Haven: Markets, Welfare, and Migrants." Working paper series. CERIS
       working paper no. 22. CERIS, The Joint Centre of Excellence for Research on
       Immigration and Settlement – Toronto. http://ceris.metropolis.net, iii. (Accessed January
       2003.)

Watkins, M. "Politics in Time and Space of Globalization." In *Changing Canada—Political
       Economy as Transformation*, edited by W. Clement and L. Vosko, 3-24. Montreal and
       Kingston: McGill-Queen's University Press, 2003.

Michael Toye and Nicole Chaland

CED in Canada: Review of Definitions and Profile of Practice

In 2002, five researchers set out looking for Community Economic Development in Canada. The Profile of CED[1] carried out by the Canadian CED Network (CCEDNet) surveyed 340 organizations from every corner of the country in an effort to ascertain the nature, size and scope of the sector. What this research found was a beautiful mosaic of community efforts unified by their identification with the title "community economic development." But what exactly does it mean?

For just about anyone involved in CED, being able to describe our work and situate it in a broader context is crucial, even more so now that CED and the social economy are getting attention at the highest levels of the federal government. While there have been a number of thorough works on community economic development in Canada, many are now ten or more years old, out of print or difficult to access. Furthermore, despite CED's growing recognition and popularity, there is still no simple, widely-accepted definition. In this light, and in hopes of furthering the discussion towards a common understanding of CED, we wanted to revisit some of these perspectives on CED, and see how they fit with the profile of CED in Canada. This chapter will review some of the literature on the concept of CED, consider a range of definitions both in the literature and in practice across the country, and present an overview of the initiatives and organizations in Canada that identify with the term.

CED as a Concept

CED draws from many fields of practice and also from social movements such as social work, cooperative development, high risk financing, equity development, anti-corporate globalization, Aboriginal rights, anti-poverty, social enterprise, community development finance, employment training, business development, adult education, land-use planning and labour and municipal sectors to name a few. Generally speaking, many people come to CED from either community development or local economic development perspectives, but rarely have a solid grounding in both. A brief look at the relationship between CED and these two fields will highlight the influences of each.

Community Development

Community development is often equated with community empowerment and community capacity building. Chekki states that "the central credo of community development is to develop the competence of the community so that it may confront its own problems."[2] As such, it implicitly transforms existing power relations, increasing influence and control over decisions affecting a community from autocratic or external sources to local, representative and accountable ones. To foster that process of change, the community development society identifies the five following "Principles of Good Practice:"

- Promote active and representative participation toward enabling all community members to meaningfully influence the decisions that affect their lives.

- Engage community members in learning about and understanding community issues, and the economic, social, environmental, political, psychological and other impacts associated with alternative courses of action.

- Incorporate the diverse interests and cultures of the community in the community development process; and disengage from support of any effort that is likely to adversely affect the disadvantaged members of a community.

- Work actively to enhance the leadership capacity of community members, leaders and groups within the community.

- Be open to using the full range of action strategies to work toward the long-term sustainability and well-being of the community.[3]

What is the "full range of action strategies?" The only limit is imagination. For most of the last forty years, Jack Rothman's pioneering trinity of locality development, social planning and policy and social action was widely accepted as describing the three models of community intervention,[4] but starting gradually in the 1980s and exploded in the 1990s. American authors such as Fisher, Hanna and Robinson, Checkoway, Dreier and Kingsley, McNeely and Gibson, have proposed a myriad of typologies and rubrics, including: community organizing, community-based development, community-based service provision, social work approach, political activist approach, neighbourhood maintenance approach, traditional politics, direct action community organizing, transformative social change, mass mobilization, social action, citizen participation, public advocacy, popular education, local services development and community building. As Checkoway points out, it is the particularities of each community that will determine which of these strategies has the most potential for empowerment.[5]

Sticking with Rothman's typology, Favreau and Lévesque broadly described the interventions that advance these strategies as community organizing.[6] Their definition of community organizing reflects many of the characteristics common to the community-based approach: a bottom-up process, with a vision of social change based on the identification of community needs and problems that will be tackled by increased democratic participation, creating new powers and services in the local community and by building on community assets rather than seeking to palliate deficits.

But the heart of recent trends in the community-based approach can be found in the recognition of the interconnectedness of social, economic and political (and, increasingly, environmental) issues. For Douglas, community development rejects the artificial divisions of community life into political and economic spheres, taking a holistic approach that treats the community as an integrated socio-economic entity within its bio-social environment: "The reality of an integrated ecosystem is respected, and problems and opportunities are approached in this manner."[7] Efforts taking this integrated and holistic approach are now often referred to as "comprehensive."[8]

Douglas described CED as a subset of community development: "The former must serve and, in effect, be grounded in practice in the latter."[9] It is understandable, then, for community developers embracing a CED approach to naturally infuse their work with the principles and approaches outlined above, grounding it in a vision of transformative social change. This can be rather different from orthodox local economic development approaches.

Local Economic Development

While Douglas placed CED as a subset of community development, he also placed it as a concept and as a field of practice toward one end of a spectrum of local initiatives that fall under the general rubric of local economic development. Fontan[10] described this spectrum as running from "liberal" approaches at one end to "progressive" at the other, with the common denominator of all local economic development activities "retaining or generating sufficient economic activity for the community's residents so that they can achieve and maintain an acceptable quality of life."[11] Of course, economic activity may increase or decline without purposeful intervention, thanks to the ever-present "invisible hand" of the market. But it is the economic development *by* the community, *for* the community that distinguishes local economic development initiatives from economic development that happens *in* the community as a result of market forces and occasional government interventions.

Perry noted that, as a program, local economic development is generally carried out by a local government or quasi-governmental agency or by a business consortium such as the local chamber of commerce. It typically follows a more liberal, rather than progressive model, involving less participation in governance by a broad range of community residents, reducing the spread of benefits and taking a less comprehensive strategy.[12] A good representation of the liberal perspective can be found in Blakely's definition:

> Local economic development refers to the process in which local governments or community-based (neighbourhood) organizations engage to stimulate or maintain business activity and/or employment. The principal goal of local economic development is to stimulate local employment opportunities in sectors that improve the community using existing human, natural and institutional resources.[13]

In his 1993 literature review of CED, Fontan described the federal government's Community Futures Program as an application of this liberal strategy[14] to improve local economies through employment development:

> Local development is aimed at increasing the community's capacity to adapt to change and at encouraging and supporting entrepreneurship. This includes the identification of market niches that may be served competitively by these communities.

> The fundamental principle of community-based economic development is the intervention of individuals who take steps at the local level to improve economic, social and environmental conditions. Job creation, in the context of local economic development, is a key element of this process which brings together those at the local level who have decided to take action and to innovate in order to combat unemployment.[15]

As one moves along the spectrum of local economic development from liberal to more progressive approaches, the extent of public participation, ownership and control increases along with the breadth of perspectives and community interests:

> Likewise, a more holistic view of the complete community economy (i.e., informal and formal) is taken as one crosses the spectrum. The role of long-range planning increases. The emphasis on community capacity building increases. While all activities along the spectrum involve development in the community, and may therefore be referred to as "local" economic development, only community economic development (and community development) are premised upon the development of the community by the community. This is the fundamental distinction.[16]

In this sense, Dennis Cutajar's "Strengthening the Downtown Management Plan: A Co-operative Approach to Community Economic Development" is a good example of a mid-spectrum, local economic development strategy.[17] This strategy, published by the University of Waterloo Economic Development Program and advertised on the website of the Economic Developers Association of Canada, describes the importance of consulting community representatives—government, business and volunteers—to revitalize the downtown as part of improving the community economy. As a participatory business development strategy, it incorporates social goals (reducing homelessness, reducing crime, expanding the library and creating a community centre), recognizing the impacts that each of these have on the business friendliness of the area.

If CED, as Douglas suggests, is found only at one end of the spectrum of local economic development approaches, the question that is raised is, "Where do you draw the line?" At what point is a local economic development strategy no longer considered CED? A look at the literature of CED definitions allows us to identify some of its distinguishing characteristics.

CED Definitions in the Literature

Is CED then the economic development of the community, in other words, community-based economic development, or community development of (among other things) the economy? The simple answer is, of course, "It depends upon whom you're asking."

In 1994, the Conference Board of Canada examined the role of the private sector in CED and defined CED as "… a strategy by which local development organizations mobilize local resources for a multi-faceted development campaign."[18] The document, however, recognizes divergent views on the ultimate goals of a CED approach:

> Some believe that CED's objective should be to create wealth and employment in communities. Others believe that CED should be about empowering local communities as an end in itself. The most successful CED initiatives in Canada have been able to integrate these two goals. These initiatives have pursued a comprehensive, multi-faceted strategy for the economic and social renewal of communities. Through the development of local resources and partnerships, local development organizations that are democratically controlled by the community have been established. These organizations mobilize local resources (people, finances, technical expertise, and real property) in order to empower community members to create and manage new and expanded socio-economic tools (businesses, specialized institutions, skills and practices). These tools have enabled communities to adapt to socio-economic change.[19]

Acknowledging the absence of a lack of common agreement on a definition of CED, Dal Brodhead suggested a checklist of key elements, most of which should be included in a CED initiative, policy or organization. It should:

- be a response to or emerge from underdevelopment and marginalization at the community level;

- pursue economic development as a way of empowering people and increasing local self-reliance;

- seek to build local capacity to plan, design, control, manage and evaluate initiatives aimed at revitalizing the community;

- incorporate a comprehensive development approach which aims at linking economic, social, cultural, environmental and other sectors of the community;

- be inclusive (not exclusive) in its outreach—enabling disadvantaged and disempowered groups in the community to create partnerships with others interested in a sustainable future for the community;

- favour medium and longer-term approaches over short-term, quick fixes typical of early job creation schemes in Canada;

- ensure that benefit accrues directly to the community at large rather than primarily to individuals within the community;

- endeavour to initiate partnerships (and joint ventures) between the marginalized segments of the population and the rest of the community.[20]

Writing at almost the same time, David Douglas also expressed many similar points, but emphasized the importance of community participation and control over the process:

> … community economic development is characterized by community-based processes and priorities. It is a process through which development of the community is pursued by the community. [P]lanning is a central activity and is based on participatory principles of community democracy. Likewise, appropriate community organizations are developed to respond to the community's priorities and values, and to facilitate the maximum access to the process and the maximum control by the community.[21]

An important way that the community pursues and takes control of its development is through the creation of accountable and democratic organizations. These are the tangible expressions of community control over the planning, design, control and management of initiatives to revitalize and develop all sectors of the community. In each of these three examples, as in much of the CED literature, "community" is understood as a limited locality, rather than a community of interest or identity. So the process of developing a comprehensive, multi-purpose strategy for all residents of the territory in question is essential. If "CED entails purposeful design and action by community residents to influence the characteristics of their local economy,"[22] then effective action will depend on a coordinated, strategic design. As Favreau and Lévesque[23] point out, discrete initiatives such as social economy enterprises can be an important part of a CED strategy, but they do not on their own constitute CED. What's required is a comprehensive plan.

The imperative for integrated and comprehensive approaches is supported by an increasing body of evidence in studies related to social capital, social inclusion, social cohesion and the social determinants of health.[24] But moving from a comprehensive plan to comprehensive action, particularly in communities with limited resources and capacity, is something else altogether. Based on work looking at comprehensive community initiatives in the United States, Torjman and Leviten-Reid concluded that what is essential in "comprehensiveness" is not comprehensive action, but a comprehensive analysis.[25] As long as the initiative is rooted in a comprehensive analysis (and therefore likely part of a comprehensive plan), it can be considered a comprehensive initiative.

While there is general agreement on the core elements of CED as expressed by Brodhead, differences in emphasis combined with the complexity of the approach and the spectrum of local realities lead to a wide range of interpretations in practice. The following section will look at some examples of how CED is understood by practitioners across the country.

CED Definitions in Practice

On the ground across Canada, a range of definitions are used for the same term, but tend to range from a liberal, economic development focus, to a focus on the improvement of social and economic conditions and empowering communities.

An example of a more liberal, local economic development interpretation of CED can be found in the Economic Developers Association of Alberta's Community Economic Development Accreditation Process and CED Training Programs. When asked for the definition of community economic development used in the program, course organizers provided the following: "The process of developing and maintaining suitable economic, social and political environments, in which balanced growth may be realized, increasing the wealth of the community."[26]

In their recent profile of women's CED, the Canadian Women's Foundation and the Canadian Women's Community Economic Development Council found that the term CED can be used to refer to a wide variety of activities, from starting a business to developing a broad-based community development plan. "CED is concerned with more than just the creation of jobs and the elimination of poverty and may address issues like housing and transportation. As a result, it has been difficult for practitioners to arrive at a clear and universal definition of CED." The definition used for the study was: "CED is local economic development that is focused on people, employment, self-employment, inclusion and sustainability. Its goal is to provide meaningful work for all, at a level of income that provides a secure livelihood, in jobs that are environmentally, socially and economically sustainable."[27]

Another attempt to provide an appropriate definition of CED was proposed by Tom Zizys for the Toronto CED Learning Network: "CED is a community-led, multi-faceted activity or strategy which seeks to improve the social and economic circumstances of a select population."[28]

Faced with the reality of this broad and divergent scope of definitions and the goal of building an inclusive movement, CED-related programs and associations such as the Canadian CED Network (CCEDNet) and the Community Economic Development Technical Assistance Program (CEDTAP) have taken a broad and inclusive approach to building capacity and fostering the growth of a movement.

To qualify for support from the CEDTAP, an organization must:

- Have a clear vision of how the initiative will contribute to the social and economic well-being of the community,

- Demonstrate that there is acceptance and support from the broader community,
- Agree to document and share lessons learned throughout the initiative.[29]

CCEDNet's definition goes beyond the improvement of social and economic conditions to include the necessity of undertaking that improvement in inclusive, holistic and participatory ways. The Network's position is:

- CED can be defined as action by people locally to create economic opportunities and enhance social conditions in their communities on a sustainable and inclusive basis, particularly with those who are most disadvantaged.

- CED is a community-based and community-directed process that explicitly combines social and economic development and fosters the economic, social, ecological and cultural well-being of communities.

- CED has emerged as an alternative to conventional approaches to economic development. It is founded on the belief that problems facing communities—unemployment, poverty, job loss, environmental degradation and loss of community control—need to be addressed in a holistic and participatory way. [30]

This definition comes closest to Brodhead's and Douglas's characteristics mentioned above, though it still does not mention empowerment or capacity building. A limitation, of course, for all of these operational definitions is their ease of comprehension and marketability. It is understandable that practitioners would seek to simplify what can be undeniably a complex concept for use in their communities and with their audience, but the risk of oversimplification is the potential loss of what makes the concept valuable. The desire to be inclusive also mitigates against explicit boundaries being drawn between what is and what is not CED.

The range of these definitions, from CED as a strategy for increasing wealth through balanced growth to CED as an alternative to conventional economic development, is an illustration not only of the liberal to progressive range of definitions that exist, but also of the pragmatic requirement of CED promoters to define their approach relative to the dominant development paradigm: economic development. The degree to which CED either strengthens economic development or seeks to replace conventional economic development, reflects the range of practice across the country, and the vision underlying those activities. CED can be undertaken as part of a transformative social change project (building on the community development approach), it can be applied to support an orthodox economic development process (the liberal local economic development approach) or it can fall somewhere in between those two extremes. While some of the immediate goals of these two approaches may be the same (such as improving economic and social conditions for a community), the long-term goals will likely differ, along with the process favoured to achieve them. As the movement and its research and evidence base grow, further debates on the strengths, weaknesses and appropriateness of these different approaches will be needed.

Among respondents to CCEDNet's profile of CED, "common to all was an understanding of community economic development as 'local action and strategies creating economic opportunities and enhancing social conditions in an inclusive and sustainable manner'."[31] So let's see what subscribers to that vision of CED look like in Canada.

Practice: Profile of CED in Canada

Until 2002, there had been no attempt to sketch out the characteristics of the CED movement in Canada as a whole. In 2002-2003, CCEDNet surveyed 364 community economic development organizations in an attempt to do this, publishing the results in the *Profile of Community Economic Development in Canada: Results of a Survey of Community Economic Development Across Canada.*[32] Those results are summarized below. This research starts the process of identifying and organizing a body of CED experience and knowledge, and assembles it in a form we all can make use of. Highlights from the *Profile* follow, along with some reflections on their significance for the CED Sector.

Method

The *Profile of Community Economic Development* is descriptive and sought to answer the question, "What is the nature, size and scope of community economic development in Canada?" Principles of participatory action research guided the research. To make the process accessible, participants were able to participate in either French or English and by telephone interview, emailed survey or a combination of both. An advisory committee allowed CED practitioners to guide and support the research throughout all stages of the process (design, data collection, data analysis, dissemination, reporting and follow-up use of the data). The survey respondents and researchers were CED practitioners themselves so that the research was guided and implemented by the informants' peers.

Approximately 1,200 organizations were identified and invited to participate in the survey by email, with about half of those being invited by telephone as well. Potential participants were drawn from CCEDNet membership, groups affiliated with the Community Economic Development Technical Assistance Program, those attending CCEDNet conferences and learning events and through personal and organizational networks, as well as organizations recommended from these initial contacts. A total of 364 surveys were completed, 294 of which provided sufficient and relevant information to be used in the analysis.

CCEDNet used a pluralistic approach to defining the CED sector. They provided a working definition of CED, but encouraged organizations to "self-identify" their involvement in CED, with a description of the activities they considered to be relevant. Survey respondents were asked to provide a mix of quantitative and qualitative data. Respondents were asked open-ended questions in order to capture the diversity and richness of their activities, practice and structure.

A Quick Look at the Results

The *Profile of CED* reported on three principal themes: the nature, size and scope of the sector. The nature of CED establishes a typology for CED organizations, their distribution and maturity, enumerates their activities, and identifies proven practices and barriers to growth. The size of the sector is quantified in terms of employees and volunteers, as well as size of budget and revenue sources. Lessons learned about the sector are revealed through comments from CED organizations about proven practices and barriers hindering success of CED in their community.

The respondents were very diverse. They included small and large operations; were incorporated as non-profit, co-operative and private agencies; and were located in both rural and urban communities. The challenge was to create a portrait of the sector while permitting people to make a reasonable comparison of particular details.

Regions outside of Ontario and Quebec were overrepresented in the response to the CED survey relative to the distribution of Canada's population. In addition, many more survey respondents were located in rural areas of Canada (47 per cent) compared with the rural share of population (28 per cent). Community economic development seems to be an important response to rural and regional disadvantage.

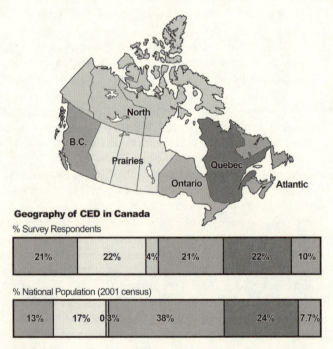

Geography of CED in Canada

% Survey Respondents

21%	22%	4%	21%	22%	10%

% National Population (2001 census)

13%	17%	0.3%	38%	24%	7.7%

Fig. 2.1

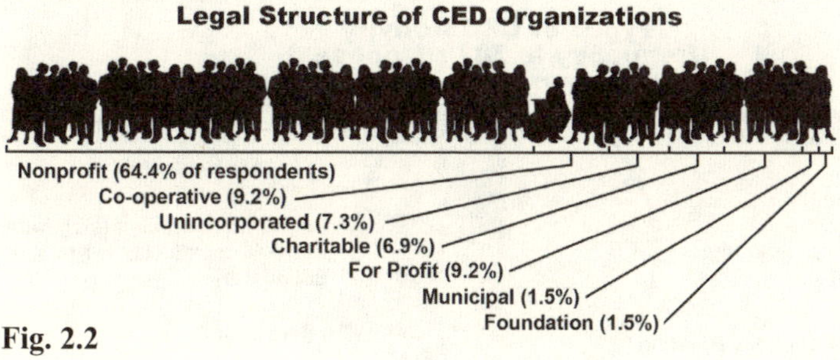

Legal Structure of CED Organizations

Nonprofit (64.4% of respondents)
Co-operative (9.2%)
Unincorporated (7.3%)
Charitable (6.9%)
For Profit (9.2%)
Municipal (1.5%)
Foundation (1.5%)

Fig. 2.2

Community economic development organizations form an important component of Canada's civil society. The majority of survey respondents were registered as non-profit societies, co-operatives, charities or unincorporated groups. "For profit" organizations, especially technical assistance providers and consulting groups, could be overrepresented in the sample. Participation in the survey included a marketing opportunity by listing services and contact information in CCEDNet's online directory. On the other hand, the existence of CEDTAP funding may contribute to the growth of consultants in the CED movement.

Nearly a third of respondents have been in operation for more than 15 years. However, over half of respondents reported that their organizations have only been in existence for the last 10 years. This speaks to recent growth in the sector, especially in BC and the Atlantic Provinces, where around 65 per cent of respondents represented organizations created since 1994.

The survey asked participants to describe their three main CED activities. The majority of respondents reported more than one activity which is consistent

Age of CED Organizations
(% of Survey Respondents, Years in Operation)

24.0% (1999-)	31.8% (1994-1998)	12.5% (1989-1993)	31.7% before 1989
0-4 Years	5-10 Years	11-15 Years	over 15 Years

Fig. 2.3

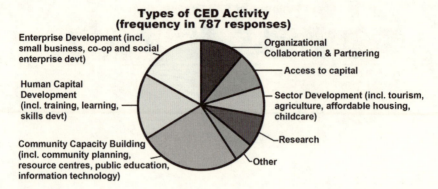

Types of CED Activity
(frequency in 787 responses)

Enterprise Development (incl. small business, co-op and social enterprise devt)

Human Capital Development (incl. training, learning, skills devt)

Community Capacity Building (incl. community planning, resource centres, public education, information technology)

Organizational Collaboration & Partnering

Access to capital

Sector Development (incl. tourism, agriculture, affordable housing, childcare)

Research

Other

Fig. 2.4

with a comprehensive approach to development, but the research was not able to report the most common mix of activities of the respondents. *The Profile* shows the responses in terms of frequency. The most common activities reported were related to community capacity building. Human capital development and enterprise development activities followed, after which came promoting collaboration, and finally activities which provided access to capital.

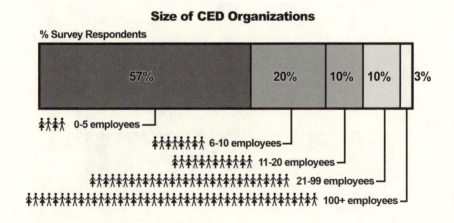

Size of CED Organizations

% Survey Respondents

| 57% | 20% | 10% | 10% | 3% |

0-5 employees

6-10 employees

11-20 employees

21-99 employees

100+ employees

Fig. 2.5

The survey also revealed the important role CED groups have in mobilizing citizen engagement and volunteer contributions to their communities. The ratio of full-time-equivalent staff to volunteers was 1 to 5.6. CED groups reported that their work involved over 19,000 volunteers, with full-time-equivalent staff of 3,410. Volunteer engagement is particularly high in the Prairies and Quebec.

The survey collected information on the respondents' annual revenue and the sources of that revenue. In total, the CED sector as surveyed has an economy valued at $194.5 million. Dollars leveraged against government funding are very high, with almost one dollar raised from non-government sources for every government dollar. This is particularly impressive given the nature of the work of most of these organizations, working in and with disadvantaged communities and populations.

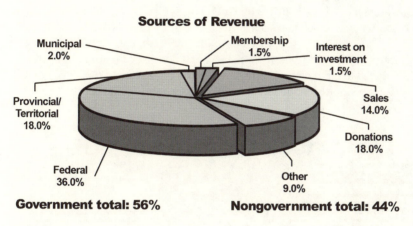

Fig. 2.6

In addition to grouping by legal identity we were able to begin to understand who the different players are in the CED sector. We grouped respondents by looking at their purpose (overall goal such as alleviating poverty) and function (such as delivering a community loan fund). While this grossly oversimplifies the variety of organizational missions and activities, it is useful in understanding the movement and different roles that organizations can play. We found that the largest grouping of respondents (35 per cent) could be differentiated from the others in that they are "single-purpose, multi-functional" organizations. This means that the organization is focused on a community of interest and implements a wide array of activities to support the betterment of that group. For example, an organization whose purpose is to improve the socio-economic conditions of women's lives may provide child care, housing, transportation and access to credit and training for women to start their own businesses. The presence of a large number that are focused on a particular community, such as mental health survivors, Aboriginals, youth, immigrants or women, could mean that existing organizations which do not have a specific mandate to serve a particular community of interest continue to exclude certain groups.

The next largest group represented in the survey are those that can be described as "single-purpose, single-function," which means that they carry out a specific service or function to a particular group of people within a community. An example of this could be a housing co-operative which has a specific purpose (provide housing to its members) but also sees itself as contributing to the larger objectives of CED.

Only 8 per cent of the organizations surveyed could say that they provide a range of functions to all residents with CED as an organizing principle. This should not be a surprising result given the lack of sustained funding for CED or the lack of a government body responsible for CED. That said, if the results are representative of the sector, the fact that such a small proportion of respondents are actively engaged in a multi-faceted approach to community economic development poses significant challenges to both practitioners and theorists. Future investments in CED, targeted to build on the existing efforts, knowledge and experience of CED groups, will be limited in their evidence base from which to build.

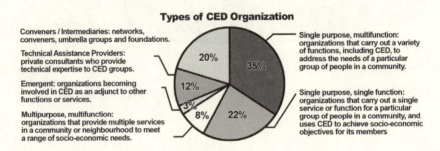

Fig. 2.7

In addition to the results originally reported in 2003, we were able to go back to the original data and examine the responses to two additional survey questions that looked at the role of CED organizations in facilitating citizen-led development: who respondents work with most frequently (stakeholder groups such as single parents, women, youth, people on low-income, homeless people, new Canadians, specific ethno-cultural groups, etc.) and in what ways their organization enables the beneficiaries of their CED activities to participate in the CED planning process (voting, consultations, etc.).

In response to the former question, 44 per cent of respondents identified one stakeholder group, 27 per cent identified two groups, and 29 per cent identified

Stakeholders (% of respondents)

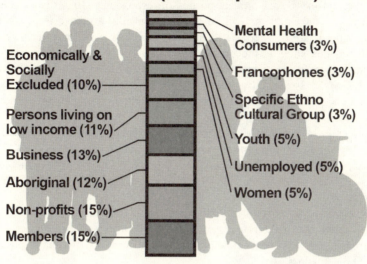

Mental Health Consumers (3%)

Francophones (3%)

Specific Ethno Cultural Group (3%)

Youth (5%)

Unemployed (5%)

Women (5%)

Economically & Socially Excluded (10%)

Persons living on low income (11%)

Business (13%)

Aboriginal (12%)

Non-profits (15%)

Members (15%)

Fig. 2.8

Participation in CED Planning Processes

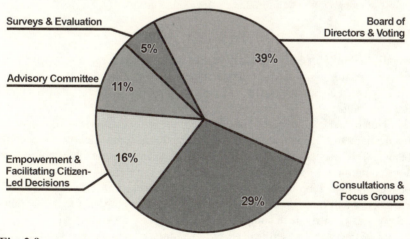

Surveys & Evaluation

Board of Directors & Voting

39%

5%

Advisory Committee

11%

Empowerment & Facilitating Citizen-Led Decisions

16%

Consultations & Focus Groups

29%

Fig. 2.9

three. The most commonly reported group was members, followed closely by non-profits, then business. A significant portion of respondents (10 per cent) simply described their stakeholders as those who are typically excluded from society. These groupings are not necessarily mutually exclusive. When direct-service recipient groups such as the unemployed, persons living on low income, Aboriginals, women and mental health consumers are combined, a total of 57 per cent of respondents reported working directly with individuals, the majority of whom are populations that experience systemic barriers to social and economic inclusion.

This number might be even higher, if "members" include the populations served. It cannot be determined whether the members category refers to organizational or individual members, but describing stakeholders as members rather than clients suggests a high level of community participation among survey respondents.

When asked in what ways their organization enables the beneficiaries of their CED activities to participate in the CED planning process, 21 per cent described three different methods of participation, 34 per cent described two and 45 per cent described one method used.

Respondents that identified consultation, surveys and advisory committees as means of participation described regular consultation at quarterly and annual general meetings, needs-assessment surveys, email correspondence, anecdotal interviews and community surveys as examples of that participation. Respondents that identified empowerment focused more on a process and approach in their answers, suggesting they "work with communities to realize their educational goals" and take a "fully inclusive, consensus-building decision-making structure and process at every stage of an initiative's development."

Conclusions

Overall, the *Profile of CED* paints a picture of a dynamic, enterprising and growing group of organizations across Canada engaged in a wide range of activities to strengthen their communities. But it also raises important questions about the CED they are doing.

Notably, the survey reveals that there are a relatively small number of organizations in Canada that can be said to be doing comprehensive, long-term planning for the social and economic renewal of an entire geographic community. More common are efforts which are limited to a community of interest or a population within a community and focus on certain aspects of social and economic renewal. It is only through partnerships that these "single-purpose, single-function" initiatives can contribute to comprehensive strategies for a given territory.

This trend may be influenced by government funding, representing over half of respondents' revenues, which is often limited to short-term projects that generate immediate, direct and measurable activity outputs for silo-specific man-dates. The dispersion of mandates and responsibilities among different departments in different levels of government means that each distinct funder will only support activities related to their limited mandate, fragmenting and multiplying the administrative burden of integrating the various activities essential to a comprehensive approach.

When CED organizations are restricted to narrowly-defined funding sources that are driven by basic activity outputs, another challenge is avoiding being reduced to a simple community-based delivery agent of government programs. Cultivating strong community participation and ownership over the organization helps ensure that it remains true to the breadth of its mission, but the resources required to cultivate that participation can be hard to find. Diversifying funding sources multiplies administrative and reporting requirements, and creating alternative sources of revenue generation, if not carefully chosen, can divert energy and attention from the mission rather than contribute to it.

The presence of government funders may also be a factor in the predominance of local economic-development-type activities (enterprise development, human capital development, access to capital and sector development) over community development ones (community capacity building, organizational collaboration and partnerships), reflecting the relative investment in those programs by governments.

Finally, one of the most important challenges for CED is measuring and demonstrating the outcomes of a comprehensive intervention in a complex system such as a community. Resources provided to CED groups for what are often short-term projects do not allow for long-term evaluation of results, or support a long-term strategy for social and economic renewal. Even if they did, the *Profile* suggests that most projects are relatively small and young (57 per cent have 0-5 employees, 50 per cent are less than ten years old), without the history or capacity to have implemented a broad evaluation framework. Improving the number and quality of outcome evaluations will be necessary to build the evidence base and thereby strengthen the practice of CED, however you define it.

Notes

1. Chaland and Downing, "Profile of Community Economic Development in Canada, 2003.

2. Chekki quoted in Douglas. "Community Economic Development in Canada: Issues, Scope, Definitions and Directions," in *Community Economic Development in Canada*, edited by David Douglas, 5.

3. Taken from http://www.comm-dev.org/, accessed October 15, 2004.

4. Rothman, "An Analysis of Goals and Roles in Community Organization Practice," in *Social Work*, 24-31.

5. Fisher, *Let the People Decide: Neighborhood Organizing in America,* 1984; Hanna and Robinson, *Strategies for Community Empowerment, Direct-Action, and Transformative Approaches to Social Change Practice,* 1994; Checkoway, "Six Strategies of Community Change," in *Community Development Journal*, 1995;

Dreier, "Community Empowerment Strategies: the Limits and Potential of Community Organizing in Urban Neighborhoods," in *Cityscape: A Journal of Policy Development and Research*, 1996, 121-159; Kingsley, McNeely and Gibson, *Community Building: Coming of Age*, 1997; see also Murphy and Cunningham (2003) for a more detailed discussion and comparison of most of these typologies.

6.   Favreau and Lévesque, *Développement économique communautaire : Économie sociale et intervention*, 1996.

7.   Douglas, 1994, 27.

8.   See Murphy and Cunningham, Kubisch et al, 2002; Torjman and Leviten-Reid; Toye and Infanti.

9.   Douglas, 3.

10.   Fontan.

11.   Douglas, 14.

12.   Perry.

13.   Blakely, xvi.

14 . Although in practice, it can certainly be said that some Community Futures Development Corporations take a more progressive approach.

15.   Employment and Immigration Canada, 1990, quoted in Fontan.

16.   Douglas, 27.

17.   Cujatar.

18.   Loizides, "The Role of the Private Sector in CED," The Conference Board of Canada,1.

19.   Ibid.

20.   Brodhead, 3.

21.   Douglas, 26.

22.   Douglas, 7.

23.   Favreau and Lévesque.

24.   Toye and Infanti.

25.   Torjman and Leviten Reid.

26.   Personal correspondence to Mike Toye, August 23, 2004. A description of the program can be found at http://edaalberta.com/CEDAP-Program.htm

27.   Canadian Women's Foundation, 9.

28.   Zizys, "CED for Toronto," Toronto CED Learning Network, 4.

29.   These are three of six total criteria, the three others involving a 20 per cent cash contribution to the technical assistance fees, agreement to administer the project, and agreement to document and share lessons learned. Taken from http://www.carleton.ca/cedtap-patdec/appform/index1_e.html, (accessed August 22, 2004.)

30.   Taken from http://www.ccednet-rcdec.ca/en/pages/home.asp, (accessed August 22, 2004.)

31.   MacInnes, Chaland and Downing, 22.

32.   Chaland and Downing.

Bibliography

Blakely, Edward and Ted Bradshaw. *Planning Local Economic Development: Theory and Practice.* 3rd ed. Thousand Oaks, California: Sage Publications, 2002.

Brodhead, Dal. "Community Economic Development Practice in Canada." In *Community Economic Development: Perspectives on Research and Policy,* edited by Burt Galaway and Joe Hudson, 2-12. Toronto: Thompson Educational Publishing, 1994.

"Building on Strengths: Community Economic Development in the Atlantic Provinces." *Summary of Conference Proceedings*, Wolfville, Nova Scotia, March 8-10, 1994.

Canadian Women's Foundation and the Canadian Women's Community Economic Development Council. "Women and Community Economic Development in Canada: A Research Report." Toronto: Canadian Women's Foundation, 2004.

Chaland, Nicole and Rupert Downing. "Profile of Community Economic Development in Canada: Results of a Survey of Community Economic Development Across Canada." Victoria, BC: Canadian Community Economic Development Network, 2003 [online]. Available from http://www.ccednet-rcdec.ca/en/docs/pubs/Profile_CED_Oct_2003.pdf

Checkoway, Barry. "Six Strategies of Community Change." *Community Development Journal* 30 no. 1 (1995) : 2-20.

Chekki, Dan. *Community Development—Theory and Method of Planned Change.* New Delhi: Vikas Publishing House PVT Ltd, 1979.

Community Economic Development Secretariat and Social Investment Organization. "CED at Work in Metro Toronto: Profiles of 40 Community Economic Development Initiatives." Toronto: Queen's Printer for Ontario, 1995.

Cutajar, Dennis. "Strengthening the Downtown Management Plan: A Cooperative Approach to Community Economic Development." *Economic Development Bulletin*, New Series, No. 7. Waterloo, ON: University of Waterloo, 2001.

Douglas, David. "Community Economic Development in Canada: Issues, Scope, Definitions and Directions." In *Community Economic Development in Canada*, edited by David Douglas. Whitby, ON: McGraw-Hill Ryerson, 1994.

Dreier, Peter. "Community Empowerment Strategies: The Limits and Potential of Community Organizing in Urban Neighborhoods." *Cityscape: A Journal of Policy Development and Research*, 2 no. 2 (1996) : 121-159. [Online]. Available from http://www.huduser.org/periodicals/cityscpe/vol2num2/ch6.html (accessed October 18, 2004).

Economic Council of Canada. "From the Bottom Up: The Community Economic Development Approach." Ottawa: Ministry of Supply and Services Canada, 1990.

Employment and Immigration Canada. "Community Economic Development and You: An Information Booklet on Community Economic Development and Strategic Planning and a Guide to Training for Community Volunteers." Ottawa: Ministry of Supply and Services Canada, 1992.

Favreau, Louis and Benoît Lévesque. *Développement économique communautaire : Économie sociale et intervention.* Sainte-Foy, QC: Presses de l'Université du Québec, 1996.

Fisher, Robert. *Let the People Decide: Neighborhood Organizing in America.* New York: Twayne, 1984.

Fontan, Jean-Marc. *A Critical Review of Canadian, American, and European Community Economic Development Literature*. Vernon, BC: Centre for Community Enterprise, 1993.

Hanna, Mark G. and Buddy Robinson. *Strategies for Community Empowerment, Direct-Action, and Transformative Approaches to Social Change Practice*. Lewiston, NY: Edwin Mellen, 1994.

Kingsley, G. Thomas, Joseph B. McNeely and James O. Gibson. *Community Building: Coming of Age*. Baltimore, MD: Development Training Institute, 1997.

Kubisch, Anne, Patricia Auspos, Prudence Brown, Robert Chaskin, Karen Fulbright-Anderson and Ralph Hamilton. "Voices from the Field II : Reflections on Comprehensive Community Change." Washington: The Aspen Institute, 2002.

Lewis, Mike. "The Scope and Characteristics of Community Economic Development in Canada." In *Community Economic Development: Perspectives on Research and Policy,* edited by Burt Galaway and Joe Hudson. Toronto: Thompson Educational Publishing, 1994.

Loizides, Stelios. "The Role of the Private Sector in Community Economic Development." Report 126-94. Ottawa: The Conference Board of Canada, 1994.

MacInnes, Colin, Nicole Chaland and Rupert Downing. "What's 'In Store': CCEDNet Profiles our Growing and Dynamic Sector." *Making Waves*, 14 no. 3 (2003): 22-25.

MacNeil, Teresa and Rick Williams. "Evaluation Framework for Community Economic Development." Ottawa: National Welfare Grants, 1995.

Murphy, Patricia Watkins and James V. Cunningham. *Organizing for Community Controlled Development: Renewing Civil Society.* Thousand Oaks, California: Sage Publications, 2003.

Ninacs, William. "Synthesizing the Research Results: Where is the Common Ground?" *Making Waves*, 4 no. 4, (1993): 18-20.

Nozick, Marcia. "Five Principles of Sustainable Community Development." In *Community Economic Development: In Search of Empowerment and Alternatives*, edited by Eric Shragge. Montréal: Black Rose Books, 1993.

Nozick, Marcia. "An Integrated Development Model for Building Sustainable Communities in Canada." In *Community Economic Development: Perspectives on Research and Policy,* edited by Burt Galaway and Joe Hudson. Toronto: Thompson Educational Publishing, 1994.

Perry, Stewart. "Yogurt on a Mission." *Making Waves*, 13 no. 4 (2002): 6-15.

Perry, Stewart. "Some Terminology and Definitions in the Field of Community Economic Development." *Making Waves*, 10 no. 1 (1999): 20-23.

Perry, Stewart and Mike Lewis. *Reinventing the Local Economy.* Vernon, BC: Centre for Community Enterprise, 1994.

Roseland, Mark. *Toward Sustainable Communities: Resources for Citizens and their Governments.* Gabriola Island, BC: New Society Publishers, 1998.

Rothman, Jack. "An Analysis of Goals and Roles in Community Organization Practice." *Social Work*, 9 no. 2 (1964): 24-31.

Savoie, Donald. "Community Economic Development in Atlantic Canada: False Hope or Panacea?" *Monograph, Maritime Series*. Moncton: Canadian Institute for Research on Regional Development, 2000 [online]. Available from: http://www.umoncton.ca/icrdr/COMMUNITY-EN.pdf

Shragge, Eric. "The Politics of Community Economic Development." In *Community Economic Development: In Search of Empowerment and Alternatives*, edited by Eric Shragge. Montréal: Black Rose Books, 1993.

Shragge, Eric. "Community Economic Development: Conflicts and Visions" in *Community Economic Development*, edited by Eric Shragge, 2nd ed. Montréal: Black Rose Books, 1997.

Smith, Ross. "Strategies, Initiatives and Models for Community Economic Development." Burnaby, BC: Simon Fraser University, 2000.

Swack, Michael. "Properties and Characteristics of a Definition of CED Based on Original/Historical Intent." Presentation at the 2003 National CED Symposium, Southern New Hampshire University School of CED, Manchester, NH. May 12-14, 2003.

Torjman, Sherri and Eric Leviten-Reid. "Comprehensive Community Initiatives." Ottawa: Caledon Institute of Social Policy, 2003 [online]. Available from http://www.caledoninst.org

Toye, Michael and Jennifer Infanti. "Social Inclusion and Community Economic Development." Victoria, BC: Canadian Community Economic Development Network, 2004 [online]. Available from http://www.ccednet-rcdec.ca/en/pages/learning network.asp (accessed October 2, 2004.)

Tremblay, Diane-Gabrielle et Jean-Marc Fontan. *Le développement économique local*. Sainte-Foy, QC: Télé-université, 1994.

Vachon, Bernard, avec la collaboration de Francine Coallier. *Le développement local : théorie et pratique.* Boucherville, QC: Gaëtan Morin éditeur, 1993.

Zizys, Tom. "Community Economic Development for Toronto." Document prepared for the Toronto CED Learning Network, 2003 [online]. Available from: http://www.torontoced.com/publications/bg/tcedln.doc

John Loxley and Laura Lamb

Economics for CED Practitioners

Despite the growing popularity of community economic development (CED), it remains under-theorized in economic, political and sociological terms.[1] On the economic side, there are two main reasons for this. First, CED is itself a vague concept open to many different definitions and approaches. This makes it difficult to develop a coherent theory to explain it. We shall return to this problem later. Secondly, orthodox economic theory has no interest in CED however it is defined. It is preoccupied with models of profit maximization, short-run efficiency and individual self-interest, within a framework that accepts perfect competition as the ideal industrial structure. Whereas industrial organizations deviate from this structure, they are considered to be less than optimal in terms of efficiency and that becomes the focal point of interest in the theory. Huge sectors of the economy in which the market plays only a peripheral role, what Bakker and Elson[2] have called the "care economy," in which women's labour figures prominently, are excluded from the analysis, even though the market economy could not function without them. The logic of this underlying competitive model is one of increasing scale, concentration and centralization, a logic which results in "inefficiency" being the norm rather than the exception. Class, gender and regional inequalities are inevitable outcomes of this theoretical model, but are treated only as irrational occurrences that would disappear if the market were given free reign. State intervention is called upon to ameliorate these inequalities, both to minimize resulting social friction and to assist the process of private accumulation. State subsidization of the private sector is intrinsic to the system and is both overt, as in the granting of concessions to attract business to a particular geographic location, and hidden, in the form of tax expenditures or state support of health, education and infrastructure, upon which the private sector is dependent.[3] Ideologically, however, the private sector is considered to be a distinct sector driven by creativity and entrepreneurial spirit, and its dependence on the state is not acknowledged in mainstream theory.

That theory makes no attempt to consider alternative, more cooperative forms of industrial organization, nor to assess what the macro, economy-wide implications of their growth or widespread adoption might be. CED would fall into this group, calling for a different approach to economic theorizing, insofar as it is driven by motivations other than private accumulation and narrow self-interest.

CED as a Challenge to Economic Orthodoxy

One of the difficulties in theorizing about CED is the eclectic nature of its definition. To some, CED covers any economic development initiative, be it private, public or community driven, taking place within some definition of community, usually a geographic one. In this view, there is no necessary inconsistency between orthodox economics and CED. For more demanding definitions of CED coming to dominate the literature, more radical departures from the orthodoxy seem called for.[4] These define CED as a social process in terms of decision-making; they replace the individual consumer with the collective community; they see the meeting of collective needs taking precedence over the satisfaction of individual consumer demands; they do not artificially split decisions about production from those about consumption, as the orthodoxy does; they take a long view of economic activities as opposed to that of short-term profit-maximization; and they see economic decisions as being inextricably linked to social, environmental, political and cultural considerations.

Within this more demanding view of CED there are two schools of thought. The first, associated with a more radical, communal tradition, sees CED as an alternative form of social organization to capitalism. The second has a more limited vision, seeing CED as a desirable and workable approach to dealing with particular problems facing communities, such as "unemployment, poverty, job loss, environmental degradation and loss of community control."[5] These problems are a direct outcome of the way in which capitalism differentially and unevenly affects certain communities and CED is seen as a way to help fix them, within the confines of the capitalist system as a whole. Adherents of the radical school are often found working alongside those of the problem-centred school on the grounds that building viable CED projects might help people see the feasibility of an alternative economic and social system based on CED principles.

The most complete set of CED principles are those underlying the Neechi model. Neechi Foods Co-op Ltd. is an Aboriginal worker-owned cooperative retail store in Winnipeg. The idea of this approach is to build a strong, inward looking, self-reliant economy which is based on goods and services consumed by people who live or work in the community. In theoretical terms it is a convergence strategy of economic development.[6] It favours cooperative ownership, small-scale production and popular control over economic decision-making. It is a holistic approach, in which the safety, health and self-respect of residents are of paramount importance.[7] The principles on which it operates are as follows: production of goods and services for local use; use of local goods and services; local reinvestment of locally generated profits; long-term employment of local residents; local skill development; local decision-making; improved public health; improved physical environment; neighbourhood stability; human dignity and solidarity among communities and businesses following these principles.

This strategy of CED can be contrasted with alternative ones which implicitly assume communities are too small to offer economic opportunities based purely on the local market, and hence should build their base on exporting goods or services. This assumes the logic of large-scale production and the logic of orthodox economics. The range of alternative economic approaches to CED are best exemplified by contrasting, in detail, export-base approaches with that of the Neechi model and it is to this that we now turn.

Export-base Approaches

Export-base approaches are a common strategy where production within the community is geared to satisfying market demand outside the community. These approaches are grounded in export-base theory, a theory of regional economic growth and development pertinent to community economic development, as a community can be considered a smaller region. Export-base theory is grounded on the assumption that all economic activities in a community are a function of export activities, and that export expansion is the primary source of economic growth. The theory postulates that growth in a community is largely determined by the success of its exports, either from an improved cost position of existing exports relative to competing areas or as a result of the development of new exports.[8]

The export base becomes instrumental in shaping the distinctive quality of the community's economy. The economic-base model conceptualizes the economy as two sectors, the export or "basic" sector and the non-export or "non-basic" sector. The basic sector consists of all economic activity whose final market lies outside the community, and the non-basic sector consists of all economic activity whose final market is local. Total economic activity is a function of export activity. Employment and income in the basic sector are a function of external demand for a community's exports.[9]

Economic-base analysis is a tool of regional economics used to examine the economic impact of export activity in a region or community. Total economic activity, Y, is modelled as a function of export activity, E, in the equation $Y = (1+k)$ E, where k is the ratio of non-basic activity to basic activity ($k = N/B$). $1 + k$ is the multiplier which will always be greater than one, assuming some non-basic activity exists. The equation explains that if export activity increases, then total activity increases by the amount of the change in export activity times the multiplier.

Export base theory is a derivative of the staple theory of growth, a Canadian theory developed to explain the economic development of Canada as a process of diversification around an export base.[10] The central concept of staple theory is the spread effects of the export sector, in other words the impact of export activity on the local economy and society. The range of investment opportunities in domestic markets or the extent of diversification around the export base is determined by the demand for factors, the demand for intermediate inputs, the possibility of further processing and the distribution of income.

Staple theory analyzes the impact of export expansion on the economy by classifying the income flows. The inducement of domestic investment resulting from increased export activity can be broken down into three linkage effects: backward linkage, forward linkage and final demand linkage.[11] A backward linkage is a measure of the extent of expenditure on community-produced inputs, including capital goods. Backward linkages are created when input requirements are comprised of resources and technologies produced or owned by the community. A forward linkage is a measure of the extent that a sector's output is sold as inputs to other sectors of the community. A final-demand linkage is a measure of the extent to which domestic industries are producing consumer or investment goods for use in the community. The greater the proportion of domestic production sold inside the region, rather than as exports, the larger the final-demand linkage effect will be. Linkages are also determined by supply-side expansion of the export sector, the degree of which depends on the relationship between staple production and the supply of entrepreneurship and complementary inputs, including technology.

If the staple or staples generate strong linkage effects which are adequately employed to the community's advantage, then eventually the economy will grow and diversify to the point where the term "staple economy" will no longer apply.[12]

The cyclical sensitivity of the region is ultimately determined by the export staple. Specifically, income elasticities of export staples are the major determinant of cyclical sensitivity in a community.[13] A region with a narrow export base is more prone to disturbances resulting from changes in income levels in other regions than a region with a broad, more diversified export base. Income elasticity of demand for the export staples is a critical determinant of vulnerability to economic fluctuations.

Export-base theory is limited in that it is only appropriate for small, isolated economies whose growth and development are dependent on export-oriented industries.[14] The theory fails to acknowledge sources of economic stimuli other than exports, such as the other components of gross regional product, including consumption, government expenditures and business investment and the volume of residential construction. Exports are neither the only nor the most important source of economic stimuli. In fact it has been found that economic activities are rarely a function only of export activities.[15]

The role and source of capital is a critical component of export-led development. As new communities typically depend on imported capital to develop their export staple industries, it is the external investors who decide on the investment projects. External investors are typically reluctant to invest in new, unproven activities where risks are greater, thus new investment goes to expanding the base rather than diversifying the local economy.[16] Resource firms do not tend to diversify, and linkages are rarely established at the point of production of the export commodity. Many of the exports are products with little or no further processing from raw material.[17] Further, profits from the imported capital typically flow out of the community, reducing linkages.

Environmental concerns may result from outside ownership of capital. Schumacher argues that community ownership is preferable in that "men [*sic*] organized in small units will take better care of *their* bit of land or other natural resources than anonymous companies or megalomaniac governments which pretend to themselves that the whole universe is their legitimate quarry."[18]

The term leakage is used as a measure of the income flows leaving a region through sources such as migratory labour, servicing of capital imports and immigrant's remittances abroad, to name a few. The development of a resource base into a staple export does not necessarily lead to community economic development. Historically, export-based economies do not diversify, and linkages are rarely established at the point of production of the export commodity. Many of the exports are products with little or no further processing from the raw material. Loxley describes staple economies as divergent, a concept introduced by C. Y. Thomas, implying that what is locally produced is not locally consumed and what is locally consumed is not locally produced.[19]

Convergence or Community-based Economic Development

A convergence or community-based approach attempts to match community needs to locally available resources.[20] This inward focused approach suggests the convergence of local use and demand through the creation of a series of industries producing "basic goods"—goods which feature prominently in the production of a wide range of consumption and investment goods.[21] The nature of the community resource base and the structure of community demand and needs determine the choice of products to be produced. Community participation and ownership are necessary components of convergence and community-based approaches because they play a part in reversing income flows, reducing income inequalities and ensuring production meets community demand and needs.[22]

A convergence approach is somewhat compatible with a subsistence strategy, as the very nature of subsistence is the convergence of local resources with need. However, a convergence strategy goes well beyond subsistence to integrate production for monetary exchange and to suggest how this might be organized.[23]

The economic theory underlying this approach perceives underdevelopment as a consequence of increasing divergence and unresponsiveness of domestic production to meeting the needs of the local community.[24] The divergence, in part, describes a lack of self-sufficiency. Foreign ownership and control of domestic resources is a key element of divergence. The economic development process transpires through economic activity with an inward focus, a convergence of a community's resource base with the community's demands and needs. Production decisions are based on the demands and needs of the community rather than demands from outside the community (exports). For example, the retailer Neechi Foods, an Aboriginal worker co-op in inner-city Winnipeg, employs community residents, sells products considered to be most needed in the community, does not sell cigarettes and subsidizes the sale of fruit to children.

The import domestic expenditure coefficient, a quantitative measure of divergence, relates the value of imports for domestic use to domestic expenditure.[25] This measurement provides relevant information on the extent of the gap between the structure of production and the structure of demand which traditional import indices, such as the measurements of import propensity (ratio of imports to GDP) and the import coefficient (ratio of imports to total expenditures), do not divulge. A community whose import domestic expenditure coefficient is close to one is described as a divergent economy, whereas a community whose coefficient is close to zero is described as a convergent economy. Disadvantaged communities typically have import domestic expenditure coefficients close to one, meaning that nearly all domestic spending is on goods and services imported into the community. The import domestic expenditure coefficient is useful for planning development strategies. For instance, development strategies based on principles of the Neechi model aim to reduce the import domestic expenditure coefficient through small business initiatives to provide goods and services consumed by those who live and work in the community.

The formation of linkages among the different production sectors is the mechanism through which community economic growth and development occurs. Staple theory, convergence theory, big push theory, as well as theoretical work by Loxley, all emphasize the importance of linkages for economic development.[26] For instance, backward linkages are created when Neechi Foods purchases moccasins and other homemade crafts made by Aboriginal women in the neighbourhood for sale in their store. Forward linkages would be created if Neechi Foods were to sell food items to a community bakery or restaurant. Final-demand linkages are formed by Neechi Foods' objective of offering a better selection of food at better prices to community residents. Neechi creates further linkages by purchasing wild rice and wild blueberries from Native communities outside of Winnipeg which are also working on building community self-reliance. The maximization of linkages and the minimization of leakages strengthens the growth and development process. Optimization is achieved to the extent that production is locally owned and profits stay within the community, and that the production output is sold to other businesses and individuals within the community.

The issue of scale is imperative to convergence and community-based approaches to community development.[27] Small-scale production is perceived as being desirable because it allows for a more spatially balanced economy, a less impersonal work environment, the possibility of community participation and control and the opportunity to tailor technology to local skill and employment levels.[28] As well, small-scale production is more compatible with the environment:

"Small-scale operations, no matter how numerous, are always less likely to be harmful to the natural environment than larger-scale ones, simply because their individual force is small in relation to the recuperative forces of nature."[29]

The emphasis on small-scale production for community development may be in conflict with microeconomic theory, which generally supports the view that economies of scale are crucial in determining the nature and levels of production. Those who support a convergence approach to community development argue that minimum-efficient scale is not as important for deciding levels of production as in the critical minimum level of production.[30] They argue that most benefits of large-scale production accrue at or below the critical minimum level of output, which may be well below output levels at which unit costs are minimized. The economic and social benefits stemming from the formation of inter-industry linkages are viewed as being more important than economies of scale in community development.[31] Nonetheless, a convergence approach acknowledges that small-scale projects will normally carry higher unit costs than larger scale projects, and that subsidies to firms may be required to compensate for the foregone benefits of large-scale production. As well, unit costs can be minimized through inter-community cooperation, minimizing capital costs through multi-usage of facilities and perhaps a shorter work week. Exports can play a pivotal role by enlarging the market just enough so that unit costs can fall to their critical minimum level. Trade outside the community thus serves a different function from that in export-base theories because exports serve only to extend domestic demand and domestic need.[32]

The higher costs of small-scale production may also be offset by external economies, in which the costs or revenues of any individual community enterprise may be improved by the existence of other enterprises in the community. External economies contribute to growth and development by improving a community's competitive cost position and can be developed through linkages as well as activities such as creating marketing organizations, credit facilities, labour-force training programs, housing projects, recreation centres and social institutions.[33]

A convergence approach faces challenges on the issues of community ownership and on its political assumptions. It is reasonable to expect fundamental opposition to approaches emphasizing community ownership from those who control the economy and those who hold power. The main challenge is that this approach requires basic and long-term state support, which it may be denied if it challenges the private sector or empowers the community to voice its demands and discontents.[34]

A pure convergence strategy is based on very ambitious political assumptions. It assumes that the political system is able to regulate or prohibit trade flows, impose taxes, take property into public sector hands, redistribute income and plan production.[35] Such a political system stands in contrast to the dominant one in present day society, in which unfettered free markets and the minimization of the role of the state are held as the formula for development. Yet, the importance of state funding to communities, state control of land and natural resources, the existence of large crown corporations and the openness to community-based approaches, provide rough proxies to some of the assumptions stated above. In Canadian society, at best only approximations of a pure convergence approach can be followed.[36]

Other CED Strategies

Between these two extremes, three other strategies of CED can be identified.[37] The first, which is really a strategy of defeatism or despair, is that of a social assistance/migration strategy, where the state and the community have effectively given up on economic development and people either survive locally on transfer payments or leave the community for other centres. This approach has characterized state policy towards some, often relatively isolated communities and underlies so-called market solutions to Aboriginal economic problems.[38] The problem with this approach is that the lack of local economic development opportunities is often assumed *a priori*, rather than concluded after detailed examination of possibilities. A second problem is that economic conditions for migrants are often little better in towns than they were in the relatively isolated communities from which they came. Market solutions are, therefore, often no solution.

The second strategy in many communities is the provision of government services which provide the main or an important aspect of economic strategy, from local government, to infrastructure building and maintenance, schools, health care facilities, policing and garbage disposal. In many Aboriginal communities, these activities account for most jobs and a high proportion of community income.

Finally, some communities pursue what economists would describe as an import substitution strategy, providing services and producing goods locally which were previously imported. The local provision of government services is particularly attractive to communities, implying that local people take over jobs previously occupied by people from outside the community. Because scale is less of an issue than the import substitution of goods, the jobs are relatively secure and long term and it also implies a greater degree of local control. The replacement of non-government services and imported products may face problems of scale but their market demand is known with a degree of certainty. Import substitution has a role in convergence strategies but the latter do not accept the existing distribution of income—and hence current market demand—as a given. Nor do convergence strategies accept that output should be driven only by the market, placing a much greater emphasis on meeting *needs* as opposed to *demand*.

The Role of Subsidies in CED

Underlying most approaches to CED is the philosophy of self-reliance and community independence. In reality, however, given that CED ventures have to compete with other, often monopolistic producers, having to accept prices fixed by them which are based on much larger scales of production and wages close to or below subsistence levels (e.g., Wal-Mart), in reality, few CED projects would be viable without some degree of subsidization. Their scale of production is usually very small, overhead costs are relatively high, wages paid have to be at socially acceptable levels, staff are often inexperienced and need training and they often face social problems not necessarily experienced by the general labour force. For all these reasons, and until prices generally in the economy are arrived at by considerations other than those of short-run, market-driven, profit maximization, CED projects will find it difficult to prosper. Many require a degree of subsidization in order to survive. Subsidies can take many forms; from someone picking up the bottom-line losses of a project, to providing a wage or training subsidy, a protected market for products at a higher than market price, physical assets at less than cost, cheap capital, a protective tariff or tax on competitors' products or help towards meeting overhead costs. All of these can be found in one form or another around the world.

In places where CED is very well established along convergence lines so that many enterprises and agencies are providing a range of goods and services, some products may be subsidized by others, so that what is called cross-subsidization is taking place. For example, a community-owned credit union may provide credit on favourable terms to other community-based projects; a locally owned restaurant may be supplied with locally produced food at higher or lower than market prices. Or, it may be the case that most locally produced products are being sold at higher prices than available elsewhere (i.e., consumers are subsidizing all the CED operations). What is the economic rationale for these various forms of subsidization?

Usually one resorts to principles of cost-benefit analysis to justify subsidization. Projects that are not commercially viable may be socially viable if the market does not accurately capture the true costs and benefits to society of the project in question. Market prices do not normally capture the true *opportunity cost* of employing resources. Thus, it is argued, in a community experiencing widespread unemployment, the true social cost of employing labour is not the wage that would have to be paid to hire workers, but rather the loss of output to society of offering these people a job. Often, that loss is zero or negligible and hence a subsidy could be justified by putting wage costs well below their market cost, thus improving the apparent profitability of the project. The state or some other entity would have to pay the project the difference between the market wage costs and the social wage cost and the rationale for this subsidy is, therefore, one of job creation. Similar arguments can be made for projects that provide training to workers, provide external economies to other sections of the community or reduce social problems in the community. The correct way to proceed is to calculate true social costs and benefits, see what this does to the bottom line of the project and limit subsidies to the amount by which they turn red ink into black ink in the accounts of the project.

In reality, these calculations are often difficult to make, and governments and politicians find them hard to follow. Where this is the case, another closely related approach may be pursued. This consists of measuring the *fiscal impact* of a project and gearing the amount of subsidy to the extent to which the project improves the fiscal position of government(s). Such improvement may come from a number of different sources. First, if the project increases employment it may reduce either Employment Insurance (EI) claims (which are expenditures in the federal government budget) or social assistance payments (usually paid by provincial or municipal governments). Secondly, workers pay EI contributions which increase government revenue as well as income, sales and other taxes. Thirdly, if projects reduce social problems, by tackling them either directly or indirectly (e.g., by putting people to work), then government spending to address social problems will go down. In theory, it is possible to add up all these positive fiscal impacts and justify government subsidization accordingly. Politicians can relate more easily to this approach and find it more accessible than justifications based on cost-benefit analyses. Though there are similarities in the two approaches, they can and will normally give different results for the amount of subsidy being justified. One potential problem with the fiscal approach is that net fiscal benefits are spread among the different levels of government, and the level of government benefiting most may not be the one that has the most subsidy available. Nonetheless, fiscal impact studies are worthwhile undertaking to justify state support for CED undertakings.

The extensive cross-subsidization of CED projects in a community through higher final sales prices, than those in neighbouring communities, is justified by reference to the jobs created by the projects which would not otherwise exist. Members of the community could probably buy the products of each individual project more cheaply elsewhere, but if they were to do so, they would lose jobs and incomes in the community and community economic and social coherence would be reduced.[39] In this respect, support for CED projects is not unlike support for fair trade products or cooperatives generally; consumers may have to pay more to support broader social goals.

Subsidies may be a feature of all alternative strategies of CED, except, by definition, a pure subsistence strategy. Thus, an export strategy may not work if production costs are too high to compete in the external market and import substitutes may need some form of protection to compete against cheaper goods and services produced outside the community. In a convergence strategy, some activities, such as housing, education and training, take on a huge importance because they immediately serve to address basic peoples' needs as well as provide sources of income, employment and linkages. Where state and third-sector funding is available for these activities (i.e., implicit or explicit subsidization), they can form the basis of a convergent CED strategy.

Another source of subsidization of projects is the voluntary labour of members of the community. This is often important and under-recognized. It is also often gendered, with women playing disproportionate roles.[40] Pursuing a convergence strategy might therefore place new demands on community members, especially women, and this needs to be recognized. Successful pursuit of the strategy might reduce other burdens on women, however, by improving child care facilities, creating job opportunities, improving incomes and reducing social problems that face them or demand their attention.

Summary and Conclusion

This contribution has attempted to throw light on aspects of the economics of CED thought to be important to CED practitioners. For that reason it has attempted to examine different philosophical approaches to CED as well as different economic strategies of implementation. Given the competing views of what CED is and how one should go about implementing it, the economics of CED cannot be separated from this broader discussion. There are no single right or wrong ways of proceeding, but the vision chosen and the strategy pursued will each have its own economic implications. Common to all approaches, when attempting to pursue CED within capitalism rather than as a replacement for it, will be the need to find sources of support for projects that allow them to compete against much larger capitalist alternatives. As the CED options expand, state subsidization may be replaced by broader consumer support through cross-subsidization, or social pricing.

Notes

1.   The economic, political and sociological theory of CED is being examined as part of the Manitoba Research Alliance on CED and the New Economy SSHRC-funded research agenda.

2.   Bakker and Elson, "Towards Engendering Budgets" in *Alternative Federal Budget Papers*. Ottawa, Canadian Centre for Policy Alternatives, 1998.

3.   O'Connor, *The Fiscal Crisis of the State*, New York, St. Martin's, 1973.

4.   See, for instance, Canadian CED Network, Home page, http://www.ccednet-rcdec.ca/en/pages/home.asp (accessed May, 2004); Loxley, *The Economics of Community Development,* Report Prepared for the Native Economic Development Program, 1986.

5.   Canadian CED Network.

6.   Thomas, *Dependence and Transformation*.

7.   Loxley, "Sustainable Urban Economic Development: An Aboriginal Perspective," *Journal of Aboriginal Economic Development*, 29-32.

8.   North, "Location Theory and Regional Economic Growth," *Journal of Political Economy*, 332-345.

9.   Davis, *Regional Economic Impact Analysis and Project Evaluation*; Hewings, *Regional Industrial Analysis and Development*.

10.   The term staple refers to the main commodity produced by a region. It is generally thought of as describing products of extractive industries. Watkins, "A Staple Theory of Economic Growth," *Canadian Journal of Economics and Political Science*, 141-158.

11.   Hirschman, *The Strategy of Economic Development*; Watkins.

12.   Watkins.

13.   North.

14.   Davis.

15.   Loxley, 1986.

16.   North.

17.   Watkins.

18.   Schumacher, *Small is Beautiful*, 34.

19.   Loxley, 1986; Thomas.

20.   Wismer, and Pell, *Community Profit: Community-based economic development in Canada*.

21.   Loxley, 1986

22.   Ibid.

23.   Ibid.

24.   Thomas.

25.   Thomas.

26.   Watkins; Thomas; Lynn, *Economic Development: Theory and Practice for a Divided World*; Loxley, 1986.

27.   Schumacher, 1974; Thomas, 1974; Wismer and Pell, 1981; Loxley, 1986

28.   Loxley, 1986.

29.   Schumacher, 33.

30.   Minimum efficient scale is that production output at which unit costs are at a minimum. The critical minimum level is the production output at which the rate of fall in unit costs, as output increases, is at its greatest. See Thomas.

31.   Loxley, 1986.

32.   Thomas.

33.   Blakely, *Planning Local Economic Development: Theory and Practice*.

34.   Shragge, Eric. *Community Economic Development: In Search of Empowerment*.

35.   Loxley, 1986.

36.   Ibid.

37.   Ibid.

38.   See Riggs, and Velk, "Native People of North America and the Dependency Issue," *McGill Working Papers in Economics*.

39.   This problem is captured graphically in the film about the experiences of Evangeline in Prince Edward Island, *We're the Boss*.

40.   Issues relating to women and CED are dealt with more extensively below in the chapter by Melanie Conn.

Bibliography

Bakker, Isabelle and Diane Elson, "Towards Engendering Budgets." In *Alternative Federal Budget Papers*. Ottawa, Canadian Centre for Policy Alternatives, 1998.

Blakely, Edward J. *Planning Local Economic Development: Theory and Practice,* 2nd ed. London: Sage, 1984.

Canadian CED Network, Home page, http://www.ccednet-rcdec.ca/en/pages/home.asp (accessed May 2004)

Davis, Craig H. *Regional Economic Impact Analysis and Project Evaluation*. Vancouver: UBC Press, 1993.

Hewings, G. J. D. *Regional Industrial Analysis and Development*. London: Methuen and Co., 1977.

Hirschman, A. O. *The Strategy of Economic Development*. New Haven and London: Yale University Press, 1965.

Loxley, John. "Sustainable Urban Economic Development: An Aboriginal Perspective." *Journal of Aboriginal Economic Development* 3, no. 1 (2002): 29-32.

Loxley, John. *The Economics of Community Development*. Report Prepared for the Native Economic Development Program, 1986.

———. "The Great Northern Plan," *Studies in Political Economy* 6, (1981): 151-182.

Lynn, Stuart R. *Economic Development: Theory and Practice for a Divided World*. New Jersey: Prentice Hall, 2003.

National Film Board, *We're the Boss*. Video. Ottawa, 1990.

North, Douglass C. "Location Theory and Regional Economic Growth." *Journal of Political Economy* 63, no.3, (1955): 332-345.

O'Connor, James, *The Fiscal Crisis of the State*. New York: St Martin's, 1973.

Riggs, A. R., and Tom Velk. "Native People of North America and the Dependency Issue." *McGill Working Papers in Economics,* April 1993.

Rothney, R. *Neechi Foods Co-op Ltd.: Lessons in Community Development*, Winnipeg, July 1992.

Shragge, Eric. *Community Economic Development: In Search of Empowerment*. Montreal: Black Rose Books, 1993.

Schumacher, E. F. *Small is Beautiful*. New York: Harper Colophon, 1973.

Thomas, Clive Y. *Dependence and Transformation*. New York: Monthly Review Press, 1974.

Watkins, Mel. " A Staple Theory of Economic Growth," *Canadian Journal of Economics and Political Science* 29, No. 2 (1963): 141-158.

Wismer, Susan and David Pell. *Community Profit: Community-Based Economic Development in Canada*. Toronto: IS Five Press, 1981.

Andrea Levy

Taking Care of Business?

In his 1994 book *Job Shift: How to Prosper in a Workplace without Jobs*, business consultant William Bridges observed that the combined effect of automation, outsourcing and the privatization of public services is to send the stable job the way of the horse and buggy. Noting that the job is itself a historically novel form of packaging the work that society needs done, he explained that the era of the secure indefinite work contract has given way to the advent of the just-in-time workforce, encompassing everyone from clerks to CEOs. Inspired by corporate executives such as AT&T Human Resources Vice-President James Meadows, who wanted all AT&T employees to regard themselves as contingent, Bridges counselled workers to recognize their uncertain status and adopt a new mindset: that of external vendors, in business for themselves.[1] In Canada, that thinking was echoed by Canadian pollster Angus Reid. Comparing the reality of the evolving labour market to a perilous circus act, he warned that the new economy holds out no guarantees of job security and advised Canadians to embrace risk and to become more entrepreneurial.[2] In a world where, as Bridges maintained, "everything is a market," the best strategy is to convert oneself, figuratively or literally, into a business. Welcome to "You & Co."[3]

Becoming a business is just what Canadians of both sexes, of all ages, from all regions and from all occupational sectors did in droves in the 1990s. Self-employment accounted for most of the net employment growth in Canada (an astonishing 79.4 per cent between 1989 and 1997).[4] By the beginning of the new millennium, nearly two-and-a-half million individuals were self-employed. Although their numbers declined in the early years of the new millennium, as of 2003, the self-employed comprised 14 per cent of the Canadian workforce—about the same proportion as the public sector.[5]

The cause of this striking phenomenon is a matter of some speculation and dispute. Coloured in part by their political inclinations, commentators cite different reasons, disagreeing about the extent to which people have been propelled into self-employment as opportunities for work in the private and public sectors narrowed, or chose to go into business for themselves because they prefer to be their own bosses.[6] But it is widely agreed that one of the explanations for this trend is the ongoing pattern of downsizing, subcontracting and privatization witnessed in the private and public sectors throughout North America in the last quarter century.

In this context, the move to self-employment is consonant with the neoliberal belief that the changes in the labour market, which are summed up in the term flexibilization—a virtual code word for the erosion of stable long-term employment and the benefits historically associated with it—are inescapable and that there is nothing that individuals or societies can (or should) do about them other than adapt.

Getting more entrepreneurial is one way of adapting. Getting poorer and more vulnerable is another. Sometimes they go hand in hand. Many researchers have pointed out that the growth in self-employment in the 1990s consisted in considerable part of precarious, one-person operations taking in significantly lower revenues than paid employees and deprived of the security attendant upon such benefits as pension plans, paid vacations, unemployment insurance and supplemental health insurance.[7]

The growth spurt in self-employment may thus be less the consequence of a renaissance of risk-taking than an expression of the broader trend towards the destabilization of work, that has been designated by such terms as "non-standard employment," the "contingent workforce," "casualization" and "precariousness"— a trend that is particularly pronounced in Canada compared with some other developed countries, but by no means exceptional. "All around the world," observes Ulrich Beck in his *Brave New World of Work*, "flexible work and insecure terms of employment are growing faster than any other form of work."[8] Fred and Harry Magdoff make the same observation, arguing along Marxist lines that the trend towards disposable labour, particularly in Europe and the United States, should be understood in terms of the universal recourse in the capitalist market system to a reserve army of labour that serves to bring down wage costs and render workers more tractable.[9] A somewhat different view holds that a significant segment of the workforce has been rendered superfluous by the technological advances of contemporary capitalism, which accounts for permanently high rates of unemployment and underemployment[10] (this is in fact one of the dominant understandings of the notion of social exclusion as opposed to traditional poverty[11]). What is undisputed is the ongoing deregulation of the labour market that is giving rise to precariousness and shutting some citizens out of the gains of economic growth.

In many of its forms, community economic development (CED) also represents an entrepreneurial response to poverty and precariousness. While going into business for oneself is typically driven by individual initiative, entrepreneurial efforts in the third sector—whether geographically oriented toward revitalizing individual poor communities, as in the case of CED, or more demographically focused on ensuring the participation of various disadvantaged groups in the labour market, as in the case of the social economy—are of a collective character, and are informed by aims different from the pursuit of personal independence and profit that at least partly underpins the You & Co. mentality. Particularly in the last ten years, new types of third-sector collective entrepreneurship have been the focus of growing attention on the part of local activists, academics and politicians concerned with finding ways and means of coping with unemployment, underemployment and various forms of social exclusion at a time when neoliberalism in theory and practice has dealt crippling blows to the welfare state throughout the advanced industrial world. In a seminal study of the social economy in the U.K., Ash Amin, Angus Cameron and Ray Hudson clearly situate the rising expectations for the third sector in the industrialized world in the context of the breakdown of the Fordist model, which has entailed growing social exclusion and the growth of non-standard employment.[12]

In this essay, I propose to explore some of these themes, particularly in the Canadian context, drawing a brief picture of the growing destabilization of the labour market, and discussing how the third sector is being harnessed to the goals of job creation. I will also offer an overview of some recent research on job quality in the third sector itself, and conclude with some reflections on a more critical approach to the issues of work and job creation than is often taken by advocates of the third sector as an instrument of economic policy.

The Destabilization of Work

Non-standard employment refers to part-time (defined by Statistics Canada as fewer than thirty hours per week) and temporary (including contractual, seasonal and casual) work, as well as self-employment (restricted in some classification schemes to own-account self-employment, that is, independent workers without employees) and multiple job holding. The category encompasses a wide range of work situations, ranging from lucrative business consulting to minimum-wage McJobs, from university teaching to dog-walking. But even the relatively value-neutral term "non-standard employment" implies a conventional employment relationship from which this type of work arrangement is a deviation.

Of course, that standard relationship, which refers to full-time work (ranging roughly from 35-44 hours) for a single employer for an indefinite term, is itself historically anomalous, arising sometime between the first decades of the twentieth century and the Second World War and applying predominantly to men (and exclusively to the West—insecurity of and in work has remained the norm for the majority of the world's population).[13] Our assumption, now increasingly uncertain, that a job comes with a measure of security and a package of benefits beyond a wage, is rooted in what is commonly described as the Fordist model—the system of mass production and mass consumption of standardized goods associated with the proposition famously tendered by Henry Ford that workers are also customers, implying that wages must be sufficiently high to permit them to purchase the consumer goods they produce. The transmutation of the employment relationship in the last quarter-century is considered by many scholars the hallmark of our own "post-Fordist" or postindustrial era, characterized by such phenomena as the decentralization of production, the dwindling of manufacturing and the massive shift to the service sector, the pivotal role played by technology and information and the advent of more flexible forms of production, accompanied by efforts to do away with what are perceived as the rigidities of labour markets.[14] Whether these changes represent a rupture, permanent or otherwise, with the postwar experience of stable jobs and relative security is, as is so much else about the nature of work and employment, the subject of a vast, intricate and recurrent debate.[15]

In Canada, non-standard employment grew apace from the mid-1970s to the mid-1990s to encompass roughly a third of the labour force and shows no signs of abating, despite strong full-time job growth in the past few years.[16] A 2003 Statistics Canada study revealed that between 2001 and 2002, the growth rate in part-time jobs (7.7 per cent) was three times higher than the growth rate of full-time jobs.[17] In addition to the 14 per cent who are self-employed, another 19 per cent are employed part-time[18] and roughly 13 per cent are employed on a temporary basis[19] (there is overlap between the various categories). Of the total, a majority are women, while ethnic minorities and youth are over-represented.[20]

The growth of non-standard employment in Canada has been the subject of much study since the 1990s. From the 1991 Economic Council of Canada report *Good Jobs, Bad Jobs* to books such as Jamie Swift's *Wheel of Fortune,* Dave Broad's *Hollow Work, Hollow Society* and the detailed portrait of precarious labour in Canada drawn up recently by researchers associated with the Community University Research Alliance on Contingent Employment,[21] Canadian policy analysts, academics, social critics and journalists have been documenting and dissecting the erosion of the traditional world of work. [22] Naturally, there is considerable debate about the forces underlying this phenomenon—particularly about the role of choice and preference in the expansion of non-standard working arrangements—as well as its implications. But there are a number of points which are widely agreed upon, and which appear to be applicable to most of the developed world.

Partly in search of higher profit margins and partly in response to competitive pressures over the last few decades, large corporations in particular have sought the latitude to quickly adjust their workforces to fit their changing requirements, as part of a bid to contain labour and other costs. This need is further fuelled by rapid technological change, which leads to accelerated obsolescence of skills and expertise. In a global market where everyone must turn on a dime in order to compete and remain profitable, firms want to be able to tailor the size and scope of their workforces to variable and shifting requirements with minimal investments in terms of benefit packages and training: With buzzwords such as "agile" and "nimble" abounding, long-term commitments become anathema. Large corporations stripped down to what they deemed their core competencies—those things most fundamental to their businesses and which they do best—and outsourcing remaining tasks, sometimes to erstwhile employees, on a pay-as-you-go basis. Governments, faced with spiralling costs and reluctant either to impose new taxes or strengthen their revenue bases by eliminating the myriad means for corporations to circumvent tax liability, followed suit, privatizing and contracting out public services.

This has certainly propelled the growth of non-standard employment. Another oft-cited factor is the combination of information technology and accelerated globalization, which, in addition to facilitating some "offshoring" (job transfer to low-wage countries), heralded the 24/7 economy and such innovations as round-the-clock customer support centres. In the service sector, consumer desire for extended shopping hours is also thought to have played a role in expanding non-standard working arrangements (we have quickly come to take Sunday shopping and 24-hour supermarkets for granted). It is also true that employees, and particularly women, have sought greater flexibility in order to be able to balance life and work. This is another factor in the growth of non-standard employment. However, there is clear evidence that a significant portion of part-time, contractual and temporary workers are involuntary participants in non-standard work arrangements who would prefer a more traditional employment relationship. From the mid-1970s to the mid-1990s, for example, the percentage of those employed part-time who reported that they accepted part-time work in the absence of full-time employment opportunities increased from 12 to 36 per cent.[23] And, according to one 2001 study, more than three-quarters of temporary workers would prefer permanent jobs.[24] One of the obvious reasons for this is that, as study after study confirms, wages are typically lower, benefits fewer and investment in training minimal in non-standard jobs.[25]

The significance of benefits in any discussion of the destabilization of work cannot be overestimated. To a significant extent, non-standard employment is precarious employment not only because those employed in non-standard working arrangements are often much less certain about the permanence of their jobs (as a rule the self-employed do not even qualify for employment insurance), but also because they are far less likely to have access to non-wage benefits such as employer-sponsored pension plans, supplemental health insurance, sick leave, disability insurance, paid vacations and so on. It is also difficult or impossible for many to take advantage of programs such as maternity leave, and the recently introduced compassionate care leave. A Statistics Canada study reported that in 2000 only 17 per cent of part-time workers and 14 per cent of temporary workers had extended medical, dental and disability insurance, compared with 58 per cent of full-time workers and 57 per cent of permanent workers; moreover, employees in non-standard jobs enjoyed less pension coverage.[26]

Non-wage benefits represent a significant cost to employers: according to Statistics Canada, the payroll cost of mandatory non-wage benefits rose from five per cent in 1961 to 12 per cent in 1998. If discretionary benefits are factored in, non-wage benefits represented a payroll cost of 36 per cent in 1998, up from 23 per cent in 1961.[27] It is not surprising then that there is an ongoing effort in both the private and public sector to roll back gains in this area. Employer-sponsored pensions, for instance, have been at the centre of recent bitter struggles by organized labour in Canada (at Air Canada and Stelco, for example). Beyond mounting direct attacks on the non-wage benefits of unionized employees, the expansion of non-standard employment is thus one way for employers to trim payroll costs.

Benefits are a crucial dimension of job quality. Consider the implications with respect to retirement, for example. This is a subject much in the news of late partly due to concerns about the consequences of the demographic shift toward an aging population and worries about the adequacy of Canada's pension fund. Retirement planning is a trendy topic in newspapers and magazines, and financial planning websites feature retirement planning calculators. "Is a million dollars enough to retire on?" financial planners muse. The figure seems absurd at first blush. However, to receive the equivalent of an employer-sponsored pension that guarantees a worker, say, 70 per cent[28] of his average salary of $50,500 (the approximate average earnings of a full-time male worker in Canada as of 2002[29]), one would need savings of $700,000 (invested at a safe annual return on capital of five per cent), a calculation that lends credence to the alarmism of financial advisors.

Although the proportion of the labour force with an employer-sponsored pension has actually increased again after falling for much of the 1990s, it still represents only about one-third.[30] Unionized workers are much more likely to have pension coverage than non-unionized workers. And people in non-standard employment are much less likely to be unionized. Prospects for those without an employer-sponsored pension plan are quite disquieting, even if the benefit-deprived do manage to put a few thousand dollars a year away in Registered Retirement Savings Plans (RRSPs). Public pensions alone are often insufficient to maintain an individual above Statistics Canada's low-income cut-offs. For a single individual aged 65 or over, the maximum Canada Pension Plan and Old Age Security benefits combined amount to a monthly income of less than $1300. Adding the applicable Guaranteed Income Supplement would leave someone living in a major urban centre more than $2000 below what is widely considered the poverty line.[31]

Drawing on research by R. N. Block and K. Roberts, Graham Lowe writes:

> Legislation and regulations governing employment standards, collective
> bargaining, health and safety, and workers' compensation were designed
> for the traditional 'standard' job. The protections they provide are
> available to a declining proportion of workers, a trend that is accelerating
> due to the weakening of employment standards in several provinces
> during the past decade.[32]

The erosion of the traditional employment relationship reflected in the expansion of non-standard employment is clearly contributing to the advent of a new sense of insecurity (exacerbated by the equally momentous dissolution of dominant family structures)[33] and the point is often made that the workforce as a whole suffers from its destabilizing impact. On the left of the political spectrum, this is viewed as a deliberate strategy to "discipline" labour, inducing docility and facilitating the extraction of concessions.

Whether orchestrated or dictated by market imperatives, the outcome is the same. Although it refers specifically to the U.S. context, this observation in a report by the organization Fair Jobs is universally applicable:

> The growth of contingent work is not just a problem for those in contingent jobs. Regular employees, however highly skilled, now face the threat that their employers may lay them off and replace them with contingent workers. This threat lessens workers' bargaining power, contributing to the weakening of unions, the persistence of low wages, and the increasing polarization of society into haves and have-nots. The prevalence of contingent work creates pervasive insecurity among American workers, families, and communities. Insecurity, in turn, increases social tension and undermines stable social relationships at every economic level.[34]

As Graham Lowe observes, in parallel with the growth of non-standard employment the meaning of "permanent" employment has changed as a result of corporate and government restructuring. "During the 1990s," he notes, "many employers sent a clear message that a lifetime job is a relic of the past."[35] Thus, just as James Meadows (proponent of the "we-are-all-contingent-now" philosophy of human resource management) hoped, the boundaries between insecure non-standard employment and the traditional job may well be fading.

The reality of non-standard employment is not, of course entirely one-sided, holding out only the prospect of anxiety and a declining living standard; the experience is far more multi-textured. Even when it comprises uncertainty and lower material returns than the traditional full-time job, non-standard employment can offer opportunities for greater time flexibility, autonomy and diversity of experience, as well as opportunities to learn and stretch one's abilities. Looking at the breakdown of the traditional employment relationship throughout the West, Ulrich Beck points out that it is a double-edged sword: on one hand, greater freedom to shape one's own life; on the other, greater insecurity, as risk is shifted from the State and the corporation to individual workers.[36] Moreover, as Lowe points out, "'standard' jobs are not necessarily the ones with the highest levels of trust, commitment, influence and communication," which he identifies as the four key psycho-social dimensions of the employment relationship.[37]

Other scholars, such as Jerald Wallulis, concur. In his study of what he calls "the new insecurity," Wallulis points out that the destandardization of work means that people are no longer prisoners of past choices; they can venture down different paths.[38] But at the same time, there is an ever-looming threat of loss of employability, along with the likely prospect of prolonged working lives to compensate for uncertain benefits and to accumulate enough for retirement. On balance, what appears most significant about the destandardization of work in the advanced industrial countries is the internalization of the core-periphery model of global development, with a heartland of highly skilled well-paid employees and a widening circle of extras and cast-aways at the outskirts; it is the defining element of a transition to a two-tier society.

Caring Inc.

The expansion of non-standard employment in Canada undoubtedly contributed to offsetting the unemployment rates of the 1990s, which decreased, according to Statistics Canada data, from the 1993 high of 11.4 percent to a low of 6.8 per cent in the year 2000. Notwithstanding the nation's stellar economic performance since the late 1990s and despite the enterprising efforts of millions of Canadians, the official unemployment rate remains (as of this writing) relatively high at 7.3 per cent, a level that would have been deemed a crisis 40 years ago, but which we, like many western societies, increasingly regard as normal and inevitable.

While continuing to trim and destabilize public-sector jobs through attrition, privatization and subcontracting, the federal government claims to be constantly seeking new ways and means to promote job creation. It is looking to initiatives in the third sector with ever greater interest, just as it has increasingly enlisted community-based non-profit organizations to provide a myriad of social services to fill the breach resulting from cutbacks to public-sector agencies.

Peter Drucker, America's leading management guru, put the third sector squarely on the neoliberal agenda in a seminal article published in the *Atlantic Monthly* in 1994. Declaring the welfare state a failure, and government ill-suited and incompetent to provide social services, Drucker consigned to the burgeoning non-profit sector the social challenges of the contemporary knowledge society. Its mission, as he saw it, was precisely to manage social problems and ensure health and welfare; but it also had a crucial second role: to build citizenship and create community in an era when, Drucker maintained, it was no longer possible for citizens to play a meaningful role in the affairs of government and the workplace could not provide for social integration. Administering the complex polity was to be left to experts. The correct attitude was one of resignation: "All we can do as citizens," he wrote, "is to vote once every few years and to pay taxes all the time." By working in the third sector, however, people could feel themselves making a difference. Noting that the relationship between the non-profit sector and government had yet to be worked out, Drucker nevertheless anticipated that "many social-sector organizations will become partners with government—as is the case in a great many 'privatizations,' where, for instance, a city pays for street cleaning and an outside contractor does the work."[39] In this, Drucker was giving theoretical expression to what governments were (and continue) doing in practice: offloading more and more responsibility onto the non-profit sector. Of course, although more nuanced in his analysis, Drucker falls within a political tradition of support for the non-profit sector precisely as a countervailing force to the expansion of state welfare—one that was vividly articulated in the United States in George Bush senior's acceptance speech at the 1988 Republican Convention, when he remarked that the "old way" of addressing social problems, namely by allocating public money, was no longer viable and that it was time for Americans to place their faith in the myriad community organizations which shine in the social firmament like "a thousand points of light."[40] Of course, outside the Anglo-American world, Western nations did not espouse the neoliberal nostrum in such an unadulterated form; but there have been ongoing reverberations everywhere.[41]

At the same time, another development brought the actual and potential economic role of the third sector onto the radar screen of policy makers and analysts throughout the advanced industrial (or post-industrial) world: receding recourse to the traditional consumer service sector as a generator of employment.

Historically, as technological advances accelerated productivity in industry, reducing the need for labour, the service sector absorbed labour power, and particularly the massive entry of women into the labour market from the 1970s onward. It now accounts for the majority of jobs in all Western nations. In Canada, the service sector's share of the total number of jobs more than doubled between 1951 and 1995[42] and today three-quarters of Canadian jobs are in the service industries. But as Jeremy Rifkin,[43] among others, has documented extensively, the service sector has itself been undergoing greater automation in recent decades. With the application of information technology, labour requirements have diminished in banking, insurance, retail and other service industries, leaving the low-productivity, unexportable, quinary and sixtenary sectors (consisting of such services as education, health care, personal care and culture) as the last bastions of job creation. With the relative decline of large-scale production in the advanced industrial economies, "the ideal product is one that only lasts until it is used for the first time, that is, consumed as soon as it is produced: meals, hairdressing, window-cleaning…."[44] And it is precisely the evanescent labour-intensive "relational services," dispensed on a person-to-person basis, that are now becoming the business—quite literally—of the third sector.

This dovetails with yet another contemporary phenomenon: the accelerating practice within advanced industrial societies of outsourcing domestic life. As Krishan Kumar observed in a critical analysis of the claims made for the post-industrial service society, the spectacular growth of the consumer service sector in the latter half of the twentieth century essentially involved a massive transfer of activities normatively carried out at home—such as cooking, cleaning, educating and caring—to the market and the State. In their new incarnations as restaurant industry, domestic services, health, education and welfare systems, they are part of the cash nexus and generate wage work.[45] As Kumar's book indicates, in the 1970s there was already discussion of the advent of the personal service society and the "increasing structural importance of social welfare and the 'caring' services,"[46] as well as concern expressed about the unintended consequences of "the professionalization of human contact."[47]

The transfer of erstwhile household activities is continuing, propelled in part by the dualization of the labour force: on one hand, there is the growing number of precariously and underemployed workers; on the other, there is the shrinking majority of the traditional full-time workforce, putting in longer hours and performing unpaid overtime to cope with the surfeit of work engendered by downsizing. Hours of work are polarizing: while the expansion of part-time and other non-standard working arrangements has many Canadians working less than a 40-hour week, others are working more. Health Canada's 2001 National Work-Life Conflict Study showed that one in four Canadian employees worked 50 hours or more per week, up from one in ten a decade earlier.[48]

Many people who are deprived of time to tend to home and family are contracting out tasks they would once have done for themselves or one another, including caring for loved ones at either end of the age spectrum. The practice of outsourcing by the corporate world and the State that has contributed to undermining job security and creating a polarized workforce is thus paralleled in the household. This, combined with the realities of a diminishing public sector, the further decomposition of traditional family structures and an aging population, engenders what are referred to in the discourse around the economic role of the third sector somewhat misleadingly as "new needs" and an expanding market for such services as home health care, child care and domestic help.

Paradoxically, then, it is in the progressive abandonment of what were once household and family responsibilities, partly owing to constraints of time and energy, that one remedy to unemployment is being sought. Job creation strategies encourage the expansion of the market into domains of activity that might otherwise remain the preserve of households by propping up consumer demand through state subsidies or acting on the supply side to ensure that services are offered at an affordable price.[49] In one European Commission document, the capacity of the "third system" (broadly synonymous with the third sector) to convert domestic activity into economic activity, thereby promoting labour market access for women, is cited explicitly as one reason (of many) it warrants support.[50] For Welfare State theorist Gosta Esping Anderson, for instance, the time crunch experienced by two-income families constitutes an opportunity to fill the employment gap with the burgeoning personal services industry.[51] And in the estimation of European researcher Mike Campbell, the third sector ("third system" in this scholar's lexicon, defined as the ensemble of cooperatives, mutual societies, associations, foundations and voluntary organizations) can make an effective contribution to "knitting together" the growing need for relational services characteristic of "dematerialized" economies with displaced workers and other job seekers.[52] In North America, a related notion was advanced by Jeremy Rifkin in his *The End of Work*; after making a compelling case for the irreversible technological displacement of consumer service jobs, he identifies the third sector as a potential counterweight, raising the possibility of paying a social wage to volunteers in the third sector who provide indispensable services to their local and national communities.

These are some of the developments that set the stage for the growing interest in and recognition of the third sector by governments in OECD countries. Wrestling with soaring unemployment in the 1980s, France was among the first to turn to the third sector explicitly as a means to alleviate the crisis of work; one notable initiative was the creation in the mid-1980s of what are called *entreprises d'insertion*, not-for profit enterprises whose primary mission is to give unemployed individuals temporary work experience in functioning businesses with the aim of facilitating their integration or reintegration into the labour market.[53] But France was not alone in conceiving the third sector as a potential agent of "employability" and generator of jobs, particularly for disadvantaged groups, through the provision of human services and the creation of social enterprises. The European Union as a whole has likewise been beset, to varying degrees, by an intractable unemployment problem (the official standardized rate for the 15 member-states prior to the May 2004 enlargement stood at 8 per cent), and by the 1990s it became European Union-wide policy to tap the employment-generating potential of the third sector or social economy, which, by the turn of the millennium, was estimated to employ nearly nine million people.[54]

The interest in the employment potential of the third sector was reciprocal. For example, in an insightful paper based on research by Eric Shragge, Pierre Hamel, Jean-Marc Fontan and others, Richard Morin notes a shift in the urban movement in Montreal in the 1980s and 1990s towards greater concern with economic development issues in face of rising unemployment and public sector cutbacks, which has been accompanied by a trend toward a more collaborative approach to the State (with all the unavoidable contradictions that implies) as third-sector organizations act in partnership with the different levels of government. Looking at Montreal's community economic development movement as an example, Morin traces a shift in emphasis from consumption to production and an emerging accent on job creation and labour market access for poor and marginalized populations.[55] In Quebec, this culminated in the establishment of a task force on the social economy, one of the primary aims of which is to generate new sources of paid employment. Again, this phenomenon is not unique to North America but partakes of a pattern evident, *mutatis mutandis*, in many of the advanced industrial economies, representing a multinational shift in the politics of urban movements.[56]

Some scholars and actors of the social economy stress that creating employment should not be construed as the primary aim, a point we shall revisit below; however, that does not prevent third-sector organizations from being seen by governments in Europe and North America above all as potential motors of job creation, and of moving people from unemployment and welfare to work. In light of an extensive study of the social economy in the U.K., Ash Amin, Angus Cameron and Ray Hudson affirm that the value of the social economy does not lie in its capacity to foster employment; nevertheless, they observe:

> Social enterprises have been welcomed as labour market intermediaries,
> facilitating the re-entry of the socially excluded into employment, not
> least because they are potentially resource-efficient and allegedly close to
> 'communities.' They are also seen as a way of contracting out to third-

      sector organizations services traditionally offered by the welfare state,
      thereby reducing the cost of welfare provision....[57]

Similarly, referring to the Quebec context, Margeurite Mendell stresses that the aims and impact of the social economy go far beyond the quantifiable target of generating new employment but she notes that provincial government support for social economy projects in the 1990s was forthcoming primarily because of an expectation that these would contribute to cost reduction and job creation.[58]

Giving Non-profits the Business

In Canada, as elsewhere, growing interest on the part of the federal government in the third sector as a motor of employment and a means of enhancing employability must be seen in the context of the drive, especially since the mid-1990s, to reduce the cost of income support in the form of employment insurance. Despite program overhauls which have resulted in billions of dollars of savings, the federal government is pursuing a policy of decreasing dependency on transfer payments by deploying carrots and sticks to induce people to engage in waged labour. This, it should be noted, at a time when GDP has grown steadily for nearly a decade but labour's share of national income, in the form of wages and salaries, has stagnated relative to corporate profits.[59]

    Taking a leaf from Rifkin's book, for example, Service Canada (formerly Human Resources and Development Canada), in collaboration with the Nova Scotia Department of Community Services, set up the Community Employment Innovation Project in Cape Breton, in part to conduct a cost-benefit analysis of mobilizing the third sector as a source of employment opportunities.[60] The project involves paying a community wage (of $300 per week plus some benefits) to individuals receiving employment insurance or income assistance who agree to volunteer in community-based projects for 35 hours per week.

    It is significant, too, that as the non-profit sector gains attention as an economic instrument, its role is conceived increasingly in business terms. In Canada, at the national level, that was demonstrated most recently in the February 2004 Speech from the Throne and the subsequent budget tabled by Paul Martin's Liberal government. Particularly noteworthy was the accent on social entrepreneurship (that segment of the third sector devoted to generating revenue through its activities, including business creation—it goes under various names, such as the social economy[61] and community entrepreneurship) and the role of non-profits in ensuring social integration through employment. Thus, while management consultants urge workers in the brave new economy to transform themselves into businesses, government prepares to reward community organizations infused with the entrepreneurial spirit.

    Martin promised to help communities help themselves, especially by supporting those who are "applying entrepreneurial skills, not for profit, but rather to enhance the social and environmental conditions in our communities right across

Canada." The speech conceives the "new approaches to community development" that go under the rubric of the "social economy" as an expression of the spirit of entrepreneurship; it goes on to promise greater access to resources for participants in this "entrepreneurial social movement" and an expansion of programs designed to assist small and medium-sized enterprises to include social enterprises.

In the subsequent budget, the general thrust of which was to perpetuate the fixation on debt reduction, the government allocated $162 million over five years to help set up regional patient capital funds (patient capital is essentially venture capital with lower and slower financial returns on investment, which are seen, in the context of community development, to be compensated by valuable social returns) and promote lending to social enterprises (the idea being to shift the form of funding from grants to investment), as well as to assist in building capacity and conducting community-based research.

Speaking in the House of Commons in March 2004, Eleni Bakopanos, Parliamentary Secretary to the Minister of Human Resources and Skills Development (a position that includes a special emphasis on the social economy) put the jobs issue front and centre in explaining the government's support for the social economy, explaining that social enterprises help communities create jobs and enhance employability, particularly for members of disadvantaged and vulnerable groups.[62] She cited as examples a neighbourhood dollar store in Halifax and the Cirque du Soleil—chosen perhaps because of the vast experience the poor and unemployed have with counting pennies and walking tightropes.

The federal government's explicit commitment to the social economy was announced under the heading "a new deal for communities." The choice of the phrase "new deal" is telling.[63] Why invoke the Depression era at a time when by all standard indicators, the Canadian economy has been booming for nearly a decade? Possibly it's because the benefits of economic growth have not been shared and are not expected to be distributed in any equitable way. The gap between rich and poor is widening and growth is no longer expected to ensure employment.[64] The phenomenon of jobless growth is well documented; with each successive recovery after a recessionary period, employment fails to return to its previous levels. There is a growing institutionalization of the polarization of wealth and resources, and unwillingness to compromise deficit reduction by investing in new social programs. At the same time there is a perceived need for a shock absorber to cushion the blow of cuts to social services and income protection systems. From this vantage point, the social economy and the third sector offer a cost-effective means to provide assistance to the growing numbers of people excluded from the benefits of growth and neoliberal restructuring, and for whom the new Canadian economy is understood to offer only a subsidiary place.

Although the adoption of the term "social economy" is new, the strategy is not. The Canadian federal government has always favoured indirect measures to stimulate employment growth over direct job creation, placing particular emphasis on fostering entrepreneurship and the creation of small businesses. Small business is endlessly touted as the key to employment growth—the You & Co. solution once again—in spite of important evidence challenging this received liberal wisdom.[65] And once again this reflects a trend across the western world. Writing in the late 1990s, Bernd Balkenhol of the International Labour Organization noted "an impressive increase" in many OECD countries in government programs designed to encourage the unemployed, welfare recipients and other disadvantaged groups to start their own businesses.[66] This has gone hand in hand with a decentralization of social assistance programs. It is in this broad context that a dizzying succession of labour force development and community economic development programs involving community-based non-profit organizations has been pursued since the 1970s, particularly at the provincial level.

Of course, the mobilization of the third sector in response to the increasing vagaries of the labour market and to the scaling back of the welfare functions of the state is also a grassroots democratic initiative, in keeping with historical traditions of mutualism and community self-help. In this context, the recent pronouncements of the federal government are perceived by many in the third sector as another victory in a protracted struggle for its recognition as a force for economic development and employment generation.[67] But this sense of achievement experienced by those in the milieu may have contributed to diverting attention away from critical analysis of the implications of continuing neoliberal policies for Canada's poor and disadvantaged. The same budget that announced support for the social economy bodes ill for social programs. The Canadian Council for Social Development judged the budget disappointing, devoid of any but piecemeal initiatives to counter growing social disparities. They point out that the objective of reducing the debt to 25 per cent of GDP within 10 years means that roughly $28.9 billion will be taken out of federal program spending, which will reach a near historic low this year of 11.8 per cent as a share of GDP.[68] The budget received similarly critical reviews from the National Anti-Poverty Organization and the Canadian Housing Renewal Association, among other organizations.

The problem here is that the loftier aspirations of the social economy and community economic development movements do not belie a convergence of laudable aims with the proclivities of neoliberal government for a *laissez-faire* approach to the dominant market economy, which conceives entrepreneurship and support for small business as the best way to address intractable problems such as structural unemployment and social exclusion. A 1992 OECD document discussing new directions in social policy hailed the transition to a State that increasingly leaves people to their own resources: "The State should no longer be considered a dispenser of largesse, but rather a partner that allows individuals to take the initiative in coping with the uncertainties of their lives and gives them the means to do so."[69] Neoliberalism is very much about shifting the burdens of cost and risk: from the employer to the employee through labour market deregulation, and from the public sector to the private sector, by encouraging organizations heavily dependent on government funding to take the initiative and strike out on revenue-generating paths.[70] Although it cannot be reduced to such considerations, the "new deal" for communities and the enthusiasm on the part of various levels of government for social entrepreneurship and a new partnership with the non-profit sector is thus informed, at least in part, by a neoliberal vision of a post-Welfare State, with the social economy, construed as the enterprising, market-oriented segment of the third sector, assigned a central role in building it. Lexicons are revealing: even the language of social policy has taken an entrepreneurial turn, with talk of social policy as a productive factor, of human capital and social return on investment. It is not an accident that business has become the dominant metaphor. It may be true, as Michael Hall, a leading scholar of Canada's third sector, observed some years ago in a different context, that "When economic thinking is the current *Zeitgeist*, you have to speak in economic terms...,"[71] but what does it say when we feel compelled to reach for the language of the market to confer a sense of importance on human development, and can it come as any surprise when the logic of business ultimately prevails and what comes to count most is the bottom line?

"Turn Your Stakeholders into Risktakers"[72]

A matter of considerable soul searching and lively debate is whether and to what extent non-profit organizations in general have been swept into the business current and, as management gurus urge, are coming to think like external vendors, seizing upon the trend towards outsourcing by corporations, governments and households to carve out niche markets and cultivate new sources of revenue. The debate is ongoing, and can only become more intense with the gradual institutionalization of third sector economic development efforts and their incorporation into State strategies for coping with the social problems exacerbated by neoliberal policies.

In 1996, an article appeared in the Charity Village newsletter discussing some of the problems facing the non-profit sector. The author commented that with the ongoing retreat of the State from the provision of services there has been an increasing blurring of the traditional roles of the private, public and non-profit sectors. The private sector has been moving in to offer services once provided by the public sector, while non-profits have been creating commercial enterprises to compete with them. What this observer concluded from these developments echoes William Bridges' exhortation to twenty-first-century workers to think like a business:

> We had all better get much more entrepreneurial very quickly. Each of us must clearly identify which products or services we are capable of providing competently, and we must learn to market those capabilities effectively, either to a series of organizations in all three sectors, or directly to end users. In many cases, this will involve the creation of new micro-businesses, often home-based and using advanced technology to compete with the big guys.[73]

In this line of thinking, the answer to the blurring of traditional roles is to collapse them altogether. Rather than protest or resist the triumph of market logic in a sector historically sheltered from it at least to some extent, it pits the non-profit sector against the private sector in a competition for market share.

But many commentators are far less enthusiastic about the blurring of roles. Various observers within and outside the third sector in Canada, as in other Western countries, are concerned that the entire third sector is being redefined in the new millennium primarily in economic terms as service providers and job creators. As governments institutionalize patterns of offloading responsibilities onto the third sector in the form of new funding and support programs for social enterprises and other initiatives, vital non-economic roles of non-profit organizations (such as advocating for social change) are overlooked or given short shrift, beyond rhetoric about the virtues of the third sector's commitment to promoting social equity. Moreover, as one particularly mordant critique of the social economy expressed the matter, social problems are being conceived of as business opportunities.[74]

The point of departure of the analysis is often the evolution of the funding environment, which is perceived to have had an adverse impact on many aspects of the non-profit sector in the last decade. Very briefly, in addition to government funding cuts, two significant shifts have been identified by scholars and activists: first, a redefinition of funding criteria to favour service providers over organizations engaging in advocacy work. In a perspicacious discussion of the problems facing non-profit organizations in the mid-1990s—particularly the conundrum of government funding retrenchment accompanied by more onerous demands for service provision—Susan Phillips noted that in the wake of (then Finance Minister) Paul Martin's 1995 budget, an interdepartmental task force was given a mandate to develop funding criteria and recommended that "groups which offer direct services be given preference over those engaged [in] advocacy" and that "funding should also depend upon how well a group's activities fit with government priorities; the extent to which it benefits the public and the ability of a group to access other funding."[75] (The same tendency was evident at the provincial level: for example, while public funding for community groups doubled in Quebec in the 1990s, it has been suggested that new funding was largely targeted to organizations that were perceived as useful to government in achieving its own priorities and which were willing to accept government contracts.)[76]

Second, in parallel with the continued practice by the State of subcontracting to the non-profit sector, there has been a noticeable shift in the type of funding organizations receive, from core funding, which affords latitude in determining the scope of activity and engaging in long-term planning, to project funding, which is earmarked for specific programs within a limited time frame but cannot be used to support the organization's operations as a whole.[77] In addition to compelling organizations to concentrate on meeting specific project requirements, sometimes at the expense of broader imperatives, and engendering constant uncertainty about the ability to maintain infrastructure (to "keep the doors open and the lights on," as one report put it[78]), the net result of the change in funding practices is to amplify the tendency for those who pay the piper to call the tune.

Much of great clarity and eloquence has been written to this effect, based on in-depth quantitative and qualitative research. Studies point to a host of undesirable consequences stemming from this destabilized funding environment: the marginalization of advocacy work as funding tends to be made available for politically neutral service provision; what is dubbed "mission slippage" or "mission drift," meaning a tendency for organizations to tailor their activities to prevailing funding priorities even at the cost of diverging from their democratically determined aims; commercialization stemming from competition for scarce funds and resulting pressure to generate revenues; bureaucratization; and an environment favouring larger over smaller organizations, among other metamorphoses. In the Canadian Council for Social Development study *Funding Matters*, researcher Katherine Scott concludes that business mentality has begun to permeate the non-profit sector, with respect both to a growing market orientation (and in some instances direct competition with the private sector) and to management practices.[79] She argues that this has contributed to the undermining of some of the very characteristics that make the third sector unique—including its very diversity, insofar as larger professional service organizations that mirror the funders themselves are better equipped to meet the complex requirements of the contractual relationship with the State (including increasingly onerous demands for accountability and evaluation that channel greater time and energy into administrative tasks), and are thus more likely to weather the rigours of the new climate.

The anxiety about the marketization of the third sector and the transformation of non-profit organizations into moral and social entrepreneurs as a consequence of changing relationships with the State and the private sector is not restricted to North America.[80] Many critics express concern about the co-optation of the third sector as part of the neoliberal bid to whittle down the Welfare State and palliate the adverse effects of growing social polarization. Drawing on some of the scholarship that is wary of the new-found enthusiasm of neoliberal governments for State-third sector partnerships, B. Mitchell Evans and John Shields conclude that the embrace of the third sector by government in Canada and elsewhere in the industrialized world is the cornerstone of a "strategy of stealth" to legitimate the retreat of the State from providing social protection and accelerate the commodification of public goods that the Welfare State had succeeded in withdrawing from the market. They emphasize the highly unequal nature of the partnerships, which are in essence contractual relationships leaving little room for autonomous decision-making. Ultimately, there is a subordination of third-sector functions to the aim of service provision and a crowding out of other essential roles, such as advocacy (helping the poor and disadvantaged make their views and concerns heard, mobilizing around specific policy issues, advocating on behalf of particular groups), mediation (building common understanding across social, ethnic, territorial and other differences) and engaging citizens in the political process, particularly at the local level. Moreover, they caution that neoliberal governments are encouraging the third sector to become more market-oriented and to behave more like businesses, with deleterious effects.

> Neoliberal restructuring assigns a key role to the third sector as an agent of the state in the production and delivery of "public goods." The contract relationship which is being developed between the state and non-profit organizations, however, is serving to transform the third sector, moving it away from its core mission, commercializing the sector's operations, and compromising its autonomy. [81]

Of course, for those in the third sector who embrace social entrepreneurship, behaving like a business is not the problem; it is part of the solution—provided the entrepreneurial spirit is enlisted in the service of socially-desirable aims. Although social entrepreneurship in theory and practice is not a direct challenge to neoliberalism and lends itself quite readily to co-optation by government and other mainstream institutions (witness the Harvard Business School's Social Enterprise Initiative[82]), there are many theorists and practitioners of community economic development, for instance, as well as many thinkers and actors involved in building the social economy in Quebec, who view non-profit business activity and social enterprises as a force for moderating the unbridled market economy while redressing some of the ills of neoliberal restructuring at the grassroots level. They regard contractual relationships with the State and even the private sector as partnerships—not without risks, but neither heralding an inevitable loss of autonomy.

In the more radical conceptions of the social economy, social or collective entrepreneurship is conceived as countervailing the pre-eminence of the market economy, complementing rather than competing with the public sector in a necessary and desirable division of responsibilities, and operating in areas neglected by both market and State. The social economy is viewed as a model of development that, although coexisting with a capitalist economy, represents a challenge to dominant arrangements by virtue of its engagement in economic activity with a view to serving the collective good rather than to the private accumulation of profit. And although it does not seek to substitute for the State, it also represents an alternative to bureaucratic State service provision by virtue of its commitment to democratic forms of internal organization and a higher degree of proximity and reciprocal understanding between the providers and users of services.[83] With this view, the social economy is a bulwark against wholesale privatization and an embodiment of the spirit of solidarity in face of the atomizing effect of the market; it seeks to strengthen the social fabric and thereby foster social cohesion. Moreover, because social enterprises are typically rooted in local communities, they are closer to citizens and can better tailor their services to real needs. In a phrase, they see the development of the enterprising role of the third sector as a means to empower the disadvantaged, enhance social cohesion, educate for citizenship and generally strengthen civil society.[84] In Quebec there has been a concerted effort to promote this vision of the social economy since the mid-1990s.[85] Indeed, it is this more optimistic view that dominates the discussion, although there have been several important critical forays, such as the wide-ranging indictment of the social economy mounted in a seminal French-language anthology edited by Louise Boivin and Mark Fortier, *L'Économie Sociale: l'Avenir d'une illusion*, and several essays in English by Paul Leduc Browne. And of course there is an energetic international debate on this question that has transpired in a vast literature, a debate which can be situated in the context of a broader discussion of such fundamental questions as the nature and future of the Welfare State, the problem of work and the causes of unemployment.

The tension between the conception of the social economy on the ground and the conception of policy makers "from above" finds a parallel in the competing visions in the 1980s of a decentralized approach to stimulating employment that French commentator Xavier Greffe characterized as "the ambiguity of local development."[86] Looking at the French context, Greffe identified two currents in the conception of local development. The first, originating in the 1970s, was embodied in a grassroots, third-sector movement seeking solutions to the problem of unemployment in a human-scale approach to development opposed to the dominant logic of profit-seeking, and emphasizing control by communities over their own affairs. The second conception was essentially the State's co-optation of the first: the alternative approach to local development was subsumed by a policy of support for small business, seen as the spearhead of economic development and an opportunity for the unemployed to create their own jobs. And while some government measures, such as making venture capital available, could lend themselves just as easily to either conception, a new dynamic took shape under the impetus of the State which was divorced from any critique of the prevailing mode of development. Greffe's description has a remarkably familiar ring, which cannot but invite the question of whether, in this instance, the past is prologue.

On the Job

One measure of the potential of the third sector to counter the drift toward a dual society is its stance in relation to the issue of work and its transformation. Two issues arise: first, to what extent are non-profit organizations and enterprises capable of creating stable, quality jobs at a time when such jobs are becoming scarcer in the private and public sector? Are they doomed to reflect existing trends toward non-standard employment and labour market polarization? Second, how do they address broader issues of an increasingly polarized labour force? To what extent do third sector practices represent a strategy of resistance to the destabilization of work, and to what extent do they constitute a compromise or accommodation? Does the social economy reinforce or challenge current neoliberal policy with respect to work? Are there other choices?

For the union movement, recourse to non-profits as a means of creating jobs and delivering social services is often viewed with a jaundiced eye as a strategy serving to undermine public-sector employment in both quantity and quality. Although there is also support for the social economy within the union movement[87] (and it should be recalled that in addition to being non-profit organizations themselves, trade unions are involved in various capacities in investing in the third sector and particularly in the traditional social economy with funds devoted to creating co-operatives[88]) there are concerns about the creation of a shadow public sector. In an analysis of the recent Liberal budget, the Canadian Union of Public Employees had this to say:

> The social economy or the "third sector" is not what we want as a model
> for community social services. We have undergone considerable
> downsizing and a loss of support for social assistance and social services.
> There has been a shift from universality to a safety net full of holes. This
> is a cut to social programs using a cheap wage strategy and a reliance on
> volunteers instead of a sound community infrastructure for these valuable
> social services. We aren't against voluntarism but voluntarism can't be
> used to replace programs for which the government has responsibility.[89]

In a similar vein, the Centrale des syndicats du Québec (CSQ), a union representing thousands of public-sector health and social service workers, took aim at the ongoing transfer of responsibilities and funds for health care and social services to the third sector and social economy, a process it dubs the "communitarization of service delivery."[90] Noting that the Quebec Ministry of Health and Social Services is continuing to incorporate community groups into the public network of service providers, the CSQ warned that this process creates a shadow public sector with inferior wages and benefits and, at the same time, by turning community groups into service providers subject to the policies and aims of the Ministry, deflects them from their fundamental mission of advocacy and community organizing. For the CSQ, the State's motives are purely economic: discount service delivery. Community organizations and social economy enterprises are "more often than not used as a palliative for an atrophied public sector," which pits the unions and the third sector against one another in unhealthy competition.

Faced with such charges, both at home and abroad, proponents of the third sector's role in generating employment tend to reply that they are responding to needs that are not currently being met, or at least not sufficiently, by the State and therefore do not compete with existing forms of public service provision. Moreover, they maintain that the public sector is poorly suited to some of these fields of activity, such as home care, given the high degree of personal interaction required, for which bureaucratic public service organizations are ill-equipped.[91] Less reassuringly, they argue that because service provision is cheaper in the third sector than the public sector, more jobs can be created with the same investment of public funds.[92] They suggest as well that the third sector plays an important role in innovating and furnishing alternative services, the design and delivery of which are subject to greater control by both the providers and consumers, thus contributing to expanding consumer choice.[93]

However, as Dominique Méda, one of the leading French philosophers of work, has observed, the avowed aim of the social economy to satisfy needs that otherwise go unmet raises the troubling issue of why society is failing to meet so many pressing needs. For her, there is a danger that in pinning our hopes on the third sector and turning our attention and energies to strengthening its scope and capacities, we are resigning ourselves to the refractory character of the private sector, in its pursuit of profit without conscience or constraint for the sole benefit of shareholders, as well as tacitly acquiescing in the ongoing withdrawal of the public sector from its social responsibilities.[94]

How valid are the fears that, in the grip of neoliberal policy makers, the third sector may engender a discount para-public sector? And to what extent can the third sector make good on its claim to create sustainable jobs that do not compete with public-sector employment? We know that the public sector in Canada shrank by approximately 9.7 per cent during the 1990s, and although it began to rebound at the end of the decade, it has not returned to its 1992 level.[95] And there are ongoing efforts to pare down the public sector. In Quebec, for example, where the social economy is the most highly organized and developed, the Parti Québécois implemented deep cuts to the public and quasi-public sector in the latter half of the 1990s, in part by encouraging early retirement; as a result, the size of the workforce shrank by 10 per cent.[96] And the current Charest government is aiming to reduce the public service by 20 per cent (16,000 jobs) in the next decade (primarily by attrition). It should be noted, too, as scholars such as Pat Armstrong have pointed out, that there are serious gender implications in the decline of public-sector employment; most of the best jobs for women have been in the public and quasi-public sectors.[97] However, it is impossible to determine how many public-sector jobs may have been or will be lost to the third sector as a result of the ability of non-profits and social enterprises to contract for services at a competitive rate by virtue of lower wages for the (predominantly female) paid staff, self-exploitation owing to a high degree of commitment to organizational goals, access to some measure of private funding, as well as the use of volunteers and community placements designed to give work experience and enhance the employability of individuals dependent on social assistance.

On the other hand, there is emerging research on the kinds of jobs the third sector provides. (For the purposes of this argument I am interested exclusively in paid employment, although of course this far from exhausts the portrait of work in the third sector; one of its unique characteristics is precisely its reliance in many instances on volunteer work, of which more than a billion hours was contributed in 2000—the equivalent of 549,000 full-time jobs.)[98] There are several different categories to consider here. First, there is employment created incidentally in the third sector as a result of the growth and expansion of non-profit organizations that employ some paid staff in addition to volunteer labour. Second, there are deliberate efforts to combat social exclusion by equipping marginalized people to enter the labour market and offer job experience through work placements. Finally, there are initiatives to encourage the formation of co-operatives and to create jobs by establishing social enterprises intended to respond to social needs that are going unmet by the private and public sectors (primarily a result of high cost which results in flaccid demand—home care is often cited in this context) and to respond to demands stemming from the time scarcity of full-time workers in the market economy.

Although calculations vary depending on what is included under the third sector or non-profit rubric, studies dating from the mid-1990s indicated that, together, Canada's registered charities (of which there are some 80,000, including quasi-public institutions such as schools and hospitals), incorporated non-profits and voluntary organizations, as well as co-operatives and other social-economy enterprises, already accounted for more than one-and-a-half million jobs.[99] And if the sector's growth trends[100] are any indication, its share of direct employment is likely to rise.

Although it is exceedingly difficult to draw a general portrait of the nature of employment in the third sector because of the extraordinary diversity of organizations that fall under the rubric and the inevitable problems of selectivity and methodology, as well as the scant research foundations on which to build prior to the turn of the millennium,[101] studies are beginning to emerge on job quality and working conditions in non-profit organizations, such as the pioneering research on "Job Quality in Nonprofit Organizations" conducted by Kathryn McMullen and Grant Schellenberg for Canadian Policy Research Networks. McMullen and Schellenberg determined that in 1999, excluding religious organizations, the non-profit sector provided jobs for about 8 per cent of the Canadian workforce, or more than 900,000 Canadians, the majority of whom are highly educated women.[102] In their research, which is doubly illuminating for providing comparative analysis with other sectors, the authors distinguish between the quasi-autonomous non-governmental organizations or "quangos" (essentially teaching institutions, hospitals and providers of public infrastructure, which are largely government funded and have a high degree of unionization) and other types of non-profit organizations, including smaller community groups. Looking at managers, professionals, technical staff and clerical staff in the non-profit sector, the study confirmed anecdotal information and other preliminary research indicating lower average hourly earnings compared with the quasi-public and for-profit sectors, extensive non-standard employment and high levels of unpaid overtime.

With respect to earnings, McMullen and Schellenberg write, "The sector lags behind both the for-profit and the quango sectors on median and average hourly earnings and on the distribution of earnings by occupation. Such pay differences are likely to be quite large when translated into annual pay."[103] As for non-wage benefits, the results of the study were more encouraging: the available information showed that while only a minority of non-profit employers offer non-wage benefits, they tend to be the larger organizations, which employ the majority of workers in the sector, with the result that just over half of non-profit employees have varying degrees of coverage. On the other hand, the scope of coverage is well below that in the quango sector. As for unionization, the non-profit sector predictably fares better than the for-profit sector and worse than the quango sector: roughly 40 per cent of employees in the non-profit sector are unionized or covered by a collective agreement, compared with 75 per cent in the quasi-public sector and 19 per cent in the private sector.[104]

With respect to non-standard employment, the study found a significantly higher level of temporary and part-time employment in the non-profit sector than in the quasi-public or for-profit sectors. As of 1999, about one quarter of the non-profit workforce was employed part-time (compared with an average of 19 per cent for the Canadian labour force as a whole), with as great a proportion of involuntary part-timers as in the other sectors (about one-third). Temporary employment accounted for 14 per cent of jobs—roughly the same proportion as for the labour force as a whole. The study revealed that although non-profits were more likely to offer benefits to temporary and part-time employees, only a little more than a quarter of them had coverage.

In a document synthesizing the findings of a series of studies of work-related issues in the non-profit sector conducted by the Canadian Policy Research Networks (including the McMullen and Schellenberg study), Ron Saunders notes that "One-third of employees in non-profit health, education and social services and non-profit culture, recreation and associations say they are dissatisfied with their wages and benefits—a larger proportion than in almost every other industry."[105] And another report entitled *The Capacity to Serve*, the initial phase of the first large-scale survey of Canadian non-profit and voluntary organizations, reveals that non-profits reported difficulties in retaining staff due to poor compensation rates and benefit packages.[106] Putting the matter rather starkly, one (anonymous) participant is cited as saying: "We can only afford to hire people who don't need to make a living."[107] While that is clearly an overstatement for the sector as a whole, it appears to be quite applicable to parts of it. For instance, a 1998 University of Guelph study of Canadian child care workers found that Canada-wide, the annual earnings of full-time teachers in non-profit day care centres were only about $2,700 higher than that of parking lot attendants, and that many child care workers had to supplement their income by moonlighting.[108]

Of course, just as certain types of non-standard working arrangements offer non-material rewards, wages and pension plans do not exhaust the question of job quality in non-profits, and all the recent research confirms that those working in the third sector typically find meaning and satisfaction in their work, which can offset the disadvantages of poorer compensation levels and relative insecurity.[109] This is the substance of the argument regarding job quality made by Mike Campbell in his discussion of the development of the third sector as a prime source for employment generation in the European Union.[110]

Moreover, the non-profit sector offers management and non-management employees greater opportunities to participate in decision-making processes. Researchers Kathryn McMullen and Richard Brisbois found a "less hierarchical model of work organization" and greater likelihood of shared decision-making and empowerment, in the original meaning of that term, in the non-profit than in the for-profit or quango sectors.[111] (At the same time, the study points out that staff in non-profit organizations are often subject to the decision-making authority of individuals and groups outside the workplace itself, such as boards of directors.)

McMullen and Schellenberg found that the proportion of non-profit employees who expressed overall satisfaction with their jobs was comparable with other sectors.[112] On the other hand, in the 2003 study *Work-Life Conflict in Canada in the New Millennium*, Linda Duxbury and Chris Higgins found higher levels of role overload (of work interfering and adversely affecting family life) in the non-profit sector than in the public and private sectors.[113] They attribute this, among other reasons, to the heavier work demands in the non-profit sector, to shift work and rigid work schedules. (Other factors to consider are the predominantly female character of the non-profit workforce, since women are more likely to experience a sense of conflicting allegiance to work and family, and the decline recorded in both the number of individuals volunteering in Canada and the number of hours volunteered.[114]) Heavier work demands often mean extra hours on the job, and McMullen and Schellenberg's study confirms the findings of other studies with respect to the prevalence of unpaid overtime in the non-profit sector (it accounts for one of every 20 hours).[115] And while they note that overtime is common in all three sectors, and particularly in the quango sector, there is more unpaid overtime among part-time workers in the non-profit than in the for-profit sector (although less than in the quango sector).

Should workers in the non-profit sector be expected to accept the moral/material trade-off—what Ron Saunders characterizes as a gap between intrinsic and extrinsic rewards?[116] And, given a choice, are they likely to, over the long haul? Saunders cites a 2003 report produced by Lynne Toupin based on consultations with management employees of a sample of non-profit organizations. The report noted that compensation and benefits are not commensurate with qualifications and performance expectations, and that while employees are often passionate enough about the work they are doing to trade off moral satisfaction for other rewards, there are limits to those compromises:

> Fewer organizations now have access to core funding and project funding tends to be short-term. Short-term funding limits organizations' ability to offer anything more than short-term contractual employment. Chronic uncertainty about funding makes it more difficult to attract and keep employees. Over time, employees wanting stability and job security will gravitate to jobs with more stable non-profits or they will go entirely outside the sector.[117]

In general then, with respect to direct employment, the non-profit sector overall offers poorer wages and benefits than the public sector and reflects many features of the broader labour market: a high degree of non-standard employment, growing insecurity and impermanence, combined with an intensification of work.

Accustomed to doing more with less, staff in the non-profit sector evidently does more *for* less as well.

The second area where non-profits are involved in job creation of a kind and employability training is welfare-to-work initiatives. These range from genuine workfare programs, in which social assistance recipients are obliged to accept work placements in order to receive their benefits, to less coercive arrangements such as subsidies for training and jobs which remain optional for the unemployed and welfare recipients. In the 1990s, numerous federal and provincial government programs were geared to job creation and placement in non-profit organizations, as well as to training, which was and largely remains the neoliberal panacea for unemployment, premised on a convenient and controvertible attribution of the problems of joblessness and precariousness to individual failings and inadequacies rather than to policy decisions or structural conditions.[118] In the context of tight funding, some non-profits have made extensive use of such programs to make ends meet, although the ethical dilemmas experienced by many organizations regarding recourse to non-voluntary labour are well documented.[119]

Whatever the successes of programs ranging from Ontario Works to Quebec's *Fonds de lutte contre la pauvreté* in enhancing employability and fostering "labour force attachment" (and they can be assumed to account for part of the national decline in the number of welfare beneficiaries from 3.1 million in 1994 to 2.1 million in 2000—nearly a 33 per cent reduction over six years), the jobs in question have typically been low-wage and temporary by design. Moreover, the types of jobs to which workfare has tended to lead have been largely precarious. As a November 1999 report noted:

> Those who obtain work are often only marginally employed and finan-
> cially insecure. Many low-wage jobs offer no fringe benefits and give
> little assurance of a steady income. Others fear layoffs or firing due to the
> seasonal or temporary nature of work, coupled with the ready supply of
> unskilled labour in some regions.[120]

Not surprisingly, this is consonant with the mixed findings in other OECD countries deploying a variety of workfare-type schemes designed to encourage or oblige unemployed individuals to participate in work in one form or another.[121]

Moreover, vocational training and skill development programs that strive to match job seekers to labour market needs run up against the serious limitations of generally low educational levels among the target groups, which virtually guarantee permanent exclusion from the high-wage knowledge-based sector of the economy. Although it is also increasingly true that post-secondary credentials are no guarantee of decent employment, and leaving aside the issue of credential inflation, nearly half of all job growth from 1991 to 2001 occurred in highly skilled occupations typically requiring university education; only one-quarter of the growth occurred in occupations requiring high school or less.[122] In a 1998 study, Jane Pulkingham and Gordon Ternowetsky concluded that evidence of success of welfare-to-work programs is mixed and inconclusive and that low education levels were an enormous barrier to training for any but precarious work.[123]

Beyond workfare, and in addition to promoting "human capital formation," community economic development (CED) strategies also aim to help people enter self-employment, set up their own businesses and establish small community enterprises. It is asserted with pride that CED-supported microentrepreneurs match or surpass survival rates for small businesses generally. Without detracting from the seriousness of the efforts or the demonstrable successes, it has to be said that the claim is somewhat less than reassuring. The failure rate for microbusiness start-ups is notoriously high (and, according to the Canadian Business Service Centre, an overall 80 per cent of business start-ups fail within the first three to five years—although there is research indicating that the survival rate among co-operative enterprises is significantly higher than in the private sector.) Moreover, employment in small businesses of 50 employees or less is typically less secure, the hours longer, wages lower and benefits fewer.[124] Moreover, small businesses are far less able than bigger firms to invest in training and technological upgrades.

Finally, there are the jobs created directly through social-economy enterprises. The employment-generating capacity of these small third-sector businesses is not insignificant, as evidenced by the case of Quebec, where the social economy is estimated to account for more than 65,000 jobs in more than 6,000 diverse businesses, more than a third of which are co-operatives. Setting aside the question of whether any portion of this employment represents a transfer from the public sector, it is useful to consider the types of jobs that are being created. And here it makes sense to concentrate on the new social economy, or what is also called the "economy of solidarity," rather than the traditional co-operative sector, since this is the segment of the social economy that has been the target of so much attention since the mid-1990s as a potential vehicle of new job creation.

One of the oft-cited examples of successful job creation in the social economy is in the area of household help. As part of the array of programs set up since the mid-1990s to support the creation and operation of social-economy enterprises, the Quebec government established the Financial Assistance Program for Domestic Help Services, which subsidizes any adult Quebecer requiring domestic help in the form of housekeeping, errands, meal preparation and so on, up to a maximum of $10 per hour, depending on income. As of 2001, there were 103 social-economy enterprises across the province providing domestic assistance services, including 42 co-operatives. About a third of the $65 million in revenues collected that year came from direct billing of customers, the rest from the government Financial Assistance program and other grants. These social-economy businesses employ more than 5000 persons, the vast majority of whom are women. Overall, excluding administrative posts, nearly half of the jobs are part-time, although there are significant regional variations.

Here, as useful and necessary as this type of work is, and as much as it contributes to fulfilling the desire of many elderly citizens to remain in their homes, it is hard not to share the concern of social critics such as André Gorz about the rise of a new servant class, and other qualms about the social economy contributing to institutionalizing a low-wage, low-skill secondary labour market. In the field of domestic services, where there is inevitably direct competition with the private sector and the informal economy, a question also arises about the extent to which the subsidized social-economy enterprises may crowd out private-sector and informal-economy contractors, thus displacing other low-wage workers.

It would be interesting to know whether there is a qualitative difference between working as a domestic in the social economy and in the informal economy or the private or public sectors. Studies of wages, benefits, working conditions and the experience of work in the social economy are now being conducted, and there is some evidence from Canada and abroad that this is indeed the case. For example, a Quebec government study reported that one-third of the subsidized domestic-help businesses had wage policies exceeding the minimum standards in the sector.[125] In the European Union, the European Commission's pilot action examining the employment potential of the third sector through the funding of a series of projects found that the third sector actually offered the best job quality in the area of personal and home care provision. Noting that this is an area where "pay is relatively low and working conditions poor" across all sectors, the report concludes that "the projects funded under the pilot action succeeded in creating job opportunities that were generally better than normal for this sector, providing more job security (even in the case of fixed-term jobs), attaching greater attention to training, health and safety and, above all, paying the minimum wage."[126] However, the report adds that there are doubts about the possibility of sustaining the jobs created via the pilot action.

In Quebec too, there are concerns about the financial viability of many of the highly subsidized enterprises, and, as in many non-profit organizations the issue of continuity of funding is a constant source of anxiety. Moreover, considering that the jobs are relatively low-paying, and many are part-time, concerns about precariousness are legitimate.

There is some doubt, for instance, about the future of an oft-cited example of social economy success: the network of *ressourceries (RRQ),* a variety of small businesses devoted to the sorting, recovery, reuse and transformation of solid waste. This network too received government support (in 1999, $22 million was allocated over five years to fund start-ups) but unlike the Domestic Help program saw its funding cut (along with financial support for a variety of environmental protection organizations) by the Liberal provincial government in March 2004. Unable to achieve economic self-sufficiency within the original time frame, partly because of underdeveloped markets for recycled goods and the relatively high cost to industry, under current regulatory conditions, of recycled materials, the *ressourceries* are now financially challenged and the fate of the 600 or so permanent and temporary jobs created by the RRQ is uncertain unless other funding is forthcoming.

The jewel in the social-economy crown in Quebec is the network of *Centres de la petite enfance*, a group of non-profit daycare centres employing some 23,000 people (making it the third largest private employer in Quebec[127]). This network was institutionalized with the introduction of Quebec's now renowned state-funded day care program, originally offered to parents at the modest cost of $5 per day (in spite of vigorous opposition, the fee was recently hiked to $7 a day under Jean Charest's Liberal government). In addition to the *Centres de la petite enfance*, providers of daycare services under the program include home-based daycares, many of which had previously operated in the informal economy, and some for-profit organizations. Although the non-profit daycare centres are administered by independent boards of directors, the program is funded almost entirely by government at great expense; as demand has increased and wages and benefits have improved, costs have spiralled to $1.3 billion annually and counting, of which government contributes more than 90 per cent.[128]

Notwithstanding certain limitations, the Quebec government program is rightly regarded as a model program in every respect, including the quality of jobs, with wages and benefits ranking among the best in the country. Many of the workers are now unionized, and they fought a successful struggle to increase their wages, which rose from an almost poverty level of about $12.50 per hour in 1999 to more than $17.00 in 2003 (with variations depending on qualifications and experience). The unionized workers also negotiated a pension plan. However, in 2004, the Charest government passed legislation to preclude the unionization of the 15,000 home-based daycare providers, thus ensuring a two-tier workforce.

In this very brief sketch,[129] I have highlighted certain issues to make the point that although the picture of work in the social economy is varied and complex, non-standard work, uncertain access to benefits, and lower rates of unionization relative to the public sector all stand out as important questions. Even if social economy enterprises succeed in honouring the commitment to pay an hourly wage that exceeds the current Quebec minimum wage of $7.45 (and the main actors in the social economy in Quebec have called for an increase in the minimum wage to $8.50 per hour), even full-time work at that rate yields an income that is scarcely enough to live on. As journalist Annick Perreault-Labelle points out in an article about "surviving on crumbs" in Quebec, the OECD defines a low-wage job as one paying less than two-thirds of the median wage. In Quebec in 2003, the median hourly wage was $15.45, which leaves any job paying less than $10.30 per hour in the low-wage zone.[130] Indeed, according to one study by researchers with Social Development Canada, many of the working poor earn wages significantly above the minimum and it is doubtful that any modest increase in the minimum wage will lift workers out of poverty.[131] This is a reminder that, in today's world, work is not necessarily an insurance against poverty. Moreover, the examples cited throw into relief the high degree of dependency on government funding, which raises the question of what happens to the jobs in the event that state financial assistance is curtailed or terminated.

The question remains as to whether there should be any reason to suppose that non-profit organizations, largely dependent on subsidies and operating in a market economy in which long-term commitments are increasingly anathema, will be more likely than other economic sectors to generate stable well-paid jobs? Can the State be expected to provide an adequate level of funding to ensure decent jobs with adequate security when it is precisely seeking a lower-cost option than the heavily unionized public sector to shoulder social responsibilities?

In a discussion of feminist issues related to the post-industrial restructuring of the Welfare State that is highly relevant to the problem of sustaining employment through the expansion of personal services, Peter Graefe summarizes the dilemma that arises from the impediments to productivity growth in human services: "If personal service productivity lags [behind] that of the economy as a whole, the relative price of these services will rise over time. These services will eventually price themselves out of the market, thus evacuating their employment-creating potential."[132] Faced with this problem, western nations have relied on two competing strategies: the neoliberal scenario, in which such services are provided to higher-income earners by low wage employees in the private sector, and the alternative social-democratic route of increased public funding of these services that helps both to democratize demand and to avert the creation of a (predominantly feminine) low-wage ghetto. Graefe points out that the obstacle to the second scenario is the aversion of most western regimes to raising taxes, which has led liberal regimes to downsize the public sector and contract out service provision functions to both private enterprises and non-profit organizations.

Under these circumstances, the main advantage of the third sector for government must lie in a greater return on investment, which is realized in part by cost-effectiveness. Because cost-effectiveness is difficult to achieve through productivity growth in the domain of human services, that leaves lower wages, longer hours and other forms of exploitation and self-exploitation. Now, it is certainly possible to argue that precisely because of its cost-effectiveness the third sector/social economy represents a desirable and practical alternative to maintaining or expanding the more expensive public sector—an option that at the same time circumvents the worst-case scenario of a low-wage precarious private sector providing services to a privileged minority. This seems to be the gravamen of Graefe's conclusions.[133] On this basis, one can stake a claim for sustained long-term funding for employment-generating service-provision by the third sector. But then we should be clear about the choice that is being made, and the obstacles to creating sustainable jobs or training for good jobs through such initiatives as social enterprises should be understood in this context. In a sense, community-based service-provision and social enterprises constitute a form of work sharing—one that cannot but generate tensions between different categories of working people and entrench certain forms of inequality.

As long as the social economy in particular positions itself as part of the solution to the contemporary employment puzzle, it is legitimate to ask how it does or might affect the larger world of work. The people who are being excluded from the spoils of growth are not only the unemployed and traditionally disadvantaged. Exclusion is being institutionalized in a two-tier society where a significant part of the labour force is itself verging on redundancy or is employed in precarious jobs. The social economy obviously cannot absorb enough workers to shift the balance of power of labour, and given its heavy reliance on government funding, it cannot be expected to provide what are traditionally considered "good jobs" at a time when the good jobs in the public sector are being restructured—often out of existence—in a bid to cut costs, and when the profitable activities privatized by the State are generally taken over by the private sector. On the other hand, it can offer meaningful work for professionals seeking a greater degree of flexibility in working hours, in addition to providing very useful opportunities for people who are marginalized to earn a living and participate in useful ways in the reproduction of society. There is no doubt, as the champions of the social economy emphasize, that there are many other benefits of social enterprises beyond their contribution to generating and maintaining jobs. The seminal European Commission study pointed for example to encouraging creativity, spillover effects that can help energize local economies, giving low-earners access to goods and services that would otherwise be out of reach. In a context of growing inequality, where certain people are excluded from social participation by virtue of their inability to compete in the labour market, strategies such as the social economy and community entrepreneurship are clearly useful and necessary. They are, like the mutualist movements which preceded them, a defensive response to conditions of insecurity, in this instance brought about by the paring down of the Welfare State. These strategies partake of a paradox, however. Much of the discourse around the social economy and community economic development revolves around the view that access to the labour market is the best hope for social inclusion and social security, which legitimates the drive toward increased dependence on the labour market at the very time when work is being destabilized and participation in wage labour is less and less likely to procure the traditional social protections.

Ultimately, in face of the generalized destabilization of work manifested in the expansion of non-standard employment and persistently high levels of unemployment, even a reformist approach to the problem of work must go beyond strategies for enhancing the employability of disadvantaged groups and creating jobs in an increasingly-commercialized third sector, the very existence of which are predicated on the neoliberal restructuring of the Welfare State and the social problems of a two-tier society. Unfortunately, discussion of the employment-generating role of the third sector/social economy is often carried on in isolation from these larger issues, which moves us onto the terrain of contesting the increasingly inequitable distribution of wealth and income.

Part of the focus within the third sector on creating jobs, as opposed to militating for policies such as generalized work reduction or guaranteed income that would render employment less central as a source of meaningful activity and income, is the deeply ingrained belief that work is and ought to remain the centre of human existence. From Karl Marx to Pope John Paul, work has been seen on all sides of the political and philosophical spectrum as that which confers dignity and makes us human. In the tradition of social Catholicism, work constitutes participation in divine creation. On the left, despite the original and often forgotten socialist goal of putting an end to waged labour, work is frequently viewed as the locus of individual self-development and political consciousness. That work has become more and more narrowly defined as paid employment has not detracted from its status as the defining fact of human life. And while this was primarily a masculine outlook, with the massive movement of women into the labour force since the 1960s it has lost its gender specificity—an important part of the feminist movement viewed women's participation in wage labour as the *sine qua non* of emancipation, and women in post-industrial societies have begun to define themselves increasingly in terms of what they do to earn a living.

Rivers of ink continue to flow on the subject of the social functions of work; much of great insight and eloquence has been said about work as a form of self development, a seat of identity, a means of social integration, a structured and structuring activity that provides essential traction,[134] a social norm measured against which non-waged workers are likely to feel a sense of marginality and meaninglessness and myriad other dimensions. There can be no doubt that many people find satisfaction and meaning in their wage work beyond securing an income, but it is also true that equally many, or more, work at jobs with little intrinsic interest and under a variety of stultifying conditions, primarily because they must. The 2003 results of Gallup's annual Employee Engagement Index poll revealed a remarkably low level of psychological commitment to their jobs among employees in the eleven countries surveyed.[135] Taken together, the number of employees who are not engaged or actively disengaged far exceeds the number of engaged employees. In Canada, for instance, 24 per cent of those surveyed were reported to be engaged, 60 per cent not engaged, and 16 per cent actively disengaged in their work. Thus, three-quarters of employees are not psychologically committed to their work—and Canada's level of engagement ranked higher than most!

I raise this point here primarily as a caveat to temper the often incautious view of waged work that underpins much of the writing on social integration through work. Indeed, the general enthusiasm for waged labour is taken by social critic Russell Jacoby as betokening the death of the utopian spirit in our time, marking our distance from the belief that the future can be different from the present.

It is undoubtedly true from the vantage point of those excluded from the labour force and in light of the documented adverse psycho-social effects of un-employment and underemployment that having a paid job is often better than not having one. Some, usually on the right of the political spectrum, argue that any job is better than none. There are echoes of this thinking in the literature on the third sector and the social economy. In a recent book on how third sector development can mitigate the inherent failings of the market, U.S. scholar Christopher Gunn asserts that in a context of high unemployment and shrinking safety nets "any job creation has to be counted as good."[136] Even, as in this case, when motivated by concern and solidarity for the unprivileged, this is a dangerous logic (thrown into relief by an article in the Berlin daily *Die Tageszeitung* which raised the hypothetical possibility that a female German welfare recipient could be threatened with termination of her welfare benefits should she refuse to accept a job in a brothel, which is a legal and legitimate enterprise in Germany). By accepting not simply the reality but the inevitability of precariousness and unemployment, as well as of the retreat of the State, it is at a loss to resist the ratcheting down of wages, and the decline of job stability and working conditions. It should be recalled, too, that the expansion of the personal-services sector is predicated precisely on a significant inequality of income within contemporary capitalist societies, which makes it worthwhile financially for the more affluent to spend a portion of their income on a variety of services provided by less-well remunerated segments of the labour force.

The question of achieving social inclusion through work is also not as simple as it can appear when premises remain unexamined. Do all jobs give those who hold them a sense of meaningful participation in society or only socially useful jobs? What constitutes a socially useful job, and why are some activities, such as care-giving, deemed socially useful only when performed within the confines of a labour contract but not outside it? In an essay discussing the results of a large-scale European research project (*Inclusion through participation* - INPART) on various schemes to activate the unemployed, three commentators question the tendency to make inclusion synonymous with employment. Extending Guy Standing's critique of workfare to other forms of "activation," they suggest that the narrow focus on employment as the royal road to social inclusion and full citizenship creates a situation in which "unemployed people's initiatives to participate in non-labour-market-related activities, which can indeed contribute to their inclusion even though they do not involve employment, are neglected or even counteracted in social policies."[137] These authors suggest that in evaluating the success of activation schemes, the actual experience of the people targeted is often of less account than quantitative measures of job placement. They conclude that the emphasis on employment as the key to social inclusion is motivated primarily by the desire on the part of policy-makers to reduce the number of people dependent on various forms of social assistance.

We should also be aware that some of our thinking about work is tautological: as a society, we define human worth and dignity excessively in terms of wage work, and regard those outside it as deprived of dignity. The conviction that work is the master key to social integration in part bespeaks our deep-seated ideas about the moral necessity to work—ideas originating in an era very different from our own. In a most interesting essay, Peter Kelvin and Joanna Jarrett traced the germs of our attitudes to unemployment and the unemployed to the Ordinance of Labourers in 1349, which forebade the giving of alms to "sturdy beggars" to compel them to work. They point out that the Ordinance was a reaction to a post-Plague labour shortage in which context every able-bodied person was needed to work and only the unfit could be spared that obligation. Thence evolved the enduring notion of non-participation in paid labour as a moral and social scourge and the belief that only the deserving (read disabled) unemployed should be granted the necessaries of life. For Kelvin and Jarrett, these lenses are entirely inappropriate to view our own era of technological displacement of work and structural unemployment.

Of course, the historical, social and intellectual basis of contemporary attitudes to work and the lack thereof is an immensely complex question which cannot be pinned to a specific event. Nevertheless, it is useful to bear in mind for argument's sake that there is no body of literature pondering the problem of the poor self-esteem and sense of social uselessness owing to the state of passive dependence among jobless trust-fund babies. But this is a long and complex debate which is beyond the compass of this essay.

Setting aside some of these more philosophical issues, in practical terms, having a job has been so central in contemporary society not only because it is the primary means of securing revenue but also because social protection in the form of benefits remains bound up with formal employment. However, flexibilization has gone hand in hand with a concerted attack on benefits so that, in effect, social protection is now being severed from work for many individuals who are left increasingly to their own devices to cope with job loss, illness, family crises, retirement. There are a number of possible responses to this. There is the neoliberal contention, heard in its most unadulterated form in Canada in the pronouncements of the Fraser Institute, that society can no longer afford the level of social protection associated with the glory days of the Welfare State—a perspective that implies the tacit or explicit acceptance of a growing population of working poor, casually employed and workfare participants and the belief that it is the role of private charity organizations in the third sector to provide the unfortunate with assistance. At the other end is the response of organized labour, which involves fighting for the preservation of existing benefits, primarily for its own members, protesting the disappearance of unionized jobs in the private and public sector associated with decent remuneration and non-wage benefits. Another response is to call for the creation of new forms of social protection that are not contingent on paid employment. At its most radical, this demand can take the form of a challenge to the very foundation of the wage-based society: advocating a decoupling of the right to an income from participation in the labour market.

This question was raised already in the 1960s by Roy Lubove in a book about the history of social security: "Must economic security remain so closely tied to stable, long-term labour force participation? Must the unemployable—dependent children, blind, handicapped, aged, able-bodied but unskilled … be penalized for the incapacity to compete in the labour market?"[138] This question is being raised urgently once again in some quarters and extended beyond "the unemployable" to encompass all those for whom the labour market no longer affords the prospect of stability or adequate income.

There are different types of proposals: from ensuring the portability of social benefits, to extending social protection to all types of non-standard work, to dissociating it from work altogether in the form of a universal citizens' income available to all adults and not contingent on participation in paid employment. Jerald Wallulis remarks that "there should be a public openness to the idea of a mechanism to buffer income and prevent the wild fluctuations in earnings that are likely in the new employment histories and struggles for employability."[139] Because everyone, including those who remain in relatively secure jobs, is increasingly vulnerable, public acceptance may be possible.

In Europe, the critique of the employment contract as too restrictive a basis for access to social protection is gaining ground among scholars and within the trade union movement. Reflecting on the transformation(s) of work in our time and drawing on a massive research project conducted by the CFDT, one of France's main trade union confederations, union leader Pierre-David Labani concludes that rethinking social protection is one of the most pressing tasks for a society in which work is no longer a guarantee against poverty and in which the spread of non-standard employment creates unstable and insecure work situations. For Labani, access to social protection must now be dissociated from the traditional labour contract.[140]

Here in Canada, a similar case is beginning to be made. In Quebec, the seminal Bernier report, commissioned by the former Parti Québécois government and published in February 2003, recommended a series of far-reaching changes to labour legislation that would extend social protection to individuals in non-standard employment situations who are economically dependent on a single employer, although they may not be "employees" as defined by the current Labour Code.[141] Affirming that a disparity in treatment based on employment status is socially unacceptable, the Bernier report advocates, for example, that temporary employees receive the same compensation as permanent and be afforded greater access to social benefits and collective bargaining. In a similar vein, a group of Ontario researchers, including Judy Fudge, Leah Vosko and Eric Tucker, presented a brief to the Law Commission of Canada, in which they used own-account self-employment as a test case to challenge the extension of labour protection to certain forms of paid work but not others.[142]

Considering the important role assigned to and assumed by the third sector/ social economy in stimulating employment and enhancing employability, it is in a privileged position to advocate for policies in relation to work that would countervail current trends toward a dual society based on a polarized labour market. As William Ninacs has argued, in order to prevent the social economy from becoming a favoured means of managing poverty, the development of social economy initiatives must be part of a broad multi-faceted offensive against unemployment and poverty...."[143]

For historical reasons that are beyond the scope of this essay, conceiving the social economy as part of a "multi-faceted offensive" is much more characteristic of scholars and activists in Europe than in North America, where attention remains trained chiefly on ways to stimulate economic growth and create new sources of employment. In Quebec, for example, the main organization engaged in promoting the social economy focuses exclusively on social entrepreneurship. In Europe, where there has been an intense meditation for several decades about the nature and place of work in contemporary western society, about the allocation of revenue and the channelling of productivity gains, about the reduction of working time and the development of a new social contract, such issues are integral to thinking about a "solidarity economy" evolving as a feasible alternative alongside the liberal market economy. In the writings of many European social analysts, the social economy tends to be conceived as one part of a multiform strategy of overall economic and social reform in reaction to the metamorphoses of labour markets that are leaving more and more people without stable or sufficient work, without job security, without benefits. It is one part of an ensemble of measures aimed not only at combating social exclusion, but also at fostering a fairer general distribution of work and income within society.

In France, for instance, the call to support the social economy often goes hand in hand with a demand for generalized work reduction, and this is true among those thinkers who continue to see work as the key to social integration and social citizenship.[144] As French economist and politician Alain Lipietz, a strong advocate of creating jobs in the third sector to meet social needs, pointed out in 1993, reducing working time for all means sharing the existing work, and sharing is the most basic form of solidarity. He presented the growth of free time for all precisely in contrast to the passing off of involuntary part-time work and other forms of precarious employment for some as work-sharing.[145] Similarly, in their public appeal for an alternative to neoliberalism in the latter half of the 1990s, a group of French economists largely committed to redefining and restoring the goal of full employment, stressed work-time reduction as an indispensable instrument.

> [A] new full-employment policy should be premised both on a significant reduction of work time and on an economic recovery plan which can certainly be "sustainable" and oriented toward social needs (development of social housing, neighbourhood revitalization, training, daycare, environmental protection…).[146]

Although it is true that if we take the long view, the number of hours worked annually has diminished by half in the last hundred years, the historic pace of work reduction has slowed in an unprecedented way in the last quarter-century. And this is so even if we decline to calculate education and training time as a part of working time, although the inclusion of training in working time would be perfectly legitimate in light of the trend toward knowledge-intensive jobs typical of the economies of the West and an educational system arguably geared increasingly toward training for employment as opposed to the traditional goals of liberal education.

In continental western Europe, many scholars and commentators single out work-time reduction, effected through any number of measures including but not limited to legislated weekly standards, as one of the keys to a more equitable distribution of wealth within society as well as to a more ecologically sustainable economy. A reduction in the number of hours worked leads to a redistribution of work and more opportunities for groups excluded from the primary labour force to enter it.

However, in contrast with Europe, where, for example, the European Trade Union Confederation supports for institution of the 35-hour week across the continent, there has been little discussion in North America of significant work time reduction as an option to counter the individualized work-time reduction (involuntary part-time, for example) occasioned by the employer-driven demand for flexibility. Although a greater number of Canadians are working more than 50 hours per week than was the case a decade ago and employees are clocking a significant amount of overtime, neither the trade union movement nor progressive political parties have placed it high on their agendas—this despite the reality of relatively shorter hours in many European countries as a result of measures such as standard five-and-six-week annual vacations, and despite evidence from the French experience of 35 hours, for instance, that reducing work time can contribute significantly to mitigating unemployment and underemployment and to contributing to a better quality of life for working people.[147]

Work time reduction is also central in the thinking of Guy Aznar, another French social theorist who sees the ongoing development of the social economy as one dimension of a necessary transition to "pluralist employment" ("*emploi pluriel*").[148] Although his arguments refer to the French context, they are more broadly applicable to the problems of precarious employment and social exclusion in the advanced capitalist economies. Aznar affirms the potential of what he calls the "associative sector" to create employment through the expansion of innovative social enterprises dedicated to providing services to individuals and local communities, with the help of government subsidies and tax credits, in areas such as environmental protection, adult education and elder care, especially in low profitability ventures which are less inviting to the private sector. For Aznar, however, who emphasizes the crucial role of paid employment as a means of achieving personal autonomy and as a basis of citizenship, job creation of this type is only viable as part of a complete overhaul of the work-based society which would include a significant reduction in the time individuals spend engaging in paid labour, as well as a diversification of the legal forms of the work contract so that people may receive an income for a wider range of activities than is currently remunerable. Although an opponent of proposals for a universal basic income or citizens' income, Aznar advocates introducing an intermittent guaranteed income that can be used to finance sabbatical years (currently a luxury of the professoriate), training and other "recharging" activities which he deems vital to human self-development.

If we are to take seriously the idea of a new model of development as advanced in the literature on community economic development and the social economy then, surely, a rethinking of the issue of work and social protection across all the sectors—private, public and non-profit—is an indispensable undertaking for scholars and social actors in Canada and Quebec. Failing to engage in a more comprehensive critique of the prevailing arrangements of the employment society leaves the case for the social economy vulnerable to the charge that, operating on the edges and in the interstices of the market economy and complementing the provision of goods and services by the State and private enterprise, it helps to provide an "out" for the depredations of neoliberalism. Concentrating energies and efforts on building a third sector specifically aimed at creating jobs by meeting unfulfilled social needs risks leaving the mainstream unchallenged as social reformers turn their attention away from the deteriorating state of affairs in the primary spheres of the economy, namely, the private and public sectors. As Dominique Méda argues, if the third sector or social economy is conceived as merely existing alongside the private sector, which is left to function according to the unfettered laws of the market, there is a danger that the private sector will become even more obsessively focused on the short-term pursuit of profit and maximizing shareholder value untempered by other considerations because the social economy will be perceived as the place to deal with the human casualties of neoliberal policies in the form of exacerbated precariousness and social exclusion.

Here in Canada, we can benefit from the pioneering work of the many European, and particularly French, social thinkers who continue to engage in a fertile meditation on potential solutions to the social problems attending the decomposition of the world of work as we have known it in the latter half of the 20th century. Their contributions promise to be useful in developing a more multifaceted and critical approach to our own society's apparent inability to assure adequate work and the concomitant social protections for all its citizens. Without question, the third sector and the social economy have a pivotal part to play in remedying this deficiency, but they remain a response to mounting social inequality, not a rampart against it. For that we require a new approach to the redistribution of work and wealth and to the legislation governing our relationships to paid employment.

Notes

I am grateful to the Social Sciences and Humanities Research Council of Canada for the post-doctoral fellowship that made the research and writing of this essay possible. I also wish to express my thanks to my post-doctoral research supervisor, Jean-Guy Vaillancourt at the Sociology department of the Université de Montréal, for his wisdom and support. This essay would not have taken shape without the encouragement of Eric Shragge at Concordia University's School of Community and Public Affairs. Our ongoing and wide-ranging discussions of social policy and strategies for change are an invaluable source of intellectual and political stimulation. Finally, I am indebted as always to John Detre for his invariably pertinent comments and constructive criticisms.

1. Bridges, Job Shift, 50-51.
2. Reid, Shakedown, see 291-304. In fairness, both Reid and Bridges are critical of neoliberal policies that throw people onto their own resources and both argue in favour of preserving social safety nets in the face of growing uncertainties of the labour market; however, they both exalt the entrepreneurial spirit as the key to extricating ourselves from the crisis of work.
3. The phrase is Bridges', 100.
4. Manser and Picot, "The Role of Self-Employment." *Monthly Labour Review*, 14.
5. Industry Canada, Key Small Business Statistics, 23. For a detailed look at self-employment in Canada, see the report by Fudge, Tucker and Vosko, "The Legal Concept of Employment," 21-36.
6. According to McCartier and Schellenberg, the majority of self-employed Canadians start their own businesses by choice rather than necessity; *The Future of Work*, 5. However, according to John Mangan, Canadian patterns suggest that labour-market difficulties may have been a significant spur; *Workers Without Traditional Employment*, 40.
7. During the 1990s, 90 per cent of new self-employment was in the "own-account" category, Manser and Picot, "Role of Self-Employment," 12. One recent study examining the period from 1988 to 1998 found that among the self-employed, earnings per worker were "well below those in other sectors, and these earnings fell increasingly, relative to those of others," Statistics Canada, "Impact of Self-Employment on Productivity Growth." See also, for example, Human Resources Development Canada, "Own-Account Self-Employment in Canada"; and Jackson, "Low Income Trends in the 1990s."
8. Beck, *Brave New World of Work*, trans. Patrick Camiller, 84.
9. Magdoff and Magdoff, "Disposable Workers," *Monthly Review*, 18-35.
10. Proponents of this argument include French social theorists André Gorz and Alain Lipietz, as well as American writers such as Jeremy Rifkin.
11. The term was initially popularized by the French left in the 1970s as a reference to the shutting out of individuals and various groups from the benefits of economic growth and from the particular social benefits that accompany participation in the labour market, although it subsequently took on board a larger set of meanings related to overlapping processes of socio-cultural marginalization. See Amin,

Cameron and Hudson, *Placing the Social Economy*, 17; Ballet, Les Entreprises d'insertion, 6-16.

12. Ibid., 2-5.

13. On the development of the full-employment society as we know it (or knew it) in the industrialized world, see for example, Gaffikin and Morrissey, *The New Unemployed*. As Dickinson and Schaeffer document, in the South the vast majority relies far more on their own ability to generate income and secure subsistence than on stable wage labour. *Fast Forward*, see especially 12-30.

14. For an excellent introduction to the concepts of post-Fordism, neo-Fordism and post-industrialism and the distinctions between them, see Allen, "Post-industrialism/Post-Fordism," chap. 16 in *Modernity: An Introduction to Modern Societies*.

15. The Marxist left in particular has been concerned to emphasize the fundamental continuity of capitalism in spite of seemingly epochal changes such as globalization and deindustrialization in the West [for an example of this genre of argument, see Clarke, "New Utopias for Old." *Capital and Class*, 131-155] although there is a tendency to negate the significance of the sea changes wrought in the advanced industrial economies in a way that seems unnecessary to uphold that view. One of the pioneering and enduringly illuminating treatments of the issues is David Harvey's *The Condition of Postmodernity*. For an excellent although now somewhat dated discussion of the debate around "new times" see Kumar, *Prophecy and Progress*. Another exceptionally lucid summary and analysis of the central issues and stakes in the debate is MacDonald's "Post-Fordism and the Flexibility Debate," *Studies in Political Economy*, 177-201. For a recent defence from the left of the value of the concept of post-Fordism see Bowring, "Post-Fordism and the End of Work," *Futures*, 159-172. This essay draws extensively on the work of Gorz, all of which is highly germane to the debate on post-Fordism.

16. How Canada compares to other western nations with respect to the proportion of its workforce employed in non-standard arrangements depends in part on the definitions employed. According to Mangan's comparative study, Australia is comparable, and Spain has an even greater degree of non-standard employment. According to some accounts, nearly one-third of the U.S. labour force works in non-standard jobs. Although the U.S. Bureau of Labour Statistics adopts a narrow definition of contingent work that, taken together with its calculations of those employed in alternative working arrangements, puts the total figure at about 10 per cent, estimates for the proportion of the U.S. labour force holding non-standard jobs in the late 1990s based on more widely used criteria range from 25 to 30 per cent. See Mangan, *Workers Without Traditional Employment*, 17 and 33, and also Hudson, *No Shortage of Nonstandard Jobs*, 2.

17. Immen, "Part-timers need support," *Globe & Mail*, C1.

18. In this case the salient evolution has been the increase of part-time employment among adult men, which has tripled since the mid-1970s. McCartin and Schellenberg, "The Future of Work," 2.

19. Lowe, *Employment Relationships*, 5.

20.   For a detailed breakdown of precarious employment in relation to the categories of sex, race and age, see Cranford, Vosko and Zukewich, "Precarious Employment in the Canadian Labour Market." *Just Labour*, 14-17.

21.   See the contributions to the Forum on Precarious Employment in the electronic journal *Just Labour* vol. 3 (Fall 2003) <http://www.justlabour.yorku.ca>.

22.   For a detailed account of the evolution of non-standard employment in Canada, see Broad, "The Casualization of the Labour Force," Chap. 3 in *Good Jobs, Bad Jobs, No Jobs and Hollow Work*, Hollow Society?

23.   McCartin and Schellenberg, "The Future of Work," 5. For a discussion of the evolution, causes and significance of part-time work in Canada, which addresses the question of the extent to which the expansion of part-time work reflects the desire of workers, and particularly women workers, for flexible working arrangements, see Duffy, "The Part-Time Solution," Chap. 8 in *Good Jobs, Bad Jobs, No Jobs*.

24.   Lowe and Schellenberg, *What's a Good Job?* CPRN Study, 13.

25.   See the discussion of temporary work in ibid., 12. Broad has synthesized some of the research on non-standard work and benefits in *Hollow Work, Hollow Society?*, see chapter 2. As one U.S. study of non-standard employment found, wage and benefit disparities between non-standard and regular full-time employment remained even when workers with similar profiles, educational levels and job descriptions were compared. Hudson, *No Shortage of Nonstandard Jobs*, 1.

26.   Cited by Saunders in *Passion and Commitment Under Stress*, 25.

27.   Marshall, "Benefits of the Job," *Perspectives on Labour and Income*.

28.   According to the prevailing view, 70 per cent of average annualized pre-tax earnings constitutes a reasonable retirement replacement income.

29.   Statistics Canada, "Average earnings by sex and work pattern." Of course, when one takes into account that the majority of people employed in non-standard working arrangements are women, the earnings gap between men and women is relevant: a woman working full-time in 2001 earned 71.6 per cent that of a man.

30.   Statistics Canada, "Retirement" in *Canada e-Book*.

31.   Statistics Canada's low-income cut-off rate for a single person living in a city with a population of over 500,000 was calculated for 2003 at $19,795. "Fact Sheet: Poverty Lines, 2003," National Council of Welfare. The 2004 benefit rates of the Canada Pension Plan, Old Age Security and the Guaranteed Income Supplement are available online at Social Development Canada's website at <http://www.sdc.gc.ca/en/cs/comm/news/2003/031217.shtml#101> and <www.sdc.gc.ca/en/isp/oas/tabrates/tabmain/shtml>

32.   Lowe, *Employment Relationships*, 12.

33.   For a discussion that links these two phenomena see Jerald Wallulis, *The New Insecurity*.

34.   "Contingent Workers Fight for Fairness," A Report from the National Alliance for Fair Employment.

35.   Lowe, *Employment Relationships*, 5.

36.   Beck, *Brave New World of Work*, 53-54.

37.   Lowe, *Employment Relationships*, 10.

38.   Wallulis, *The New Insecurity*, 114-16.

39. Drucker, "The Age of Social Transformation," *The Atlantic Monthly*, 76.

40. Salamon notes that in the U.S., this antagonistic pairing of the non-profit sector and the State dates back to the end of the Civil War, "The Case of America," in *Third Sector Policy at the Crossroads*, 19.

41. On this point, see, for example, the various contributions to *Third Sector Policy at the Crossroads*. The situation on the European continent is likely to take a turn for the worse following the recent wave of public sector privatization and downsizing discussed by Hailimi in "Dans l'étau des privatisations," *Le Monde Diplomatique*.

42. Glenday, "Lost Horizons, Leisure Shock," in *Good Jobs, Bad Jobs*, 11.

43. Rifkin, *The End of Work*, see especially Chap.10, "The Last Service Worker."

44. Craib cited in Wallulis, *The New Insecurity*, 87-88.

45. Kumar, *Prophecy and Progress*, 244-45.

46. Ibid., 196.

47. The phrase is Wachtel's from his *The Poverty of Affluence*, 259. Critics such as Illich and Gorz have meditated on the potentially perverse effects of an intensified commercialization of the realm of domestic life. This is a prominent theme in works ranging from Illich's *The Right to Useful Unemployment* to Gorz's *Misères du present, richesse du possible*. This is highly pertinent to the whole discussion (below) of the employment-generating potential of the third sector/social economy. Indeed, where enthusiasts see in the development of the social economy a countervailing realm to the market, the most trenchant critics make a case for the social economy as part and parcel of the ultimate triumph of the market:

> Parenting, learning, socializing, taking care of oneself and each other, building networks of trust and contributing to the social solidarity on which both regional economies and flexibly specialized corporations depend could all qualify as work in a post-Fordist economy, thus satisfying critics of social exclusion by extending the socially normalizing, economically rationalizing logic of capital into hitherto uncommodified regions of life.

Bowring, "Post-Fordism and the end of work," *Futures*, 170. I have discussed this point in "Reflections on Work," in *Social Economy*.

48. Duxbury and Higgins, *The 2001 National Work-Life Conflict Study*, xv.

49. For one defense of this logic that attempts to engage with various criticisms, see Gautié, *Les Politiques de l'emploi*, 184-92.

50. European Commission, *The New Actors of Employment*, 29.

51. Esping-Anderson's perspective is summarized by Peter Graefe in "Broadening the Options," 2-3.

52. Campbell, *The Third System Employment*, 5.

53. For an extended description of this initiative, see Ballet, *Les Entreprises d'insertion*.

54. Of the overall job total, associations provide 71 per cent, cooperatives 25.7 per cent and mutual associations 3.1 per cent, although the proportions vary from country to country, European Commission, *New Actors of Employment*, 8-9.

55. Morin, "Urban Movements and Social Economy: Towards a New Kind of Solidarity?"

56. See Mayer, "The Changing Scope of Action," in *Possible Urban Worlds*, INURA.

57. Amin, Cameron and Hudson, "The U.K. Social Economy," 13.

58. Mendell, "The Social Economy in Quebec," 9.

59. See Jackson, "Paul Martin's Economic Record," Alternative Federal Budget. For a different interpretation and conclusions, see Fisher and Hostland, "The Long View," in *The Review of Economic Performance*.

60. For an extensive description of the project see Greenwood et. al., *The Community Employment Innovation Project*.

61. The term "social economy" is far more common in Europe than in North America. Variously defined, it tends to refer broadly to economic activity that is motivated by social aims rather than profit and conducted for the benefit of stakeholders such as employees and clients rather than investors. Social enterprise surpluses are typically reinvested in the business, or in the case of cooperatives, redistributed. Some definitions exclude enterprises that are completely dependent on grants, making some form of earned income a decisive criterion. More democratic decision-making practices tend to be another defining feature of what is included under the social economy rubric, as is autonomy from the State in matters of management. The broader definitions tend to correspond to a wide range of community economic development activities. As a practice and an object of policy, the social economy overlaps in many respects with community economic development, although the latter is seen to have a specific territorial focus. [See Lewis "Common Ground; CED & the Social Economy—Sorting Out the Basics," *Making Waves,* 7-11.]. Quarter uses the term as an umbrella category embracing the entire third sector including the entire range of non-profit organizations ["The Social Economy and the Neo-Conservative Agenda" in *The Social Economy*, 55-58]; however, in the milieu, the definition of the social economy appears to be increasingly restricted to the entrepreneurial segment of the third sector. The terminology tangle is unlikely to be resolved given the geographical and conceptual diversity at issue. The federal government's adoption of this nomenclature comes in the wake of a concerted effort to promote the social economy in theory and practice in Quebec, where it has been the object of policy initiatives since the mid-1990s. Thenceforth, an array of programs was set up to provide assistance and support for the creation and operation of social economy enterprises. For English-language overviews of the development of the social economy in Quebec see for instance Mendell, "The Social Economy in Quebec" and Ninacs (with the assistance of Toye), "A Review of the Theory and Practice of Social Economy/Économie Sociale."

62. House of Commons, Debates, 1550, 1555, 1600.

63. The phrase "new deal for communities" is also used in the U.K. in reference to a government program of partnerships, in particular with the voluntary sector, to revitalize distressed neighbourhoods; worklessness tops the list of problems to be tackled. One commentator from the U.K. characterizes it as a workfare program for the unemployed that relies on the social economy, although the author himself is inclined towards a positive view of such developments as the harbinger of a new form of welfare governance, Smith, "Green Citizenship," 15-16.

64. See the highlights of a recent Statistics Canada study of wealth and poverty in Canadian cities that confirms previous evidence of growing inequality in Canada throughout the 1990s in Galloway, "The rich got richer…" *The Globe and Mail*, A-10.

65. See Finlayson and Peacock, "Gauging the Economic Contribution of Large and Small Businesses," *Policy Perspectives*.

66. Balkenhol, "Enterprise Creation by the Unemployed," 1.

67. This is the thrust of the editorial in the May 2004 issue of *Making Waves*; Lewis, "The End of the Beginning," *Making Waves*, 2-3.

68. Canadian Council on Social Development, "Budget gives Social Development Department little to do."

69. Cited by Greason in "Décentraliser pour mieux privatiser," *Relations*, trans. Levy, 202.

70. As Scott emphasizes, the importance of government funding, the primary source of support for the third sector in Canada, "cannot be overstated." For her detailed discussion, see "Portrait of the Nonprofit and Voluntary Sector," Appendix B in *Funding Matters*.

71. Hall, "Comments" in *The Emerging Sector*, 80.

72. Title of an article on social entrepreneurship in the U.S. publication *Nonprofit World*, 16.

73. Jamieson, "Canada turns a corner," *CharityVillage NewsWeek*.

74. Boivin and Fortier, Introduction, in *L'Économie Sociale*, 22.

75. "Redefining Government Relationships."

76. Bernier and Dallaire, "What Price Have Women Paid for Health Care Reform?" in *Exposing Privatization*, 130.

77. On this point, see for example Hall et al., *The Capacity to Serve*, 20.

78. Roberts, *We Can't Fundraise Anymore*, 8.

79. Scott, "Portrait of the Nonprofit and Voluntery Sector," *Funding Matters*, see especially, 151-153.

80. See, for example, Anheier and Kendall, eds., *Third Sector Policy at the Crossroads* and the proceedings of the conference Moving from Income Support to Work, held at the John F. Kennedy Institute of the Freie Universität in Berlin in June 2003, published under the title *From Welfare to Work*.

81. Evans and Shields, "Neoliberal Restructuring and the Third Sector," 2.

82. See the Web site at http://www.hbs.edu/socialenterprise/whatis.html.

83. The conflicting conceptions of the social economy began to be elaborated and discussed, in terms that find echoes in the current discussion, more than a century ago when French economists attempted to classify the emerging co-operative movement and expressed divergent opinions about whether it constituted simply a discrete element of the system of producing or a force for social transformation. See Ninacs, "A Review of the Theory and Practice of Social Economy," 3.

84. For dissenting remarks on whether State-dependent, service-delivering non-profit organizations and enterprises can legitimately or usefully be included in the civil society category concept, see Dekker, "When Nonprofitness Makes No Difference," in *Third Sector Policy*, 66-67.

85. See, for example, the extensive writings of Lévesque, for instance, "Economie sociale et solidaire dans un contexte de mondialisation." See also Neamtan, "The Social and Solidarity Economy," trans. Anika Mendell. Highly relevant in this context is the discussion of the contrast between the reformist and utopian perspectives on the social economy by Fontan and Shragge in "Tendencies, Tensions and Visions," in *Social Economy*.

86. Greffe, *Décentraliser pour l'emploi,* Chap. 4.

87. See for example the cautiously positive assessment presented in 1997 by Aubry, then the chief researcher for Quebec's Confédération des Syndicats Nationaux (CSN), "Quel rôle pour l'économie sociale?" *Possibles*, 65-81.

88. For an overview of the issues and some of the literature on union/third sector relations in (English) Canada see the briefing note prepared by the Manitoba Voluntary Sector Initiative, "Summary of Research on Relations."

89. "Paul Martin's first budget as PM ignores pressing needs," Canadian Union of Public Employees (CUPE).

90. Centrale des syndicats du Québec (CSQ), "Un bon état de santé, 20-22.

91. See, for example, Campbell, *The Third System Employment,* 24.

92. Ibid., 25.

93. See, for example, Smith, "Green Citizenship and the Social Economy," 15-16.

94. Méda's reflections on the social economy were published in the context of a special issue of the journal *Transversales* devoted to a discussion of the third sector prompted by the tabling of a 1999 report on the third sector as an economy of social solidarity by Lipietz, one of France's pre-eminent political ecologists and elected representative of the French Green party to the European Parliament, "Risques et limites du tiers secteur," *Transversales*.

95. The public sector accounted for roughly 3.1 million jobs in 1992, for 2.8 million in 2001 and for 2.9 million in 2003. Statistics Canada includes all three levels of government in its calculations, as well as crown corporations and public institutions such as hospitals and universities, Statistics Canada, "Employers."

96. Bernier and Dallaire, "What Price Have Women Paid?" 139-40.

97. Armstrong, "The Context for Health Care Reform," in *Exposing Privatization*, 32-33.

98. *Connecting with Canadians.*

99. Dow, *Backgrounder on the Literature on (Paid) Human Resources*, 4-6.

100. From the late 1960s to the late 1990s, the number of registered charities alone more than tripled; Hirshhorn, *Emerging Sector*, 11. And see Scott, "Portrait of the Nonprofit and Voluntary Sector," Appendix B in *Funding Matters*, 166.

101. For a discussion of the challenges that face(d) researchers see Betcherman, et al., *The Voluntary Sector in Canada.*

102. Three-quarters of non-profit workers are women, and workers in the sector tend to be highly qualified, with about one-third in professional occupations and nearly 60 per cent possessing post-secondary education. McMullen and Schellenberg, *Job Quality in Non-Profit Organizations*, Canadian Policy Research Networks Research Series, 10-11.

103. Ibid., 34.

104. McMullen and Brisbois, *Coping with Change*, 33.

105. Saunders, *Passion and Commitment Under Stress*, 47.

106. Hall et al., *The Capacity to Serve*, 33.

107. Cited in ibid., 29.

108. The Guelph study is one of a variety of studies and statistical surveys, the findings of which are summarized by Dow in his comprehensive review of the research on paid employment in the non-profit sector conducted in the period from 1997 to 2001, *Backgrounder*, 20-22.

109. See, for example, Hall et al., T*he Capacity to Serve,* 33.

110. Campbell, *The Third System Employment and Local Development*, 25-26.

111. McMullen and Brisbois, *Coping with Change,* 27.

112. McMullen and Schellenberg, *Job Quality in Non-Profit Organizations*, 42.

113. Duxbury and Higgins, *Work-Life Conflict in Canada in the New Millennium,* 22.

114. Saunders refers to the 2000 National Survey of Giving, Volunteering and Participating, which revealed a 13 per cent decrease between 1997 and 2000 in the number of persons volunteering and a drop in hours volunteered equivalent to 29,000 full time, full-year jobs, *Passion and Commitment Under Stress*, 56.

115. McMullen and Schellenberg, *Job Quality in Non-Profit Organizations*, 22. Based on his review of previous research, Dow writes: "One of the most frequently mentioned HR sore points for the voluntary sector concerns the extent of unpaid overtime, and how common the expectation is that employees will continue to provide it without demurring," *Backgrounder,* 37.

116. Saunders, *Passion and Commitment Under Stress*, 47-50.

117. Cited in ibid., 54-55.

118. For a critical discussion of the "gospel of training" espoused by Canadian policymakers in the 90s, see *The Training Trap*, eds. Dunk, McBride and Nelsen.

119. For example, the examination of human resource issues in the third sector undertaken by Betcherman et al. in 1998 revealed that 40 per cent of organizations reported that they would be unwilling to participate in workfare-type programs; *The Voluntary Sector in Canada*, 39.

120. *Lessons Learned.*

121. See, for example, the discussion of the European INPART (inclusion through participation) project by Valkenburg, Lind and van Berkel, "Work and Inclusion," *Transfer*.

122. *Connecting with Canadians.*

123. Pulkingham and Ternowetsky, *A State of the Art Review*.

124. See for example, "How Much Do Small Business Employees Earn?", Industry Canada.

125. Thouin and Chagnon, *Portrait des entreprises en aide domestique*, 44.

126. European Commission, *New Actors of Employment*, 14.

127. "Centres de la petite enfance."

128. Lefebvre, "Quebec's Innovative Early Childhood," *Policy Options*, 54.

129. For a useful summary of some of the issues and research findings, see Fournier, "L'amélioration des conditions de travail passe par le syndicalisation."

130. Perreault-Labelle, "Survivre avec des miettes," *Jobboom*, 18.

131. Fleury and Fortin, "Canada's Working Poor," *Horizons*, 52.

132. Graefe, "Broadening the Options," 3.

133. Graefe is cautiously optimistic; he contests some of the assumptions that underpin the dilemma of the service economy, including the widely accepted thesis of inherent impediments to productivity growth in human services, and he is concerned to emphasize the possible variations on the two post-industrial trajectories that can conceivably represent a resolution of the dilemma, including community economic development and the building of the social economy in Quebec. However, his assessment of the latter's success in bypassing the low road of flexible low-wage service provision is guarded.

134. The fertile notion of traction is explored by Haworth and Evans in "Meaningful Activity," in *Unemployed People*, 243-45.

135. The overall survey results are summarized in an article devoted to the particularly high level of disengagement among British workers published in Gallup's online journal "Great Britain's Workforce Lacks Inspiration," *Gallup Management Journal*.

136. Gunn, *Third Sector Development*, 53.

137. Valkenburg, Lind and van Berkel, "Work and Inclusion," *Transfer*, 8-9.

138. Cited in Wallulis, *The New Insecurity*, 62.

139. Wallulis, *The New Insecurity*, 83.

140. Labani, "Les mutations du travail," 107 ff.

141. The report is available online at http://www.travail.gouv.qc.ca/actualite/travail_non_traditionnel/Bernier2003/. Predictably, the recommendations met with vehement resistance from the business community and there is little chance they will be adopted by Jean Charest's Liberal government.

142. Fudge, Tucker and Vosko, *The Legal Concept of Employment*, see especially 105 ff.

143. Ninacs, "A Review of the Theory and Practice of Social Economy," 26.

144. For an excellent and succinct overview of a number of the recent French debates around work see Laville, "The Future of Work."

145. Lipietz, *Vert espérance*, 53.

146. Ramaux, "La 'pleine activité' contre le chômage," in *Pour un nouveau plein emploi*, 103.

147. On this point see for example, Hayden, "International Work-Time Trends," 28-30. Plans by the conservative government of Jacques Chirac to undercut France's 35-hours legislation brought hundreds of thousands of French workers into the streets in protest in February and March of 2005.

148. See Aznar, *La fin des années chômage*.

Bibliography

Allen, John. "Post-industrialism/Post-Fordism." In *Modernity: An Introduction to Modern Societies*, edited by Stuart Hall et. al. Malden, MA: Blackwell, 1996.

Amin, Ash, Angus Cameron and Ray Hudson. *Placing the Social Economy*. London and New York: Routledge, 2002.

————. "The U.K. Social Economy: Panacea or Problem." Synopsis for EuroConference on Social Capital: Interdisciplinary Perspectives, University of Exeter, 15-20 September 2001, 13 <http://www.ex.ac.uk/shipss/politics/research/socialcapital/papers/amin.pdf> [12 August 2004]

Anheier, Helmut K. and Jeremy Kendall. *Third Sector Policy at the Crossroads: An International Nonprofit Analysis*. London and New York: Routledge, 2001.

Armstrong, Pat. "The Context for Health Care Reform in Canada." In *Exposing Privatization*, 32-33. Aurora, ON: Garamond Press, 2001.

Aubry, François. "Quel rôle pour l'économie sociale?" *Possibles,* Vol 21, no. 2 (Spring 1997): 65-81.

Aznar, Guy. *La fin des années chômage*. Paris: Syros, 1999.

Balkenhol, Bernd. "Enterprise Creation by the Unemployed: The Role of Micro-finance – An ILO Action Program." Paper for the International Conference on Self-employment, Burlington, 24-26 September 1998.

Ballet, Jérome. *Les Entreprises d'insertion*. Paris: Presses universitaires, 1997.

Beck, Ulrich. *Brave New World of Work*, trans. Patrick Camiller. Cambridge: Polity Press, 2000.

Bernier, Jocelyne and Marlène Dallaire. "What Price Have Women Paid for Health Care Reform? The Situation in Quebec." In *Exposing Privatization*, edited by Pat Armstrong et al. Aurora, ON: Garamond Press, 2001.

Betcherman, Gordon et al. *The Voluntary Sector in Canada: Literature Review and Strategic Considerations for a Human Resources Sector Study*. Ottawa: Canadian Policy Research Networks, April 1998.

Boivin, Louise and Mark Fortier. Introduction in *L'Économie Sociale: l'Avenir d'une Illusion*. Montréal: Fides, 1998.

Bowring, Finn. "Post-Fordism and the End of Work." *Futures* 34 (2002): 159-72.

Bridges, William. *Job Shift: How to Prosper in a Workplace without Jobs*. Reading, MA: Addison-Wesley Publishing Company, 1994.

Broad, Dave. "The Casualization of the Labour Force." In *Good Jobs, Bad Jobs, No Jobs: The Transformation of Work in the 21st Century*, edited by Ann Duffy, Daniel Glenday and Norene Pupo. Toronto: Harcourt Brace & Co., 1997.

Campbell, Mike. *The Third System Employment and Local Development, volume 1 Synthesis Report*. Leeds Metropolitan University: Policy Research Institute, August 1999.

Canadian Council on Social Development, "Budget gives Social Development Department little to do," 23 March 2004, <http://www.ccsd.ca/pr/2004/budget.htm> [25 May 2004].

Centrale des syndicats du Québec (CSQ). "*Un bon état de santé, c'est une affaire publique.*" Union health and social services platform, June 2001.

"Centres de la petite enfance: Un milieu qui fourmille de projets." Comité sectoriel de main-d'œuvre économie sociale et action communautaire. <http://www.csmoesac.qc.ca/uploads/cahiers_es/296_13.pdf> [4 June 2004].

Clarke, Simon. "New Utopias for Old: Fordist Dream and Post-Fordist Fantasies." *Capital and Class* 42 (Winter 1990): 131-155.

The Community Employment Innovation Project, Social Research and Demonstration Corporation, December 2003. <http://www.srdc.org/english/publications/ceip_implementation_report.pdf> [14 April 2004].

Connecting with Canadians: Pursuing Service Transformation. Final Report of the Government On-Line Advisory Panel (10 December 2003) <http://www.gol-ged.gc.ca/pnl-grp/reports/final/final13_e.asp> [18 June 2004].

"Contingent Workers Fight for Fairness," A Report from the National Alliance for Fair Employment. <http://www.fairjobs.org/fairjobs/contingent/cwffe_execsum.php> [20 May 2004].

Cranford, Cynthia, Leah F. Vosko and Nancy Zukewich, "Precarious Employment in the Canadian Labour Market: A Statistical Portrait." *Just Labour* [Electronic Journal] Volume 3 (Fall 2003). <http://www.justlabour.yorku.ca/cranfordetal_justlabour.PDF>.

Dekker, Paul. "When Nonprofitness Makes No Difference." In *Third Sector Policy at the Crossroads*, edited by Jeremy Kendall and H. K. Anheier. New York and London: Routledge, 2001.

Dickinson, Torry and Robert K. Schaeffer. *Fast Forward: Work, Gender and Protest in a Changing World*. Lanham, MD: Rowman and Littlefield Publishers, 2001.

Dow, Warren. *Backgrounder on the Literature on (Paid) Human Resources in the Canadian Voluntary Sector*. Report prepared for the Voluntary Sector Initiative, August 2001. <http://www.vsi-isbc.ca/eng/hr/pdf/rod_sept26_lit_review.pdf> [8 May 2004].

Drucker, Peter. "The Age of Social Transformation." *The Atlantic Monthly*. November 1994.

Duffy, Ann. "The Part-Time Solution: Toward Entrapment or Empowerment." In *Good Jobs, Bad Jobs, No Jobs,* edited by Ann Duffy, Daniel Glenday and Norene Pupo. Toronto: Harcourt Brace & Co., 1997.

Dunk, Thomas, Stephen McBride and Randle W. Nelsen, eds. *The Training Trap*. Winnipeg/Halifax: Society for Socialist Studies/Fernwood Publishing, 1996.

Duxbury, Linda and Chris Higgins. *Work-Life Conflict in Canada in the New Millennium*. Final Report, Health Canada. October, 2003. http://www.hc-sc.gc.ca/pphb-dgspsp/publicat/work-travil/pdf/report_2_e.pdf [4 April 2004].

Duxbury, Linda and Chris Higgins. *The 2001 National Work-Life Conflict Study: Report One*. Final Report, Health Canada, March 2002, <http://www.phac-aspc.gc.ca/publicat/work-travail/pdf/rprt_1_e.pdf> [4 April 2004].

"Economie sociale et solidaire dans un contexte de mondialisation : pour une démocratie plurielle," Cahiers du CRISES, November 2001. <http://www.crises.uqam.ca/cahiers/ET0115.pdf> [14 May 2004].

Eric, Volker, Margit Mayer and Jens Sembale, eds. *From Welfare to Work*. Berlin: December 2003.

European Commission. *The new actors of employment — Synthesis of the pilot action 'Third system and employment': 1997-2000*. Luxembourg: Office for Official Publications of the European Communities, 2003.

Evans, B. Mitchell and John Shields. "Neoliberal Restructuring and the Third Sector: Reshaping Governance, Civil Society and Local Relations." Ryerson Polytechnic University Centre for Voluntary Sector Studies Working Paper Series no. 13, July 2000.

"Fact Sheet: Poverty Lines, 2003," National Council of Welfare. <http://www.ncwcnbes.net/ htmdocument/principales/povertyline_e.htm> [12 April 2004].

Finlayson, Jock and Ken Peacock. "Gauging the Economic Contribution of Large and Small Businesses: A Reassessment." *Policy Perspectives,* vol. 10, no. 4 (August 2003).

Fisher, Tony and Doug Hostland, "The Long View: Labour Productivity, Labour Income and Living Standards in Canada." In *The Review of Economic Performance and Social Progress, 2002: Towards a Social Understanding of Productivity*, edited by Keith Banting, Andrew Sharpe, and France St. Hilaire. Montreal and Ottawa: Institute for Research on Public Policy, 2002.

Fleury, Dominique and Myriam Fortin. "Canada's Working Poor," *Horizons* [Electronic Journal] vol. 7, no. 2 (December 2004). <http://policyresearch.gc.ca/v7n2_e.pdf>.

Fontan, Jean-Marc and Eric Shragge. "Tendencies, Tensions and Visions in the Social Economy." In *Social Economy: International Perspectives and Debates*. Montreal: Black Rose Books, 2000.

Fournier, Jacques. "L'amélioration des conditions de travail passe par le syndicalisation." Summary of a roundtable discussion on Working Conditions and Unionization in the Social Economy held in Montreal in January 2003, Web site of the Regroupement québécois des intervenants et intervenantes en action communautaire (2 May 2003). <http://www.rqiiac.qc.ca/fr/interaction_communautaire/journal/ article_theme.asp? section=3&Id_theme=1&Id_articles=732> [22 March 2004].

"Forum on Precarious Employment." *Just Labour* vol. 3 (Fall 2003). http://www.justlabour. yorku.ca>.

Fudge, Judy, Eric Tucker and Leah Vosko. *The Legal Concept of Employment: Marginalizing Workers*. Research paper, Law Commission of Canada, 2002.

The Future of Work: Non-Standard Employment in the Public Service of Canada, Research Directorate Policy, Research and Communications Branch, Public Service Commission, March 1999.

Gaffikin, Frank and Mike Morrissey. *The New Unemployed: Joblessness and Poverty in the Market Economy*. London: Zed Books, 1992.

Galloway, Gloria. "The rich got richer…" *The Globe and Mail*, Thursday, 8 April 2004, A-10.

Gautié, Jérôme. *Les Politiques de l'emploi: les marges étroites de la lutte contre le chômage* Paris: Librairie Vuibert, 1993.

Glenday, Daniel. "Lost Horizons, Leisure Shock." In *Good Jobs, Bad Jobs, No Jobs,* edited by Ann Duffy, Daniel Glenday and Norene Pupo. Toronto: Harcourt Brace & Co., 1997.

Gorz, André. *Misères du present, richesse du possible*. Paris: Éditions Galilée, 1997.

Graefe, Peter. "Broadening the Options: Inflecting Quebec's Post-Industrial Trajectory." Paper for the 2003 Annual Meeting of the Canadian Political Science Association, Dalhousie University, Halifax, 29 May 2003.

Greason, Vincent. "Décentraliser pour mieux privatiser." *Relations* (September 1998), 22.

"Great Britain's Workforce Lacks Inspiration." *Gallup Management Journal*, 11 December 2003. <http://gmj.gallup.com/content/default.asp?ci=9847> [12 April 2004].

Greffe, Xavier. *Décentraliser pour l'emploi*. Paris: Economica, 1988.

Gunn, Christopher. *Third Sector Development*. Ithaca and London: Cornell University Press, 2004.

Hailimi, Serge. "Dans l'étau des privatisations." *Le Monde Diplomatique* (June 2004).

Hall, Michael. "Comments." In *The Emerging Sector: In Search of a Framework*, edited by Ronald Hirshhorn. Ottawa: Canadian Policy Research Networks, 1997.

Hall, Michael H. et al. *The Capacity to Serve: A Qualitative Study of the Challenges Facing Canada's Nonprofit and Voluntary Organizations*. Toronto: Canadian Centre for Philanthropy, 2003.

Harvey, David. *The Condition of Postmodernity*. Oxford: Basil Blackwell, 1989.

Haworth, John T. and Stephen T. Evans. "Meaningful Activity and Unemployment." In *Unemployed People*, edited by David Fryer and Philip Ullah, 243-245. Stony Stratford: Open University Press, 1987.

Hayden, Anders. "International Work-Time Trends: The Emerging Gap in Hours." *Just Labour* [Electronic Journal] Volume 2 (Spring 2003): 28-30. <http://www.yorku.ca/julabour/volume2/hayden_justlabour.PDF>.

Hirshhorn, Ronald. *Emerging Sector: In Search of a Framework*. Canadian Policy Research Networks, 1997.

Hollow Work, Hollow Society? Globalization and the Casual Labour Problem in Canada. Halifax: Fernwood Publishing, 2000.

House of Commons. Debates. 37th Parl., 3rd Sess., no. 32. 30 March 2004. http://www.parl.gc.ca/37/3/parlbus/chambres/house/debates/032_2004_03_30/han032-e.htm [15 May 2004].

"How Much Do Small Business Employees Earn?" Industry Canada, <http://strategis.ic.gc.ca/epic/internet/insbrp-rppe.nsf/en/rd00694e.html> [4 June 2004].

Hudson, Ken. *No Shortage of Nonstandard Jobs*. Washington, DC: Economic Policy Institute Briefing Paper, December 1999.

Human Resources Development Canada, "Own-Account Self-Employment in Canada: Lessons Learned," Final report, Evaluation and Data Development, Strategic Policy, November 2000, <http://www11.hrdc-drhc.gc.ca/pls/edd/edd_brief.document?p_site=EDD&cat=LLS&sub=OASEC> [7 May 2004]

Illich, Ivan. *The Right to Useful Unemployment*. London: Marion Boyers, 1978.

Immen, Wallace. "Part-timers need support." *Globe & Mail*, 17 October 2003, C1.

Industry Canada, *Key Small Business Statistics*. Ottawa: Industry Canada, April 2004.

Jackson, Andrew. "Low Income Trends in the 1990s," Canadian Council on Social Development, January 2001, <http://www.ginsler.com/documents/Low_Income_Trends_in_1990s.html> [4 April 2004].

———. "Paul Martin's Economic Record: Living Standards of Working Families and Prospects for Future Prosperity," Alternative Federal Budget 2004 Technical Paper #2, 10 December 2003. <http://www.policyalternatives.ca/afb/afb2004-martin-eco-record.pdf> [23 May 2004].

Jamieson, Doug. "Canada turns a corner—part three: looking ahead." *Charity Village NewsWeek*, 23 September 1996, <http://www.charityvillage.com/cv/research/rsta18.html>[20 March 2004].

Kelvin, Peter and Joanna E. Jarrett. *The Social Psychological Effects of Unemployment*. Cambridge: Cambridge University Press, 1985.

Kendall, Jeremy and H. K. Anheier. *Third Sector Policy at the Crossroads: An International Nonprofit Analysis*. New York and London: Routledge, 2001.

Kumar, Krishan. *Prophecy and Progress: The Sociology of Industrial and Post-Industrial Society*. London: Penguin, 1986.

Labani, Pierre-David. "Les mutations du travail. Entreprises, parcours professionnels et identités sociales." *Esprit* no. 288 (October 2002).

Laville, Jean-Louis. "The Future of Work: The Debate in France." Oslo: FAFO Institute for Applied Social Science, 1999.

Lefebvre, Pierre. "Quebec's Innovative Early Childhood Education and Care Policy and Its Weaknesses." *Policy Options* (March 2004).

Lessons Learned – Reconnecting Social Assistance Recipients to the Labour Market. Ottawa: Social Development Canada, November 1999). <http://www11.sdc.gc.ca/en/cs/sp/edd/reports/1999-000436/page06.shtml> [10 June 2004].

Lévesques, Benôit. "Economie sociale et solidaire dans un contexte de mondialisation: pour une democratic plusielle." *Cahiers du CRISES*. November 2001. http://www.crises.ugam.ca/cahiers/ETO115.pdf [14 May 2004].

Levy, Andrea. "Reflections on Work, the Social Economy and the Dangers of Carefare." In *Social Economy: International Debates and Perspectives*, edited by Eric Shragge and Jean-Marc Fontan. Montreal: Black Rose Books, 2000.

Lewis, Mike. "Common Ground; CED and the Social Economy—Sorting Out the Basics." *Making Waves*, vol. 15, no. 1 (May 2004): 7-11.

———. "The End of the Beginning." *Making Waves*, vol. 15, no. 1 (May 2004): 2-3.

Lipietz, Alain. "Risques et limites du tiers secteur." *Transversales* no. 57 (May/June 1999).

———. *Vert espérance : L'avenir de l'écologie politique*. Paris: Éditions la Découverte, 1993.

Lowe, Graham. *Employment Relationships as the Centrepiece of a New Labour Policy Paradigm*. Ottawa: Canadian Policy Research Networks, April 2002.

Lowe, Graham S. and Grant Schellenberg. *What's a Good Job? The Importance of Employment Relationships*, CPRN Study No. W/05. Ottawa: Canadian Policy Research Networks, 2001. <www.cprn.com/documents/2289_en.pdf> [10 May 2004].

MacDonald, Martha. "Post-Fordism and the Flexibility Debate." *Studies in Political Economy* 36 (Autumn 1991): 177-201.

Magdoff, Fred and Harry Magdoff. "Disposable Workers: Today's Reserve Army of Labor." *Monthly Review* (April 2004): 18-35.

Mangan, John. *Workers Without Traditional Employment: An International Study of Non-Standard Work*. Cheltenham, U.K. Edward Elgar Publishing Ltd., 2000.

Manitoba Voluntary Sector Initiative, "Summary of Research on Relations between the Voluntary Sector and Organized Labour," January 23, 2001, <http://www.voluntarysector.mb.ca/library/BN-RS5W.pdf> [29 May 2004].

Manser, Marilyn E. and Garnett Picot. "The Role of Self-Employment in U.S. and Canadian Job Growth," *Monthly Labour Review* (April 1999).

Marshall, Katherine. "Benefits of the Job." *Perspectives on Labour and Income, Online Edition* vol. 4, no. 5. Ottawa: Statistics Canada, 23 May 2003. <http://www.statcan.ca/english/studies/75-001/00503/hi-fs_200305_01_a.html> [7 May 2004].

Mayer, Margit. "The Changing Scope of Action in Urban Politics." In *Possible Urban Worlds*, edited by INURA [International Network for Urban Research and Action]. Basel, Switzerland: Birkhäuser-Verlag, 1998.

McCartier, Michel and Grant Schellenberg. *The Future of Work: Non-Standard Employment in the Public Service of Canada*. Research Directorate Policy. Research and Communication Branch, Public Service Commission, March 1999.

McMullen, Kathryn and Grant Schellenberg. *Job Quality in Non-Profit Organizations*. Canadian Policy Research Networks Research Series on Human Resources in the Non-profit Sector, no. 2, January 2003, pp.10-11.

McMullen, Kathryn and Richard Brisbois, *Coping with Change: Human Resource Management in Canada's Non-Profit Sector*. Ottawa: Canadian Policy Research Networks, December 2003.

Méda, Dominique. *Le Travail, une valeur en voie de disparition*. Paris: Aubier, 1995.

Mendell, Marguerite. "The Social Economy in Quebec." Paper for the VII International CLAD conference held in Panama, 28-31 October 2003.

Morin, Richard. "Urban Movements and Social Economy: Towards a New Kind of Solidarity?" Paper presented at ISA Congress in Brisbane, Social Movements and Social Classes Research Committee (no. 47) Panel 8 - Social Movements and Democracy II, July 2002.

Neamtan, Nancy. "The Social and Solidarity Economy: Towards an 'Alternative' Globalization." Trans. Anika Mendell. Background Paper for the Symposium on Citizenship and Globalisation organized by The Carold Institute, Vancouver, 14-16 June 2002.

Ninacs, William. "A Review of the Theory and Practice of Social Economy/Économie Sociale in Canada." SRDC Working Paper Series 02-02, August 2002.

"Paul Martin's first budget as PM ignores pressing needs." Canadian Union of Public Employees (CUPE) Web site (23 March 23 2004). <http://www.cupe.ca/www/fedbud04/9395> [12 May 2004].

Perreault-Labelle, Annick. "Survivre avec des miettes." *Jobboom*, vol. 6, no. 2 (February/March 2005).

Pulkingham, Jane and Gordon Ternowetsky. *A State of the Art Review of Income Security Reform in Canada* (Part B: Labour Market Policies: Delineating and Evaluating Work/Employment Incentives), IDRC Working Series Paper #4. Ottawa: International Development Research Centre, 1998, <http://www.idrc.ca:8080/socdev/pub/social/contents.html> [15 May 2004].

Quarter, Jack. "The Social Economy and the Neo-Conservative Agenda." In *Social Economy: International Perspectives and Debates*, edited by Eric Shragge and Jean-Marc Fontain, 55-58. Montreal: Black Rose Books, 2000.

Ramaux, Christophe. "La 'pleine activité' contre le chômage: les chemins de l'enfer peuvent être pavés de bonnes intentions." in *Pour un nouveau plein emploi: Appel des économistes pour sortir de la pensée unique*. Paris: Syros, 1997.

"Redefining Government Relationships with the Voluntary Sector: On Great Expectations *and* Sense and Sensibility." Ottawa: Voluntary Sector Roundtable, November 1995, <http://www.vsr-trsb.net/publications/phillips-e.html> [7 April 2004].

Reid, Angus. *Shakedown*. Toronto: Doubleday Canada, 1996.

Rifkin, Jeremy. *The End of Work*. New York: G.P. Putnam's Sons, 1995.

Roberts, Linda J. *We Can't Fundraise Anymore and Other Realities of Small, Community-based, Nonprofit Agencies – the Canadian Context*. Paper prepared for the NCVO 5th Researching the Voluntary Sector Conference, London, U.K. 7-8 September 1999.

Salamon, Lester. "The Case of America." In *Third Sector Policy at the Crossroads: An International Nonprofit Analysis*, edited by Helmut K. Anheier and Jeremy Kendall. London and New York: Routledge, 2001.

Saunders, Ron. *Passion and Commitment Under Stress: Human Resource Issues in Canada's Non-profit Sector – A Synthesis Report*. Ottawa: Canadian Policy Research Networks, January 2004.

Scott, Katherine. "Portrait of the Nonprofit and Voluntary Sector." Appendix B in *Funding Matters: The Impact of Canada's New Funding Regime on Nonprofit and Voluntary Organizations*. Ottawa: Canadian Council on Social Development, 2003. <http://www.ccsd.ca/pubs/2003/fm [12 March 2004].

Smith, Graham. "Green Citizenship and the Social Economy." Paper for the ECPR Joint Sessions, Uppsala 2004.

Statistics Canada. "Average earnings by sex and work pattern," <http://www.statcan.ca/english/Pgdb/labour01b.htm> [15 May 2004].

Statistics Canada. "Employers." *Canada e-book 2002*. http://142.206.72.67/02/02e_002-e.htm and <http://www.statcan.ca/english/Pgbd/govt54a.htm>

Statistics Canada. "Impact of self-employment on productivity growth in Canada and the United States" *The Daily,* Thursday, 28 August 2003, <http://www.statcan.ca/Daily/English/030828/d030828d.htm> [4 May 2004].

Statistics Canada. "Retirement" in *Canada e-Book*, <http://142.206.72.67/02/02e/02e_009_e.htm> [4 May 2004].

Thouin, Daniel and Jocelyne Chagnon, *Portrait des entreprises en aide domestique*. Quebec City: La Direction des communications du Ministère du Développement économique et régional, 2002. <http://www.mic.gouv.qc.ca/publications/cooperatives/Portrait_EESAD.pdf> [4 May 2004].

"Turn Your Stakeholders into Risktakers." *Nonprofit World* 20, no. 4 (July-August 2002): 16.

Valkenburg, Ben, Jens Lind and Rik van Berkel. "Work and Inclusion." *Transfer* vol. 7, no. 1 (2001).

Wachtel, Paul. *The Poverty of Affluence*. New York: The Free Press, 1983.

Wallulis, Jerald. *The New Insecurity: the End of the Standard Job and Family*. New York: State University of New York Press, 1998.

Workers Without Traditional Employment: An International Study of Non-Standard Work. Cheltenham, U.K.: Edward Elgar Publishing, 2000.

Jean-Marc Fontan, Pierre Hamel,
Richard Morin and Eric Shragge

Urban Perspectives on CED Practice: The Montreal Experience

Les corporations de developpement économique communautaire (CDECs) are the organizations that have played a leading role in shaping Community Economic Development (CED) practice in Montreal. They are highly institutionalized, para-governmental organizations that balance the demands from government programs that they implement while responding to diverse needs and situations at the local level. The CDECs were the outcomes of strategies to rebuild neighbourhoods faced with poverty and loss of jobs related to industrial restructuring and subsequent decline. Historically, these traditional working-class neighbourhoods had experienced periods of economic decline and expansion related to capitalist cycles. The 1980s were different. This time, factory closures marked an end to an industrial era and a huge loss of blue-collar jobs that were often unionized and once relatively stable. At the same time, this period marked a severe assault on social programs and heralded a redefinition of the role of the state. There were many cutbacks in benefits and services, but more important, the new dominant ideology argued that market forces and international competition drove economic development rather than local democracy or state-initiated-and-led economic revitalization schemes. In this context, leaders of community organizations and their allies in trade unions began to search for new directions. It seemed to them that neither traditional market nor state driven, top-down approaches were going to respond to this serious crisis. Local organizations took up the challenge, brought different individuals to the table and launched CED organizations in Montreal. This marked a shift for community organizations in two ways. First, they began to engage in discussions and deal with economic questions and, second, they became involved in partnership structures with local unions, business and government. With these changes the

CDECs began a new form of local development with an emphasis on partnership and new forms of governance.

This chapter will examine the evolution and development of the CDECs, from their beginnings through their rapid institutionalization as para-governmental organizations. The experience in Montreal has demonstrated how CED can grow from a local base and become transformed by state policy and actions that create conditions of stability, but at the same time they have been able to maintain some degree of autonomy to respond to local situations. We will explore several questions. The first is the role that the CDECs play in supporting and developing both CED and the development of the social economy. With the building of these institutions, there has been a process of standardization of their programs. What impact has this had on local development? Second, democratic participation in local organizations has deep roots in the traditions of Montreal's community organizations. How has democratic control of the CDECs changed with their evolution? Finally, the CDECs emerged in a period of transformation in which neoliberal policies underpinned many government programs and approaches. They are a product of this period, but also have challenged the new underlying values by supporting innovative and democratic practices that come from local organizations. This tension will also be explored.

CDECs: Bottom-up to Top-down

In this section we will describe the different stages of development of the CDECs in Montreal in three phases. The first phase corresponded to their emergence and the processes around the political construction of this social innovation. The second phase is related to the negotiation and processes of the institutionalization of these organizations. The third phase corresponds to their adaptation to the provincial-institutional context and the struggle to preserve organizational identity and relative autonomy.

Phase 1: The emergence

CED in Montreal represents a departure for community organizations. It brought them into the field of economic development and into formal partnerships with unions, business and other local actors. The new practices were based upon building local consensus on strategies for revitalization of declining neighbourhoods through economic development. The CDECs have also inherited the traditions of urban community movements, particularly the demands of local organizations to participate in the administration and policies that shape their neighbourhood. As a consequence, the early structure of the CDECs incorporated this principle into their structures.

The first three CDECs were initiated in 1984 and 1985 by coalitions of community organizations.[1] The first CED initiative took place in Pointe St. Charles, a working-class neighbourhood home to many older industries that suffered decline since the 1960s. The neighbourhood has a long tradition of both grassroots and labour organizing. Its citizens created the first popular health and legal clinics, popular education centers, and initiated campaigns to promote the needs and the interests of the poor and working-class residents. In addition, its residents pioneered the development of co-operative housing. With the economic decline and continuing high levels of unemployment, new initiatives were put in place to find solutions. A coalition of organizations put together a report that argued for a community economic development strategy as a way to revitalize the area and create jobs. Further, the report argued that the local citizens had to take charge of both the planning and implementation of this process.[2] The Pointe St. Charles Economic Program (PEP) was founded in 1984. This initiative, although modified in many ways over the years, was the model for much of what followed. The concept of local partnership across interests and subsequently building a consensus on the direction for local economic development was a controversial departure from the traditions of the community sector. PEP committed itself to a program of economic revitalization, job creation and training. It benefited from substantial grants from both the provincial and federal governments. Yet its growth and success created conflict with some local groups, who criticized its growing professionalism and declining democracy. The latter was because of the shift from the tradition of direct participation of citizens to the newer practices of local individuals entering into formal partnerships with representation from each of the groups in the partnership structure. Similar CED processes occurred in two other old industrial neighbour-hoods with strong community traditions.

During the first three years of their existence, the Montreal CDECs received start-up funding mainly from the provincial government, and complementary funding from the federal government and the municipal administration to provide specific services. Some of the monies were allocated for the organization's operation, and another portion was for venture capital that was made available to small and medium enterprises at very low interest rates. By the end of the 1980s, to ensure better bargaining power with the state the inter-CDEC committee was created, first informally and then formally a few years later. It was and still is a consultative committee that represents the CDECs in their negotiation with the three levels of government.

The CDECs were put in place to:

- Often through the management of risk capital funds to start new businesses,

- Facilitate the training and placement of the unemployed into the labour market.

- Initiate processes to bring actors together to finds ways to support local development and to change the defeatist mentality that was pervasive after many years of economic divestment.

To realize the last objective of local mobilization, partnerships that represented different actors were preferred to large-scale "popular" participation. Representatives of local organizations including unions, local business and some of the public institutions located in their territory were elected to the boards of the CDECs through a system of electoral colleges. Thus, the CDECs can be described as intermediary organizations. They are governed by a management structure that includes representatives of different interest groups in their neighbourhoods.[3] These partnership structures were innovative and were designed to build a broad-based consensus for defining local action.

Phase 2: The institutionalization process

With all three in place and a couple of others beginning, in 1990 the administration of the City of Montreal brought together representatives of the provincial and federal governments to collaborate in the establishment of a common policy to support local economic development. In their discussion, it was decided that these new organizations (CDECs) should be the conduits for local strategies of revitalization, and they should be more formally recognized and supported. The product of this process eventually led to the creation of a total of seven CDECs during the 1990s.

In an action plan published,[4] the Montreal municipal administration, formed by the social democratic Montreal Citizens' Movement (MCM),[5] decided to extend the development of CDECs to every neighbourhood except the downtown core. This city administration believed that these organizations had the capacity to play an innovative and dynamic role in the promotion of local economic development. This plan became the basis of an agreement between the three levels of government that then recognized and financed the CDECs. Through this process, the first three were consolidated, two were enlarged and two others were put in place. This brought the number of CDECs to seven, each one covering an average of three local districts (the territory gathering these districts is called an "arrondissement"[6]). In contrast to the local processes that resulted in the creation of the first three CDECs, the others were initiated through a top-down process with little participation at the beginning from local groups and citizens. Local participation followed the creation of the organization.

To coordinate the implementation, funding and evaluation of the CDECs, the three levels of government—municipal, provincial and federal—formed a "Comité d'harmonisation." This committee, following from the experience of the original CDECs, assigned three basic objectives to them: job creation, integration of the unemployed into the labour market and local mobilization. Specific funding envelopes were linked to the realization of each of these objectives. Through this process, the role of governments as program funders and program evaluators was strengthened. This committee became the place of negotiation between the CDECs and the governments for resources and as a way to coordinate and to plan the respective roles and contributions of different government departments. Between 1990 and 1996, with the creation of the new organizations, the Inter-CEDC committee enlarged its membership and its function grew in importance. It represented the CDECs in negotiation with the provincial government and their other funding agencies.

One of the concerns of the Comité d'harmonisation was to evaluate the progress of the CDECs in relation to pre-established goals. In 1995, it developed an annual evaluation framework for the activities of the CDECs. From that time on, the CDECs planned their actions making reference to this framework. One of the results of this process was an attempt to standardize the CDECs' agendas and programs, but tensions resulted between the Comité d'harmonisation and several CDECs that intended to implement specific development projects in their own communities. The tensions were based on the degree to which these CDECs wished to maintain their own pre-defined priorities that did not necessarily follow from the government-defined guidelines. Over the years, there has been a resolution in which the CDECs can write their own action plan reflecting local priorities.

Phase 3: Becoming part of the provincial network

The third phase is characterized by an increase of direct governmental control of the CDECs[7] that occurred in two steps. In 1997, the provincial government initiated a reform of both its employability and social assistance programs, on one hand, and its programs to support local economic development, on the other. These changes were both consolidations of employment programs taken over from the federal government and regionalization of economic development programs across the province. These were to be administered through new local organizations, decentralized to regional and large municipalities, and called "Centre local d'emploi" (CLE; Local Employment Center) and "Centre local de développement" (CLD; Local Development Center). Prior to this restructuring, the CDECs that had worked in both areas had demanded along with others in the community sector more comprehensive and socially-oriented development policies. Ironically, the provincial government responded positively in some respects which threatened the very existence of the CDECs, who reacted to the possibility of losing their mandate. Further, this reform was a top-down process and it undermined the processes of bringing local players together around development issues. The CDECs, through their inter-CDEC committee, developed a position that defended their role and mobilized local support. Through a complex process of negotiation with the municipal and provincial governments, they reached a compromise in which they were to take on the functions of the new local development centres and some employability programs of the new local employment centres. Thus, the CDECs saved themselves as intermediary organizations.

The structures of CDECs changed in fundamental ways. The city of Montreal was to be served by one CLD, which was incorporated in 1998. There were nine main organizations given mandates to carry out the functions of the CLD locally. The CDECs received these mandates and thus became part of a city-wide organization with direct accountability to the provincial government via the Ministère d'État aux Affaires Municipales et à la Métropole. The shift here is significant, as the provincial government became the primary funder of and policy definer for these organizations. Both the Montreal-wide organization and the local ones (which continue to be called CDECs) have their own governing bodies based on a representative partnership structure. At the local level, each CDEC kept an independent board similar to its previous structure, but City councillors were added.

Since December 2003 a new law, Bill 34, now determines the method by which local representatives become members of CDEC Board of Directors. This law limits the participation of individual members of the local population in the governing structures of the CDECs. As before, each sector of representatives, whether community, institutional, or business sector, is divided into named electoral colleges. Each electoral college then names the representatives who will sit on the Board of Directors, and these are approved at the annual general meeting. Another electoral college made up of the elected officials, informally referred to as the *comité des élus*, also names the municipal and provincial elected officials that will sit on the Board of Directors. However, these do not have to be approved at the annual general meeting. Moreover, the *comité des élus* is the largest electoral college on the Board of Directors. While the other colleges are made up of two representatives, the *comité des élus* at the minimum doubles in size and subsequently plays a more prominent role on the Board of Directors. This change reduces the power of the local community to shape the direction of the CDECs. Coupled with the control of funding and the programmatic direction of the provincial government, this furthers the process of institutionalization and turns these organizations into extensions of that level of government with less accountability to the local district. However, within these limits, there are still some opportunities for innovative and democratic initiatives.

Program Administration

The CDECs have become the local organizations that administer a variety of government programs and investment funds. The criteria for these programs are determined in provincial ministries but there is some local flexibility in their implementation. The types of programs and their entrepreneurial orientation play a major role in shaping the practice and in orienting the CDECs towards specific economic projects rather than building a wider vision of neighbourhood revitalization and other possible community development practices. By 2004, the CDECs under the Ministry of Economic and Regional Development, administer the following programs: the Fonds local d'investissement (local investment fund) the Fonds de développement des entreprises d'économie sociale (the fund for the development of social economy enterprises) and the program, Jeunes Promoteurs (the young entrepreneurs program).[8]

The objective of the Fonds local d'investissement is to stimulate local entrepreneurship through access to capital for the creation and expansion of business initiatives in the traditional and social economy. As such, it seeks to support the development of jobs and economic activity. Though eligibility criteria may vary among CDECs, all new initiatives or businesses seeking to expand and that subscribe to the orientations of the CDECs and their investment policies may apply for financial assistance. Whether it be start-up or expansion capital, the financial assistance provided, combining funding from the government of Canada and of Quebec as well as from the CDEC, is usually a loan or a loan guarantee that does not exceed 50 per cent of the cost of the admissible expenses for project. The maximum is $25,000 for the traditional economy. However, projects undertaken in the social economy may receive financial assistance for up to 80 per cent of the admissible expenses. The Fonds local d'investissement does not provide funding in the form of subsidies.

The Fonds de développement des entreprises d'économie sociale seeks to stimulate the creation of sustainable businesses within the social economy and of employment opportunities by offering financial support to such initiatives. This fund defines social economy as activities and organizations initiated by collective endeavors that respect the following principles: service to members or collectives, autonomous management, democratic decision-making processes, primacy of persons and work over capital in the distribution of surpluses and revenues, and participation. Further, social economy enterprises produce services and goods that are financially viable and that create durable employment opportunities. They may be not-for-profit or co-operatives operating in any sector of the market. This fund offers access to capital in the form of grants for up to 80 per cent of the cost of admissible expenses combining all financial assistance provided by the federal and provincial government as well as by the CDEC itself.

The objective of the program Jeunes Promoteurs is to promote entrepreneurship and to provide financial assistance among youth aged 18 to 35 years by facilitating the launch of a first or second business. Those seeking admissibility to this program must be Canadian citizens or landed immigrants residing in Quebec, they must possess experience pertinent to the project they are undertaking, and they must be committed to working full-time on their initiative. This program offers financial assistance for feasibility studies and the amounts allotted for this cannot exceed 75 per cent of the admissible expenses, and provides start-up capital for up to 50 per cent of the expenses admissible under the program. Finally, the program will cover up to 100 per cent of the costs for any training necessary for the realization and sustainability of the project.

The CDECs also administer the Mesure de soutien au travail autonome, a program in partnership with Emploi-Quebec, which is mandated by the Ministère de l'Emploi, de la Solidarité sociale et de la Famille. The objective of this program is to offer financial and technical assistance to persons seeking to develop a microenterprise or to become self-employed. As such, it seeks to create employment opportunities, to diversify local economies and to promote financial autonomy. Those eligible for the program must have received some form of government financial assistance or must be a worker with precarious status, must possess the profile of an entrepreneur and must be able to make a financial contribution of 20 per cent to the total costs of the project. The financial support provided by this program consists of a weekly contribution and of reimbursement for the costs of child care for up to 52 weeks. The program further provides technical assistance and training.

The Société locale d'investissement pour le développement de l'emploi (SOLIDE) is another fund that is administered by the CDECs though in collaboration with the commissioners of economic development of the boroughs in Montreal. This fund is supported by multiple partnerships that include the City of Montreal, the Government of Quebec, and the Fonds de solidarité des travailleurs du Quebec, and is offered by the Direction de l'aménagement urbain et des services aux enterprises of the boroughs. The objective of this fund is to support new businesses and those in expansion by providing loans that range from $5000 to $50,000 in order to create and maintain jobs in the boroughs.

Finally, the CDECs administer the Fonds de developpement Emploi - Montréal in collaboration with the City of Montreal, the Fonds de la solidarité des travailleurs du Québec, la Société de développement industriel du Québec, and the government of Quebec and of Canada. This fund was established to equip Montreal boroughs with a tool for economic development and therefore seek to simulate entrepreneurship in the manufacturing and industrial sector. Further, the fund seeks to foster employment opportunities and to promote local hiring of the unemployed. This fund provides access to capital in the form of loans that range from $50,000 to $100,000.

These are the basic programs administered by the CDECs, though some have an additional program that will vary according to the employment needs of the local borough. They tend to target persons with low incomes or who are on the margins of the labour market. For instance, CDEC Centre-Nord also administers the Budget d'initiatives locales which is established in partnership with Emploi-Quebec in order to support local employability initiatives.[9] Similarly, CDEC (CDN-NDG) administers the program *FACILE*, which seeks to create jobs by supporting the development of microbusinesses for persons with low incomes.[10]

What are the results of these programs? We have drawn the following from the annual reports of RESO, the largest of Montreal's CDECs and from CDEC CDN-NDG[11] to illustrate the type of practices during their respective fiscal year 2002-2003. It is important to note that despite the social orientation of the CDECs, the largest amount of their support is given to private business development. Through the department of Services aux enterprises, and their different programs, RESO invested over $700, 000 in 21 projects that generated over $4,700,000 of revenue and have maintained or created about 175 jobs in the South-West, using the program Soutien aux travailleurs autonomes (STA). This program provides support to autonomous workers, RESO accepted to support 22 projects and approved 16 business plans. Through the program Jeunes Promoteurs RESO accepted to support 11 projects and 455 jobs were consequently created. Through the local investment program Fonds local d'investissement (FLI), RESO supported four new projects that required a total investment of $185, 000 (35 jobs), and through FDEM program, it supported three new projects requiring a total investment of $300,000, which created or helped maintain 61 jobs. In terms of social economy and community development, RESO supported ten new projects.

The CDEC CDN/NDG is a smaller organization. Its Action Plan of 2003-2004,[12] stated that through its support to businesses it supported the development of 16 initiatives. Twelve of these were through FLI. The majority of its new projects for that year were to support individual enterprises, including 25 for Jeunes Promoteurs and 50 for Soutien aux travailleurs autonomes (STA). In addition, the CDEC provided support for five new social economy projects.

The programs administered by the CDECs are directed by government policy that centres on job creation, business growth and diversification of the economy. At all levels of government, provincial, federal and municipal, the language of community economic development is one of entrepreneurship and employability. As such, the programs approach problems of poverty and social inequality as issues that are to be re-dressed through market-driven initiatives to foster social integration and social inclusion, by improving the employability of local populations and by supporting local entrepreneurship and job creation. Though this has long been the mandate of CDECs, it now occurs within a context of government programs that are a part of a larger agenda that seeks to transform the economic and social landscape to make it competitive and in sync with market-driven economic visions. The three levels of government for which the CDECs administer programs promote the necessity of "adjusting to the new global economic environment."[13]

The mandate of the organizations has shifted in emphasis less oriented to job training and integrating those excluded from the labour market into training and jobs and toward entrepreneurship as a means of job creation. This includes the administration of a "social economy" fund that was used to develop businesses with a social vocation. At the local level an action plan is prepared and herein is the flexibility, but it exists within narrower boundaries. In addition, these changes represent a shift in the configuration of power. The role of the federal and municipal governments has become less important, and the main funding body is the provincial government. The municipal level plays a role mainly through the participation of locally-elected officials. The federal government, until the announcements of the Martin budget of 2004, supported specific projects on a limited basis. This will change with new resources promised by the federal government but the exact mechanisms have not been defined. The provincial government has consolidated its power through the funding of decentralized structures, integrated into a wider plan of socio-economic reform. Thus, the CDECs face new relationships with provincial ministries whose visions go beyond the local and sees the role of CDECs and similar organizations as part of their network of government services and strategies implemented at the local level.

Specific Projects Supported by the CDECs: From Traditional Economics to Alternative?

Most of the work of the CDECs tends to be either small business development or work in the social economy. The CDECs, in the neoliberal context, have supported the shift toward the dominance of the market—an entrepreneurial strategy—as the path for social development. One underlying assumption is that social integration/ insertion can be achieved through business development and/or job training and related experiences for the unemployed. The business development is usually on a relatively small scale. First and foremost, businesses are assessed for their market viability. This does not necessarily imply that profit must be made, but that there is income generation that in the long term will allow the business to be "sustainable." Social development is present as well but market viability is a prerequisite. This creates a tension because social and cultural development becomes subjected to market criteria. Within this some local projects have created new ways of contributing to their local communities. The following are examples:

> The coopérative de solidarité en environnement la maison verte, sup-
> ported by CDEC CDN-NDG, is a community-based, member-owned co-
> operative offering environmental products, services and education.
> Through its cooperative structure of worker, consumer and community
> membership, it provides ecologically sound, sustainable products and
> technologies and whole foods. Further, in partnership with other groups,
> they are also committed to promoting outreach, education and social
> action to foster and inspire environmentally healthy and sustainable
> practices. As such, it seeks to offer society an example of an organization
> that successfully engages in economic activities using reasonable profits
> to sustain their activities, to provide an alternative to consumerism and
> excessive consumption and to improve their community and protect and
> respect their natural environment. This project is supported by the social
> economy funds.[14]

CDEC Rosemont-Petite-Patrie supports the Corporation de développement le Dauphin, which took over Cinéma Le Dauphin when Cineplex Loews Odeon opted to close the theatre. Cinéma Le Dauphin was the last existing neighbourhood movie theatre in Montreal operating in a cultural landmark. The theatre was consequently renamed Cinéma Beaubien and is now run as a non-profit organization. It has maintained the eight jobs that exist at the theatre and created ten additional ones while contributing to the revitalization of the district.[15]

CDEC Centre-Sud-Plateau Mont-Royal also supports the Festival International Nuits d'Afrique, a project in the social economy. The Festival seeks to showcase the talent and culture of Africa, the Caribbean and Latin America with an annual eleven-day festival of celebration, music and art.[16]

The following projects are examples of larger-scale economic development supported by CDECs. The second example below provides an example of how a

CDEC can support a larger-scale development that plays a role in economic revitalization. The third example provides an example of high tech development, which is the exception to most business development supported by the CDECs. The larger-scale developments tend to face more pressures from the market and are not socially driven or accountable to wider social and political actors. They do, however, create jobs and other spin-offs and as such are tools of revitalization:

> RESO supports a project for the survival of Agmont, Inc. Agmont is a manufacturer of circular knit fabrics. Agmont specializes in producing cotton, nylon, poly, lycra and specialty blend knitted fabrics including micro fibers. This company has been in operations for over 30 years in the traditional economy. The South-West, the borough in which RESO is located, has been hit by the loss of hundreds of jobs with the close of a prominent plant in the area. As such, to safeguard against the loss of further jobs, RESO is part of a project to ensure that Agmont, Inc. remains financially viable and in the area.[17] (It is interesting to note that Agmont formally closed in 2002 when there was a successful union drive and re-opened under new ownership without the union later that year.)

CDEC Rosemont-Petitie-Patrie also supports Technopôle Angus, which is an attempt to revitalize a portion of what once was the Angus Yards in order to create 2000 jobs over ten years. The yards already host various businesses in the manufacturing, industrial, services, electronics, biotechnology and social economy sectors that will become a part of the Technopôle Angus run under the auspices of the Société de développement Angus, a non-profit organization in collaboration with partners in the traditional economy. Technopôle Angus seeks to be an engine for development in the borough.[18]

CDEC Centre-Sud-Plateau Mont-Royal supports Dynapix Intelligence Imaging, which specializes in image analysis for the biomedical, health and drug discovery industries. As such, it has created a software program that accelerates the biomedical discovery process and improves clinical diagnoses, scientific analysis of digital images by adapting itself to a wide variety of biomedical images.[19]

Discussion

In this concluding section, we will discuss several issues that are raised by the evolution, the role and the directions of the CDECs, as well as the type of practices that they support. The first question is: What type of CED practice has emerged in and with the support of the CDECs? The answer to this is complex because of the variety of outcomes, but there is one observation that can be made. The CDECs were put in place with a vision of neighbourhood revitalization, which included holistic development as a means of responding to unemployment, poverty and urban decay. This included a development process for a district of the city. However, as we have seen from the programs administered by the CDECs, the strategy that has been given priority is to use individual and some collective, socially-oriented enterprises as the means to do this. Business development, both within the traditional and the social economy, is preferred over a more comprehensive vision of development. There is an overlap between the wider vision and narrower support for entrepreneurship, but with little planning taking place at the level of the borough for ongoing economic and social development, the specific initiatives are left to individuals, small collectives and what can be supported in the market. The CDECs have become local organizations to support and to promote social and traditional business development with a reduced vision of the economic and social development of the district. It is clear that the tools and programs that are supported by government leave little opportunity for this wider vision.

Democracy based on the participation of local organizations and citizens was a cornerstone of the development of the CDECs. This tradition is deeply rooted in the community sector in Quebec. The structures that were created by the CDECs extended the possibility for residents and local organizations to have a voice in shaping local economic and social development through participation in the structures of the CDECs. With each transformation, this control has been diminished and there are two reasons for this. First, control of policy has shifted away from the local. In the evolution of the CDECs, we have seen the government play a central role, particularly in funding these organizations. At first, three levels of government were involved and over the years the CDECs became more directly under the control of the provincial government with narrowing mandates and foci linked to funding programs and budget envelopes. Thus the choices of program became increasingly shaped by policy and related funding. The role of the organization is to act as a transmission belt to the local district. This does not imply that there is no flexibility or room to adapt programs to local conditions. However, the parameters are decided outside the organizations. Further, the evaluation criteria are linked to programs and success is defined within those boundaries. Thus, accountability is upwards in relation to measurable outcomes. With these processes gaining prominence, local control is diminished and the boards and local communities have to adapt to programs rather than shape them. We are not arguing that there is no power at the local level, but it is limited and shaped from the outside. The CDEC can administer the resources in a way that can respond to local conditions, but the range of interventions has narrowed and the tools are reduced and homogenized. This limits democratic choices that could be developed within a global budget rather than a programmatic one.

Second, the structure of representation has been a key element in the way the different parts of the local community can participate in the CDECs. The electoral college system was the means established to do this. In theory it is a democratic process in which all organizations and individuals can choose their representatives on the board through meetings of their colleges. For example, representatives of community organizations that were members of the CDEC would meet and select their representative(s) on the board of directors. A similar process would happen for business, labour and citizens at large. Participation in this process is very uneven, with some electoral colleges able to mobilize good representation and others with very few participants. More important, the principle of this structure is to represent the points of view and interests on the board of directors of the CDEC. The colleges did not function as places for groups to discuss positions and the board member for the most part represented their own point of view. Participation is hard to sustain unless there is staff working on this process on an ongoing basis. The formal democratic structure is one that had potential but in practice is less successful. With the change brought in by Bill 34, the representation of the electoral colleges was undermined. Organizational representatives and residents now have even less formal power to control the CDECs. With elected officials in the majority on CDEC boards, the control will be far more with the government. Thus, because of the changes in the way the CDECs are funded and the structure of governance, there is much less accountability to the local district. The staff of the CDECs can administer the programs with flexibility and attempt to support local initiatives, but this is increasingly within the boundaries of a para-governmental organization, which is accountable upwards rather than locally.

The CDECs were put in place in a period of economic transformation. These changes were part of the process of globalization and major shifts in where and how production took place. De-industrialization and shifts in production to countries in the South, where wages and regulation are diminished, left working-class neighbourhoods in the North with huge levels of unemployment and poverty. At the same time governments have actively supported neoliberal policies as a way to intervene in these situations. It is incorrect to talk about the state disappearing under neoliberalism but the state has played an "activating role."[20] Local organizations become participants in the restructuring process, taking over a variety of functions at the local level. This was supported by the state by funding programs or by putting in place structures in which local actors could actively participate. Peck and Tickell argue:

> In the asymmetrical scale politics of neoliberalism, local institutions and
> actors were given responsibility without power, while international
> institutions and actors were gaining power without responsibility: a form
> of regulatory dumping was occurring at the local scale, while macrorule
> regimes were being remade in regressive and marketized ways.[21]

The analysis implies more than cuts in the welfare state, but it implies a reorganization of the relation between the market and the state. Greater opportunities for the market with less government interference are opened. The market then becomes the means of addressing some social problems that were the fallout from the restructuring described above. In Quebec, workfare and an ideology of social inclusion through work was the policy orientation through this period.[22] Wage labour was to be the means of social integration for the poor, and the community sector developed tools to accomplish this—either through training programs or economic development.

CED in Montreal emerged in a period in which the direction of the state policy was in many ways consistent with neoliberal ideology and practices.

However, the community sector did not necessarily share the same ideology. Its response assumed that neither state nor the market was responding adequately to the problems of unemployment and poverty, and alternative approaches were required. The convergence with government policy was through the idea of social inclusion through work. Thus CED was motivated by job creation, first and foremost. It also became a tool of social innovation in some circumstances. The projects described above are examples. CED then has to be seen as practice that develops in a tension between the neoliberal policies and the creation of socio-economic alternatives. The CDECs are sites of conflict between contestants of unequal power. The government has the resources and programs and has used its policy prerogatives to impose an entrepreneurial agenda that gives priority to traditional economic development with support to the social economy. The CDECs have survived several restructurings and remain as important local players but with each round of change reducing their autonomy and their accountability to the local district. Whether or not the CEDCs will be able to support alternative practices, that are themselves democratic, and create new forms of economic development, depends upon the initiatives from below. Local groups working on ecological or cultural alternatives have been able to get support and resources from the CDECs as long as their projects have an aspect that is economically viable. Herein lies a limit. Social development and a variety of new community projects are faced with huge problems of funding unless they are to become subcontractors to government agencies. The space for social innovation is narrowed and the place where there are limited openings is through CED and the social economy.

The CDECs in Montreal are pulled in many directions but the strongest player in determining their future and in shaping their orientation is the provincial government through the mandates and programs and funds provided. Perhaps the most important counterweight to the pressures from above is the practical initiatives from below. Particularly in the older working-class neighbourhoods, there continues to be some innovative and democratic projects that are a continuation of the earlier community traditions. For the most part, the districts that have a longer tradition of active citizens and related organizations have been able to pressure the CDECs through their participation on the boards to respond with greater flexibility to local agendas. Thus, the actions of local community actors who are engaged in the issue of economic development have moderated the strong forces at play in the shaping of the orientation of the CDECs. These tend to be locally based and limited to specific projects, and do not necessarily contribute to a broader alternative vision of socio-economic development. The CDECs have thus played a democratizing role in the processes of the development of the local economy by creating an opportunity for a wide range of actors to participate in the decision-making. Because of the strong consensus that views economic development as the strategy for social inclusion, an alternative vision for social development has not emerged from the CDEC structures and processes. Despite the presence and support of specific projects, a model that challenges the assumptions of the current economic direction with its notions of growth, work and consumerism has not emerged from the CDECs. However, they remain an organization that, with pressures from local organizations, can contribute democratically to social development that responds to local needs with innovation.

Notes

1. See Morin, "L'expérience montréalaise des corporations de développmenet économique, *Coopératives et développement*, 13-29; Hamel, *Action collective et démocratie locale*.

2. See Fontan, "Pointe St. Charles—Building a Community Voice," in Shragge (ed.) *Community Economic Development: In Search of Empowerment*, 76-92; and Gareau, *Le programme économique de Pointe St. Charles, 1983-1989.*

3. See Morin, "Communautés territoriales et insertion socio-économique en milieu urbain," in Klein and Lévesque (eds.), *Contre l'exclusion: repenser l'économie*, 247-265.

4. See Silvestro, *Le développement économique communautaire dans un contexte métropolitain.*

5. The MCM was created in 1974 by a coalition of popular and community groups and the trade union movement. This municipal party took power in 1986. Its program supported local democracy with a strong voice in neighbourhoods. Their practice once in office was dominated by a technocratic approach and centralized leadership.

6. By the end of the 1980s,the Montreal municipal government divided the city in nine arrondissements. By 1990, only two arrondissements did not have a CDEC organization, including the city centre.

7. See Fontan and Shragge. "CED in Montreal:Community versus State Control," in Shragge (ed.), *Community Economic Development: In Search of Empowerment* (2nd ed.) 87-109.

8. Ministere du developpement economique et regional.

9. CDEC Centre-nord.

10. CDEC Cote-des-Neiges/Notre-Dame-de-Grace.

11. CDEC Cote-des-Neiges/Notre-Dame-de-Grace. *Resume Rapport d'activites*; Regroupement economique et social du Sud-Ouest. *Rapport Annuel 2002-200.*

12. CDEC Cote-des-Neiges/Notre-Dame-de-Grace. *Plan d'action.*

13. Ministry of Industry and Minister responsible for the Economic Development Agency of Canada for the Regions of Quebec. 11.

14. CDEC Cote-des-Neiges/Notre-Dame-de-Grace. *Resume Rapport.*

15. Corporation de dveloppement economique communautaire Rosemont-Petite-Patrie. *Rapport d'activites.*

16. CDEC Centre-sud. Plateau Montreal.

17. Regroupement economique et social du Sud-Ouest. *Rapport Annuel.*

18. Corporation de développement economique communautaire Rosemont-Petite-Patrie. *Rapport d'activites.*

19.   CDEC Centre-sud. Plateau Montreal.
20.   Wohlfahrt, "The Activating State in Germany," 12-20.
21.   Peck and Tickell, "Neoliberalizing Space," in Brenner and Theodore (eds.), *Spaces of Neoliberalism,* 39.
22.   Shragge, "Community Organizations in Transition: Labour Regulators or New Options for Work?" *in From Welfare to Work,* 88-97.

Bibliography

CDEC Centre-nord. http://www.cdec-centrenord.org.

CDEC Centre-sud. Plateau Montreal. http://www.cdec-cspmtl.org.

CDEC Cote-des-Neiges/Notre-Dame-de-Grace. *Resume Rapport d'activites 2002-2003,* 31 mars 2003.

CDEC Cote-des-Neiges/Notre-Dame-de-Grace. *Plan d'action 2003-2004.* 3 avril 2003.

Corporation de developpement economique communautaire Rosemont-Petite-Patrie. *Rapport d'activites 2003-2004. Resultats au* 30 septembre 2003.

Fontan, Jean-Marc. "Pointe St. Charles—Building a Community Voice." In *Community Economic Development: In Search of Empowerment,* edited by Eric Shragge, 76-92. Montreal: Black Rose, 1993.

———— and Eric Shragge. "CED in Montreal: Community versus State Control." In *Community Economic Development: In Search of Empowerment,* edited by Eric Shragge, 87-109. Montreal: Black Rose Books, 1997.

Gareau, J. M. *Le programme économique de Pointe St. Charles, 1983-1989, la percée du developpement économique communautaire dans le Sud-ouest de Montréal.* Montreal: Les Presses de L'IFDEC, 1992.

Hamel, P. *Action collective et démocratie locale: les mouvements urbains montréalais.* Montréal: Presses de l'Université de Montréal, 1991.

Ministere du developpement economique et regional. www.mreg.gouv.qc.ca.

Ministry of Industry and Minister responsible for the Economic Development Agency of Canada for the Regions of Quebec. Government of Canada.

Morin, R., "L'expérience montréalaise des corporations de développmenet économique communautaire; à la croisée des chemins," *Coopératives et développement* 26, no. 2: 13-29.

————. "Communautés territoriales et insertion socio-économique en milieu urbain." In *Contre l'exclusion: repenser l'économie,* edited by J. L. Klein and B. Lévesque, 247-265. Sainte-Foy/Montréal: Presses de l'Université du Québec/Association d'Économie politique, 1995.

Peck, J. and A. Tickell. "Neoliberalizing Space." In *Spaces of Neoliberalism: Urban Restructuring in North America and Western Europe,* edited by N. Brenner and N. Theodore, 39. Oxford: Blackwell, 2002.

Regroupement economique et social du Sud-Ouest. *Rapport Annuel 2002-2003 1ᵉʳ avril 2002 au* 31 mars 2003.

Shragge, Eric. "Community Organizations in Transition : Labour Regulators or New Options for Work? " In *From Welfare to Work : Non/profits and the Workfare State in Berlin and Los Angeles*, edited by V. Erick, M. Mayer and J. Sebale, 88-97. Berlin: Free University of Berlin, 2003.

Silvestro, M. *Le développement économique communautaire dans un contexte métropolitain: le cas de Montréal*. Études, matrériaux et documents 14. Montreal: Département d'études urbaines et touristiques, Université du Québec à Montréal, 2002.

Wohlfahrt, N. "The Activating State in Germany: Beyond the Hartz Commission." In *From Welfare to Work: Nonprofits and the Workfare State in Berlin and Los Angeles*, 12-20, edited by V. Eick, M. Mayer and J. Sembale. Berlin: Free University of Berlin, 2003.

Melanie Conn

"Why Women?"

Women-centred CED is fundamentally different from mainstream community economic development (CED) because it adapts the framework to accomplish changes for women. A women-centred approach is a more radical form of CED because it challenges deeper and more systemic elements of economic and social inequality. Globalization has augmented the significance of social and political action because of the dramatic increase in poverty and decrease in options for women and their families. There is an opportunity now for women involved in women-centred CED to take a leadership role to advocate for systemic change and to implement effective policies and programs.

On a warm September evening in 1996, an enthusiastic audience packed a Vancouver theatre to see *Who's Counting?*[1], a film that demystifies and critiques the productivity formulas used by governments the world over to create economic policy. The first section of the film shows the fallacy and impact of discounting women's unpaid work in the Gross Domestic Product. A huge cheer broke out when Marilyn Waring (the author of the book on which the film is based) urged the audience to demand "What about women?! What about women?!" as a more effective screen for the allocation of economic resources.

The audience exuberance was not so much in response to the question itself but to the credibility Waring ascribed to it. Exposing the myth that productive work must involve monetary exchange, thereby excluding unpaid domestic and reproductive activity has been an important dimension of women's movement activity worldwide for more than forty years. It is also the issue that sets the stage for women to consider community economic development as a strategy for implementing change in their own lives and in their communities.

In British Columbia in the late 1980s, WomenFutures CED Society conducted workshops with women's groups around British Columbia to explore the potential of CED for women. There were important learnings from the experience but a spontaneous activity turned out to be a remarkable tool for describing the enormous contribution of women's unpaid work to the community.[2] It was the first morning of a workshop in a small rural community and women were travelling from all over the region to attend. At the last minute, there were many phone calls from participants to confirm or revise arrangements so they could be there.

To help participants make a mental transition to the workshop, the facilitators asked women to choose partners and describe the activities they had put aside in order to attend. The exercise turned out to be an extremely effective way to reveal and validate the daily work that women do—child care, food preservation and preparation, home maintenance, emotional nurturing, financial management, volunteering at the safe house or for the arts council—to support the market economy, to keep their families out of poverty and to improve the quality of life in the community and in the region. For ten minutes, each woman identified herself, not as an inactive spectator or dependent in the economy, but as a significant contributor.

It was a perfect introduction to the workshop where participants created group pictures of "what the community would look like if women were at the centre." The pictures were colourful and lively illustrations of how women would implement their dreams. They wove their concerns about health care, youth, environmental crises and cultural issues into plans for economic and social renewal. Nodes of co-operative activity—community gardens, kitchens, housing, farmers markets—radiated energy and spinoffs. Networks of small businesses and support services provided local employment and supplies. Streams and mountainsides flourished and also hosted appreciative tourists. And everywhere there were children—at school, at play, at home, at rest.

During the next eight years, WomenFutures facilitated dozens of workshops and eventually documented the experience in *Counting Ourselves In: A Handbook About Women's CED*.[3] The Handbook explained that while every community has a unique set of geographical, social and economic circumstances, women were forming *communities of interest* and their analysis was guided by common principles.[4] Some had already been incorporated into mainstream CED theory and practice, such as:

- establishing holistic, multiple-bottom-line objectives;

- developing and building on collective assets; and

- ensuring inclusivity and participation in project and community planning to benefit individuals, their families and ultimately the whole community.

Other principles were unique to women and their organizations and included:

- redefining productivity to include unpaid and paid work;

- starting with women's lives, their strengths and perspectives; and

- working from a community-based women's organization.

The innovation was to integrate a women-centred approach into CED—a development strategy that recognizes the relationship between economic and social development and respects a bottom-up approach to planning and implementing activities.

Women-centred CED as an Anti-poverty Strategy

The WomenFutures experience showed that when women initially became interested in CED, they were often already involved in the women's movement and/or with other social and political movements that were confronting the root causes of inequality and social injustice. CED was an attractive option because it offered positive and concrete models for dealing with the disproportionate social and economic vulnerability of women, many of whom are even more deeply marginalized because they are visible minorities, new immigrants or Aboriginal— or by factors such as age, ability or sexual orientation.

Numerous sources cite the percentage of women living in poverty in Canada as almost 20 per cent of the entire population of adult women in the country, between 2.2 and 2.8 million.[5] Sole-support mothers are even more likely to live below the regional low-income cutoff lines established by Statistics Canada. Children are poor when their mothers are poor: children are one-third of people dependent on social assistance benefits.

Pan-Canadian women's organizations have decades of experience with an approach to social change that focuses on women's daily lives and their multiple responsibilities. While employment-related activities are a significant element of women-centred CED, projects and programs that have developed over the past twenty years responded initially (and still do) to basic and urgent needs of women in their communities, often focusing on emergency and affordable housing, community kitchens and gardens, child care and informal savings groups.[6]

CED strategies at work

The Antigonish Women's Resource Centre is a typical example of the approach. Based in a small, ethnically diverse rural community in Nova Scotia, the Centre plays a central role in the lives of women and in the community, by offering services such as crisis counselling, referrals, information and advocacy, support groups, a library of print and resource materials, affordable housing initiatives and immediate poverty-relief and literacy. The Centre also runs On the Road to Employment, a pre-employment program for women that so far has provided a basis for 75 per cent of its participants to obtain employment, return to school or seek further training. The program focuses on "life skills" or personal development (e.g., communication, building self-esteem, healthy living) and on practical job skills (e.g., basic computer training, job search, first aid). Participant evaluations consistently describe the importance of the personal development component as the key factor in their ability to build on the specific job-related elements.

In Western Canada, the West Kootenay Women's Association (WKWA) has designed a similar approach to integrate social and economic development, but with a focus on co-operative enterprise. Founded in 1972, WKWA has the distinction of being the oldest rural women's centre in Canada, and it has operated a host of innovative programs and services for women over the years. The Co-operative Ventures Training Workshops provided a group-oriented experience for women to identify and nurture their abilities to conceive and implement strategies to benefit themselves and their communities. While there were sessions on co-operative development topics such as venture identification, marketing and business structures, the program also created opportunities for women to talk about the painful experience of living in poverty and to work toward a more positive sense of themselves and their abilities. The organization has always been careful to attend to the activities that women's centres have learned are essential for participation. These include practical supports such as on-site child care, bus tickets, lunches and socializing time.

MicroSkills in Toronto is another example of an organization that integrates social and economic objectives in its program design. This remarkable organization has served women, immigrant and racial minorities since 1984, providing settlement, employment and self-employment services. The Women's Enterprise and Resource Centre (WERC) was established in 1998 to create a comprehensive and supportive learning environment for low-income, immigrant and racial minority women to become self-employed. In addition to business development training and access to a fully-equipped business resource centre, WERC provides innovative opportunities for women to train as home child care workers and to acquire information technology skills. Employment-related services are complemented by an extensive range of other supports: single-parent groups, leadership skills development, an immigrant women's information network and practical supports, such as on-site child minding and contingency funds for transportation and other emergencies.

These organizations, and others with a similar commitment to building CED projects on a foundation of practical support for women, are confident that the approach is necessary for women to participate in and to benefit from the programs offered. At the same time, women's organizations are facing an enormous challenge to sustain their CED activity and to keep their doors open. In Nova Scotia and British Columbia, provincial funding for women's centres has been withdrawn; Service Canada (formerly Human Resource and Skills Development Canada) has eliminated women as a target for services; funding for social programs has been reduced. Staff and volunteers spend countless hours preparing proposals each year for "new" projects to incorporate revised funding priorities and frameworks. Numerous organizations have closed down or drastically reduced their activities as a result of funding changes. In common cause with others in the non-profit sector, women-centred CED organizations advocate for multi-year funding for core services to ensure a stable base for programs.

The Challenges for Self-employment

The environment for women-centred CED presents obstacles that prevent women who receive social assistance from engaging in self-employment. Although there are exceptions, in many provinces any income from the operation of a business must be reported and the amount is then deducted from their monthly benefits. Without a policy that allows women to operate their business in a reasonable fashion (e.g., to use income from sales to purchase inventory and pay creditors), they are discouraged from trying. In addition, there is no transition from social assistance to independence; thus budding entrepreneurs lose their medical, dental and other benefits all at once, putting too much pressure on the new enterprise and its operator.

Neither policy makes sense in the context of business planning and knowledge which suggests that new entrepreneurs should not expect a business to break even (match expenses with income) for eighteen months to three years. It is as appropriate and necessary to invest in the individuals who are pouring their energy and hope into self-employment as it is to support the organizations that are assisting them.

Furthermore, at the same time that women have increased their participation in the workforce, the downsizing caused by globalization has led to the decline of full-time, full-benefit jobs and the rise of self-employment, part-time, temporary and casual work. As a result, women are more likely than men to become contingent workers. The designation of self-employment as "non-standard work" by Service Canada (HRSDC) means women choosing this option do not have access to training or employment programs.[7]

Giving Women Credit

It is not surprising that credit programs are an element of many women-centred CED activities. Back in 1985, when WomenFutures was just beginning to offer workshops about women and CED, a women's centre board member requested an informal pre-workshop discussion about women's access to credit. As it happened, the classroom booked for the discussion gradually filled until every chair was taken and women were sitting on the tables. An amazing round of stories ensued as women told about their unsuccessful attempts to borrow money from banks and credit unions. Without assets to use as collateral for a loan or a credit history in their own name, they repeatedly encountered the advice to "get your husband to sign" or to put the amount required on their credit card. There was clearly a need for a new approach to support women's need for credit, especially as there was such an appetite to become involved in various types of income-generation.

Both the WKWA and MicroSkills have incorporated credit for women in their programming: WKWA is associated with Habondia, a women's loan organization; and MicroSkills has recently established a fund to make small loans to graduates from its self-employment program.

As with other women-centred CED, credit programs start with women's circumstances and build on their strengths and creativity. Based in Thunder Bay,

PARO Centre for Women's Enterprise has operated a peer-lending community loan fund since 1995. PARO organizes circles of four to seven women who meet monthly to exchange advice, provide support, approve and guarantee each other's loans and monitor payments. Once the group members have approved a loan, it is disbursed by one of five partnering Community Futures Development Corporations.[8] Since the Fund was established, almost $200,000 has been disbursed through thirty-five circles; some circles are nine years old and have members who have borrowed thousands of dollars for their businesses. PARO provides a network of additional supports including a weekly e-newsletter, networking dinners, marketing events and the operation of PARO Presents, a store where members can sell their products. In 2000, the organization opened PARO Centre to house its administration and an incubator for women's businesses with shared space, equipment and access to many other resources, including a child care corner.

Women who complete a micro-credit program may graduate to a mainstream lending institution once the small loan has been repaid and the owner has a more "acceptable" credit and business history. However, there has not been a noticeable change in the policies of financial institutions reluctant to provide small loans because of the low rate of return in relation to the administration expenses. Women continue to see the banks as unwilling or unable to recognize the ability and dependability of the women who need to borrow. As a result, there continues to be a need for micro-credit programs, especially when combined with women-centred, holistic, micro-enterprise programs, and the organizational and administrative support required to sustain them.

Many jurisdictions require social assistance recipients to report loans as income, a policy which completely nullifies their utility and greatly frustrates practitioners and would-be entrepreneurs.

Empowering Process

In the early days of women-centred CED, much of the energy went into learning about economics and alternatives. WomenFutures experimented with many different ways to create a comfortable environment for women to share their opinions about economic issues and to create new strategies. Providing opportunities for women-only discussions has been a basic—and profoundly effective—method for inviting women to participate in challenging the economic status quo.

Language has been an important element of the learning process. WomenFutures discovered that workshop titles like "Women and Community Economic Development" did not have much meaning for women. Names that resonated more were "Making the Economy Work for Us" or "Counting Women In." It was also useful to keep a running glossary of unfamiliar words that came up in a workshop: globalization, privatization, gross domestic product and so on. These methods help to demystify economics and encourage women to ask questions and share what they know about local and international conditions.

As they have become more experienced in CED, women have contributed to the language of the field, inventing the phrase "multiple bottom lines"[9] to convey the holistic approach women bring to their project planning. Using a cost-benefit analysis, women's organizations can demonstrate how child care is an economic stimulator and an investment in the health of the community rather than a drain on the economy. Quality of life issues can be factored into tourism and business attraction strategies. Support for small loans for self-employment can be justified because they increase the multiplier effect. Employing just such compelling arguments, the Chetwynd Women's Resource Society in Northeast British Columbia has taken the lead in building a half-million-dollar farmers and artisan market that will also house their new women's centre.

Women have brought their expertise of working with women and in other social movements to women-centred CED work. Popular education methodology was integrated into the development process, as illustrated by a number of handbooks, manuals and other tools. Finding the conventional entrepreneur guides to be absurdly unrelated to the realities of women's lives (e.g., one standard self-assessment asks: "Are you prepared to put aside the demands of your family in order to focus on your business for the first three years?"), women's organizations created their own training materials. In 2001, Nova Scotia-based Women's Economic Equality (WEE) Society published *Tea You Could Trot a Mouse On*, a two-volume manual about CED; it covers a gamut of topics and is extremely accessible in language and presentation.[10]

Women-centred CED emphasizes the resources or assets women bring to their attempts to build better lives for themselves and their families and to contribute to their communities. The Canadian Women's Foundation has sponsored the development and sharing of the Sustainable Livelihoods framework,[11] which supports women's organizations to research and understand women's asset development. PARO and other women's organizations have used the Sustainable Livelihoods model as a framework to assess and develop a range of human, social, personal, physical and financial assets, covering every aspect of a woman's life (e.g., increasing self-confidence, balancing family and work and strengthening social networks). The women involved in the West Kootenay Women's Association talk about the importance of the "abundance model" as an alternative to the "scarcity model;" the former provides a foundation for the discovery of personal strengths and abilities as well as the development of cooperation instead of competition.

Social Enterprise

Social enterprises are generally defined as businesses that use business to achieve a social mission (e.g., a business that employs people with employment barriers or one that is started by a non-profit society to generate revenue for its other programs). As such, they are the basis of the social economy, a sector of increasing interest in many jurisdictions, including the federal government. Several of the organizations already described are engaged in social enterprise on a small scale by selling handbooks, manuals and other publications. MicroSkills generates independent revenue by selling part-time training as part of its business services and offering a range of technology support and other services to the community.

Atira Housing Society in the Lower Mainland of British Columbia has been managing housing for women at risk since 1999 and uses social enterprise to meet its mission. Recently, the organization purchased a property management company which it operates, using the profits to support Atira's other activities. One of those activities is itself a fledgling social enterprise: an artisan co-operative with residents of Bridge Housing in Vancouver's downtown eastside who would otherwise be homeless or living in shelters.

Compagnie F is a women's organization based in Montreal that originated in a women's centre called "Le centre des femmes d'ici et d'ailleurs" (a multi-cultural women's centre). In 1997, women who wanted to work specifically on women's economic development started Compagnie F to establish services for independent workers and micro-entrepreneurs who were trying to achieve financial and professional independence. The group works with women of all origins who earn a low income, offering training (pre-pre-entrepreneurship and start-up), coaching in marketing, promotion and also networking activities in their social enterprise, Café Réseau.

The Café was founded in 2000 to create a convivial space for micro-entrepreneurs to work, network, meet, promote their product or service, obtain access to equipment (computers, fax, photocopies) and plug into Compagnie F's resources. It is also a showcase for micro-entrepreneurs, including women artists who have participated in entrepreneurship training for young women artists. The café is a window into Compagnie F, which frequently becomes a door for women into the other programs the group operates on its own and in partnership with other organizations, such as community financing through ACEM (Association communautaire d'emprunt de Montréal) and mentoring in partnership with SACO-CESO (Canadian Executive Service Organization).

The social enterprise strategy is attractive for organizations since it promises a degree of self-reliance. It also allows organizations to experience the process of business start-up and operations; and it creates tangible opportunities for new community and government partnerships. Given the new language and structures involved, it is an excellent capacity-building activity.

However, balancing business goals (to maximize profit) and non-profit goals (to increase individual and collective well-being) is a complex undertaking. As a result, the risk of failure that confronts every entrepreneur can be higher for those organizations engaging in social enterprise. As well, the group is likely to have less business experience than those with a conventional focus. Expectations need to be specific (e.g., "We do not expect profits from the business for two (or three or five) years"; "We expect revenues from the business to supplement other income from grants, not to be the sole source of funds"). Otherwise, it is likely that outcomes will disappoint supporters and/or create enormous stress on the enterprise participants.

The Éko Café/Boutique in Point St. Charles, Montreal, is a good example of a social enterprise that has moved through a process of development towards sustainability, confronting many challenges en route. Started by young mothers as a workplace for women to balance their home and community responsibilities with paid work, Éko Café/Boutique is a worker co-operative currently employing twelve members. The co-operative has multiple functions: a restaurant that features organic and fair trade products, a natural food store, a site for education about nutrition and natural health, a children's play area and an art exhibit space. The co-operative received generous financial support for start-up and initially employed twenty-six worker members. When there was a significant deficit at the end of the first year, drastic measures were taken by members to restructure the enterprise: reducing hours, establishing differential wages and introducing a mechanism for members to invest in the business. As well, a training program in customer service and sales was developed. Given the commitment of members and the clarification of procedures and objectives, funding agencies maintained their participation in re-capitalizing the enterprise.

There is great interest in social enterprise as a model for women-centred CED. At best, it is a way to explore the potential of the model as another way to integrate social and economic objectives. At worst, it is being promoted as a way to rationalize the withdrawal of public funds for social services and to create a context where it is the responsibility of the community to maintain social health with the assistance of benevolent private-sector partners. As with any strategy, it is important to be clear about the long-term goals and impacts.

The Profile of Women-centred CED

Until recently, women-centred CED organizations and projects have functioned in isolation, not playing a vital role in the women's movement. In the face of globalization, cutbacks and the sheer magnitude of the task facing them, women's centres have barely been able to address the basic needs presented by women in their communities. Status of Women Canada has been a significant support, providing funding for a number of projects across the country in recognition of their potential to challenge systemic barriers facing women. In the last few years, the Canadian Women's Foundation has made a considerable and valuable contribution to women-centred CED through its granting programs and the annual National Skills Initiatives. The NSIs brought hundreds of women together to examine the potential of CED as a framework for participating more formally in economic development in the community.

There is no question about women participating in the CED sector. Individual women have been active in CED, many involved in programs that supported women in particular ways, but women's issues continue to need a voice. Overall, women-centred CED has run on a parallel track with the generic CED sector, intersecting at CED conferences or other events. Encountering the "why women?" question has continued to be a common experience. As one practitioner once said: "Women are in the same building but we walk down a different corridor."

A recent experience at a pan-Canadian CED conference illustrates the dynamic. For the past several years, women have presented workshop sessions about women-centred CED at national CED conferences. The participation by women is always enthusiastic; useful information is exchanged and new connections are made. Participation by men has been welcome, although limited. Therefore, an invitation to the Women's CED Council[12] to participate in a panel about concrete ways to build a pan-Canadian *Communities First Agenda* was a good opportunity to show that an analysis of economics and sexism is the context in which CED can confront and reverse women's systemic marginalization, including the deeper and different forms of discrimination and inequity experienced by immigrant women, Aboriginal women, women with different abilities, senior women and others. In short, the goal was to show that such an analysis increases CED's strategic importance and accounts for the Council's commitment to it.

Women share many elements of the vision of the mainstream CED sector such as access to community-based financing for CED or multi-year funding for CED organizations. However, the pressing issues raised by the Council panelist were related to the root causes of the marginalization of women: access to child care for women who require it for their families; reinstatement of funding for women's organizations; the application of gender analysis of government and non-government programs to look at the differential impact of policies on women and men; and the elimination of social assistance policies that restrict participation. Changing the statistics that consistently identify women and their children as the country's most impoverished sector depends on addressing these issues. Presenting the context for women-centred CED activity and advocacy in the larger arena was an important step. As a significant follow up, the Autumn-Winter 2005-06 issue of *Making Waves*[13] focused exclusively on Women and CED.

The Future for Women-centred CED

One consultant in the field notes that CED practitioners are more fearful than they used to be about taking risks; they are concerned that if they press their organizations to challenge policies or if they propose projects that extend beyond the usual boundaries, they could jeopardize their jobs as well as their organization's viability. Organizations play a vital role in supporting CED and women-centred CED; it is a serious concern if they are weakening. For that reason, many of the recommendations of the various studies throughout this article focus on the critical importance of investing in women's organizations as well as in the others that promote and implement CED strategies.

Women-centred CED has a strong history of results and a role in contributing to the meaningful development of communities. There are also a number of positive circumstances that are encouraging and point to opportunities to move the field of women-centred CED forward:

• There is a healthy debate underway about the social economy: what it is, what it accomplishes, and how it complements CED as a strategy of social justice and economic empowerment. Developments in Quebec over the last ten years have catapulted social economy from a grassroots strategy into a federal budget item, and there is no question that the Women's March Against Poverty in 1995 was instrumental. Whether social economy is defined as volunteer activity, collectives founded on values of autonomy, solidarity and democratic decision-making, or a still wider range of social enterprise, women feature among its leading practitioners and will play a major role in developing the strategy.

• Anti-globalization consciousness is increasing among youth who are outraged about the international and domestic impacts of economic restructuring. While protests and demonstrations are legitimate expressions of their perspective, they are also seeking positive alternatives. This means women have many potential new allies who recognize the problems facing communities, are interested in CED as a solution and appreciate the value of women's experience as community-builders and organizers. These are the future practitioners of women-centred CED and it is crucial to invite them to identify priorities for action.

• There are now dozens of examples of women-centred CED to examine and learn from: employment training, self-employment, co-operatives, financing, asset development, food security, housing, child care, health care. Many have also given rise to effective resources and tools. It is important to supplement the research undertaken in the past two years with an overview of the successes and challenges of these initiatives, in order to help practitioners and organizations mobilize around common interests and needs, both technical and political.

• Many women's organizations are defined by a specific cultural, ethnic or lifestyle perspective. Their CED work is based on solidarity within this perspective and focuses on confronting barriers to employment or participation because of racism or discrimination in relation to other factors. Their experience enriches the knowledge about women's contribution to the community and needs to be understood and integrated more effectively with the overall analysis and practice of women-centred CED and that of the whole sector.

• Solid partnerships have been developed to understand more about women-centred CED, its contribution and its potential role. The Canadian Women's Foundation, CEDTAP and Status of Women Canada have supported efforts to build knowledge and support; CWF has initiated research and activities while the other two organizations have generously funded projects. These relationships contribute to the credibility of women-centred CED and form a base to gather more support. Good links are also being developed with organizations such as the Canadian CED Network, Community Futures Development Corporations and the

Canadian Co-operative Association, promising opportunities to integrate a women-centred approach with other CED activities.

• While there is abundant anecdotal evidence that women-centred CED contributes to social justice and economic development, it is time to develop methodologies that make the argument more forcefully to policy-makers and other decision-makers. There are a number of useful frameworks for measuring impact: the Social Determinants of Health, the United Nations Human Development Index, Genuine Progress Indicators, the Social Return on Investment. The challenge is to ensure that any measurement method incorporates the analysis and experience of women-centred CED.

There is no doubt that the passion, commitment and expertise of women involved in women-centred CED have brought enormous depth and scope to the field as a whole. It is time to acknowledge the strength and significance of the work. As women assume more leadership roles, we can be confident that questioning the importance of a women-centred CED focus will become a distant memory.

Notes

I wish to express my appreciation to the members of the Canadian Women's CED Council and to a number of other women who reviewed this chapter and contributed their experience and words of wisdom.

1.   *Who's Counting,* National Film Board of Canada.
2.   See Conn and Alderson, *WomenFutures.*
3.   WomenFutures, *Counting Ourselves In.*
4.   *Community of interest* is generally used in CED to identify a group of people connected to each other by a need to solve common problems, develop skills and share common practices. However, the phrase is frequently interpreted as implying self-interest which can then be used to discount the focus and analysis. The Women's CED Council prefers *women-centred CED* to describe a strategy that starts with a focus on women and their lives.
5.   Statistics Canada, Canadian Women's Foundation, Canadian Association of Social Workers.
6.   Information about women-centred CED activity in Canada is fully documented in the March 2004 study of Women's CED in Canada conducted by Interface on behalf of the Canadian Women's Foundation and the Women's CED Council.
7.   See Robinson, Cormier and Lockyer. *Northern Opportunities for Women.*
8.   Lockyer, "Our Piece of the Pie." This report provides detailed information about the formation and administration of lending circles.
9.   See WomenFutures, *Counting Ourselves In* and Conn and Alderson, "Making Communities Work," *Community Economic Development Perspectives.*
10.   *Tea you could trot a mouse on.*
11.   See Murray and Ferguson. *Women in Transition Out of Poverty.*

12. The Women's CED Council (WCEDC) was formed in 2002 by an association of women who are CED practitioners from across the country. Its mandate is to advance women-centred CED as a means of reducing poverty and improving the lives of women, their families and their communities. The Council was the initiating partner in the research projects cited above with the Canadian Women's Foundation and Status of Women Canada, and plans to continue to take a leadership role in providing a focus for research and other support for women-centred CED.

13. *Making Waves* is a quarterly published by the Centre for Community Enterprise based in Port Alberni, British Columbia.

Bibliography

Conn, Melanie and Lucy Alderson. "WomenFutures: Reflections on Community Economic Development." In *Community Economic Development in Canada*, edited by Eric Shragge. Montreal: Black Rose Books, 1997.

———. "Making Communities Work: Women and Community Economic Development." In *Community Economic Development Perspectives on Research and Policy*, edited by Burt Galaway and Joe Hudson. Toronto: Thompson Educational Publishing.

Counting Ourselves In: A Women's Community Economic Development Handbook. Vancouver: WomenFutures CED Society and the Social Planning and Research Council of BC (SPARC), 1993.

Lockyer, Rosalind. *Our Piece of the Pie: A Recipe for Developing a Women's Community Loan Fund.* Thunder Bay, ON: PARO: 1999.

Making Waves. Autumn-Winter 2005-06.

Murray, Janet and Mary Ferguson. *Women in Transition Out of Poverty: An Asset-Based Approach to Building Sustainable Livelihoods.* Canadian Women's Foundation Women and Economic Development Consortium, January 2001.

Robinson, Marina, Shannon Cormier and Rosalind Lockyer. *Northern Opportunities for Women: A Research Report.* PARO Centre for Women's Enterprise and the North Superior Training Board/Comité de formation du Nord Supérieur. October 2004.

Statistics Canada, Canadian Women's Foundation, Canadian Association of Social Workers.

Tea you could trot a mouse on. Women's Economic Equality (WEE) Society, Hubbards, NS: 2001.

Waring, Marilyn. *If Women Counted: A New Feminist Economics.* San Francisco: Harper Collins, 1988.

WomenFutures. *Counting Ourselves In: A Women's Community Economic Development Handbook.* Vancouver: WomenFutures CED Society and the Social Planning and Research Council of BC (SPARC), 1993.

National Film Board of Canada. *Who's Counting: Marilyn Waring on Sex, Lies & Global Economics,* 1996.

Wanda Wuttunee

Making Space: Aboriginal Perspectives of Community Economic Development

Preliminary Exploration of First Nations Values and CED

For First Nations peoples in Canada to participate in an evolving partnership with the rest of Canadians, fundamental shifts of relationships within Canada must continue to occur as recommended in the final report of the Royal Commission on Aboriginal Peoples (1996). Vital issues of governance, capacity-building and economic development including community economic development (CED), are part of the healing process that will result in First Nations peoples' full participation and contribution to Canada.

Change-makers in First Nations communities are hard at work. Their impact is becoming much more evident as educated First Nations leaders take up leadership opportunities and as more young people become educated and committed to change in their communities. Where are those bright lights in the communities and how do they live their dreams? Case studies in this chapter profile the current experience for several prairie communities.

CED stresses local control over important elements of the economy in promoting development of communities.[1] A great deal of money goes into rural and urban communities, but often very little of it stays. The profits that are made often quickly leave the community, so CED focuses on building linkages between producers and consumers. Community development proposals seek to plug some of those holes by encouraging local production, use of local goods and local employment. Profits are to be reinvested locally, and local skills, health and the physical environment improved. In the process, the community gains more control over its future, since it controls decisions critical to the success of a CED strategy.

Loxley notes important CED guiding principles that contribute to circulation of income within the local community resulting in less income drain, stronger economic linkages within the local community, less dependency on outside markets, greater community self-reliance and restoration of balance in the local economy. These include:

- Use of locally produced goods and services

- Production of goods and services for local use

- Local reinvestment of profits

- Long-term employment of local residents—reduced dependency on welfare and food banks and opportunities to live more socially productive lives, with increased personal and community self-esteem—with more wages and salaries spent in the local community

- Training of local residents—geared to community development for higher labour productivity, greater employability in communities with high unemployment and greater productive capability of economically depressed areas

- Local ownership and control—cooperative ownership and control with grassroots involvement that will improve community self-determination

- Physical environment—healthy, safe and attractive neighbourhoods that demonstrate ecological sensitivity

- Neighbourhood stability—with dependable housing, where there is long-term residency and a basis for long-term community development

- Human dignity—self-respect, community spirit, gender equality, respect for seniors and children that comes with personal and social pride and dignity

- Support for other CED initiatives—mutually supportive trade among organizations with similar community development goals.[2]

For First Nations peoples, CED offers a place for important tradition, culture and wisdom while incorporating selected successful mainstream development approaches. Each community will develop its own blend of priorities, ideally working with leadership that is in step with community goals, goals which change over time. Working with community strengths and dreams generates needed support for CED projects. Again, sensitive leadership must be in tune with community rhythms for the sake of community-held dreams and aspirations. The next point of exploration is First Nations philosophies.

Contemplating core values for First Nations peoples is complex, but these ideas form the core by which some First Nations peoples make sense of their place in the world and their perspectives on life. Common themes exist across First Nations communities within a diversity of practice and experience. These variations exist and Mohawk scholar T. Alfred urges:

Working within a traditional framework, we must acknowledge the fact that cultures change, and that any particular notion of what constitutes

"tradition" will be contested. Nevertheless, we can identify certain
common beliefs, values and principles that form the persistent core of a
community's culture.[3]

Unrealistic lists may attempt to encompass *all* traditional values that speak for
every indigenous person, but the context and essence of values is dynamic and
complex and cannot be distilled to a single list. Indeed, many First Nations peoples
turn away from traditional teachings and seek guidance from other religions of the
world due to the long influence of missionaries. Despite the limitations inherent in
listing core values, it is a place to begin a discussion of First Nations philosophy
and its fusion with CED perspectives. It is a superficial means by which to begin
communicating about the very essence of First Nations society, which can only
truly be understood through living it and talking to people who are living it.

Knowing the limitations of "writing" about core values does not mean that
using this approach strips all meaning. It sets the stage, begins a dialogue on the
written page that draws on the experience of First Nations scholars and provides
illumination and encouragement for greater understanding. The following list draws
on the teachings and words of several elders and authors, some who wish to remain
anonymous and some who allow their names to be noted. These values have been
handed down from elders to share with the community and come from the Creator,
recorded by authors but not attributed to one source.[4] Dockstater deals with this
issue. He notes that it is inappropriate to attribute a list like this to any one person
or source, nor to ceremonial knowledge out of cultural context.[5]

- Honouring all creation by showing respect
  Love of Creator and for all living things that come from the Creator is
  demonstrated by showing respect from the moment one rises in the
  morning to when one retires in the evening.
- Treasuring knowledge as wisdom
  Reflection, acknowledgement, seeking guidance and respecting the
  quality of knowing and the gift of vision in ourselves and in others
  demonstrates wisdom. Wisdom encompasses the holistic view,
  possesses spiritual quality and is expressed in the experiential breadth
  and depth of life.
- Knowing love is to know peace
  Caring, kindness, hope, harmony and cooperation are fundamental
  values. Caring and sharing are shown to one another with an ethic of
  generosity, collective/communal consciousness and cooperation, while
  recognizing the interdependence and interrelatedness of life.
  Recognizing the valuable gifts of the individual, the community and all
  nations leads to harmony and cooperation. Honouring the individual and
  the collective by thinking for yourself and acting for others.
- Courage and bravery is demonstrated in facing challenges with honesty
  and integrity
  The goal is to protect the quality of life and inherent autonomy of
  oneself and others. Life may then be lived in an atmosphere of security,
  peace, dignity and freedom.

- Cherishing yourself as a sacred part of creation is humility
  Honour all of life that is endowed with the same inherent autonomy,
  dignity, freedom and equality. Listen and learn from others and do so
  with a sense of modesty and sensitivity.
- The truth is to know all of these things.

To know all of these values is to have balance in one's life. With Statistics Canada's indices of mounting despair within the Aboriginal community overwhelming efforts made toward a healthy society, hope for many First Nations peoples lies in incorporating a holistic approach to development that honours a First Nations perspective. In reviewing the literature, it is obvious that striving for a healthy population occupies the priorities of many First Nations communities, making self-sufficiency through CED a significant strategy.

First Nations peoples who live in urban settings have a range of connection to their traditional values from non-existent to strong. Many urban-based programs, organizations and individuals continue to follow traditional teachings. Many hold true to their traditional values while living in a contemporary society with many pressures in opposition to traditional values.

An informal survey of a Mohawk reserve community in the early 1990s asked about the importance of traditional values in today's society.[6] The results point to the significance of these values in their community. Ninety-seven per cent believed in responsibility for all of creation; more than 80 per cent placed importance on extended family, respect for inner wisdom, and the importance of educating their young people; and more than 70 per cent honoured the sacredness of children, the importance of family unity, wisdom of the past and sharing and cooperation. Traditional values have a place in today's society and are critical to a complete and thorough understanding of First Nations peoples. The interconnectedness of politics, economy, land and culture cannot be disregarded, be it at the local, regional or national level, in First Nations or mainstream organizations.

The gift of land and the responsibility it entailed was meant to protect Mother Earth for future generations and to honour, maintain and protect the cycle of creation. This connection has been tested over the years. First Nations people were forced to live on reserves under treaty and obliged to attend residential schools under a government policy of assimilation. Métis people lived wherever they could since they were not welcomed by Europeans or by First Nations. Nomadic lifestyles of the Inuit were curtailed and community life dominated by church and government. They were forced off the land and into communities, often for the education of their children.

For some First Nations peoples in Canada, today's commitment to Mother Earth is so obvious that it is odd even to speak of. While the connection to a life on the land is almost gone in most communities, some maintain their link by trapping, hunting, fishing and berry-gathering on the weekends and in the summers. These are seen as important times for family and for personal rejuvenation. The words "sustainable development" are not used and instead wisdom and knowledge passed through the generations are relied upon to protect the land from overuse and permanent damage.

In some communities, Christianity is influential and traditional ties to the land may be described more in line with Christian teachings. For some Christians, there is a belief in dominion over all living creatures that may also be accepted by First Nations members. For others, the disconnection to traditional teachings may result from generational impacts flowing from residential school experiences, migration to the urban setting and lack of interest. In many cases, Aboriginal peoples do not hold legal title to their traditional lands, or do not have their rights recognized, and are unable to prevent damaging economic development undertaken by corporations.

In summary, this section references information adding to an understanding that is rich in texture with far-reaching values and relationships shaped by struggle, necessity and connection with life. A set of values that stand together have been enumerated. They cannot be individually singled out as more or less important in understanding CED from Aboriginal perspectives. They are integral to a holistic view that is still relevant in a contemporary analysis of the people and their development experience.

We see the end result of these challenging experiences. It is a people where many are marginalized, struggling to hold onto meaningful personal and community identities that capture shared values and honour existing diversity in ways that truly represent their place in Canadian society. Sickness, dysfunctional family situations, poverty, disenchanted youth and lack of control over resources are only some of the obstacles facing First Nations peoples. Hope, faith, dreams, clarity of leadership, education and persistence encourage healing change for all Aboriginal peoples.

Exploring Economic Values in Historical and Contemporary Settings

Thirty-five to forty per cent of First Nations people live on reserves (small pieces of land set aside under treaties). The balance live in rural and urban communities. Those who live on reserves and have status, fall under the jurisdiction of the federal department of Indian and Northern Affairs which negotiates funding agreements for governance, housing, social services and economic development. When status Indians leave their reserves, the jurisdiction of the federal government is less clear and the benefits they are able to claim generally decrease. The Royal Proclamation of 1763 and the British North America Act (1867) outline the federal government's responsibility to Aboriginal peoples. Provincial governments have consistently refused to provide special services to off-reserve status Indians—although this situation is slowly changing across Canada.

Métis people have no formal relationship with the federal government and today are eligible for the same level of services as all Canadians. Inuit people have a similar relationship with Indian and Northern Affairs and receive funding through territorial and federal agreements. Once a status Indian leaves the reserve, usually all Indian Affairs services are denied and there may be difficulties in replacing these services with provincial and municipal services. Provincial governments differ in the amount of responsibility they are willing to pick up from the federal government for these people, as usually there is no additional federal funding forthcoming.

The basis for the current situation in Aboriginal society is derived from the historical relationship between Aboriginal peoples and Canadian governments as articulated by government policy. Of particular interest here is understanding the deterioration of a meaningful Aboriginal economy that prospered prior to European contact and then dwindled by the end of the fur trade. It was then that Aboriginal peoples became a "liability" as Europeans sought to expand ownership and control across the country.

Aboriginal leaders were aware of the changes that were occurring. The government signed treaties seeking a way to open up the land to settlers at all costs, and leaders in the Aboriginal community signed treaties wanting to ensure future survival and a partnership that would benefit all parties involved. Scholars from within the Aboriginal community make the following observations:

> Aboriginal peoples have always had a strongly held value of self-sufficiency. We have always wanted to take care of ourselves. We have always acted to ensure that we can do this. As you can see there were many ways in which they prevented us from taking care of ourselves.

> Prior to contact with European newcomers, Aboriginal peoples were self-sufficient. Trade and commerce played an important part in the lives of many tribal communities. It was not until the imposition of foreign values that these practices were curtailed. Our ancestral leaders conducted mutually beneficial trade relationships, supported whole communities, negotiated among themselves and laid the foundations for productive, fulfilling societies before their skills and practices were cut short by invading strangers. The records of the treaty negotiations in the late 19th century are filled with the testimony of Indian leaders who knew of the world that was being built around them and who actively attempted to obtain the tools necessary to survive and thrive in the emerging market economy.

> We read the Council minutes of the traditional chiefs of the Iroquois Confederacy and hear the chiefs asking, repeatedly, of the Indian agents about the value of their investments and the size of their bank accounts in Ottawa. We see them asking to use their own money to establish loan funds for small businesses instead of being used exclusively for social welfare.

> [I]n the records of the fur trade, we read of constant bargaining over the price of furs by Aboriginal peoples and the Hudson Bay Company (HBC). The Indians were always asking for more than the HBC was

willing to pay. The HBC was forced to put into place a rather compli-
cated system. Indians understood extremely well how the system worked
and for whose advantage it was built. They usually got their prices.[7]

The context for surviving and thriving as communities continued to change.
Legislation including the Indian Act, was enacted for the benefit of Canadians
without focus on Aboriginal peoples, to their detriment. Treaty lands were small,
removed from markets in most cases, of poor quality with limited opportunities
for meaningful participation in the Canadian economy. While charged with
introducing agriculture as an alternative for self-sufficiency, government agents
regularly did poor jobs in providing farming implements and supporting marketing
possibilities. If anything, many consistently undermined the efforts of the
government and Aboriginal peoples. If opportunities arose to participate in the
Canadian economy, often Canadians were unwilling to conduct business to any
great extent with Aboriginal peoples.[8]

The Canadian government policy of a social safety net for its citizens changed
in the early 1920s with the Depression and became broadly available to all
Canadians, including Aboriginal peoples by the 1960s. Instead of trying to develop
programs of education, training and support for encouraging positive contributions
by Aboriginal peoples to the economy, the government chose to use the welfare
program as the dominant means of addressing the negative impacts of the residential
school system, colonialism, marginalization and general deterioration of Aboriginal
peoples. Dr. Fred Wien, scholar and head of the Royal Commission on Aboriginal
Peoples (RCAP) Economic Development section, comments on this urgent situation:

> For the on-reserve population in Canada as a whole, 37 per cent were
> reliant on social assistance by 1981, a figure that grew to 45 per cent by
> 1995. Projected in the future and taking account of anticipated demo-
> graphic change, the rate of dependence on social assistance is expected to
> reach 60 per cent by the year 2010....

> We are now caught in a cycle where costs for welfare and related
> remedial measures continue to grow while funds for economic develop-
> ment stagnate or are reduced.... The amount allocated for what might be
> called social problem spending (social assistance, health, housing,
> policing) has grown from 30 to 40 per cent of total spending in the period
> between 1981/82 and 1995/96. The amount allocated for economic
> development (broadly defined to include items such as economic
> development, business development, and land claims) decreased from 10
> per cent to 8 per cent, while the proportion allocated to education and
> training, has grown slightly from 19 to 22 per cent.

> The overriding impression left by these figures, and by the experience of
> Aboriginal communities across the country, is that governments continue
> to meet economic distress with income support payments rather than
> investing in the often more difficult measures that would rebuild
> Aboriginal economies.

> We desperately need to break out of this cycle.[9]

In recent decades, Aboriginal peoples have pushed for government policies to achieve a stronger, more self-reliant economic base. The first major statement on the issues came in reaction to the 1969 white paper and was prepared by the Manitoba Indian Brotherhood (MIB). Its report, *Wahbung: Our Tomorrows*, states:

> In developing new methods of response and community involvement it is imperative that we, both Indian and Government, recognize that economic, social and educational development are synonymous, and thus must be dealt with as a "total" approach rather than in parts. The practice of program development in segments, in isolation as between its parts, inhibits if not precludes, effective utilization of all resources in the concentrated effort required to support economic, social and educational advancement.
>
> In order that we can effect changes in our own right, it will be necessary to develop a whole new process of community orientation and development. The single dependency factor of Indian people upon the state cannot continue, nor do we want to develop a community structure that narrows the opportunities of the individual through the transferral of dependencies under another single agency approach.
>
> The transition from paternalism to community self-sufficiency may be long and will require significant support from the state, however, we would emphasize that state support should not be such that the government continues to do for us, that which we want to do for ourselves.[10]

The report gave voice to Aboriginal peoples that had been muffled and led to a chorus of protest for change across the country. Revised policies advocated by Aboriginal leaders focused on community development as part of a holistic and comprehensive approach. Healing for individuals, safeguarding Aboriginal rights to land and resources while developing cultural and human resources were priorities developed by and for Aboriginal peoples. Proposed changes for increased self-sufficiency highlight ways to build on the strengths of Aboriginal and mainstream society. Local input dictates the emphasis placed by communities on individual or communal interests adding to the appropriateness of independence and self-governance.

An example of sensitive capacity-building is discernible through Aboriginal-controlled education institutions developing to meet the challenge of educating a population that has many needs. Rather than just limiting options to skills that are transferable to an urban setting, programs also meet specific community needs.[11] Other shifts in strategies also include a shift in emphasis to the community level in other areas of economic development with *more local control*.

As noted, while federal and provincial governments try to assist in making positive change, Aboriginal peoples have visions too, and have increasingly taken control in directing the means to attain those goals. As outlined by RCAP, a major shift in approach and investment of funds by government and the private sector is essential and will facilitate personal development and healing within the Aboriginal community that precedes meaningful growth and independence, goals at the heart of CED. Continuing on the present path, according to Wien and RCAP, will cost millions in social assistance costs and in the end will be more costly than spending millions of dollars on the Aboriginal community infrastructure. The clear message is that education, training and other RCAP recommendations will truly build capacity, allowing the Aboriginal community to take on the challenges of the new millennium.[12]

These authors contemplate a partnership of healing and CED built on greater understanding of the need for substantive change by the Canadian public. In the end, working together will result in betterment for all Canadians and, most importantly, for all Aboriginal peoples. All have an important role to contribute to this process. In the words of Ovide Mercredi, former Grand Chief of the Assembly of First Nations:

> It is no longer acceptable to be just complainers about our social and economic conditions. It is no longer enough just to blame others for our pain and misery. What does it take? How many pennies does it take to stop family violence in our homes? How many dollars does it take to prevent child abuse in our communities? We must begin the healing process for the recovery of our First Nations peoples with whatever resources we have. It must start with us, here in our hearts. Yes, we will need outside support, but we have to do everything we can on our own, too.
>
> For some time our people have been trying to find ways of being more self-sufficient. It is quite apparent to us that in order to reach that objective, we are going to need the help and cooperation of the Canadian people and the corporate or business communities.
>
> Unlike some other First Nations leaders, I do not believe in absolute sovereignty or independence for our people, because I think it is impossible to close our minds and our hearts to the experiences of other people in this country. We cannot pretend that we are the only human beings on this planet or that we are totally independent ... not a single nation-state is absolutely sovereign in terms of its economic policy....
>
> We live in an era of interdependence. We have to come to the realization, as First Nations, that we have to lift ourselves up, and in the process reach out to other Canadians and their governments to help us elevate our social and economic conditions. We must eliminate poverty and suffering so that we can contribute to a common vision of economic and social progress for all the individuals that should benefit from sharing our Mother Earth.[13]

An examination of the current approaches to CED in Aboriginal communities reveals critical differences with Western approaches, including the role of community in decision-making, the role of elders, spirituality and the connection to the land. These distinctions are not always easily identified by an untrained observer nor are they present in every community, but they are important to recognize because they do exist. Where they do not exist in communities that reflect a more mainstream orientation, these distinctions may be recaptured through future goals.

The debate regarding resource development is ongoing, with opinions occupying all points on the spectrum within the communities. The issues are often where CED should take place and how it should occur. Many leaders are cognizant of the damage that has been done to their lands due to economic development and are very cautious about the projects that are supported. Other communities place more emphasis on employment in making economic development decisions, while balancing that with the impact on the environment. Some communities pass all projects for review by elders' councils, where the elders draw upon traditional knowledge in considering the project's appropriateness. This process screens out projects that may be profitable but do not meet the community's standards regarding its responsibility toward Mother Earth. Elders often play an active role in guiding their urban and rural communities to determine a balance in CED that makes sense in their communities.

The CED approach is reflected in current federal government policy. It fits well into the context calling for broader initiatives to develop institutional capacity at the national or sectoral levels. RCAP concluded that CED's focus on local circumstances from a local perspective is holistic and is harmonious with Aboriginal world views. In particular, CED is a comprehensive approach that integrates social and economic goals. Resources on all levels are identified with community support and a reasonable economic development plan is crafted. The focus is on such things as stimulation of local businesses for job creation, while building social and physical resources including training, education, housing, transportation, public infrastructure, culture and leisure.

RCAP concluded:

> The CED approach, which recognizes the local community as a legitimate location for development effort, requires that communities be able to engage in a planning process to articulate social and economic needs and goals, identify institutions that need to be founded or supported, and identify development strategies consistent with local cultural, social and economic conditions. It requires that the community have in place a governance process to provide legitimacy and a basis for implementing plans.

> The federal government has been sympathetic to CED, but it has experienced difficulty translating that attitude into official action. Budgets for CED and the resulting activities are inadequate, and real control over budgets and development still eludes communities. The Commission's community case studies revealed hamlet councils and related boards with very limited capacity to pursue job creation, training, or community planning. While the need will vary with the size of the community, at a minimum, Aboriginal communities should have some

capacity to support economic development in terms of organization, staff resources and training.

[I]n a review of the experience with CED in the United States, Stewart Perry reported that perhaps the most significant lesson ... is that CED must be carried on under local direction, according to local priorities, and by mobilizing local resources first. That is quite different from conventional development policy that begins with central decisions in the economic core areas about what should happen in the peripheral regions.[14]

Relevant recommendations for this discussion focus on the economic development context in which CED occurs. Fred Wien summarizes these strategies in his Royal Bank/CANDO contribution:

• Regain control over the levers that govern their economies through realization of self-government. All levels of government are urged to make room for an Aboriginal order of government.

• Rebuild Aboriginal nations as the basis for bringing together a critical mass of resources that allow for economies of scale.

• Build institutional capacity on the basis of legitimate authority (within the nation), appropriate rules and procedures within a safe and secure environment for potential investors.

• Expand lands and resources through establishing clear legal interests.

• Recognize Aboriginal and treaty rights as one means for expanding lands and resources.

• Build Aboriginal businesses through improved access to capital; advice for entrepreneurs; and improved access to markets.

• Support traditional economies including trapping, hunting and fishing.

• Overcome barriers to employment, through expanding available jobs, appropriate education and training, improving information networks to bring jobs and people together, partnering with major employers and improving child care.

• Develop new approaches to income support programs that help people break the cycle of welfare dependence.[15]

The need for mainstream CED strategies in harmony with Aboriginal community goals for economic independence through appropriate means is recognized. For example, RCAP recommends development of natural resources using small-scale, environmentally friendly techniques that will allow for flexibility in exploiting natural resources that multinational corporations do not currently exercise. Additionally, developing a stronger traditional or subsistence economy, involving living on the land and with the land, is suggested as being economically viable since material goods and specialist services are provided in a renewable fashion. These activities also provide meaning for many Aboriginal peoples living in communities. Several examples of strategic effort within a CED framework by Aboriginal leaders will be outlined in the next section.

Wealth Creation in a CED Context

Two examples of strategic effort will be examined within the CED framework. The material comes from a recent research project on the Canadian prairies in which the communities and contributing individuals are anonymous. The following profiles set out critical facts about their efforts for these two communities referred to here as Manitoba Grand Council and Saskatchewan First Nation.

Manitoba Grand Council (MGC) occupies three treaty areas and covers 2.5 million hectares. Membership totals more than 30,000 with 16,700 living in 26 communities. MGC operates with a $400 million budget for governance and economic development with employment for many of its citizens. It is the largest tribal council in Manitoba and is a significant player at the national level. Political issues are key, along with supporting youth to develop through healthy lifestyles, education and opportunity. Careers that are of particular interest include trades, medicine, nursing, engineering and commerce. While completed grades for citizens living on-reserve are rising rapidly, education levels still lag behind other First Nations.

The will of the people directs the MGC, and their strength and resilience is noted as key to their nation's continued independence and further achievements. According to the operations manager, the organization is developing more tools for greater effectiveness, including moving to business plans in a number of key programs in order to more effectively meet the needs of its membership.

MGC supports education, health, youth, elders and cultural initiatives. Annual and business planning sessions began in 2000 with internal, external and environmental scans followed by an analysis of strengths, weaknesses, opportunities and threats to success. It also encourages business development with the assistance of an economic development advisor. It plays an active role in the Manitoba economy through the Manitoba Development Corporation. Owned equally by its member First Nations, MDC has invested in real estate, the hotel and service industries, construction, security, employment referral services and janitorial services. Strength in unity is the MDC philosophy.

In the 1980s, MDC pooled its resources and built an office building and signed long-term leases with the Grand Council, Indian and Northern Affairs Canada and Medical Services Branch. Today it owns four office buildings. It also started a security and janitorial service company and has secured major contracts with large resource corporations. In the 1990s, MDC purchased the Manitoba Inn to capitalize on a hotel and meeting facilities opportunity that would provide employment for its members. The inn boasts 108 rooms, conference and banquet facilities, nightclub, lounge, cold beer and wine store, with a restaurant and pool. It now owns several more hotels. Additional projects include acting as developer and operator for a local casino, a joint venture with a large construction company in development of a natural resource project and partnering with other tribal councils in business ventures such as a golf course and a local airlines.

The community of Saskatchewan First Nation (SFN) is a small community of 4,400 hectares located less than 30 minutes from a city. Ten years ago it received $800,000 from Indian Affairs for an on-reserve population of approximately 150 people. This was the bleak situation that existed when a new chief was elected. Through focus on building healthy lifestyles and economic prosperity, things have improved immensely. A recent community survey noted that 20 per cent of their community membership have completed Grade 12, and 26 per cent have trades and post-secondary experience. There is 13 per cent unemployment with the balance employed, self-employed, going to school or retired. Social assistance is drawn by 16 per cent and 62 per cent earn employment income.

In order to meet the challenges facing his community, the chief and two council members have worked on various governance and economic initiatives to move the community forward. A Community Sustainability Plan describes the level of economic activity that SFN is seeking to achieve. Fiscal performance under a governance and administration program improved accountability and fiscal responsibility from near bankruptcy to a negotiated Financial Transfer Agreement (with increased flexibility based on credible past performance) and a $4-million budget in 2004.

Community services include a medical clinic, a children's headstart program and school. There is a volunteer fire department and a band office. One entrepreneurial band member owns a stable, the first of many small businesses. All houses have water, sewer and natural gas, one of the better improvements over the last ten years. Partnerships mark SFN's approach to development, ranging from a mechanical company to a golf course creating 40 jobs and catering to 250 golfers per day. Future projects include developing tourism opportunities, a casino, a hotel with convention facilities, a golf club house and a golf course expansion. Other plans include a condominium project along the golf course and residential lot development. Land will be leased to suitable projects. Partnerships with local communities are enhancing tourism and infrastructure for the entire region. Its plans and future goals outstrip its size but demonstrate what can be accomplished with imagination.

The complexity of CED in Aboriginal communities is demonstrated in the exploration of closely connected concepts of politics and business. Developing institutional and leadership capacity supports healthy governance and allows for a strong economic contribution, these two leading organizations have encouraged this development in several ways. Research has concluded that separation of business and politics leads to more effective business operations.[16] MGC and SFN leaders acknowledge the complexity of the relationships between politics and business. The process of decision-making includes MGC's board made up of political leaders from their First Nation members and SFN with its small leadership who are integrally involved in the economic process. There is an interconnection between the political position and balancing the wealth and profit goals of a development corporation. Governance and leadership are supportive of business through effective intervention and lobbying of industry and government by Chief and Council.

Rather than a potential tension existing between traditional values and capitalism, these groups describe the relationship more as an integrated values partnership in keeping with CED's objectives. "Community capitalism" is the term used in the MDC. Communities suffer from high unemployment and they expect their leadership to create business and employment opportunities with the benefits returning to the communities. SFN states that their development corporation's profits are reinvested in community culture and language after career opportunities have been created for its citizens. While profit and risk would be the end of the analysis for mainstream businesses, analysis at SFN includes the fit with community values, the impact on the community environment and long-term benefits. All note an effort to reach consensus in these matters so everyone understands what is planned. Inherent to the concept of community capitalism, is the nurturing of a particular business culture that incorporates the best of business and traditional values.

The focus is on profits, jobs and proper business questions through consensus building and the participation of elders. Elders monitor meetings to ensure they are conducted in a good way and will intervene to remind participants of their duties and responsibilities to the community. For MDC, it took more than twenty-four years to develop this business culture. It has taken a decade to establish trust, a track record of successful partnerships and development, professional management and effective communication. There has also been consistency in board leadership through a number of board members having a long record of re-election, which has translated to consistency in an approach to investment and business development. This maturity in approach has evolved where competition among band businesses is encouraged, and there are no lingering ill effects against the winning bidder. Often companies partner and are working for competitors at the same time.

These case studies demonstrate that CED is more than jobs and income, it is community wealth generated from corporate profits that go back to communities and it is wealth generated for individuals. With this understanding, these groups demonstrate common strategic planning approaches that accommodate internally-generated ideas and external opportunities. For SFN, a land-use plan designated land for residential and commercial development as a result of community consultation. Commercial development projects must blend in well with the natural beauty of their community and create jobs and revenue streams that support self-sufficiency.

While the community had approved the idea for a golf course for some time prior to the chief of SFN's tenure, it was successfully resurrected and recently completed. Other large projects, including the casino, RV park, hotel and training centre, with a total of 500-600 jobs, were partner investments or lease opportunities that were seized by the community. Other revenue sources include business tax and a community improvement fee from the blanket taxation of alcohol, tobacco and fuel that will contribute to self-sufficiency. While more moderate proposals might have made sense for such a small community, demonstrating lower unemployment and a small land base, the community endorsed the supported proposals. That is CED at its best.

SFN's recent success is the result of a long period of reconstruction after the community came close to requiring third party management. The basic needs of the community were met, goodwill with surrounding communities and a strategy of partnership were developed. For a small community with limited access to capital, it has bylaws and policies in place to assuage the needs of funders who include other First Nations, private investors, banks and the federal government.

These two communities go after investment opportunities. MDC identified jobs in an urban setting for their youth and invested in a number of hotels. Their experience is that companies will approach their membership for partnering in ventures especially where Aboriginal people are given bidding priority through set-aside programs, while Aboriginal entrepreneurs will seek industry partners based on their interest in a sector and need for capital and management expertise.

For SFN, partnering or leasing land has meant opportunities beyond the regular imagination of its members. Active leadership has focused on partnering, including lobbying for projects that require funding and leasehold projects that they do not own. MDC builds on trust and collaboration and a willingness to work together within its own membership and with industry partners.

Community and privately-owned businesses are seen as ways to obtain a better quality of life in the communities. In an organization such as Manitoba Grand Council, that encompasses many communities, there are more privately owned businesses. For SFN, the prediction is that entrepreneurs will grow in the future, given the economic opportunities forecast. While profits are important, all businesses require a service and community focus—a factor in their success.

Employment must include career and advancement opportunities; members want access to good careers so that they can provide comfortably for their families. Other families in Saskatchewan provide quality of living that these SFN community members are striving for as part of more sustainable, self-reliant communities. In small communities, community-owned businesses are the economic drivers and are thus essential for a CED strategy. This activity occurs within the context of outreach to surrounding communities so that a solid network is built.

Strong governance and accountability practices and procedures are in evidence in this case study group. For example, MDC's board is composed of each chief from the affected First Nations. The Grand Chief sits as chair of the MDC. He works with the MDC's CEO, on identifying or cultivating investment opportunities. Investment guidelines and policies guide the work of the development corporation. SFN's governance system is dictated by its small size. It has an economic development committee that includes the chief and its two council members. Its constitution empowers chief and council to make economic decisions on behalf of the community and the community recently approved the Land Management Act, a property tax bylaw and a community improvement fee that facilitates community governance. The accountability norm is set by standard business practices for the development corporation work of MGC and FSN and developed over a period of years. All investment opportunities are examined by the management team and brought to the board (made up of community members).

In MDC's practice, full board approval is sought for an investment and then often it is the management board (a subset of the whole board) that gives further guidance and approval to MDC's management team. In the last five years, the board has given unanimous support to fully vetted initiatives. Elders participate on the management board and at the chiefs' level there is a council of elders. The whole SFN community's approval is sought to go forward within investment guidelines and full information disclosure. Once approval in principle is obtained, the SFN Economic Development committee carries out its mandate quickly and decisively. Accountability is open and transparent and these groups use a variety of regular communication tools to keep shareholders and citizens apprised of their activities. For example, SFN holds regular monthly staff meetings and elders meetings, and circulates weekly newsletters to members. MDC has an annual report, regular newsletters and community meetings. MGC has a web-based newsletter and informal reporting to the Grand Chief and council.

Hand-in-hand with governance structure and accountability practices, is a well-planned management strategy. Critical elements in MGC's successful strategy include consistency in leadership, separation of business and politics and community empowerment. Long experience contributes to corporate memory and solid development philosophy and goals. Business is more efficient when not impeded by undue political influence and MDC supports communities who take the initiative to grow their own development corporations. They also attribute their success to pragmatic political leaders who understand successful CED and who are light on rhetoric.

With young leadership, SFN enjoys the benefits of educated, experienced leaders who do not carry emotional baggage such as the residential school experience. Their approach is different and translates into a future focus rather than a focus on past negativity. SFN's chief notes: "We have programs to help members handle the past. The focus for me is on the positive ... partnerships, employment opportunities, and job creation. What can we do to make a difference rather than pointing a finger and blaming someone else?" SFN has full community support to build a sustainable community. "By going big, we create a sustainable community," according to the chief. Through thorough discussion, there is more understanding, less politics and less debate.

Each community leader has a particular vision of success with elements being clear and unique, yet with much in common. Success is shared with their citizens through dividend policies, employment practices and skill development. Success expands beyond the boundaries of their own community or organization to fellow leaders and colleagues through sharing of experiences and to future generations by expressing visions for the future.

Success for MGC is focused on youth and education. In order to significantly improve the socio-economic situation in their area, they need to create 585 jobs per year for ten years if they wish to attain 50 per cent employment. They now focus on industries with high employment needs and they are fast tracking interested band citizens into suitable educational opportunities. With a critical consistency of approach, employment and successful businesses generating wealth and reinvestment of that community wealth are all indicators of success.

Four-hundred band citizens are employed in community-owned businesses. There is a high turnover in entry-level positions, but these people have gone on to better jobs or training institutions so they too are part of MGC's success. Their investments are generating profits and creating community wealth that are reinvested in more jobs and improved social programming. It is a consistent cycle that brings increasing success as measured in terms of progress over time and focus on positive change. An important indicator also includes comments from community members who say, "We're proud of this accomplishment."

At SFN, focus is on self-sufficiency, employment opportunities for healthy, employable people and stability of revenue sources. The chief notes: "We were once known as the hardest-working community around. We need to get our pride back like in the sixties. Our success is being talked about in the media and the community is taking a lot of pride in that." A vision of success is SFN's focus on community involvement, consensus and the use of elders in ways that successfully combine traditional and non-traditional ways. Their vision requires that specific steps be taken knowing that not everybody's needs can be met at once, so a longer strategic approach makes sense. SFN is open to partners and working cooperatively with as many people as possible. Leadership takes direction from their community and then moves aggressively to make it happen with integrity. Sometimes it is difficult to maintain time frames and standards but the effort to do so pays off in the long run.

Sharing success is fundamental to the visions this group strives to achieve. In terms of profit distribution and reinvestment of retained earnings, MDC has determined a formula for each dollar of net profit 33 per cent is paid as dividends to shareholders; 33 per cent is for new investments and 33 per cent to upgrade investments and assets. SFN's investments will bring profits for distribution in the future. There will be no per-capita program. The chief comments, "We want to make our people proud so the next generation will see the success and carry it forward. We will invest in schooling, post-secondary students, the elders program, enhanced health care, our language and in infrastructure, such as paved roads."

Finally, each group shares their experience with their colleagues and dreams for their community's future. According to the Grand Chief, some of the old ways were short-sighted and often ignored youth investment or wealth creation. Job creation based on short-term projects did not address unemployment issues effectively.

> If "children truly are our future," then we need to stop the rhetoric and devise a long term plan focusing on sustainability. Opportunities for training youth and creating wealth in the community are essential. It is wealth that will allow us to be independent, self-reliant. It's a new approach to economic development that is much more supportive of success.

For these organizations, the future of their communities is bright. MDC sees effective capacity-building of their economic development officers and of young people as an important part of the future that will make a big difference. In twenty years, they will be formalizing the next five-year plan and will be a major economic block in the province of Manitoba, alongside other First Nations corporations. By 2024, SFN's development plans will be realized and their community will be a driving force of economic prosperity. Any member who wants to work will have a job. Income and education levels will be much higher in the community. There will be good recreation facilities and a stronger language component. There will be a stronger business relationship with the non-Aboriginal community than we have currently. A framework for leadership will be in place with accountability at its heart.

These insights are from leaders in a community, a community of tribal councils focusing on governance and development. Their experience highlights diversity in success, goals and achievements and is very similar to any cross-section of economic initiatives across Canadian society, more specifically, among participants in Aboriginal economies across the country. These case studies trace the evolving maturity of Aboriginal leadership in the area of effective long-term strategic planning and implementation within a CED framework.

Once the basic infrastructural needs of their communities have been met, education and jobs dominate all efforts. Success is accomplished within a context flavoured with consistent community direction, active participation and thus community ownership for their respective and collective successes. The most skilled expertise is accessed and incorporates a blend of individually and collectively oriented approaches to business development. These leaders are carrying their communities forward with skills that are becoming more common in Aboriginal communities. They are young, educated and aggressive in meeting the economic demands of their communities. They are using solid business tools, including community input and consensus—true economic warriors that from a CED perspective demonstrate ways for their community members to realize their development needs, finance local projects and take control and ownership of their economic destiny.

Notes

1. John Loxley, "Sustainable Urban Economic Development." *Journal of Aboriginal Economic Development*, Vol 3, No. 1, (2002) 29-32.
2. Ibid.
3. Alfred, *Peace, Power, Righteousness*, xvii.
4. See also Newhouse, "Modern Aboriginal Economies;" Alfred, 134; Black, *Redefining Success in Community Development*.
5. Dockstater, *Towards an Understanding of Aboriginal Self*-government, 9.
6. Alfred, 22.
7. Newhouse and Jetté, (1997). "CANDO Statement on the Economic Development Recommendations of the Royal Commission on Aboriginal Peoples," in the *Cost of Doing Nothing*, 3.
8. Ibid., 2.
9. Wien, "The Royal Commission Report: Nine Steps to Rebuild Aboriginal Economies," in *The Cost of Doing Nothing*, 3-4.
10. RCAP. *Looking Forward: Looking* Back, 795-96.
11. Ibid., 794-795.
12. See RCAP, 1996; Royal Bank/CANDO, 1997.
13. Mercredi and Turpel. *In the Rapids*, 145-46; 154-55.
14. RCAP, 1996, 845-846.
15. Wien, 11-23.
16. Kalt and Cornell, *What can tribes do?*

Bibliography

Alfred, Taiaiake. *Peace, Power, Righteousness: An Indigenous Manifesto*. Don Mills, ON: Oxford University Press, 1999.

Anderson, Robert. *Economic Development Among the Aboriginal Peoples in Canada*. Ontario: Captus Press, 1999.

Black, Sherry Salway. *Redefining Success in Community Development: A New Approach for Determining and Measuring the Impact of Development*. The Richard Shramm Paper on Community Development: The Lincoln Filene Centre, 1994.

Carter, Sarah. *Lost Harvests: Prairie Indian Reserve Farmers and Government Policy*. Montreal: McGill-Queen's University Press, 1990.

Dockstater, Mark. "Towards an Understanding of Aboriginal Self-government: A Proposed Theoretical Model and Illustrative Factual Analysis." PhD diss., Osgoode Hall Law School, York University, 1993.

Elias, Peter. *Northern Aboriginal Communities:Economies and Development*. North York: Captus Press, 1995.

Johnson, Chief G., Kluane Tribal Council, Burwash Landing, Yukon. Personal communication. April 27, 1993.

Kalt, Joseph, and Stephen Cornell. *What Can Tribes Do? Strategies and Institutions in American Indian Economic Development*. Los Angeles: University of California, 1993.

Loxley, John. "Sustainable Urban Economic Development: An Aboriginal perspective." *Journal of Aboriginal Economic Development* 3, no. 1, (2002): 29-32.

Mercredi, Ovide, and Mary Ellen Turpel. *In the Rapids: Navigating the Future of First Nations*. Toronto: Penguin Books, 1993.

Newhouse, David. "Modern Aboriginal Economies: Capitalism with an Aboriginal Face." In National Round Table on Aboriginal Economic Development and Resources, 1993.

———. "Sharing the Harvest: The Road to Self-Reliance." In National Roundtable on Aboriginal Economic Development and Resources, 90-100. Ottawa: Royal Commission on Aboriginal Peoples, 1993.

———. "From the Tribal to the Modern: The Development of Modern Aboriginal Societies." Submission to the Royal Commission on Aboriginal Peoples. Ottawa, 1992.

———, and C. Mount-Pleasant Jetté. "CANDO Statement on the economic development recommendations of the Royal Commission on Aboriginal peoples." In *the Cost of Doing Nothing: A Call to Action*. The Joint CANDO-Royal Bank Symposium, Toronto, Ontario, 1997.

Royal Commission on Aboriginal Peoples. *Looking Forward:Looking Back*. Vols 1, 2 and 3. Canada Communication Group. Ottawa, 1996.

Wien, Fred. "The Royal Commission Report: Nine Steps to Rebuild Aboriginal Economies." In *The Cost of Doing Nothing: A Call to Action*. Toronto: CANDO-Royal Bank Symposium, 1997.

David Newhouse

Aboriginal Economic Development in the Shadow of the Borg[*]

There has been a great deal of development and change in Aboriginal communities since 1966, the year the Hawthorne Report, *A Survey of Contemporary Indians of Canada*,[1] was released. The Hawthorne Report examined about seventeen different Aboriginal communities across the country and documented their social and economic conditions in the early 1960s. The report described contemporary social thinking about how these communities ought to be developed and what strategies the Government of Canada ought to follow over the next short while. The main idea of the Hawthorne Report is that of treating Aboriginal as citizens-plus. While this idea was rejected by governments, Aboriginals took it up and have been pursuing it through a variety of means ever since. So, forty-odd years down the road, we are beginning to see some changes, but I also think that it is useful for us who work in Aboriginal community economic development to step back and to think about what it is we are involved in. That is the context of this chapter; forty years after the Hawthorne Report, when the path that we have chosen is beginning to bring results and introduce new challenges.

My interest as an academic is to document, examine and reflect on the transitions in Aboriginal society that I see going on around me. As a society, we are starting to move away from the time of great pain and to lay the foundations for what I have come to call "modern Aboriginal society." Across the country, I see a strong desire to build First Nations communities on a foundation of Aboriginal tradition, custom and ideas. Accomplishing this goal is difficult, a result of our position as Aboriginal peoples—a small minority within an environment dominated

---

[*] In the TV show, *Star Trek: The Next Generation*, Captain Picard never defeats the Borg, he only keeps them at bay. He does that through clever resistance based on a strong understanding of self and a strong desire to survive. He is firm in his belief that humankind will survive.

by Western[2] ideas. The arena of Aboriginal economic development is an excellent example of the challenges facing us as we try to act upon our desire to use our own ideas as the basis for collective public and community action.

In 1996, a small magazine started by Rolland Bellerose, a young man from Alberta, began to explore Aboriginal economic development. *Aboriginaltimes* has grown from a small local publication to one that is now included as a monthly insert in the *Globe and Mail*, Canada's national newspaper. The masthead says that *Aboriginaltimes* is "a national business and news monthly magazine which explores the issues and experiences of Aboriginal People."[3] Issue #2, from October 1996, states that

> *Aboriginal Times* is produced with the spirit and intent of sharing and participating! [It is] a communication bridge that will link Aboriginals and Corporate Canada together in a meaningful and beneficial way ... we provide an unprecedented way to inform the public of information pertinent to the Aboriginal Business community.[4]

Since then, consistent with its mission, the magazine has evolved into an unabashed supporter of Aboriginal business and economic development. It contains columns on partnerships, business opportunities, training programs, movers and shakers, natural resources, upcoming events of all sorts: snippets of Aboriginal history, political commentary, education opportunities and advertisements from governments, businesses, services, government policy. Its editorial policy is optimistic, pro-development, pro-business, pro-Aboriginal. In tone, it differs little from other business magazines in other sectors of the Canadian economy, but four decades ago, such a magazine would have been unthinkable and undoable.

In another part of the country, we see another example of something that a few decades ago would similarly have been undoable. A few years ago, I had the opportunity to undertake a case study of the development of the economy at Six Nations of Grand River and to think about the challenges that this community was facing. I was struck by what I saw and heard. The economy itself was booming: new business start-ups were at an all-time high; people were consuming. There was buzz within the community as this new entrepreneurial spirit began to affect it. The council was publicly musing about the need for zoning bylaws for commercial enterprises, particularly in view of a rather disastrous tire fire. Local small business people said:

> We don't need regulations. We can regulate ourselves. Regulations will increase the cost of doing business. And we're not sure that as a Band Council you have the authority to regulate small business. More regulation will make it difficult to start new businesses or attract new ones to Six Nations.

For economists, these statements ought to sound very familiar. The two situations were illustrative of the situation facing those working in the field of Aboriginal economic development: on one hand, we want to be proponents of more of it, like those described in *Aboriginaltimes*. On the other, we are somewhat taken aback when we see the old classical economic debates being replicated in front of our eyes. Aboriginal economic development, driven as it is by aboriginal values, is expected to be different.

In several places around the country, we are starting to replicate the classical debates about regulation of private enterprise, the appropriate mix of public and private enterprise, the role of government in the economy, the influence of culture on development goals and practices and, in some cases, the goals of economic development itself. It is uplifting to see possibility of great improvement in the material life of Aboriginal peoples, but at the same time it is dispiriting to realize that we have not been able to escape the conflicts that will inevitably accompany this improvement.

With the history of Aboriginal-European-Canadian relations dancing in my head, I also wonder if economic development is the just latest solution to the "Indian problem": Instead of being in need of civilizing, Aboriginals were now in need of development. Were we, as individuals involved in the field, helping to reinforce a view of Aboriginals as problems that need to be solved? As we are all aware, there is a long history of European-Canadians[5] seeing "Indians" as problems. Much research has been done to define the particular nature of the Indian problem and to influence public policy in an effort to solve the problem. "Indians are problems" and "Indians have problems" may serve as the simple summary of the status of Indians in Canadian society.

It should come as no surprise that, predominantly, we see Aboriginal economic development through the lens of deficiency: there isn't enough of it or it's of the wrong kind. We see it as secular manna: more of it will solve many problems within the Aboriginal community. Public policy officials, academics, both theoretical and applied, and politicians of all stripes and hues have turned their attention to the problem: The Harvard Project on American Indian Economies, headed by professors Joseph Kalt and Stephen Cornell, has been exploring the conditions that make for successful economic development. The York University project on strong Aboriginal communities, headed by Professor Cynthia Chataway, is also looking at successful communities and how they can be fostered. The Royal Commission on Aboriginal Peoples (1996) considered increasing the level of economic development for Aboriginal peoples to be part of its fundamental goals. Furthering economic development has become the solution to the poverty of Aboriginals. Sometimes the problem was that the state wasn't doing enough; other times the state was doing too much. Which view dominates public policy depends on the political predilection of the observer.

Since the 1960s, Aboriginal peoples have had the attention of the development apparatus of the state, have been the objects of effort by the development community and its cadre of professionals and have launched development efforts themselves. Yet the problems of low income, inadequate housing and poor labour force participation continue to persist. In each decade since the 1960s, a new generation of policy researchers and analysts prepares a new set of solutions. The latest view, expressed by Cornell and Kalt, in *What can Tribes Do? Strategies and Institutions in American Indian Economic Development?*, sees economic development as requiring the support of appropriate governing institutions, and the latest efforts are focused on improving the governance of Aboriginal communities.

The 1996 RCAP final report identified the Aboriginal economic development problem and proposed the latest set of solutions: more land, more capital, improved education and training, more development institutions, sectoral strategies, better governance. Yet, in essence it differs little from the solutions proposed in the early 1970s. The RCAP solution may be more sophisticated, more nuanced, better researched and based upon Aboriginal experience, ideas and desires, but I am starting to question, not the solution, but the production of the solution and the ideas behind it. I am starting to see that there is a complex of ideas that drives the production of solutions. The solutions being proposed for Aboriginal economic development come out of the international development community, which for the last fifty years has been working hard in other areas of the world to solve problems faced by Africans and people in other areas of the "Third World." Many of these efforts have also been remarkably unsuccessful.

As Aboriginal peoples living in Canada, we inhabit a society dominated by the ideas of capitalism and the market. There are strong connections and interdependencies between economy, governance, law and social order. The connection between development and democracy is often invisible: we discuss economic development in the context of governance, never in the context of democracy. We work in a sea of Western ideas about the economy and its development, government and its role, economic and social institutions, and social order. And, for the most part, these ideas have become part of the fabric of our everyday lives and define what we see as the natural order of things.

We also encounter a concept which MacPherson calls "Possessive Individualism." This notion conceives of

> the individual as essentially the proprietor of his own person and capacities, owing nothing to society for them. The individual was seen neither as moral whole nor as part of a larger social whole but as an owner of himself [*sic*].[6]

Furthermore,

> the individual ... is free inasmuch as he is proprietor of his person and capacities. The human essence is freedom from dependence on the wills of others, and freedom is a function of possession. Society becomes a lot of free equal individuals related to each other as proprietors of their own capacities and of what they have acquired by their exercise. Society consists of relations of exchange between proprietors. Political society becomes a calculated device for the protection of property and for the maintenance of an orderly relation of exchange.[7]

MacPherson's idea leads us to the conception of society as based on the notion of exchange and the polity as a the means by which exchanges can occur in an orderly fashion and in which property is protected. The idea of an exchange society becomes our market society. MacPherson's conception of society is at odds with some Aboriginal ideas of society and the sense of community and interdependence inherent in traditional thought.

We also encounter the idea of "progress," arguably one of the most important ideas of the modern age. And an idea that we hold, usually, unconsciously and unquestioningly. Progress implies that there is a pattern of change in human history, that we can know this pattern and that it consists of irreversible changes in one direction. This direction is toward improvement from a less to a more desirable state of affairs. The path towards improvement is generally that which the West has followed.

These are the ideas that motivate our actions as economic developers working in the context of early 21st-century capitalism in Canada. These are the ideas that the education system has brought to the table and presented to us as the ideas to be followed. Aboriginal ideas about the nature of economies have not been part of the education of our children nor of European-Canadian children. Aboriginal ideas have been absent and considered unworthy of serious discussion outside the realms of anthropology.

During the last fifty years, European-Canadians—and I would dare say humankind—and Aboriginal peoples have come to see market society and capitalism as offering the best option for improving human welfare. Since the end of the Second World War, we have also adopted grand strategies for fostering its adoption as the fundamental solution to the problem of poverty. As Aboriginal peoples, we have also come to believe in the idea of progress as postulated by the West, although there is a healthy discussion about what progress entails and a strong desire to create a more holistic definition, one that does not define progress entirely in the material.

The ideas that have animated Aboriginal economic development efforts here have been used in other areas of the world. A 1949 economic mission of the International Bank for Reconstruction and Development to Colombia described its mission thus:

> We have interpreted our terms of reference as calling for a comprehensive and internally consistent program.... The relationships among various sectors of Colombian economy are very complex and intensive analysis of these relationships has been necessary to develop a consistent picture.... This, then, is the reason and justification for an overall program of development. Piecemeal and sporadic efforts are apt to make little impression on the general picture. Only through a generalized attack throughout the whole economy on education, health, housing, food and productivity can the vicious cycle of poverty, ignorance, ill health and low productivity be decisively broken. But once the break is made, the process of economic development can become self-generating.[1]

The report called for improvements and reforms in all aspects of the Colombian economy. The representation of the country's social and economic reality was new and radical. The approach to development was comprehensive, integrated and planned. The report outlined development goals, quantifiable targets, investment needs, design criteria, methodologies and timeframes and sequences for activities.

In its last paragraphs, the report comments on the emerging development approach:

> One cannot escape the conclusion that reliance on natural forces has not produced the most happy results. Equally inescapable is the conclusion that with knowledge of the underlying facts and economic processes, good planning in setting objectives and allocating resources, and determination in carrying out a program for improvements and reforms, a great deal can be done to improve the economic environments by shaping economic policies to meet scientifically ascertained social requirements....
>
> Colombia is presented with an opportunity unique in its long history. Its rich natural resources can be made tremendously productive through the application of modern techniques and efficient practices. Its favorable international debt and trade position enables it to obtain modern equipment and techniques from abroad. International and foreign national organizations have been established to aid underdeveloped areas technically and financially. All that is needed to usher a period of rapid and wide-spread development is a determined effort by the Colombian people themselves. In making such an effort, Colombia would not only accomplish its own salvation but would at the same time furnish an inspiring example to all other underdeveloped areas of the world.

When we deconstruct this statement, we see within it ideas at play in our own work in economic development in aboriginal communities today. The statement says that economic development/salvation is possible. It is a complex task, but there are tools that have been created for such a task (planning, science, technology, development organizations, etc.). These tools have worked in the West and are neutral and universally applicable. They are also desirable. Before development, there was only darkness and natural forces, which did not produce "the most happy result." Development brings light and the possibility of meeting "scientifically ascertained social requirements." Colombians need only to wake from their lethargic sleep and follow the only path to salvation.

What began to occur here, in 1949, was the promotion of a development ideal, an ideal that was later to become seen as the normal course of evolution and progress. The ideal was expressed in language creating a discourse of development which in turn created a social reality.

Escobar, in *Encountering Development*, writes:

> The system ... establishes a discursive practice that sets the rules of the game: who can speak, from what points of view, with what authority, and according to what criteria of expertise; it sets the rules that must be

followed for this or that problem, theory, or object to emerge and be
named, analyzed and eventually transformed into a policy or a plan.

Development has dealt with a myriad of objects over the years: initially
poverty, insufficient technology and capital, rapid population growth,
inadequate public services, then adding cultural attitudes and values,
other racial, religious, geographic or ethnic factors which were believed
to be associated with underdevelopment. These elements were brought to
attention from a widening array of experts: development organizations,
universities and research centres and local indigenous institutions. Over
time, the entire cultural, economic and political geography of indigenous
peoples was brought into the gaze of the expert.

However, we would be remiss if we ignored the role of power in the creation of
objects for study. Power was concentrated in the hands of experts: economists,
demographers, educators, experts in agriculture, public health, management,
government. Institutions, such as the UN, have the moral, professional and legal
authority to name subjects and define strategies; lending agencies had power that
came with capital. The experts—economists, demographers, educators, technical
experts in agriculture, public service, health and law—conducted their observations,
prepared their theories, assessments and programs in institutional bases that are
not part of the local indigenous community.

What we see emerging out of this discourse is a notion of diagnosis and
prescription: a diagnosis of underdevelopment, an examination to find the type
and level of underdevelopment, and the prescription of a cure; all of this occurs
through the observations of experts. What is missing from this approach is people,
more particularly the knowledge of local people.

We can begin to see that one of the effects of these assumptions has been the
increasing institutionalization and professionalization of development and the
establishment of the development industry: development becomes an important
process, too important to be left to those who know little about it. A huge research
industry has also sprung up to provide the observational data for the diagnosis and
prescription of problems and solutions. A politics of knowledge emerges which
allows experts to classify problems and formulate polices, to pass judgement on
entire social groups and forecast the future, in short, to produce a set of truths and
norms about them. Knowledge becomes real and useful only when produced by
experts. Local knowledge becomes displaced.

An African scholar, quoted by Escobar says:

our own history, culture and practices, good or bad, are discovered and
translated into the journals of the North and come back to us re-conceptu-
alized, couched in the languages and paradigms which make it all sound
so new and novel.

In this way, the development discourse sets the modern against the traditional. The
traditional must be transformed into the modern. The traditional becomes an obstacle
to the establishment of the modern. Development must always lead to the modern.

This notion of transformation, present in the 1950s, is still present today. Somehow the indigenous must be transformed. Escobar comments:

> Development was conceived as a top-down, ethnocentric and technocractic approach which treated people and cultures as abstract concepts, statistical figures to be moved up and down in the charts of "progress."

> Development was conceived not as a cultural process (cultural was a residual variable, to disappear with the advance of modernization) but instead a system of more-or-less universally applicable technical interventions designed to deliver some "badly needed" goods to a "target" population.

This is the development world that Aboriginal people encounter: a world of scientific modernism, of economic policy and instruments, strategic interventions, research, technology, technical assistance, human resources, capital resources, land and labour. The Borg of development threatens to absorb and transform us.

The rise of development fosters a view of social life as a technical problem, as a matter of rational decision and management to be entrusted to a group of people whose specialized knowledge equips them well for the task. The development professional becomes a valued person. Development also assumes a teleology to the extent that it presumes that the underdeveloped will sooner or later be reformed. It reproduces the separation between reformers and those to be reformed by keeping alive the premise of the underdeveloped as different and inferior, as having a limited humanity in relation to the dominant group. The development gaze aims not to simply discipline individuals but to transform the conditions of their lives—to create a productive normalized social environment.

What is also created is a relationship between the developers and the developing: a dance that locks both into a difficult and troubling relationship. The developer has the power, ideas, capital, technology; the developing, wishing access to these things, needs to play their assigned role. Given this social and political reality, can development occur?

There are some encouraging signs.

The development paradigm, despite its almost universal application, is showing some edgy willingness to accommodate other objectives. What are called alternative development theories are at least being discussed. A new category of development theories called "people-centred theories" is starting to appear. The original development theories focused their attention on economic growth and economic transformation, they did not attempt to explain the political and cultural changes that occur during the development process. Only recently have they come to include political and cultural considerations. There is also a rejection in some places of the universalist assumption.

The resistance of Aboriginal peoples to the universalism embedded in development is starting to be felt. The desire to use CED as a fundamental approach as well as the desire to use traditional knowledge as the basis of social action are all excellent indicators that the Borg are slowing a bit. The strong desire of Aboriginal peoples to maintain a distinct cultural identity and to have this identity reflected in and respected in the marketplace is also a strong indicator. The gathering up of power and capital through the land claims and treaty process is providing the means to do more than resist. The creation of Aboriginal institutions of research and advocacy is creating a strong aboriginal technical presence to counter the presence of outside experts.

Yet, I think that this is not enough. The Borg are too powerful to resist in the usual fashion. For Aboriginals, the way forward is I think through traditional thought and knowledge. This thought and knowledge has been systematically excluded from the discursive world of development. Now is the time to put it into the system. Can we have improvements in our material lives without being absorbed? Are there ways to make the market society conform to indigenous ideas about society? How do we prevent the uneven distribution of wealth that we see around us? How do we create economies of respect and reciprocity?

The Department of Social and Economic Affairs of the United Nations in a 1951 report entitled *Measures for the Economic Development of Underdeveloped Countries* expresses the kind of thinking we need to fight against:

> There is a sense in which rapid economic progress is impossible without painful adjustments. Ancient philosophies have to be scrapped: old social institutions have to disintegrate; bonds of caste, creed and race have to burst; and large numbers of persons who cannot keep up with progress have to have their expectations of a comfortable life frustrated. Very few communities are willing to pay the full price of economic progress.

The report suggested that economic progress extracts a cost: the total transformation of a society. The development Borg are bent on creating this transformation and recreating us in their image. Is resistance futile? If not, then how does one resist?

I believe that we resist through stating and restating our own objectives as Aboriginal peoples: for cultural distinctiveness, for societies based upon traditional ideas, values and customs, for sustainable development, for equitable distribution of wealth, for the idea of progress that is broad and multi-faceted, for communities that are more than markets.

We need, I believe, to develop a regime of understanding and practice that affirms, fosters, expands and translates Aboriginal understandings of progress into individual and collective action that works to create an economy that affirms Aboriginal cultural identities and the autonomy of cultures and that sanctions social structures and values. We start by conceptualizing development in positive contributory terms, acting out of strongly held values and ideas about how society and economy ought to operate.

Traditional thought requires first of all an acknowledgment of strengths, of what can be contributed. It requires that one's actions are based on these strengths. Aboriginal thought requires us to pay attention to our strengths, to build upon those strengths, to use our strengths as the centre, to act on our strengths and balance the strength of our ideals. This is the most difficult part of the task that we have as Aboriginal development workers.

The most difficult challenge we face is that we are attempting to do undertake these tasks in an environment in which we ourselves are only now beginning to reaffirm these ideals, and only now beginning to discover that they can make a difference in our lives. And we are doing this in an environment in which we are standing under the gaze of the development community, and the development experts.

We are also pulled in different directions by our own desires for a material life. We want to be consumers, we want to consume in the same way as those around us. At the same time, we see that a life of consumption is not the life that we would build for ourselves if we were going to build a life founded upon traditional thought.

I think that this is one of the important educational efforts that we can make as universities and as academics: to reflect upon the practice that we are engaged in, so that we do not engage in practices unconsciously, so that we ask critical questions about what we are doing and what we are proposing, so that we begin to be able to engage the Borg more thoughtfully.

We can then return to *Aboriginaltimes* and see it not just as the unconscious acceptance of the Borg but as an important statement about sharing and aboriginal vision. The danger remains, however, that in the struggle to overcome the time of great pain, we unconsciously accept the transformation as represented by the Borg.

Notes

Adapted from a talk at the Sharing Voices, Value(s) Added conference on Aboriginal economic development, College of Commerce, University of Saskatchewan, March 2002.

1. Hawthorne, ed., Indian Affairs Canada, 1966
2. I use the term West, Western, to describe a suite of ideas emanating from the philosophical traditions of western Europe and North America, primarily those which arose after that historical period called by European historians "the Enlightenment."
3. *Aboriginaltimes* 5, No. 11, October 2001. Calgary, AB: Cree-Ative Media.
4. *Aboriginaltimes*, No. 2, October 1996. Calgary, AB: Clicks and Bits Publishing.
5. I always have a problem choosing a term to describe the collective of Canadians who are not of aboriginal culture or heritage. For the majority of time in the history of Canada, the cultural heritage of this group has been European and I've chosen the term European-Canadian. Sometimes I use the term "white" but those who would be called white don't like to have attention drawn to the colour of their skin, so out of respect, I use "European."
6. MacPherson, 3.
7. Ibid.

Bibliography

Cornell, Stephen and Joseph Kalt. *What can Tribes Do? Strategies and Institutions in American Indian Economic Development*. University of California at Los Angeles, 1992.

Dyck, Noel. *What is the Indian "Problem"? Tutelage and Resistance in Canadian Indian Administration*. St. John's, NL: Memorial University, 1991.

Escobar, Arturo. *Encountering Development: The Making and Unmaking of the Third World*. Princeton, NJ: Princeton University Press, 1995.

MacPherson, C. B. *The Political Theory of Possessive Individualism: Hobbes to Locke*. Oxford: University Press, 1962.

Martinussen, John. *Society, State and Market, A Guide to Competing Theories of Development*. Halifax, NS: Fernwood Publishing, 1995.

Pollard, Sidney. *The Idea of Progress: History and Society*. Middlesex: Penguin, 1968.

Rahnema, Majid and Victoria Bawtree. *The Post Development Reader*. Halifax, NS: Fernwood Publishing, 1997.

Smith, Dean Howard. *Modern Tribal Development: Paths to Self-Sufficiency and Cultural Integrity in Indian Country*. Walnut Creek, CA: Altamira Press, 2001.

Supply and Services Canada. "Sharing the Harvest, The Road to Self-Reliance." *The Report of National Round Table on Aboriginal Economic Development and Resources*. Royal Commission on Aboriginal Peoples, 1993.

Kathryn Church

Working Like Crazy on *Working Like Crazy*: Imag(in)ing CED Practice through Documentary Film

If I were a witch I'd get heard.
(Susan Ashby, courier, A-Way Express)

Taking Off

Air Canada Flight 01 is late taking off. Weather reports warn of strong headwinds over the Bering Sea and suggest the prudence of loading more fuel. So says the Captain. Could he not have kept that little gem to himself? I am already nervous about the daunting journey ahead: eighteen flying hours until I reach Taipei City (via Tokyo). There I will be met by an organizer for the fifth Asian NGO Forum, an event at which I am a guest. One of my duties will be to screen and discuss *Working Like Crazy*. It is the prospect of sharing this rare documentary—subtitled in Mandarin through the efforts of my Taiwanese colleagues—that has me on the tarmac. Released by the National Film Board of Canada in 1999, the film profiles six psychiatric survivors[1] who work in survivor-run community businesses.[2] Their stories reveal not just the contradictions of survivor economic development but the multi-dimensionality of the survivor community. They challenge prevalent notions of the "mentally ill," and create the film's anti-discriminatory message:

- Laurie Hall's incredible journey has taken her from the isolation of a psychiatric hospital to executive director of A-Way Express Couriers.

- Diana Capponi has transformed the grief and rage of family violence into a passion for justice as the director of the Ontario Council of Alternative Businesses (OCAB).

• Courier Susan Ashby's love of animals has transformed her in the eyes of the neighborhood children from the "cuckoo lady" to the "rat lady," a title she much prefers.

• Patricia Fowler is surprised to have lived into her 40s. But she has fought a crushing sense of worthlessness to become indispensable as OCAB's administrative assistant.

• Scott Benness was told by the vocational rehabilitation counselors that he could do nothing. Now he's proving them wrong.

• Graham Brown uses his work to fight against depression and sleeping his life away. It's all part of his plan, "the plan to get back to being a man."

These characters take the viewer into three Toronto sites: A-Way Express Couriers, The Raging Spoon diner and catering company, and Fresh Start Cleaning. Foreshadowed by the economic activities of The Mad Market in the 1960s, initiatives such as these became particularly prominent in the 1990s as entrepreneurialism in Ontario proliferated. Toronto was a hot spot but small cooperative ventures appeared in several other communities as well. Jump-started by supportive funding policies, they were strengthened by the work of the Ontario Council of Alternative Businesses (OCAB). Founded in 1993, OCAB is an umbrella organization for the six to eight economic initiatives that operate at any given time in various parts of the province. Its intent is to provide hands-on assistance with business development and community organizing including producing resource materials, identifying and supporting leaders and influencing legislation and policy.[3]

The plane finally pulls away from the terminal. As it lumbers heavily down the runway, I reflect on *Working Like Crazy*'s extraordinary trajectory.[4] In four short years, it moved from its Toronto origins to regional screenings/discussions across Ontario, and from there into the hands of mental health activists half-way around the globe: Northern Ireland, Scotland, England and now Taiwan. Having been there from the beginning, I know that another cast of characters—hidden somewhat behind the scenes—orchestrated this passage. In Canada, the project was conceived and implemented by a handful of psychiatric survivors loosely organized as the In-Your-Face Learning Academy.[5] Key players were Diana Capponi and Laurie Hall (both introduced above), and David Reville, former city/provincial politician who now runs his own consulting firm. These survivor leaders partnered with me and two independent filmmakers: Gwynne Basen in Montreal and Laura Sky (SkyWorks) in Toronto. Together we constituted the reference group for the film's development and distribution.

As the only "non-survivor" member of the Learning Academy, my role was to help "bridge" the filmmakers with the survivor community, and to translate for them some of the complexities of that culture. As a researcher/ally of the psychiatric survivor movement, my task was to analyze and document what happened. Over the past number of years, I have written several articles describing psychiatric survivor economic development as an approach that emphasizes human process: flexible organizations, peer training and participatory management.[6] I have written plain language texts that describe this approach as "the business behind the business," [7] and I have been part of a determined attempt to define CED evaluation criteria that takes it into account.[8]

My contribution to this book leaves behind the foundational work of articulating and legitimating "model" CED practice from the survivor standpoint, for the pressing and complex matter of its public reception. *Working Like Crazy* is the vehicle for my investigation. In the following pages, I tell two tales about the film's distribution. The first highlights key lessons that the reference group derived from collaborating to organize the Ontario tour.[9] The second builds on the group's "Brit-tour" experience to make policy suggestions.[10] These tales are intended to take up the potential of community economic development for advocacy and organizing not just locally but internationally. By "working like crazy" to create and promote *Working Like Crazy*, the reference group demonstrated the implications of CED practice for broad-scale knowledge and policy development.

Encountering the Audience/s: Three Dilemmas

In 2000, filmmaker Laura Sky received funds from the Trillium Foundation that enabled SkyWorks to undertake the dissemination of *Working Like Crazy* by organizing a series of regional screenings across Ontario. She hired me and David Reville to join her as project consultants.[11] With a vital organizational interest in this process, Diana Capponi proposed that film distribution become a leadership development exercise for the survivor "stars" of the film. In response, our plan mobilized consultant/survivor panels for two screenings in each of seven sites: one co-sponsored with a local self-help group for psychiatric survivors; the other intended for mental health professionals and open to the public. These meetings enabled us to encounter a range of audiences whose reactions to the film I have crystallized into three themes.[12]

Probing the politics of laughter

What most surprised the consultant team about the *Working Like Crazy* screenings was the emergence of laughter as a consistent and puzzling dimension of audience response. As soon as I noticed it, I began to track the laugh-lines in the film, keeping notes about who laughed where. My analysis of this data points to humour as a faultline along which psychiatric survivor and professional/student audiences form two solitudes.[13] Much of the survivor humour—delicious to "insiders"—is opaque to "outsiders."[14] The question that emerged was whether professional and survivor audiences were even "seeing" the same film.

Most survivor audiences responded with laughter from the very first spoken lines of the film, rising to Laurie's softly asserted "Screw that (unemployment)! We'll make our own businesses," or Susan's wry description of schizophrenia as a condition in which "You don't get much privacy." The film fostered "insider" recognitions and a sense of hope. Explaining why they liked it, one survivor noted that "at no time when I was watching it did I feel helpless." Responses such as these were a tremendous confirmation that the filmmakers' standpoint truly was that of the survivor community rather than the psychiatric establishment.

"Outsider" responses were noticeably different and, in a sense, more complex. Members of these audiences—mostly students or mental health service providers—were slower to laugh, laughed less throughout the film and laughed in different places than did survivor audiences. For example, a Toronto audience comprised of graduate students in policy studies was quiet throughout an entire screening. "They seem to think about 'mental illness' as a uniformly serious topic," I wrote to my colleagues, "and therefore didn't know whether it was okay to laugh when something struck them as funny. They were worried about being politically incorrect." The film gave an audience of psychology students what appeared to be their first exposure to the psychiatric survivor sense of humour. So divergent is the film's portrayal from what they had been taught that these viewers—and many more—had trouble believing the main characters were actually "crazy." In their failure to perceive our "stars" as capable of a full range of human emotions, we discovered the prejudices of professional training.

Curiously enough, psychiatric survivors in one small city did not laugh when Laurie recalls attempts made by nurses in the mental hospital to "correct" her supposedly wrongheaded lesbianism. Either they heard this as a serious story (although Laurie's amused telling spares viewers the obvious pain of her circumstances) or sexual orientation was not an open topic in this location. By contrast, highly sensitized to issues of gender and sexualities, Toronto graduate students were openly responsive to the intersection of sexual politics and psychiatric treatment at the heart of Laurie's story.

Psychiatric survivors and mental health audiences alike laughed when Susan recalls taking her rat for a walk, an event that transformed her in the eyes of the neighborhood kids from the Cuckoo Lady to the Rat Lady. "So, the pets have been important," she asserts to the camera, telling her truth but completely missing its pathos. This is one of the film's most complex moments. Laughter generated here was so full of nuances that it was difficult to read in any audience. But there is no doubt that some of it was at Susan's expense—for it lacked the grief and rage that would actually have honoured her analysis.

Changing the subject

Working Like Crazy is structured by atypical stories as well as de-medicalized sites, interactions and images of the "mentally ill." Despite this, many viewers insisted on posing questions within the established psychiatric framework. The film invited viewers to "talk about it otherwise." Yet, they reproduced familiar conversations and debates—tracing paths of thought, speech and feeling that are as worn as old linoleum. They resolutely discussed what they already knew how to discuss rather than what they saw/felt or were coming to know differently. By contrast, the consultant team was very much in the mood to challenge dominant discourses. We wanted to change the subject.

Resistance to our desire was most pronounced among people who reacted to *Working Like Crazy* as "anti-psychiatry." The most dramatic examples of this happened with bureaucrats and educators. So, for example, the coordinator of a program in a prominent university insisted on screening the film personally before allowing it to be viewed by psychiatry interns. His response was that it did not reflect recent changes in the treatment of "mental illness." Consequently, the Department of Psychiatry did not sponsor a screening—even for the purpose of generating debate! Health Canada took a similar position when I approached them to consider financial support for the film's cross-Canada distribution. After viewing it, their representative accused us of taking up a one-sided, 1950s view of psychiatry that was polarizing, conflictual and divisive to the field of community mental health. I disagreed but that did not change the fact that no assistance was forthcoming.

The positioning of *Working Like Crazy* in relation to psychiatry and its treatment system remains one of the film's most contentious features. The stories portrayed unsettled entrenched power relations of the mental health field. One way to re-establish order is to de-legitimize them as "anti-psychiatry." But it is important not to allow the psychiatry/anti-psychiatry debate to set the terms for discussion (again). Treatment issues are merely part of the complex backdrop—historical and current—against which survivors do economic development. What is more important, what the film does well is to show psychiatric survivors creating community life by addressing their needs for employment and a decent income. What the consultant team tried to do in the regional screenings was challenge our audiences to drop the standard, predictable talk about "the mentally ill" long enough to have that conversation.

Promoting collective action

One of the advantages of community economic development—rarely spoken or written of in mainstream literature—is the opening it gives marginalized people to appropriate the powerful discourse of business in an increasingly entrepreneurial culture. At their best, survivor-run businesses help people to slowly redefine themselves, moving from identifications as "mental patients" and "welfare recipients" to "employees"—whether as couriers, cleaners, carpenters, caterers or business developers and managers. This shift can be very positive in opening up de-pathologized subject positions from which people can become active in re/constructing their lives. However, it is not without substantial risks. Primary among them is that communities of vulnerable people might uncritically do business development according to private sector values: individual initiative, competition and fiscal profit as the bottom line measure of success.

Although clearly forced to struggle with this worldview, the psychiatric survivor vision of CED is to "use the economy to build the community" rather than the other way around. However, because *Working Like Crazy* was created as a "why to" rather than a "how to" on economic development, it did not explicitly communicate this distinction. Doing so became an important part of the consultant's role in post-screening discussions—and an ongoing source of discomfort. Too often, we started out from a position of appearing to promote small business development as a panacea for the ills of the economically excluded. Because this idea is already active in both disability and service provider communities, it took hard work to (again) begin to "change the subject."

In one city, for example, a woman talked about the frustrations of cycling through mental health difficulties, having and losing jobs, ending up unemployed and on social assistance. A man then stood up and endorsed entrepreneurship as a good option for people in her (and his) situation. He had found his own small business a useful way of coping. This point was then further entrenched by comments from service providers involved in conventional CED. As facilitators, while affirming whatever success these viewers had achieved, we struggled to shift discussion away from the single entrepreneur, single job approach and into the collective nature of alternative businesses.

Working Like Crazy generated a strong flow of stories about poverty, the difficulties people face earning an income and questions about changes to vital social assistance and disability pension benefit plans. It became clear that the reason so many people were drawn to business development was that they were unemployed, stripped of adequate state assistance and thrust onto meager personal resources. The consultant team soon realized that we should have gone into the distribution process with a more explicit plan for addressing these realities. With hindsight, we saw the opportunity to do some organizing around the provincially imposed "cap" on the earnings of people who receive benefits. Disability benefits issues were ripe for coalition building and political education. Throughout the screenings, we discovered the need to develop strategies for leadership in this area and to mobilize on a broader basis.

Imagining a Better World: Three Recommendations

In 2001, after almost a year of organizing and fundraising, I spent two weeks with Laura Sky and three psychiatric survivors (Diana, Laurie, Patricia) travelling with *Working Like Crazy* to Belfast, Edinburgh, Hull, Brighton and London. We came away with rich impressions about users of mental health services in these cities, about the systems that claim to support them and the policies that shape their lives. When you travel, you expect to be confronted with language and customs that are strange to you. However, I was struck more by similarities than differences. Upon my return, I crystallized those impressions into three key recommendations pertinent to fostering survivor economic development:

We need good income and benefits policies.

As in Canada, service recipients in Britain are generally poor and unemployed. They are boxed into public "benefits" schemes that use "caps" and clawbacks to punish them for part-time earnings. They are afraid to risk employment of any sort. This may be the reason why some were unsettled by images of working survivors and the optimistic tone of *Working Like Crazy*. Many service recipients who attended the screenings were intrigued by the notion of starting their own business, especially the possibility of more flexible hours and less discrimination than mainstream employment. Most assumed, however, that they would be single entrepreneurs, and that they would be required to be financially self-sufficient in both start-up capital and subsequent revenue production. And that seemed like a tall order.

On each occasion, we worried that the film was feeding people's imaginations around the possibilities of "doing business" without adequately portraying the material base on which its examples depend. To clarify, the situation in Ontario is precisely the same as in the U.K.—both in terms of people's hopes and structural barriers:

- People on welfare/disability pension are allowed to earn only $160 before they face deductions on their earnings of 75 cents on the dollar. If you are making $10.00 per hour, you have reached your limit after only 16 hours. After that, your net gain is $2.50 per hour.

- If employees work enough hours to come off the pension, they lose their prescription drug card. Fear of having to wait to be reinstated or having to pay for very expensive drugs keeps most survivors from working more hours.

- Most survivors who work in alternative businesses are on both the Ontario Disability Support Program and Canada Pension Plan (CPP). CPP has never said clearly whether a claimant can work, even as a volunteer. It often depends upon the person's worker but the fear is that any earnings will trigger a reassessment of the person's disability status. For many that fear is also a deterrent.

- CPP is taxable income. A psychiatric survivor with a small amount of earned income plus CPP benefits is looking at more tax than they can generally afford.

In the face of these restrictions, the primary reason that psychiatric survivors are working in survivor-run businesses in Ontario is political. In the 1990s, through "kitchen table" research, accessible documentation, advocacy and public relations, they were able to sell the notion that it is legitimate for employees to support themselves using both social assistance and income earned by performing permanent part-time jobs.

Similarly, survivor businesses operate using a combination of public dollars and employee-generated revenues. In general, grant moneys from the Ministry of Health cover core administrative expenses while employees generate the revenue to pay their own salaries. The advantage is that survivor businesses cost the Ministry less than other community initiatives and certainly less than institutional services. One study shows that service use by people involved in survivor businesses reduces hospital inpatient days, crisis contacts and number of hospital admissions. Conservatively, the estimated savings are roughly $13,000 per survivor per year. That adds up to big savings for the system.

To summarize, psychiatric survivor businesses in Ontario operate on a hybrid public-private model. They generate independence but do not presume complete self-sufficiency either for the individual or the business. This arrangement is far from perfect. Perfect would be a guaranteed annual income; almost perfect would be a substantial increase in the rate of pension benefits; headed in the right direction would be the following basic policy suggestions:

- Raise the limit on allowable earnings for people on disability pension;

- Graduate the clawback on earnings over the allowable limit;

- Rapidly reinstate people who go off benefits in order to work and find themselves in difficulty;

- Separate the prescription drug card out as a benefit independent of living pensions;

- Establish consistency between levels of government in benefit regulations.

We need policies that support independent psychiatric survivor initiatives.

Mental health professionals at our U.K. screenings were much like their Canadian counterparts: cautiously curious, never openly hostile—even in response to the scenes that some have labelled anti-psychiatry—and seemingly genuine in their desire to understand community economic development. They are boxed into an uninspiring "range" of vocational program options—none of which deliver much in the way of "real work for real pay." By contrast, all of the talk about CED sounded promising. People got excited and, for the most part, that was a good sign.

Service providers are essential allies and a fundamental resource for survivor economic development. But their eagerness in this area makes me uneasy. As in Canada, providers in the U.K. tended to take up business development as a new edge of the service system, as a set of activities that could expand their program options and professional expertise. I do not see it that way. From my perspective, the real professional opportunity here is to use business development to re/direct resources to the larger project of building the psychiatric survivor sector.

In the 1990s, the Ontario government bought into economic development as a mental health strategy in a big way. This gave psychiatric survivors and other vulnerable communities access to fresh sources of funding and new ways of defining themselves to the public. While struggling with the private sector values that accompany the provision of goods and services, they have attempted to advance "the business behind the business" of local economics. This (somewhat hidden) agenda goes beyond the income/profit, work/jobs and skills training agenda to encompass broader processes of social and political development. It includes organizing, advocacy, knowledge creation and leadership development.

In each of these spheres, survivor control is a core principle. The point is not to segregate (or ghettoize) this community but to build group skills, strength and solidarity by ensuring against a reliance on professional experts. By implication, evaluators have to wean themselves off individual "improvement" as the primary criterion for success and take a closer look at group formation and functioning. Thus, what interests me about the businesses that I have studied in the past few years is what happens when you bring people together who share a similar life experience in a collaborative effort for change. In that collectivizing, participants have a powerful opportunity to begin to analyze what has happened to them, and to formulate new and different kinds of expectations and demands.

There are tremendous implications here for professional practice. Over the past number of years, funding policies in Ontario have forced psychiatric survivors into becoming partners with service-provider organizations in order to stay alive. The intent is to minimize the number of transfer agencies but the effect has been the growth of an entrenched partnership culture that precludes or is suspicious of independent survivor activity. At least in the beginning, provider-user partnerships are important for strong economic development; however, it is essential that user groups be able to enter and leave these relationships of their own volition.

To summarize, successful survivor economic development requires policies and funding mechanisms that support the formation and growth of democratically run, local self-help groups and the substantive participation of their members in decisions that shape the mental health system. What this achieves over time is the emergence of local survivor leaders capable of taking on a range of projects, including economic development.

We need a broad-based policy agenda.

A decade ago, Jean-Marc Fontan divided his review of the CED literature into dominant and contesting definitions. He referred to the dominant definition as liberal local development: processes that "are aimed at repairing the economic fabric of the private sector in order to create jobs." He referred to the alternative definition as progressive local development: processes that "invest the economy with social concerns."[15] This is an important distinction that was not clearly articulated by those promoting economic initiatives in the U.K. mental health field. In fact, "social firms"—the vanguard of this movement—appear to be a prime example of the dominant liberal type: They are about employment and they have a market orientation.[16]

Given people's desperate need for income, and the systemic barriers that exclude them from regular employment, it is difficult to dispute the "goodness" of this agenda. And yet, buying into approaches that emphasize work/jobs alone leads to "repair" strategies that ignore deep structural inequities. As brilliant and hopeful as it sometimes is, CED is no adequate substitute for using enlightened macro-level economic and fiscal policies to address the crises of jobs and poverty. It should not deflect us from engaging with more political responses to economic deprivation.

I hardly need say that millions of people face enormous problems of poverty and unemployment, globally as well as locally. Realistically, survivor-run businesses will have only a marginal impact on the mental health piece of this situation. By even trying them out, practitioners risk appearing to support neoconservative policies that dismantle state-supported social service provision in favour of individual self-reliance through entrepreneurship. So, even as we turn our attention to economic development, we must continue to fight for access and high quality support in the beleaguered areas of health and community/social services, subsidized housing and criminal justice.

In the world that I imagine, we would also recognize the learning needs/capacities of psychiatric survivors and turn our attention to education. My particular interest is to see policy development and practice in support of survivor-run businesses as sites of informal (non-credentialed) learning and the creation of knowledge rooted in the survivor standpoint. Several years ago, with colleagues from Montreal, I completed a study of what we call "social learning" accomplished through community organizations by people who are excluded from the labour market. We found that sites such as A-Way Express foster informal learning in three ways:

- Organizational learning refers to the ways in which community organizations learn to build programs that will fly in the new economy while retaining their historical concerns for social and economic justice.

- Solidarity learning refers to the identifications that are formed and the strategies that are developed simply because these settings bring together people who are typically isolated.

- Identity learning refers to the new sense of self that emerges as a result of participant immersion in organizational culture and their contact with other participants.

Learning such as this occurs spontaneously and incidentally in survivor-run businesses. It occurs at the level of ordinary, taken-for-granted personal interactions, and in the context of friendships between employees. Because it is central to the liberating potential of these organizations, my colleagues and I would like to see the learning dimensions of CED recognized, preserved and actively enhanced. In fact, the art of survivor-directed CED is to work the tension between its regulatory agenda—often emerging in tension with state funding requirements—and its liberatory agenda—often emerging informally through social learning.

To summarize, in keeping with my continuous plea for the broad view it is important that service providers press governments for more progressive income and benefits policies. It is important that we foster the growth of survivor groups and survivor leaders. It is important that we open funded spaces within the system, by allocating certain lines of our own agency budgets to survivor contractors and by lobbying for the funding of separate survivor-directed initiatives. Most of all, it is important that we move the work of economic development into the hands of the survivor community. If we do not transfer power and resources, all we are engaged in here is creating a new piece of the existing service system that will continue to operate to our advantage.

Landings

The return trip is easier: a mere ten hours of flying from Taipei to Vancouver and then the Red Eye to Toronto. Uncomfortably awake for most of the journey, I have plenty of time to review and analyze a flood of impressions. My hosts worked me hard during the NGO Forum: two formal papers,[17] two film screenings with discussion, visits to two psychiatric hospitals, and a day-long visit to a family-based community organization engaged in building a water-delivery business for their "mentally ill" members. [18]

Like their Canadian and British counterparts, Taiwanese audiences were enthusiastic about *Working Like Crazy*. However, even more sharply I perceived the importance of a cultural interpreter who could take viewers beyond just the translation of words. My talks contextualized the film in terms of the social relations that shaped its production, most significantly, a well-established psychiatric survivor movement whose actions call for new forms of professional and bureaucratic practice. Without this background, it would have been even more difficult than it was for viewers to take in the images they were seeing.

There is no psychiatric survivor movement in Taiwan. (Indeed, martial law for the entire population ended a scant decade ago.) There is no history of survivor leadership or action independent of professional services and/or family support. The work of service providers remains heavily defined by the psychiatric establishment—faithfully reproduced in Taiwan by practitioner-training in North American and European universities.[19] Perhaps this explains why I identified only one laugh-line from audiences in Taipei. "He's just checking to see if I'm taking my medication," says Scott of the ten minutes his psychiatrist spends with him every three months. Then, turning a rueful grin to the camera declares "I can *do* that!" This quip elicited a surge of merriment particularly from the film's more medicated viewers.

But more often than not I was confronted with polite silence or disbelief. "What you are showing us is utopia," my viewers declared. They looked for (without finding) the medical presence they expected would govern the business sites. Where did professional intervention occur? How was it organized? I was asked pointed questions about the economics of the businesses. How did they possibly sustain themselves? Where did the money come from? And I was told that "our mentally ill" were too low-functioning to figure as potential workers in such initiatives. Here, then, was a different configuration of familiar themes: intriguing absences of laughter intersecting with fresh refusals to change the subject in ways that, again, call for collective action and enlightened policies.

How will this process begin? Carried by whom? According to my hosts, the necessary desire and determination lie with the family-member associations. "You have marked an important footprint on the development of Taiwanese family self-help movements," I was told. "They saw themselves in your presentation and gained strength from it. We will continue to work with them. You have become a common language for us."[20] This is a daunting thought, particularly since my journey to Taipei reawakened previous wonderings. Does *Working Like Crazy* portray a utopian vision? Is it more an act of imagination than documentary reality?

As fate would have it, while pondering these questions I saw A-Way Express courier Susan Ashby on the street. Package in hand, head down against a bitter wind, she was clearly en route to a delivery. The encounter caused me to recall one of her most potent onscreen comments: "If I was a witch I'd get heard," she declared. However I manage to resolve my questions about filmic representation, the magic of *Working Like Crazy* lies in its proliferation of Susan's voice and her story on three continents.

Notes

1. "Psychiatric survivor"is the term of choice among leaders of the mental health self-help groups that I have worked with in Canada. It replaces terms such as "patient," "client," "consumer," and "consumer/survivor" in my vocabulary. In this chapter I also use "service user" and "service recipient" because these terms were operant in the U.K.

2. These particular descriptions are taken from the National Film Board of Canada promotional material for *Working Like Crazy.* The film was a co-production of the National Film Board and Skyworks Charitable Foundation in association with TV Ontario, with the participation of the Ontario Council of Alternative Businesses, Ontario Ministry of Health and Long-Term Care, the Centre for Addictions and Mental Health and the Trillium Foundation. The film can be ordered from the NFB: www.nfb.ca.

3. While several key resources are listed here, a complete bibliography of references for psychiatric survivor economic development (published and unpublished) can be obtained from the author at k3church@ryerson.ca.

4. I have not included here any description of the film's development. While I cannot do justice to that process in this chapter, I can say that it took two years of hard work. Our labours during the first year focused on situating the filmmakers to learn the key players, sites, issues and politics of the psychiatric survivor community. It was during this time that they identified the characters and stories they wanted to feature in the film. The focus of the second year was filming and editing from rough cut to final print. Strategic discussions and fundraising were ongoing activities across both years.

5. I wish to acknowledge the efforts of Dr. Mary Chambers and Carol E. Kelly in Northern Ireland, Dr. Steve Tilley in Edinburgh, David Glenister in Hull, and Dr.

Tessa Parkes in Brighton. I wish to acknowledge the significant role played by Dr. Frank Wang in getting me to Taipei City, and translating the formal papers that I gave; also to Debra Tien, Executive Director of the Career Foundation which hosted the Asia Forum. Special thanks to Jung-Che Chang, my translator for the week who also opened my eyes to his Taipei. My trip was financially supported by the Canadian Trade Office in Taipei with gratitude to Sumeeta Chandavarkar, General Relations Deputy Director.

6.　　Church, "Business (not quite) As Usual," in *Community Economic Development*; Church, "Strange Bedfellows" in *Social Economy*.

7.　　Church, *Because of Where We've Been*.

8.　　Lachance, Church, Shragge and Fontan, *Appropriating evaluation*.

9.　　Laurie Hall established an electronic listserv for the *Working Like Crazy* reference group in September1999. The key themes of the film's Ontario tour emerged in this conversational space, in the witty, pungent and uncensored dialogue that it enabled between members. The listserv facilitated our strategic discussions about points of resonance between the film and our audiences, and significantly enhanced our leadership and mutual support.

10.　　I wrote this second tale initially at the request of the Scottish Development Corporation. I wish to acknowledge their financial support of the work and their permission to publish a revised version of it in this volume.

11.　　I wrote this section of the chapter for SkyWorks' final project report to the Trillium Foundation. It was part of a larger document also called "Working like Crazy on Working like Crazy" with David Reville and Laura Sky as co-authors.

12.　　For the purposes of this chapter, I eliminated one theme that was present in the original Trillium report. It described the reference group's discussion about who should "represent" the film in the community screenings. At issue was whether Laura and I, and to a lesser extent David, were adequate for the task given our "outsider" status with the survivor community. We believed ourselves capable – not an easy point to make in the world of survivor politics. The resolution in favour of the mixed teams was a capitulation that led to some good outcomes but did not completely satisfy my longing for a different, less essentialist position on the question of "Whose voice/knowledge is this anyway?" In fact, it was the moment in which I realized that I needed to leave the borderland location in which I worked with(out) the survivor community to establish a broader, more diverse base for my work as a producer of anti-oppressive knowledge. The complexities of this process are such that I have not featured it in this writing.

13.　　I first observed this dynamic in the early '90s when, in the course of my doctoral research, I studied a provincial consultation on community mental health services legislation. In this forum service providers often accused service users of "bad manners." Conflicts arose between the two groups because each operated from a behavioral code (linguistic styles, body postures, voice tones, speech habits) that was different from the other. The pivotal issue, acted out indirectly in all kinds of interactions, was whether and how deeply personal and emotional experience would be included as a form of knowledge. My analysis of the *Working Like Crazy* laugh-lines recognizes and enhances this phenomenon. Do people laugh out of fear, anxiety, hostility, compassion and/or recognition? These points give access to complex social and power relations portrayed in the film.

14.   For a good discussion of insider/outsider distinction, see Uma Narayan, "Working together across difference: Some considerations on emotions and political practice." *Hypatia*, 31-47.

15.   Fontan, *A Critical Review of Canadian, American and European Community Economic Development Literature.*

16.   This characterization is based primarily on remarks made by Dr. Bob Grove in his presentation to the *Working Like Crazy* screening workshop in Brighton, England.

17.   The first paper was about "mad people's history" in English Canada, while the second focused on the process of critical autobiography as social science.

18.   The name of this organization is the Hsin-I Rehabilitation United Families/ Caregivers Association.

19.   Ironically, while attending the NGO Forum and discussing the conditions affecting marginalized groups in Taipei, I had the odd experience of attending a "wine 'em and dine 'em" recruiting soiree hosted by the University of Toronto in a swank downtown hotel.

20.   With his inimitable style, Dr. Wang made this comment in our email correspondence after the event.

Bibliography

Church, Kathryn. "Business (not quite) As Usual: Psychiatric survivors and Community Economic Development in Ontario." In *Community Economic Development: In Search of Empowerment*, edited by Eric Shragge. Montreal: Black Rose, 1997.

———. *Because of Where We've Been: The Business Behind the Business of Psychiatric Survivor Economic Development.* Toronto: Ontario Council of Alternative Businesses, 1997.

———. "Strange Bedfellows: Seduction of a Social Movement." In *Social Economy: International Perspectives and Debates*, edited by Eric Shragge and Jean-Marc Fontan. Montreal: Black Rose, 2000.

Fontan, Jean-Marc. *A Critical Review of Canadian, American and European Community Economic Development Literature.* Vancouver: CCE/Westcoast Publications, 1993.

Lachance, Elaine, Kathryn Church, Eric Shragge and Jean-Marc Fontan. *Appropriating Evaluation: A Guide to Critically Examining Our Practice.* Ottawa, Human Resources Development Canada, 1999.

Narayan, Uma. "Working Together Across Difference: Some Considerations on Emotions and Political Practice." *Hypatia* 3, no 2, (1988): 31-47.

Working Like Crazy. Ottawa: National Film Board, 1999.

Jill Hanley and Luba Serge

Putting Housing on the CED Agenda

Introduction

The right to decent housing is protected in Article 25(1) of the Universal Declaration of Human Rights, adopted by the United Nations in 1948. Housing offers physical shelter from the elements, is often a central focus of socializing with family and friends, is a site of economic production and reproduction and has important cultural and social significance. Housing, by all accounts, is a fundamental human need— this much is widely agreed upon.[1] What to do about this fact is where the debate begins.

Although housing is considered an integral part of community economic development (CED) in the U.S. tradition, the same cannot be said within Canada. Here, the CED emphasis has been much more on entrepreneurship and creating local employment. The housing and CED movements in Canada are nearly completely separate, a situation markedly different from the community development corporation (CDC) movement south of the border. In this chapter, we will discuss the links between housing and sustainable social, community and economic development, the core concerns of CED. And the current housing and homelessness crisis can only be seen to have effects contrary to the goals of CED.

So why have the two movements remained so distinct? This is a question that may be answered to some extent when we turn to housing as a political issue, considering the ways in which the government and community movements have interacted over the years in the struggle around housing policy. Just as the CED movement experiences tension between a more technical liberal approach and a more empowerment-oriented progressive approach, so has the housing movement. For many years, community groups were able to rely upon government funding and even direct intervention to address housing concerns. With the end of federal funding in 1993, however, the housing movement has been pushed to re-examine its approach and return to being more political, emphasizing housing as a tool of empowerment for social and community development. As the CED movement faces the same challenge, this may be a good time to bring the two movements together, encouraging both to broaden their visions and their bases of potential support.

Links Between Housing and CED

There are many ways that housing has an impact on the issues of concern to CED activists and professionals, whether social, economic or environmental. Good housing not only provides a springboard from which community members are better able to pursue their interests but the housing itself provides opportunities for employment, training and other forms of social and economic activities. It is widely recognized, for example, that the housing industry and housing investment play a critical role in the macro-economy of Western nations[2] and local economies concurrently. There is also wide recognition that housing plays a significant role in individual and community social outcomes and experiences.[3] Levels of educational achievement, access to employment, physical and emotional health and degree of social integration or exclusion have all been linked to housing conditions.[4] Without the benefit of decent housing for participants or for the community surrounding them, CED projects will have difficulty succeeding.

Social Links

Good housing has positive social impacts on the individual, group and community levels, all of which, in turn, improve their economic chances. For individuals, good quality housing and a healthy living environment contribute to both mental and physical health.[5] Asthma and tuberculosis are linked to poor-quality and over-crowded housing, for example, and physical injuries can occur due to poorly maintained buildings. Mental health is improved with a sense of not only physical security but also security of tenure. Decent housing has also been linked to better educational attainment, underscoring the negative impacts of children changing schools as a result of losing their housing, experiencing housing-related stress and even just being unable to find a quiet place to study. There is a similar effect among adults interested in pursuing their educations.

For some populations, housing is also closely linked to necessary social services.[6] For example, it is often social housing that provides the structural adaptations necessary for Canadians with physical disabilities to live independently, and social housing is increasingly an important support for older single women living alone.[7] State subsidies are essential for the many group homes providing non-institutional care for people with physical and intellectual disabilities, for people living with mental illness, for young mothers, for the elderly, for women fleeing from domestic violence or for people attempting to conquer their addictions.

Housing is also a basic element in individuals' ability to integrate socially into their communities. Social networks of friendship and mutual aid are often formed among neighbours and well-located, stable housing contributes to people being able to properly access community amenities (such as health centres, schools, stores, leisure). Having reasonably-priced housing means more money left in the budget to look after other basic needs and, in the best of scenarios, social and leisure outings. Finally, decent housing has been linked in a very fundamental way to people's self-esteem. In this society, your housing says something about your achievements and your life situation.

On a group level, community organizations can be strengthened through their involvement in housing. To begin with, housing is perhaps one of the easiest issues around which to mobilize. Getting people involved via a housing issue is one way to build solidarity and skills to be turned in the future toward other social projects—CED, for example. The multi-faceted nature of housing also offers opportunities for strengthening ties of cooperation between local organizations. Housing projects raise issues of environment, food security and a host of other social rights. Groups defending these different issues can get involved in housing projects, contributing to the housing but also having the opportunity to further their own agendas.

Housing also offers many social benefits to communities. Improved housing can improve security in a neighbourhood; not only do people feel safer when a neighbourhood is kept up, but they are also more likely to take action if something appears to threaten the security or well-being of their place of belonging. A study of the impact of renovations and social housing in Montreal neighbourhoods found that not only did renovations increase security in the housing through generally improved conditions and enhanced security measures (e.g., locks on main doors and intercom systems) and a more positive outlook on the part of residents of renovated units, but also increased mutual help and surveillance in housing co-ops.[8] Good housing helps people feel proud of their neighbourhood and increases their interest in making it a long-term home. Community housing projects can also integrate green space and leisure areas for the use of the whole neighbourhood.

Economic Links

Economically, there are again many benefits from housing. Investment in housing generates employment. For example, it has been estimated that for each new housing unit built, between three and six person-years of employment over a five-year period are created.[9] Investment in renovations has been estimated to result in even more employment. Furthermore, housing has an important impact on the financial situation of individuals. Those with affordable, adequate and decent housing will find it easier to maintain employment, relieved of the stress of unstable housing, frequent moves or missed work to deal with housing crises. Stable housing also contributes to the maintenance of the social networks that are key to finding work. Well-located housing, with easy access to public transportation, makes it easier to find and get to work as well. A study of women's economic participation and housing concluded that:

> at the most basic level, secure, quality housing is a prerequisite for
> women to upgrade their education, participate in training programs or
> enter the labour force. Securing decent and affordable housing can be the
> first in an incremental series of steps towards women's personal achieve-
> ment, including labour force participation.[10]

Community groups can use housing development to contribute to their training and employment objectives. For example, housing projects have often been used as opportunities to train local residents in the construction trades. The Co-operative Housing Association of Eastern Ontario took up this approach in 1998 with its Youthworks summer employment program through which co-op teenagers learn to do basic maintenance and upkeep on housing,[11] and we will discuss an example from Winnipeg below. Local exchange networks, whether formal or informal, can also be facilitated through the establishment of community-oriented, affordable and stable housing.

Improved housing in a neighbourhood often brings investment in local services (public and commercial), although there is a fine line between improving a neighbourhood for the benefit of its residents versus starting on the slippery slope to gentrification. Additionally, in lieu of the private sector profiting from the jobs and economic spin-offs related to housing, housing could be developed with more socially-oriented economic goals in mind.

Andrew Jackson sums up well the varied impacts that housing has on the economy:

> Housing is a major part of the economy and has an impact on the cyclical
> pattern of economic and employment growth, for good and for bad....
> [T]he housing system influences long-term growth and the spatial
> distribution of growth through its impacts on business investment
> decisions and the location decisions of workers. The housing system is
> also a critical intervening factor between the matching of workers and
> jobs and the efficient and equitable functioning of the labour market. The
> neighbourhood sorting of households by income can create barriers to
> employment for low-income workers.[12]

While social and economic links are significant, housing is also an important factor for the environment, one concern of CED that is increasingly neglected.

Environmental Links

Sustainable development, a core value of CED, is a term that has been popular ever since it surfaced in the Brundtland Report in 1987. It involves, "meeting the needs of the present without compromising the needs of future generations."[13] The environment is central to this concept, and one aspect that is often overlooked when it comes to the environment is housing. In fact, the types and design of housing that Canadians have built in the past 40 years has changed very little, particularly in terms of environmental impact. The suburban single-detached house is still the norm in Canada.

Community-oriented housing offers an opportunity to work environmental considerations into residential development, reducing what has been termed the "ecological footprint,"[14] or use of natural resources. The basic principle of this concept is that land area is consumed to support the needs of individuals. This land not only provides raw materials but it is also affected by energy use and waste production. Often, the land we affect is not local, consumption patterns often having global effects. According to Wackernagel and Rees, "Housing alone accounts for 21 per cent of the total size of the Canadian citizen's ecological footprint...."[15] Energy use and waste consumption are issues not only in the construction and maintenance of the house, but also through the everyday living done by the resident. Planners, architects and builders can make decisions to minimize the environmental impacts of housing through its construction and maintenance.

A recent Canada Mortgage and Housing Corporation report suggested the following components of a "sustainable collectivity" to be sought through housing development planning—a concept which is also one of the goals of CED: sustainable protection of the environment, urban planning that supports public transportation, urban densification, "village centres" within neighbourhoods, healthy local economy, adequate treatment of waste water and runoff, water conservation, energy efficiency and, finally, the proverbial reduce, reuse, recycle.[16]

Current Housing Dilemmas

Canada can be considered to be in the midst of a serious housing crisis. The 2001 census revealed that 16 per cent of Canadians are considered to be in "core need,"[17] without access to suitable, adequate and/or affordable housing,[18] and the mayors of Canada's major cities have sounded the alarm bell on the housing situation.[19] As we will see below, however, housing need affects some segments of the population more severely than others. Housing difficulties are more likely to affect marginalized social groups such as woman-headed households (especially those with children), newcomers to Canada, as well as First Nations.[20] The basic housing precariousness experienced by these specific groups puts them at greater risk for the ultimate difficulty in housing—homelessness.

Woman-headed households

Housing is very much a women's issue. As the majority of the poor, women around the world find access to housing a struggle.[21] In Canada, women represent a disproportionate number of the poor (15 per cent are poor) and it is more often single mothers (52 per cent) and lone senior women (42 per cent) who lack adequate income,[22] a reflection of men's greater earning power.[23]

Not surprisingly, this disproportionate level of poverty among women and girls translates into disproportionate difficulty in securing decent, adequate and affordable housing (16 per cent overall[24]). Among single people over 65 years old (the majority of whom are women), 53 per cent experience core housing need while 50 per cent of lone parents with children under 18 (again, the majority of whom are women) experience core housing need.[25] Other factors intersecting with gender, such as racism, disability, illness and addictions, render particular women's housing situation even more vulnerable.[26] Women's organizations and housing organizations have long demanded attention to the gendered nature of housing problems, but recently there have been organized campaigns to pressure the government into action,[27] as well as women-centred housing projects that incorporate economic development programs to address the poverty issues underlying women's difficulties in housing.[28]

Newcomers to Canada

International migrants (including immigrants, refugees and undocumented individuals) also face particular issues around housing, compounded by the intersection of several social factors. Recent immigrants are more likely to be low income than Canadian-born individuals (a gap which has widened in the past twenty years).[29] As more and more non-Europeans migrate to Canada, there is less acceptance of their credentials and past work experience, often related to flat-out racism. Language ability is another factor that influences job outcomes.

The discrimination seen in employment also plays out in housing. Add to this that immigrants may have fewer social networks to help them find decent, adequate and affordable housing and that they are more likely to live in major metropolitan areas where housing costs can be very high,[30] and it becomes easy to understand that one-third of immigrants living in Canada for fewer than five years are in core need.[31] Overall, 21 per cent of immigrants face housing difficulties but among those with precarious status (e.g., refugee claimants, temporary visas) it is 43 per cent.[32]

With culture so central to people's sense of home and use of space, the increasing ethnic diversity in our cities raises a further issue of housing design and, even more importantly, social cohesion among residents of a neighbourhood. Given the centrality of housing to the settlement process, not to mention all the other social indicators discussed earlier in the chapter, the interests of immigrants in housing must not be neglected.[33]

First Nations and housing

One of the groups that experiences constant socio-economic difficulties, including housing problems, are Canadian Aboriginal households. According to the 2001 Census, non-reserve Aboriginal households had incomes that were 20 per cent less than non-Aboriginal households.[34] The impact of poverty is felt on many levels. Aboriginal persons die a decade earlier than the average population and infant mortality rates are double the average,[35] the rate of suicide of Aboriginal male youth is five times that of Canadian youth while that of Aboriginal female youth is eight times higher,[36] participation in post secondary education is only half of that of Canadians[37] and there is an increased risk of homelessness.[38]

According to the 2001 census almost one-quarter of Aboriginal non-reserve households were in core housing need compared to 16 per cent of non-Aboriginal households. The proportion of Aboriginal households experiencing core need varied by region, ranging from 18 per cent of Aboriginal households in Quebec in core need (compared to 14 per cent of non-Aboriginal households) to 44 per cent in Nunavut (compared to 17 per cent of non-Aboriginal households). While shelter costs are not collected by the census for on-reserve households, these were "more than twice as likely to live in crowded conditions, and 3.3 times as likely to live in housing in need of major repair, with the household unable to afford acceptable housing" when compared to non-reserve Aboriginal households.[39]

There is growing evidence of the link between poor housing conditions and chronic illness among this population. For example, one study revealed that infants in Nunavut were found to have a level of respiratory disease six times the national average, attributed to overcrowding and a high rate of yeast in mattresses that were often put on floors to lodge more people.[40] Another study examining increased rates of asthma and Chronic Obstructive Pulmonary Disease (COPD) in the Aboriginal community concluded that many communities "suffer from overcrowding and inadequate water and sewage systems, exposing residents to harmful environmental toxins and infectious agents."[41]

Homelessness

The changes in the population affected by homelessness have resulted in a shift in the explanation of its causes. No longer seen as the result of personal failing (e.g., alcoholism), homelessness is now seen as a convergence of trends ranging from structural causes (e.g., economic factors such as growth in involuntary part-time, low-paid employment or policy gaps in the social safety net) to individual risk factors such as poverty, sexual or physical abuse, having been in child-protection care, prison, drug or alcohol misuse and poor mental or physical health.[42] In Canada, a diverse group ranging from those with mental illness, the elderly, families, women, youth, the urban Aboriginal population, as well as workers, find themselves homeless. For example, a study found that in Calgary, 50 per cent of the absolute homeless—that is, those literally without a home—were working part-time or full-time.[43]

The discussion of structural factors inevitably includes access and availability to affordable housing. A widely cited analogy likens the pursuit of affordable housing and homelessness outcomes to a game of musical chairs. When there are not enough "chairs" to go around, the weak and disadvantaged are not as quick to lay claim to a chair when the music stops.[44] In Canada, advocates have largely situated homelessness as a housing problem, a perspective that is confirmed by research. One review of studies dealing with homelessness concluded: "Every study that has looked has found that affordable, usually subsidized, housing prevents homelessness more effectively than anything else. This is true for all groups of poor people, including those with severe and persistent mental illness and/or substance abuse."[45]

While for many, if not the majority, homelessness is easily resolved by access to decent, affordable housing, for others, the lack of stable housing is related to a complex series of problems, such as substance use or mental illness, and housing that includes services are needed. Nonetheless, projects such as that of Pathways to Housing in New York City, where persons are offered immediate access to individual, permanent, independent apartments, are proving to be highly successful. Most clients of Pathways have substance-use issues, many have mental health problems, yet the only condition is that they abide by the terms and conditions of their leases and meet with a staff member at least twice a month. Evaluations of this "housing first" model have revealed that a variety of indicators (e.g., housing stability, hospitalizations, employment, etc.) show that this approach is more successful than those that require abstinence and/or a gradual transition to individual housing.[46] "In fact ... getting stably housed is increasingly being recognized as a prerequisite to other steps in reconnecting with the community...."[47]

Federal Government Response to Housing Issues

The types of housing dilemmas reviewed above are not entirely new; the profit-oriented capitalist system of housing production and distribution cannot adequately house all members of society without government intervention and/or provision,[48] a fact recognized even by those on Canada's political right.[49] The federal government has long intervened in social housing, but there has always been a tension between (a) supporting market mechanisms for housing and (b) creating social housing outside the market.[50]

Although housing falls under provincial jurisdiction, the federal government began in the late 1940s to directly provide residual housing to those most disadvantaged in society as well as to war veterans. Overall, however, the Canadian state preferred to use market mechanisms to intervene in housing, investing more over time in both rental and home ownership through such mechanisms as mortgage guarantees, tax breaks for owners and direct subsidies for construction.[51]

Traditionally, Canadian housing policy has had two main orientations: (a) "eliminating perceived inefficiencies of the housing market"; and (b) "concern with issues of equity and social justice in housing."[52] Not to be underestimated is the influence of the classic Keynesian theory of stimulating the economy via state spending on infrastructure and public goods such as housing. These forces have combined in Canada to create "social housing"— a term generally defined as state-subsidized non-profit housing with collective ownership.

Federal housing policy

Before the Second World War, the government did little to intervene in the housing market. In the 1930s, tenant struggles demanding fair treatment and legal protections were the purview of left-wing groups, the Communist Party and unions.[53] The Canadian government's housing legislation prior to the Second World War was generally intended to support private production and home ownership. By the end of the Second World War, however, Canada was facing a serious housing shortage due to lack of maintenance and new construction since the Depression. In response, the National Housing Act was amended in 1944 to support private housing development and improve access to credit for Canadian homebuyers. The Canada Mortgage and Housing Corporation (CMHC) was established in 1946 to administer the Act.[54]

There remained interest among activist groups such as the Co-operative Union of Canada, the Canadian Union of Students and the Canadian Labour Congress for public and non-profit housing, but their demands went, for a time, unanswered.[55] Although a National Public Housing program was adopted in 1949, it faced significant political and ideological resistance, and public housing construction remained stalled until 1964. Between 1949 and 1964, only 11,624 units of public housing were built, an average of only 0.7 per cent of annual housing construction.[56]

In the mid-1960s, there came a realization among the public and among policy-makers that the "golden age" being enjoyed by many was failing to reach a significant proportion of the population. Poverty had not been eradicated and housing affordability found its way onto the public agenda. Pressure was mounting for more effective state intervention in housing. The 1964 amendments to the National Housing Act supported the twinning of construction of public housing and inner city commercial development with urban renewal through the 1964 Public Housing Program.[57] Between 1964 and 1978, 164,000 public housing units were built in Canada, most of them managed by provincial authorities with a 50/50 cost-sharing arrangement with the federal government.[58]

In 1969, however, and despite the boom in public housing construction, a federal task force confirmed that "housing is a universal need, yet the private market on which Canadians have relied is anything but universal in its present scope and applications."[59] Still, the CMHC seemed unable to fill the void. Housing advocate groups were ready with alternatives. The Co-operative Housing Foundation (CHF)'s negotiations with the federal government over the next few years would change the direction of Canadian housing policy.[60]

The 1973 oil crisis and subsequent recession led to a reassessment of state involvement in a range of social policy arenas, housing included. Federal officials were interested in reducing the state's financial obligations and in addressing the stigma and public concerns related to the "concentration of poverty" created by large-scale public housing projects. Partly in response to negotiations with the CHF—but also under pressure from the NDP who held the balance of power in parliament at the time[61]—1973 amendments to the National Housing Act changed the funding structures for public housing and allowed subsidies for third-sector (non-profit) housing initiatives.[62] Housing co-operatives and housing owned and managed by non-profit organizations became important new partners in providing affordable housing to Canadians. The Canadian government had adopted the concept of "social housing" but as the 1970s went on, they cut back on overall funding for housing.

Lack of support for social housing continued into the 1980s. The election of the Conservative Mulroney government in 1984 drove neoconservative politics home in Canada. By 1986, the CMHC was asserting that its role was to assist "in developing a climate of stability for the private market so that it can function effectively."[63] Assisting those who could not afford market rates was a secondary concern. Construction of public housing slowed considerably and during this period third sector housing made up 80 per cent of new social housing, marking a withdrawal of the state from this sector.[64]

The Conservatives, however, left the full elimination of funding to new social housing to the Liberals. Their 1993 budget heralded the end of an era in Canadian housing policy. In that year, the federal government ended funding for new social housing and made clear its intention to transfer responsibility to the provinces by capping its spending on existing projects. Many provinces responded with housing cutbacks of their own.[65]

Current policy initiatives and trends

Housing subsidies in Canada have been scaled back in the past two decades, to the point that today many people question whether there is a future for Canadian social housing at all, despite the federal government's recent return to modestly funding what they term "affordable housing." There has been successful pressure to shift social housing from a program conceived as a "universal" program which should serve all Canadians, to a "targetted" one which would require that beneficiaries be subjected to needs-testing based on such factors as income and health problems.

We are at a critical crossroads in Canadian housing policy with changes in policy that are historic in scope. National coalitions have brought significant pressure to bear on the federal government, arguing that their neglect of social housing has contributed to our current crisis.[66] Despite the negotiation of the federal government's feeble return to the financing of subsidized housing, the prospects for social housing in Canada continue to seem limited. The next few years will undoubtedly be a time when community-based housing organizations will have to take serious stock of their organizing strategies and policy demands. Unfortunately, early estimates suggest that the provinces and the third sector will not be able to keep up with the need for affordable housing,[67] and the funds injected by the Affordable Housing program seem unlikely to make the difference[68] for the 21 per cent of Canadians currently paying more than 30 per cent of their income for housing.[69]

The federal role in homelessness has taken a slightly different course and reflects the political ambivalence in dealing with homelessness as a housing problem. Following a declaration in November 1998 by the Big City Mayors Caucus of the Federation of Canadian Municipalities that homelessness was a national disaster and calling upon the federal government to take action, the federal government, in 1999, established a National Secretariat on Homelessness (NSH), and launched the National Homelessness Initiative. This initiative, renewed for a second three-year period in 2003, includes support for communities to strengthen capacity and develop new responses, an urban Aboriginal strategy and a fund for small and rural communities. It is based on a "continuum of supports" approach to planning for homelessness, but in the three-year period did not offer funding for permanent affordable housing, and the primary focus has been meeting emergency needs such as shelter beds.[70]

Community Response to Housing Issues: Social Housing

There is quite a debate as to whether governments intervene in social housing for the welfare of citizens or whether they do so to preserve social order and contribute to socio-economic stability. Regardless of their motivation, "No government is likely to take the requisite action to provide housing for those who require societal intervention unless there appears to be a policy advantage or unless the pressure for action on the government in power is so strong that it can no longer be resisted."[71] Apart from social concerns, economic development of communities and economic profit for private developers are perhaps the most common policy advantages considered by government for intervening in housing. As we will see in the rest of this section, social housing, the very definition of which is a subject of debate, is but one aspect of government intervention in housing and one that frequently requires community organizing before action is taken.

Defining Social Housing

"Social housing" implies that the state is involved in the provision of housing, whether directly, in state-owned and managed developments, or indirectly, through state-funded, non-governmental organizations. Richard Morin and Francine Dansereau suggest the following "zones of consensus" in defining social housing:

1. Non-profit management: social housing generally refers to housing that is collectively owned and managed outside of private market provisions. Rents are usually below market rates.

2. Allocation is according to a socially defined need or social solidarity rather than according to ability to pay or according to profit-maximization.

3. It is subject to political decisions and governmental control or public accountability as a function of its reliance on state subsidies.[72]

Other characteristics of social housing vary across jurisdictions and the proportion of social housing within the overall housing stock varies widely between countries. In Canada, social housing is only approximately 5 per cent of the total stock,[73] while social housing makes up 15 to 40 per cent of housing in the European Union.[74] As well, the organizations involved in producing and managing social housing vary; municipal, provincial or federal governments may be responsible or third sector secular or religious charities, community organizations, community development corporations or co-operatives might be involved. Procedures for determining eligibility for social housing and determining rent levels vary according to the priorities and ideologies of those managing social housing.

The three most common types of social housing found in Canada are public housing, community housing and co-operative housing, distinguished principally according to who paid for them, who owns them and who manages them. Public housing is paid for by government investment (sometimes from all three levels) and owned and managed by a government agency, usually at the municipal level. All units are usually subsidized so that tenants pay 30 per cent of their income in rent and most projects target low-income families or people over 65 years of age. Community housing may have government capital and operating grants, but the mortgage is paid by the non-profit organization that owns and manages the project. The boards of these organizations usually have professional, community and tenant representatives. Rents vary according to funding programs. Community housing is often the formula used to accommodate populations with special needs (e.g., transitional housing for homeless persons, supported living for people with disabilities). Co-operative housing is funded in a similar fashion to community housing, but it is owned and managed by a non-profit co-operative association entirely controlled by the residents of the project. Each resident household has the right to contribute to decisions about the project and the responsibility to contribute to its maintenance.

A recent shift in the definition of social housing includes a move away from the centrality of the concept of "collective ownership" and a willingness to include other types of housing that benefit from government subsidies.[75] In recent interviews, some people in the community sector said they were willing to consider subsidized private rental housing, subsidized individual home ownership (especially when it is non-profit and the affordability is protected by resale formulae) and private rent subsidies to individual households as forms of social housing.[76] This shift is sometimes related to a greater ideological openness to market provision of housing and sometimes to a pragmatic acceptance of the limits of the current neoliberal political context.

Community organizing for housing
Regardless of their specific definitions of social housing, those active in the housing movement share the belief that collective action is necessary in order to make progress in a number of different areas related to housing. The analysis is similar

to that of CED activists' identifying inequalities in the system and concluding that it is only community mobilization and action that will redress it, whether through pressuring the government or organizing to provide autonomous alternatives.

From this perspective, organizing is about changing the balance of power, relying upon democratic principles of participation and a good dose of political strategy. Community organizing can also have the benefits of sharing technical and analytical skills with participants through popular education. At its very best, community organizing brings people together to build a common vision; at the same time, it can be difficult, slow and sometimes may even seem ineffective. The technocratic approach can sometimes get things done more quickly, and many people are uncomfortable with the basic underlying conflict that is inherent in community organizing.[77]

Around housing issues, there are four major areas of organizing: tenants' rights, housing management, housing development and housing policy. Tenants' rights organizing is usually undertaken by local housing committees whose focus is on informing tenants of their rights and then helping them to defend them. The focus tends to be on private housing and on landlord/tenant relations. Local housing committees (or more general grassroots social rights organizations) use popular education to inform residents of a building, block or neighbourhood and may use a combination of individual and collective action to address problems. For example, tenants in a building with cockroach infestation might go together to insist that the city inspectors fine the landlord, or they might write a petition to the landlord threatening to go en masse to file legal complaints. This is often the first form of involvement for community activists and it sometimes leads to mobilization around broader issues.

An awareness of tenant rights often leads to a desire for tenant involvement in the housing management. In private housing, tenants can create an association to negotiate with the landlord and, in ideal situations, contribute to decision-making. In public and community housing, the goal is often to have effective tenant representation on the board of directors that controls the project. Having board reps is often combined with a tenant committee, as well. Housing co-operatives are the ultimate form of tenant control where they collectively manage all aspects of the project. Co-operatives are usually also an example of the next form of community organizing for housing, community development.

In the community development of social housing done from an organizing perspective, prospective tenants and community members come together to plan and implement the construction or renovation of a housing project that meets their common objectives around such things as affordability, community control, neighbourhood revitalization and particular physical adaptations. This approach usually links the physical housing interest to broader quality of life issues in the neighbourhood (i.e., transportation, green space, community gardens, municipal services). Social housing development is undertaken by non-profit organizations with a variety of mandates: housing-specific, population-specific, neighbourhood-oriented, economic development and so on.

Finally, most of the other three forms of organizing will at some point come to consider the focus of this last form: housing policy organizing. Municipal, provincial and federal governments all have housing laws, policies and regulations that form the legal framework for important issues such as tenants' rights and levels and forms of investment in social housing. Often done through coalitions made up of those involved in the first three forms, policy organizing uses such approaches as lobbying, research, direct action and media work to influence government decision-makers. Popular education or public outreach to build support for their policy positions is another important aspect.

In the next section, we can see ways that community organizing has resulted in innovative housing projects that bridge the social and the economic.

Case Examples: Housing Projects Bridging Social and Economic Objectives

Housing projects, both large and small developments, have increasingly tried to integrate wider social and economic components into their planning. Projects can be developed with a variety of issues at heart, for example, housing specific clienteles with responses to their particular needs, addressing local employment issues or contributing to overall community social and environmental sustainability.

In Montreal, the LéZarts housing co-operative illustrates this clientele-specific approach. The co-op was developed to answer the need for affordable housing and studio space for young artists, whose low and precarious incomes make the cost of both a studio and housing prohibitively expensive. After five years of development, the co-op transformed an abandoned factory into 33 units in 2002 with a design that permitted integration of studio space within individual residential units. Furthermore, collective services were added and include conversion of an uninhabitable basement into gallery space, technical (e.g., sharing of tools and equipment) and career support (e.g. applying for subsidies or preparing a portfolio) for residents, as well as outreach activities, such as workshops, in the wider community.

Other projects have leveraged the potential employment and training opportunities that housing development represents. For example, the Victoria Cool Aid Society, in renovating a fifteen-bed shelter for women, obtained funding to involve the intended clientele in the construction phase. The clients of the project, women aged 19 to 45—many of whom were homeless, working in the sex trade and dealing with mental illness—were not only trained in basic carpentry but also gained marketable skills, enhanced job readiness and self-esteem through paid work experience, tutoring and counselling.[78]

On a larger scale, the North End Housing Project (NEHP) in Winnipeg is an example of a Comprehensive Community Initiative (CCI). These initiatives seek neighbourhood revitalization through a holistic approach that includes community organization, rehabilitation of infrastructure, expansion of local economic potential and strengthening social networks.[79] The NEHP was developed to address housing needs in a community with low incomes, high unemployment, poor housing conditions and a high percentage of renters.[80] It not only attempted to interrupt the cycle of residential neglect and decline by renovating a critical mass of properties but, as described by Lawrence Deane,[81] by favouring a rent-to-buy approach, the NEHP sought to "capture rents that normally would have leaked out of the community to absentee landlords." By 2004 it was estimated that the community was "capturing" $379,000 annually in rental charges. Furthermore, previously unemployed residents of the community carried out the renovation work. Between 1999 and 2003 NEHP paid "approximately $1.96 million in renovation wages almost entirely to local trainees who were previously unemployed." Other initiatives included a Salvage Shop that recycled building material that within six months was generating $3,000 in monthly sales. Finally, part of the initiative included job training for members of an Aboriginal street gang that approached NEHP to help break the cycle of crime and incarceration. Upon release from long-term prison sentences, members were unable to find employment due to criminal records, little education and "unconventional appearances." A program was developed that included life-skills counselling and training. Ten participants renovated three houses in the first year but "the most significant result of this initiative is that there have been no re-arrests from any gang-related offences in the 29 months since this program started."

A final example is an innovative project that has been developed in British Columbia that has combined sustainable development goals (e.g., use of renewable energy sources such as wind, solar and geo-thermal heating) with Aboriginal social values and designs. The Seabird Island Project includes features of sustainable development such as rainwater collection systems, site planning that resulted in smaller building footprints, as well as design that promotes healthy housing (e.g., low emission paints, non-toxic building materials) as well as adaptability to changing needs. Aboriginal design elements include a spiritual healing garden. The project was built by the Seabird First Nation construction team to "further reduce costs as well as develop their capacity to build, maintain, and operate their new homes."[82]

These projects are just a few examples of the ways in which the housing movement has been incorporating CED values into its projects. These innovations are relatively recent and suggest that greater opportunities exist for collaboration for those working on CED and those who, up until now, have been primarily concerned with the "bricks and mortar" of housing.

Putting Housing on the CED Agenda

Housing is a fundamental human need and fundamental human right, access to which is mostly dependent on private market forces. Whether or not you have decent, adequate and affordable housing is largely a function of how much money you have. Housing is also key to our economy, representing massive investment by individuals and a large number of jobs that could be channelled to social ends rather than profit. A CED perspective can enhance the conception of social housing projects beyond "bricks and mortar" and basic affordability to create spin-off opportunities for related CED projects (construction, suppliers, maintenance, management, etc.).

As early as 1968, Hans Blumenfeld urged us to recognize the possibility that our preoccupation with housing may simply be a diversion from the more important issue of households' inadequate income: "What we call the problem of slum housing is just the housing aspect of poverty. We have not yet been able to house everyone properly because we haven't yet eradicated poverty."[83] Thirty-five years later, we are as far as ever from that goal. Putting housing on the CED agenda may be one way to help answer these community and economic questions: Do Canadians have a *right* to decent and affordable housing? If so, how will this be provided for? Who will control it? Who will pay for it? Who will define what is decent and what is affordable?

At a time when housing need in Canada remains high—rent and other housing costs rise unabated, construction of affordable rental units is rare and discrimination remains current—these questions are as important as ever. The will to expand social housing exists; it is the financing that is scarce. Community groups organizing for social housing are maintaining pressure on municipal, provincial and federal governments for renewed and sustained funding of social housing. Activists will be keen to ensure that CED foundations' investment in riskier alternative small businesses will not shift to housing. However, given its protected equity in the form of a physical entity, housing projects can more easily seek financing from private sources. With care, competition can be avoided. In fact, the housing movement itself may have a contribution to make in terms of financing other housing projects and perhaps even CED businesses. Many social housing projects are coming to the end of their mortgages and while some may need major reinvestment to repair and renovate units, many also now own valuable assets.

There is potential to develop new projects, applying lessons learned over the last few decades in housing and in CED to develop projects that meet unanswered needs. In the current context, the potential for innovation in social housing is high; the experience and skills of CED practitioners stand to make important contributions. It is important that, as CED approaches are being developed in communities, housing—often the major function of neighbourhoods and the anchor for people living in communities—not be ignored but rather integrated where possible. The examples cited in this chapter illustrate that housing not only meets fundamental needs but can leverage employment and can integrate other functions, such as space for work, in its design.

Notes

1. SPR Associates Inc., *Canadian Women and Their Housing,* Canada Mortgage and Housing Corporation, *Canadian Housing Observer.*

2. Miron, "On Progress in Housing Canadians," in *House, Home and Community, 7-21.*

3. Malpass, "Housing Policy: Does It Have a Future?" *Policy and Politics,* 217-28.

4. Jackson, *Home Truths.*

5. Ibid.

6. McClain, "Housing as a Human Service," in *House, Home and Community,* 220-38; Ogilvie, "The State of Supported Housing for Mental Health Consumers," *Psychiatric Rehabilitation Journal,* 122-31.

7. Cooper and Rodman, "Accessibility and Quality of Life in Housing Cooperatives," *Environment and Behavior,* 49; Spector, "The Hidden Housing Problem," *Canadian Housing,* 27.

8. Bernèche et al., *Le rôle des interventions publiques en habitation.*

9. CMHC, *Economic Impacts of Residential Construction.*

10. Johnson and Ruddock, *Building Capacity.*

11. CHAEO, *CHASEO Member Services.*

12. Jackson, 57.

13. WCED, *Our Common Future.*

14. Wackernagel and Rees, *Our Ecological Footprint.*

15. Ibid., 21.

16. CMHC, *Développement de collectivités durables.*

17. Households are considered to be experiencing "Core Housing Need" if they fail to meet one or more of the following standards (CMHC 2003). "Adequate" housing requires only regular upkeep, has hot and cold water, an indoor toilet and bath or shower. "Suitable" housing meets national occupancy standards (2 people/ bedroom, children of opposite sex in separate bedrooms after age five, 1 bedroom for each couple or person over 18). And "affordable" means a household spends less than 30 per cent of its income on housing (including utilities).

18. CMHC, *Canadian Housing Observer.*

19. Federation of Canadian Municipalities (FCM), *National Housing Options Paper;* FCM, *A National Affordable Housing Strategy.*

20. CMHC, *Canadian Housing Observer.*

21. United Nations Human Settlement Program (UN Habitat), *The Habitat Agenda.*

22. Statistics Canada, *Persons in low income before tax.*

23. Evans, "Divided citizenship? in *Women and the Canadian Welfare State,* 91-116; Reitsma-Street et al., *Housing Policy Options for Women Living in Urban Poverty.*

24. CMHC, *Special Studies on 1996 Census Data: Housing Conditions of Women and Girls, and Female-led Households.*

25. CMHC, *Canadian Housing Observer.*

26. Reitsma-Street et al., CMHC, *Special Studies on 1996 Census Data: Housing Conditions of Women and Girls,* 3.

27. Federations des femme du Québec (FFQ), *Revendications de la Marche mondiale des femmes.*

28. See, for example, the "Entre Nous Femmes" housing project in British Columbia: http://www.sfu.ca/cscd/gateway/sharing/chap2.htm

29. Picot, *The Deteriorating Economic Welfare of Immigrants.*

30. CMHC, *Special Studies on 1996 Census Data: Housing Conditions of Immigrants.*

31. CMHC, *Canadian Housing Observer.*

32. CMHC, *Special Studies on 1996 Census Data: Housing Conditions of Immigrants.*

33. Chicoine and Charbonneau, "Le processus de reconstruction des réseaux sociaux des femmes immigrantes dans l'espace montréalais."

34. CMHC, *2001 Census Housing Series Issue 6: Aboriginal Households.*

35. Sin et al., "Asthma and COPD Among Aboriginals in Alberta, Canada" *CHEST.*

36. Canada, *National Aboriginal Youth Strategy.*

37. Thiessen, *Policy Research Issues for Canadian Youth.*

38. Mayor's Homelessness Action Task Force, *Taking Responsibility for Homelessness.*

39. CMHC, *2001 Census Housing Series: Aboriginal Households.*

40. CMHC, *National Housing and Research Committee.*

41. Sin et al.

42. Edgar et al., *Services for Homeless People*; Avramov, *Coping with Homelessness.*

43. Eberle and Serge, "From Housing … to Homelessness," in *Homeless in Europe, The Newsletter of FEANSTA.*

44. Koegel et al., "The Causes of Homelessness," in *Homelessness in America.*

45. Shinn and Baumohl, "Rethinking the Prevention of Homelessness," in *Practical Lessons.*

46. Gulcur et al., "Housing, Hospitalization, and Cost Outcomes for Homeless Individuals, *Journal of Community and Applied Social Psychology*, 171-86; Tsemberis et al., "Consumer Preference Programs for Individuals Who Are Homeless," *American Journal of Community Psychology*, 305-17.

47. Rog and Holupka, "Reconnecting Homeless Individuals and Families," in *Practical Lessons.*

48. Rose, *Canadian Housing Policies.*

49. Desrochers, "Shattering Shelter Myths," *The Gazette.*

50. Bacher, *Keeping to the Marketplace.*

51. Miron, "Private Rental Housing," *Urban Studies*, 579.

52. Miron, "On Progress in Housing Canadians," in *House, Home and Community*, 15.

53. Bennett, *Shelter, Housing and Homes.*

54. Hulchanski, *Canada's Housing and Housing Policy.*

55. Chouinard, "The Uneven Development of Capitalist States," *Environment and Planning A*, 1291-1308.

56. Morin and Dansereau, *L'Habitation sociale: les clientèles et leur vécu.*

57. Unfortunately, as early as 1968, it had become clear that this 'slum clearance' almost always resulted in more expensive rent, and more apartments were destroyed than created (Blumenfeld 1968).

58. Morin and Dansereau, 14.

59. Federal Task Force on Housing and Urban Development, *Report of the Federal Task Force on Housing and Urban Development*, 14.

60. In March 1968, the Co-operative Union of Canada, the Canadian Union of Students and the Canadian Labour Congress had come together to form the CHF, the first national organization for the co-operative housing movement (Chouinard 1990).

61. Hulchanski, "New Forms of Owning and Renting," in *House, Home and Community*.

62. Carter, "Current Practices for Procuring Affordable Housing,"*Housing Policy Debate*, 593-631.

63. Hulchanski, *Canada's Housing and Housing Policy: An Introduction*.

64. Morin and Dansereau, 14.

65. Carroll and Jones, "The Road to Innovation, Convergence or Inertia." *Canadian Public Policy*, 277-93.

66. Hanley, "De tout avec ben d'la sauce: Community Organising for Social Housing in Immigrant Neighbourhoods" (PhD thesis).

67. Skaburskis and Mok, "The Impact of Withdrawing Subsidies for New Rental Housing. *Housing Studies*, 169-94.

68. MacNeil and Warnock, *The Disappearance of Affordable Housing in Regina*.

69. CMHC, *2001 Census Housing Series. Issue 1: Housing Affordability*.

70. Human Resources Development Canada, *Evaluation of the National Homelessness Initiative*.

71. Rose, 3.

72. Morin and Dansereau, 4-6.

73. Connelly Consulting Services, *Guaranteeing a Future*.

74. Morin and Dansereau.

75. Vaillancourt et al. *Portrait des politiques de logement social au Québec à la fin des années 1990*.

76. Hanley.

77. For a good overview of community organizing, see Shragge 2004.

78. Best Practices Agencies and L. Serge, *Documentation of Best Practices Addressing Homelessness*.

79. Kubisch and Stone, "Comprehensive Community Initiatives," in *Rebuilding Community: Policy and Practice in Urban Regeneration*.

80. Brown et al., "Shared responsibility."

81. Deane, "Rebuilding a neighbourhood."

82. CMHC, *Building a Sustainable Future*.

83. Blumenfeld, "Est-il possible de loger convenablement tout le monde?" in *Une Ville à vivre*, our translation, 15.

Bibliography

Avramov, Dragana, ed. *Coping with Homelessness: Issues to be Tackled and Best Practices in Europe*. Aldershot, Hants, England: Ashgate Publishing, 1999.

Bacher, John C. *Keeping to the Marketplace: the Evolution of Canadian Housing Policy*. Montreal: McGill-Queen's Press, 1993.

Baum, Alice S. and Donald Burnes. *A Nation in Denial: The Truth About Homelessness*. Boulder: Westview Press, 1993.

Bennett, Arnold. *Shelter, Housing and Homes: a Social Right*. Montreal: Black Rose Books, 1997.

Bernèche, Francine, M. Shaw, L. Serge, M. Monfort et C.O'Neill. *Le rôle des interventions publiques en habitation dans l'amélioration de la sécurité et la prévention de la criminalité à l'échelle des quartiers montréalais*. Montréal: Société de développement de Montréal, 1997.

Best Practices Agencies and Luba Serge. *Documentation of Best Practices Addressing Homelessness*. Ottawa: Canada Mortgage and Housing Corporation, 1999.

Blumenfeld, Hans. "Est-il possible de loger convenablement tout le monde?" in *Une Ville à vivre: Une Colloque sur l'habitat urbain d'aujourd'hui et de demain*, edited by Institut canadien des affaires publiques (ICAP), 13-25. Montréal: Éditions du jour, 1968.

Brown, Jason, Nancy Higgitt, Susan Wingert and Larry Morrissette. "Shared Responsibility: Building Sustainable Communities in Winnipeg's Inner City." Paper presented at Adequate & Affordable Housing for All: Research, Policy, Practice International Conference, 24-27 June, Toronto, 2004.

Canada Mortgage and Housing Corporation (CMHC). *2001 Census Housing Series, Issue 1: Housing Affordability Improves*. Research Highlights. Ottawa: CMHC, 2003.

———. *2001 Census Housing Series Issue 6: Aboriginal Households Research Highlights*. Socio-economic Series, Issue 04-036. Ottawa: CMHC, September 2004.

———. *Building a Sustainable Future: Seabird Island First Nation Sustainable Community Demonstration Project*. Ottawa: CMHC, 2004.

———. *Canadian Housing Observer*. Ottawa: CMHC, 2004. [Online] Available at: http://www.cmhc-schl.gc.ca/en/cahoob/

———. *Développement de collectivités durables: Élabouration du rôle du gouvernement fédéral pour le 21e siècle*. Ottawa: CMHC, 2000.

———. *Economic Impacts of Residential Construction Research Highlights*. Socio-economic Series, Issue 69. Ottawa: CMHC, 2000.

———. *National Housing and Research Committee*. Working Group on Housing and Population Health Spring Meeting, May 4, 2004. Montréal, Quebec. Ottawa: CMHC, 2004.

———. *Special Studies on 1996 Census Data: Housing Conditions of Immigrants. Research Highlights*. Ottawa: CMHC, 2001.

———. *Special Studies on 1996 Census Data: Housing Conditions of Women and Girls, and Female-led Households*. Research Highlights. Ottawa: CMHC, 2002.

Carroll, Barbara W. and Ruth J. E. Jones. "The Road to Innovation, Convergence or Inertia: Devolution in Housing Policy in Canada" *Canadian Public Policy* 26, no. 3, (2000): 277-93.

Carter, Tom. "Current Practices for Procuring Affordable Housing: The Canadian Context." *Housing Policy Debate* 8, no. 3 (1997): 593-631.

Chicoine, Nathalie and Johanne Charbonneau with Damaris Rose and Brian Ray. "Le processus de reconstruction des réseaux sociaux des femmes immigrantes dans l'espace montréalais." *Recherches Féministes* 10, no. 2 (1997) : 27-48.

Chouinard, Vera. "The Uneven Development of Capitalist States: 1. Theoretical Proposals and an Analysis of Postwar Changes in Canada's Assisted Housing Programmes." *Environment and Planning A* 22, no. 10 (1990): 1291-1308.

Connelly Consulting Services. *Guaranteeing a Future: The Challenge to Social Housing As Operating Agreements Expire.* Ottawa: CHRA, 2003.

Cooper, Matthew and Margaret Rodman. "Accessibility and Quality of Life in Housing Cooperatives." *Environment and Behavior* 26, no. 1 (1994): 49.

Co-operative Housing Association of Eastern Ontario. *CHASEO Member Services.* Ottawa: CHASEO, 2004. [Online] Available at: http://www.chaseo.org/services.html

Deane, Lawrence. "Rebuilding a Neighbourhood: Housing and Comprehensive Community Development." Paper presented at Adequate & Affordable Housing for All: Research, Policy, Practice International Conference, 24-27 June, Toronto, 2004.

Desrochers, Pierre. "Shattering Shelter Myths." *The Gazette*, 29 June 2002, final edition, B7.

Eberle, Margaret and Luba Serge. "From Housing… to Homelessness." *Homeless in Europe, The Newsletter of FEANSTA*, Spring, 2004.

Edgar, Bill, Joe Doherty and Amy Mina-Coull. *Services for Homeless People: Innovation and Changes in the European Union.* FEANSTA. Bristol: The Policy Press, 1999.

Evans, Patricia M. "Divided Citizenship? Gender, Income Security, and the Welfare State." In *Women and the Canadian Welfare State.* Edited by Patricia M. Evans and Gerda M. Wekerle, 91-116. Toronto: University of Toronto Press, 1997.

Federal Task Force on Housing and Urban Development. *Report of the Federal Task Force on Housing and Urban Development.* Ottawa: Information Canada, 1969.

Fédération des femmes du Québec (FFQ). *Revendications de la Marche mondiale des femmes.* Montréal: FFQ, 2000.

Federation of Canadian Municipalities (FCM). *A National Affordable Housing Strategy.* Ottawa: FCM, 2000.

———. *National Housing Options Paper.* Ottawa: FCM, 1998.

Fontan, Jean-Marc. *A Critical Review of Canadian, American and European Community Economic Development Literature.* Vancouver: Centre for Community Enterprise, 1993.

Front d'action populaire en réaménagement urbain (FRAPRU). *Femmes et logement au Québec.* Montréal: FRAPRU, 2004.

Government of Canada. *National Aboriginal Youth Strategy.* December. Ottawa: Queen's Press, 1999.

Gulcur, Leyla, Ana Stefancic, Marybeth Shinn, Sam Tsemberis and Sean N. Fischer. "Housing, Hospitalization, and Cost Outcomes for Homeless Individuals with Psychiatric Disabilities Participating in Continuum of Care and Housing First Programmes." *Journal of Community & Applied Social Psychology* 13 (2003): 171-186.

Hanley, Jill. "De tout avec ben d'la sauce: Community Organising for Social Housing in Immigrant Neighbourhoods." PhD thesis. Montreal: Ecole de service social, Université de Montréal, 2004.

Hulchanski, J. D. *Canada's Housing and Housing Policy: An Introduction*. Vancouver: UBC, 1988.

———. "New Forms of Owning and Renting." In *House, Home and Community: Progress in Housing Canadians, 1945-1986*, edited by John R. Miron, 64-75. Ottawa: CMHC, 1993.

Human Resources Development Canada (HRDC). *Evaluation of the National Homelessness Initiative: Implementation and Early Outcomes of the HRDC-based Components, Final Report*. Ottawa: Strategic Evaluations, Evaluation and Data Development, Strategic Policy, 2003.

Jackson, Andrew. *Home Truths: Why the Housing System Matters to All Canadians*. Ottawa: Canadian Housing and Renewal Association, 2004.

Johnson, Laura C. and Allison Ruddock. *Building Capacity: Enhancing Women's Economic Participation through Housing*. Ottawa: Status of Women Canada, 2000.

Koegel, Paul, Audrey Burnam, and Jim Baumohl. "The Causes of Homelessness." In *Homelessness in America*, edited by Jim Baumohl. Phoenix: Oryx Press, 1996.

Kubisch, Anne C. and Rebecca Stone. "Comprehensive Community Initiatives: The American Experience." In *Rebuilding Community: Policy and Practice in Urban Regeneration*, edited by John Pierson and Joan Smith. Hampshire, UK: Palgrave, 2001.

MacNeil, Della and John W. Warnock. *The Disappearance of Affordable Housing in Regina*. Regina: The Council on Social Development Regina, 2000.

Malpass, P. "Housing Policy: Does It Have a Future?" *Policy and Politics* 27, no. 2 (1999): 217-28.

Mayor's Homelessness Action Task Force. *Taking Responsibility for Homelessness: An Action Plan for Toronto*. Toronto: City of Toronto, 1999.

McClain, Janet. "Housing As a Human Service: Accommodating Special Needs." In *House, Home and Community: Progress in Housing Canadians, 1945-1986*, edited by John R. Miron, 220-38. Ottawa: CMHC, 1993.

Miron, John R. "On Progress in Housing Canadians." In *House, Home and Community: Progress in Housing Canadians, 1945-1986*, edited by John R. Miron, 7-21. Ottawa: CMHC, 1993.

———. "Private Rental Housing: The Canadian Experience." *Urban Studies* 32, no. 3 (1995): 579.

Morin, Richard and Francine Dansereau. *L'Habitation sociale: les clientèles et leur vécu, le modes de gestion, les solutions de rechange. Synthèse de la littérature*. Montreal: INRS-Urbanisation, 1990.

Ogilvie, Rita J. "The State of Supported Housing for Mental Health Consumers: A Literature Review." *Psychiatric Rehabilitation Journal* 21, no. 2 (1997): 122-31.

Picot, Garnett. *The Deteriorating Economic Welfare of Immigrants and Possible Causes*. Ottawa: StatsCan, 2004.

Reitsma-Street, Marge, Josie Schofield, Brishkai Lund and Colleen Kasting. *Housing Policy Options for Women Living in Urban Poverty: An Action Research Project in Three Canadian Cities*. Ottawa: Status of Women Canada, 2001.

Rog, Debra J. and C. Scott Holupka. "Reconnecting Homeless Individuals and Families to the Community." In *Practical Lessons: National Symposium on Homelessness Research*. Washington: U.S. Department of Housing and Urban Development and U.S. Department of Health and Human Services, 1999.

Rose, Albert. *Canadian Housing Policies (1935-1980)*. Toronto: Butterworth, 1980.

Shinn, Marybeth and Jim Baumhohl. "Rethinking the Prevention of Homelessness." In *Practical Lessons: National Symposium on Homelessness. Research Prepared for U.S. Department of Housing and Urban Development and U.S.* Washington: Department of Health and Human Services, 1999.

Shragge, Eric. *Activism and Social Change: Lessons for Community and Local Organising*. Peterborough, ON: Broadview Press, 2004.

Sin, Don D., Heather Wells, Lawrence W. Svenson, and S.F. Paul Man. "Asthma and COPD Among Aboriginals in Alberta, Canada." *CHEST* 121, no. 6 (2002).

Skaburskis, Andrejs and D. Mok. "The Impact of Withdrawing Subsidies for New Rental Housing: Projections for Toronto and the Rest of Ontario." *Housing Studies* 15, no. 2 (2000): 169-94.

Spector, Aron. "The Hidden Housing Problem: Housing Affordability Among Older Single Women Living Alone." *Canadian Housing* 15, no. 1 (1998): 27.

SPR Associates Inc. *Canadian Women and Their Housing, 1997*. Ottawa: Canada Mortgage and Housing Corporation, 1998.

Statistics Canada (StatsCan). *Persons in low income before tax, prevalence in percent*. Ottawa: StatsCan, 2004.

Thiessen, Victor. *Policy Research Issues for Canadian Youth: School-Work Transitions*. Ottawa: Applied Research Branch, Strategic Policy, HRDC, 2001.

Tsemberis, Sam, Linda Moran, Marybeth Shinn, Sara Asmussen, and David Shern. "Consumer Preference Programs for Individuals Who Are Homeless and Have Psychiatric Disabilities: A Drop-In Center and a Supported Housing Program." *American Journal of Community Psychology* 32, no. 3/4 (2003): 305-17.

United Nations Human Settlements Programme (UN Habitat). *The Habitat Agenda: Istanbul Declaration on Human Settlements*. Geneva: United Nations, 1996. [Online] Available at: http://www.unhabitat.org/unchs/english/hagenda/index.htm

Vaillancourt, Yves, Marie-Noëlle Ducharche, Robert Cohen, Claude Roy, and Christian Jetté. *Portrait des politiques de logement social au Québec à la fin des années 1990. Le Logement social, une composante importante des politiques sociales en reconfiguration: État de la situation au Québec*. Montréal: LAREPPS, 2000.

Wachernagel, M. and W. Rees. *Our Ecological Footprint: Reducing Human Impact on the Earth*. Gabriola Island: New Society Publishers, 1996.

World Commission on Environment and Development (WCED). *Our Common Future*. Geneva: WCED, 1987.

Mark Roseland

Curtain Call: In Search of a Missing Actor for Sustainable Community Development

In Nelson, British Columbia, a 1.11 hectare parcel of lakefront land located downtown was placed on the market by BC Buildings Corporation in 2001. Some of the proposed bids for the property included developing the land for big-box retail purposes. A group of local residents recognized the significance of this property, not only for its value as a prime development site, but also for the ability of development on this property to influence the design and function of future development on Nelson's waterfront as a whole.

This familiar scenario is played out in communities across Canada and many other countries on a regular basis. Our quality of life is closely related to the design and nature of the homes, neighbourhoods and communities in which we live. Recognition of the link between quality of life issues and the environment has been at the foundation of the rapid expansion of sustainable development planning on a global and local scale over the last decade.[1] However, the market has been slow to respond to sustainable development planning initiatives. While there are numerous examples of sustainable development plans, there are few examples of urban developments that are comprehensive reflections of those community plans. The purpose of this chapter is to discuss market mechanisms that help move from sustainable community planning to sustainable community development.

Current realities and trends toward a more influential role for the private sector and a more entrepreneurial approach to local government[2] have combined with the increased use of market mechanisms to guide, reward, monitor and penalize private-sector involvement in planning decisions and development projects.[3] This suggests that new approaches are needed to orient these influences toward sustainable community development.

In order to achieve specific land-use planning goals, there is a need for more flexible economic evaluation processes and a broader range of market-based approaches to achieve more complex objectives.[4] These new approaches need to be responsive not only to the market, but to proactive community participation as well—local social structures are powerful forces in the determination of urban processes.[5]

Community economic development (CED) is a means of addressing sustainable development at the community level (i.e., sustainable community development). This chapter argues that to fulfill the planning potential of sustainable community initiatives, the market has to respond with private-sector proposals and initiatives that advance sustainability. In most cases, however, there is missing a market actor to function in this capacity.

As well, seemingly ordinary local planning and development decisions can have significant impacts on global environmental sustainability.[6] Although local governments are not the only agencies charged with community planning and development, they are the only locally elected, representative and accountable bodies responsible for community decision-making. This makes them critical players in the movement toward sustainable communities.[7] Indeed, it is clear that if the agreements reached at the Earth Summit in Rio in 1992 and in Johannesburg in 2002 are to be implemented, most, if not all will require concerted action at the local level.

A prerequisite of sustainable community development is understanding the global context for local development and, to put these local matters in context, I begin with a brief discussion of sustainable development.

The Development Significance of Sustainable Development

In 1987, the World Commission on Environment and Development (WCED) report *Our Common Future* brought the concept of "sustainable development" squarely into the arena of governments and publics around the world.[8] This global audience has pinned its hopes on sustainable development as a solution to urgent environmental and societal problems where business-as-usual has failed.

The current debate over the Kyoto Accord on climate change illustrates that the mainstream view of the environment today is sharply different from what it was twenty-five years ago, when environmental problems were almost universally regarded as minor, technical, soluble and politically uncontentious. They were considered by-products of economic growth and social progress which further applications of growth and progress would duly solve, as increasing wealth created the resources, and improved technology the means, to solve them.

By 2000, throughout the industrialized world, governments and parties of both left and right were acknowledging that environmental problems are indeed very serious, requiring solutions which are not merely technical, and which may not be available at all without significant social and economic change. The vehicle for this shift has been the concept of sustainable development, which has succeeded in overcoming the conflict between environmental protection and economic growth that characterized the environmental debates of the 1970s and early 1980s. It accepts that protecting the environment requires fundamental change in the direction of economic progress and the institutions of government policy. But it argues that this is compatible with continued economic growth in a (regulated) global capitalist system. In this sense, sustainable development represents a "historic compromise" between the ideology of capitalism and its environmental critique, which has enabled a single environmental discourse of development, used by all manner of governments, businesses and environmental organizations.[9]

One might believe today that sustainable development has finally come of age. Born—publicly, at least—in the 1987 report of the UN's (Brundtland) World Commission on Environment and Development, the child of the global agenda at the Rio "Earth Summit" in 1992, stumbled awkwardly toward maturity with the Johannesburg World Summit on Sustainable Development[10] and the 2005 Kyoto Accord on climate change, sustainable development seems to have survived even the shift to a "post-September-11" world.

More people are using the term "sustainable" today than ever before, but most often it is used to simply mean "surviving," "staying afloat" or "not going out of business," rather than any integrated notion of simultaneously achieving economic, social and environmental objectives.

Some in the environmental movement might look askance at equating sustainability with economic survival, but with the end of the Cold War and the absence of any credible alternative to capitalism, it is clear that serious attempts to promote sustainable development must honour this basic capitalist and biophysical reality: nothing is sustainable if it is not here next year. For better or worse, this has not changed since Adam Smith published the *Wealth of Nations* in 1776.

What has changed, however, is an emerging recognition that a contemporary view of sustainable development has to blend this basic desire for economic prosperity with multiple bottom-line objectives. Staying in business is undoubtedly necessary, but it is no longer enough. We have obligations to the planet and to each other and to future generations. Business depends upon our commitment to these obligations (e.g., environmental stewardship; a healthy, educated and peaceful population) and fulfilling these obligations depends upon our ability to create and distribute wealth is in such a way that society and nature become more stable and secure, not less so.

Gated communities within gated countries will not lead to long-term global prosperity and security. Genuine "homeland security" requires us to "do development differently."[11] Much of the debate over the meaning of sustainable development focuses on the tension between the economic necessity for material growth and the ecological reality of limits. In the years since *The Limits to Growth*[12] was published, few researchers have seriously explored the implications of this concept for social organization, work and community economic development.[13] Ryle notes that "ecological limits may limit political choices, but they do not determine them." The heart of the growth issue, Ryle continues, is simply that

> underlying the social democratic advocacy of economic expansion is the
> fact that within a capitalist market framework, "growth" is indeed the
> prerequisite of much else: especially, of the provision of welfare services
> and the creation of jobs, and of national economic status vis-á-vis other
> capitalist powers. Thus the critique of growth becomes a critique of
> capitalism and the market … an alternative would have to find new, non-
> market-based means of providing employment and of meeting welfare
> needs.[14]

Just as sustainability has prompted a shift in our transportation and energy planning away from the traditional concerns with increasing supply to the new focus on managing demand, we must also shift our economic development emphasis from the traditional concern with increasing growth to *reducing social dependence on economic growth,* or what we might call EDM—economic demand management.[15] This has distinct implications for sustainable community development, particularly regarding employment and community economic development. As Norberg-Hodge puts it:

> The most urgent issue today, however, isn't whether people have oranges
> in cold climates, but whether their wheat, eggs, or milk should travel
> thousands of miles when they could all be produced within a 50-mile
> radius. Individuals are becoming dependent for their everyday needs on
> products that have been transported thousands of miles, often unnecessar-
> ily. The goal of localization would not be to eliminate all trade but to
> reduce unnecessary transport while encouraging changes that would
> strengthen and diversify economies at both the community and national
> levels. The degree of diversification, the goods produced, and the amount
> of trade would naturally vary from region to region.[16]

Community Capital

There are myriad ways to understand and conceptualize community.[17] In terms of sustainable community development, however, we are discovering that it is useful to think of community in terms of assets, or *capital.*

All forms of capital are created by spending time and effort in transformation and transaction activities.[18] During the last few years there have been several efforts to describe sustainable development in terms of three or four types of capital.[19] For example, Canada's National Round Table on the Environment and the Economy is using a capital model based on four types of capital.[20]

Recent explorations by the SFU Centre for Sustainable Community Development and others are attempting to create a notion of *community capital* as a foundation for sustainable community development.[21] Our perspective on community capital (Figure 14.1) includes natural, physical, economic, human, social and cultural forms of capital.[22] Strengthening community capital for sustainable community development means focusing attention on these six forms of capital:

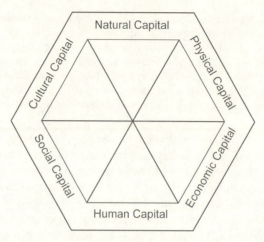

Figure 11.1 *Community Capital is the foundation for sustainable community development. Each triangle represents the ways we can strengthen that form of capital.*[23]

Minimizing the consumption of essential natural capital means living within ecological limits, conserving and enhancing natural resources, sustainable resource management (soil, air, water, energy, agriculture, etc.), cleaner production and minimizing waste (solid, liquid, air pollution, etc.).

Improving physical capital includes focusing on community assets such as public facilities (e.g., hospitals and schools) water and sanitation, efficient transportation, safe, quality housing, adequate infrastructure and telecommunications.

Strengthening economic capital means focusing on making more with less: maximizing use of existing resources (e.g., using waste as a resource), making the money-go-round (circulating dollars within a community), making things ourselves (import replacement), making something new (creating a new product), trading fairly with others and developing community financial institutions.

Increasing human capital requires a focus on areas such as health, education, nutrition, literacy and family and community cohesion; basic determinants of health such as peace and safety, food, shelter, education, income and employment are necessary prerequisites.

Multiplying social capital requires attention to effective and representative local governance, strong organizations, capacity-building, participatory planning, access to information and collaboration and partnerships.

Enhancing cultural capital implies attention to traditions and values, heritage and place, the arts, diversity and social history.

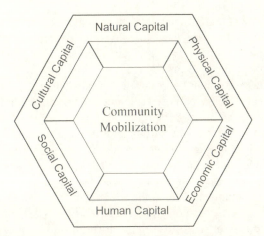

Figure 11.2 *A Framework for Sustainable Community Development. Sustainable development requires mobilizing citizens and their governments to strengthen all forms of community capital. Community mobilization is necessary to coordinate, balance and catalyze community capital.[24]*

Strengthening these six forms of community capital is the foundation for sustainable community development.[25] Applying the concept of sustainable development to North American communities requires mobilizing citizens and their governments to strengthen all forms of community capital. Community mobilization is necessary to coordinate, balance and catalyze community capital (Figure 14.2).

The community capital approach to sustainable community development approach requires some relatively new thinking about broad questions of community sustainability and self-reliance, and more specific innovations concerning community ownership, management, finance, organization, capacity and learning.

Using Market Mechanisms to Address Market Failure

Land-use planning rarely addresses long-term or life-cycle costs, so taxpayers often end up paying the hidden costs of development infrastructure (roads, sewage, etc.). Citizens in many communities see something wrong with this picture, but the solutions commonly proposed rarely speak to the underlying issues.

Although many communities have attempted to stop or slow growth, the critical issue for most communities is the pattern of growth, not the pace of growth. Communities which attempt to halt further development by prohibiting growth in their own jurisdictions merely shift development to neighbouring areas—where controls are looser and more conducive to further sprawl. Moreover, future development presents an invaluable opportunity to remedy the status quo. If communities do not want to be frozen in their current automobile-dependent patterns, they need to exploit new growth to their advantage by filling in underused space to make their urban areas more compact.[26] One key to changing growth patterns is rethinking the property tax system.

Sustainable communities require that we go beyond the notion that land is a mere commodity.[27] However, even in conventional economic terms, land is a peculiar commodity in that its supply cannot increase, no matter how high the price.[28] As demand for land grows, the wealth of landowners tends to grow regardless of how well or how badly they use the land. In his 1879 classic *Progress and Poverty,* Henry George proposed a solution to this dilemma: taxing away the *value* of land produced by anything other than private efforts. Such a land value tax would keep private landowners from unfairly capturing the benefits of natural resources, urban locations and public services. George also believed that this tax would force landowners either to put their land to its "highest and best" use themselves, or make it accessible to someone who would.[29]

While such comprehensive public approaches are essential, it is clear that other approaches must be developed and employed as well that are complementary and nimble. The market works well enough (beautifully, some would say) for private purposes, but when we are talking about the common good its failings become readily apparent.[30] While the land market generally functions well for individual property owners, it responds to price signals that reflect conventional understandings of "highest and best" use. Therefore, if left solely to its own devices, the market will substitute financial capital for other forms of capital[31] (e.g., converting agricultural land to shopping centres and depleting natural capital, or developing on sacred sites and depleting cultural capital). Its more egregious failings will be rectified by protected area designations, parks, agricultural land reserves and so on. However, as the Nelson example illustrates, there are more subtle market failures that have a huge impact on community sustainability, for example by influencing the amount of private (automobile) versus public transportation, or the amount of local employment and wealth creation versus economic leakage.

While sustainability requires comprehensive public-sector responses in regard to factors such as planning, taxation and services, it also requires complementary private sector approaches that are more entrepreneurial. "Normal" private sector actors do not generally concern themselves much with the common good, unless they are bigger players worrying about "reputation management," since the return on investing for the common good is rarely as high as the return where maximizing profit is the sole criterion. If the public sector sent the right signals (e.g., through shifting to green taxes, carbon taxes, etc.), we could expect more sustainably-oriented private initiatives; therefore, this is an extremely critical public agenda item. However, waiting for the day when the tax system rewards sustainable behaviour could be a very long wait, and in the meantime we are rapidly depleting natural and other forms of capital (e.g., losing ecologically and culturally significant parcels of land) to unsustainable development.

We therefore need a private actor with a sustainability outlook to use market approaches for the common good. Since the public sector does not seem to have the necessary resources, inclination, or will to strengthen community capital for sustainable development, we need to develop an actor who does have those qualities.

Such an actor would quietly, quickly and aggressively seek to control strategically significant land for sustainable purposes using market mechanisms (e.g., ownership). While this would be a new actor on the local stage, we have some valuable CED models we can learn from, such as socially-responsible investment funds, community development corporations and community land trusts. The most promising of these may be the community land trust (CLT).

Lessons from the Community Land Trust Model

The community land trust model stems from the ancient view of the earth as something naturally given, or God-given, to all people in common—something which, like the air above it, can never be owned in any absolute sense by individuals. A community land trust is not simply a land trust that happens to be in a community. As developed by the Institute for Community Economics,

> A community land trust is an organization created to hold land for the benefit of a community and of individuals within the community. It is a democratically structured nonprofit corporation, with an open membership and a board of trustees elected by the membership. The board typically includes residents of trust-owned lands, other community residents, and public-interest representatives. Board members are elected for limited terms, so that the community retains ultimate control of the organization and of the land it owns. [32]

The CLT acquires land through purchase or donation with an intention to retain title in perpetuity, thus removing the land from the speculative market. Appropriate uses for the land are determined in a process comparable to public planning or zoning processes, and the land is then leased to individuals, families, cooperatives, community organizations, businesses or for public purposes.

One of the greatest attractions of the community land trust model is that it is inherently flexible. Although there are characteristics common to all CLTs, each land trust writes its own bylaws and defines its own goals, priorities and structure. It is precisely because of this flexibility that the CLT model can link multiple objectives such as affordable housing and environmental protection.

Because communities vary, CLTs vary both in the emphasis that they place on specific issues and interests and in the strategies and techniques that they use to realize their goals. CLTs in rural areas are working to provide access to land and decent housing for low-income people, to preserve family farms and farmland and to facilitate sound, long-term land and forest management. Urban CLTs have formed to combat speculation and gentrification, to preserve and develop low- and moderate-income housing, and to maintain useful urban open spaces.[33] Several geographically decentralized communities or "units" might be quite different in size, structure and even purpose, but all could be strengthened under the umbrella of a single regional land trust.[34]

There are more than 125 CLTs in operation or development in both rural and urban areas in the United States, plus a few in Canada.[35]

> Land-use planning and environmental protection, placed in the hands of
> CLTs, would ... seem to satisfy those critics of traditional restrictions on
> use who decry the confiscatory nature of zoning and other police-power
> regulations, and who fear the centralization of land-use planning in
> higher and higher units of government.[36]

The CLT represents a means of "returning the power to plan and develop to local hands."[37]

However, the primary limitation of the CLT from a sustainable development perspective is that it makes little impact on the large concentrations of property and power which now abound in North America, and thus does not affect the pattern of landownership and institutional framework of land tenure outside of the CLT's domain. Like other CED models, CLTs are limited in their ability and scope; they often rely on government funding; they have limited organizational capacity to expand beyond day-to-day management; they lack long-term professional capacity (vs. short-term volunteer capacity); and they are fully absorbed with managing their existing properties and therefore lack capacity to be aggressive or expansive. As non-profit entities, CLTs also often find it difficult to sell or exchange assets easily. Existing CED models are therefore limited in their ability to transform development on a large scale, and sustainable development requires large-scale transformation of the development process.

In Search of a Missing Actor

What is needed is a new market actor that can ultimately take on this large-scale, strategic, sustainable, community development function, particularly with respect to site control and land assembly. This actor's role would be to acquire and hold strategically significant land for a limited period of time (e.g., 18-24 months), and during that time transform the site (e.g., by undertaking the necessary planning, design, rezoning, covenanting, business planning, community organizing, etc.). It would then convey or dispose of that land to another actor (e.g., a municipal government, green developer, co-housing group, etc.) with some certainty that the parcel of land in question will be developed in a more rather than less sustainable way (e.g., mixed-use housing and homegrown commercial rather than sprawling big-box retail).

The best form for this actor (e.g., a CLT, a CDC, a development trust, a real estate fund, etc.) is something we are currently trying to determine through our research. However, we can illustrate its potential by a brief examination of real estate development in British Columbia.

Real estate development in BC is a well-established, financed and mature area of economic activity. The bulk of private capital in recent years has been flowing to projects in the urban areas of the Lower Mainland of Vancouver and the Southern Vancouver Island areas near the provincial capital of Victoria. Although property development activity has been robust, there has been a dearth of projects that could be described as "green" (e.g., using LEED standards), especially in rural areas. More importantly, sustainable community development standards (sometimes referred to as Smart Growth) have been filtering into some urban developments but have been lacking in smaller communities. Additionally, there are an increasing number of ecologically sensitive areas that are lacking a stewardship champion, as well as abandoned developments in smaller communities that were once economic drivers but are now contaminated scars.

The real estate development landscape in BC includes: traditional developers ready to move capital to projects with financial potential, investors and financial institutions eager to consider land transactions that capitalize on the natural beauty of BC, land trusts (The Land Conservancy, Nature Trust, Nature Conservancy, Ducks Unlimited) working to protect areas for conservation, environmental NGOs that advocate for sustainable community development and public-sector players creating public policy to encourage land stewardship. What is missing is an actor to play a role in understanding and implementing sustainable market-based land acquisition and property development mechanisms, particularly for strategically significant properties that demonstrate sustainable community development opportunities. This is especially critical with respect to culturally significant sites with First Nations partners, ecologically sensitive areas and brownfield sites requiring land rehabilitation.

The site described earlier in Nelson, BC, serves to illustrate the role of this missing actor. The Nelson group was ultimately successful in purchasing the property; their purpose as owners is not to develop the land themselves, but to enact a form of site control on the land. When the best development proposal for the site is identified, the local group will arrange to sell the land to that developer.

Similar sites exist in many communities in Canada and around the world. Like the Nelson site, which could either become a big box Wal-Mart or a mixed-use neighbourhood with a park and community centre, they are strategically significant for the future of those communities. We have identified numerous other sites in British Columbia which illustrate these kinds of strategically significant developments, including:

- A 740-square-metre commercial building on the main strip of a small town, built to a very high green building standard. With the right ownership and management, it could become a centre for consumer awareness of green building.

- Three waterfront properties for sale in a coastal community that will almost double the size of the town, if fully developed, and fundamentally change the demographics and character of the entire area. The municipality has designated various public amenities and types of development for this land in its Official Development Plan.

- A heritage building located in a major city.

• A former residential school—a symbol of cultural loss—which the First Nations community wants to turn into a cultural and business centre that is an asset to the rejuvenation of their people.

• A potential community forest.

The Nelson example is inspiring, but also raises a number of interesting questions. The people in Nelson had to invent their strategy from scratch, and are stuck with major land holding costs as they find themselves in the risky role of novice developers. How many communities with similar properties at stake are unable to muster the financial and human resources necessary to control their destiny? How much more successful would Nelson and other communities be if they were able to call upon this missing actor to provide technical, legal and financial expertise, and/or organizational development and management capacity?

In Vancouver's Downtown Eastside, for example, the Woodwards department store building sat vacant for more than ten years despite numerous attempts to develop the property. It was not until the City of Vancouver purchased the site that community planning processes began. How different could it have been had our missing actor been identified and created?

The SFU Centre for Sustainable Community Development (www.sfu.ca/cscd) is actively engaged in a series of research projects on market mechanisms, site control and strategic sustainability designed in part to identify, and create, this missing actor.

This missing actor—a new CED tool·to promote sustainable community development—could be the key to building sustainable neighbourhoods. With good design and appropriate resources, it could operate in a range of jurisdictions, even a range of countries. With any luck, this missing actor might also demonstrate the true significance of sustainable development's "historic compromise" by transforming capitalism to serve sustainability, rather than to subvert it.

Notes

This chapter is based upon research funded in part by the Social Sciences and Humanities Research Council and by Canada Mortgage and Housing Corporation. Sean Markey, Sean Connelly, and Rick Kohn provided much-appreciated intellectual support.

1.   International Council for Local Environmental Initiatives (ICLEI), *Accelerating Sustainable Development*.

2.   Osborne and Gaebler. *Reinventing Government*.

3.   Choe, "The Promise and Pitfalls of Public-Private Partnerships in Korea," *International Social Science Journal*, 253-59; C. E. Di Leva, "The Conservation of Nature and Natural Resources." *Review of European Community and International Environmental Law*, 84-95.

4.   Corkindale, "Land Development in the United Kingdom." *Environment and Planning* A, 2053-2070; Williamson, "Re-Engineering Land Administration Systems." *International Journal of Applied Earth Observation and Geoinformation*, 278-89.

5.   Imrie, Thomas and Marshall, "Business Organizations, Local Dependence and the Politics of Urban Renewal" *Urban Studies*, 31-47.

6.   See Newman and Kenworthy, *Sustainability and Cities*; Wackernagel and Rees, *Our Ecological Footprint*.

7.   Roseland, *Eco-City Dimensions* and *Toward Sustainable Communities*.

8.   World Commission on Environment and Development. *Our Common Future*.

9.   Jacobs, "The New Politics of the Environment," in *Greening the Millennium*.

10.   International Council for Local Environmental Initiatives; K. Otto-Zimmermann, "Local Action 21: Motto-Mandate-Movement." *Local Environment* 7, 465-69.

11.   Roseland, *Toward Sustainable Communities*.

12.   Meadows, et al. *The Limits to Growth*.

13.   See Meadows, et al. *Beyond the Limits*.

14.   Ryle, *Ecology and Socialism*.

15.   Roseland, *Toward Sustainable Communities*.

16.   Norberg-Hodge, in *Small is Beautiful*.

17.   Throughout this chapter the term "community" is used to refer to geographic communities (i.e., communities of place as opposed to communities of interest, race, business, etc.) with a shared destiny, and represented by a municipal, local or band form of government.

18.   Ostrom, *Social Capital*.

19.   Goodland, "Sustainability," in *Encyclopedia of Global Environmental Change*; Rainey, Robinson, Allen and Christy, "Essential Forms of Capital for Sustainable Community Development." *American Journal of Agricultural Economics*, 708-15.

20.   National Roundtable on the Environment and the Economy (NRTEE), *Environment and Sustainable Development Indicators*.

21.   See Roseland, "Natural Capital and Social Capital," in *Communities, Development, and Sustainability*, 190-207; Roseland, "Sustainable Community Development," in *Progress in Planning*, 73-132; Hancock, "People, Partnerships and Human Progress." *Health Promotion International*, 275-80.

22.   The term "community capital" more conventionally refers to economic or financial capital. For example, in the U.S., National Community Capital is a network of more than 150 private-sector community development financial institutions (CDFIs) that provides financing, training, consulting and advocacy for CDFIs. Active in all 50 states, the National Community Capital network invests in small businesses, quality affordable housing, and vital community services that benefit economically disadvantaged people and communities. National Community Capital is committed to leading the community development finance system to scale through capital formation, policy and capacity development. Details at: http://www.communitycapital.org/.

23.   Roseland, *Toward Sustainable Communities*.

24.   Ibid.

25.   Ibid.
26.   Lowe, *Shaping Cities*, 105.
27.   Canadian Institute of Planners (CIP). *Reflections on Sustainable Planning*.
28.   With a few notable exceptions, such as Boston's Back Bay area, built on fill, or
       that city's massive "Big Dig" project to bury a major freeway system and "create"
       new land over it.
29.   Brown, ed., *Land Use and Taxation*.
30.   Daly and Cobb, Jr., *For the Common Good*.
31.   Roseland, 2005.
32.   Institute for Community Economics (ICE), *The Community Land Trust Handbook*.
33.   Ibid.
34.   International Independence Institute (III), *The Community Land Trust: A Guide to
       a New Model*.
35.   Institute for Community Economics (ICE), www.iceclt.org.
36.   Davis, "Reallocating Equity," in *Land Reform, American Style*.
37.   Ibid.

Bibliography

Brown, H. J., ed. *Land use and Taxation: Applying the Insights of Henry George.* Cambridge,
    MA: Lincoln Institute of Land Policy, 1997.

Canadian Institute of Planners (CIP). *Reflections on Sustainable Planning: The Implications
    of Sustainable Development for Planning and the Canadian Institute of Planners.*
    Ottawa: CIP, 1990.

Choe, S. C. "The Promise and Pitfalls of Public-Private Partnerships in Korea." *International
    Social Science Journal* no. 172 (2002): 253-59.

Corkindale, J. "Land Development in the United Kingdom: Private Property Rights and
    Public Policy Objectives." *Environment and Planning* A 31, no. 11 (1999): 2053-70.

Daly, H. E. and J. B. Cobb, Jr, *For the Common Good: Redirecting the Economy Toward
    Community, the Environment, and a Sustainable Future.* Boston: Beacon Press, 1989.

Davis, J. E. "Reallocating Equity: A Land Trust Model of Land Reform." In *Land Reform,
    American Style,* edited by Charles Geisler and Frank Popper. Totowa, NJ: Rowman
    and Allanheld, 1984.

Di Leva, C. E. "The Conservation of Nature and Natural Resources through Legal and
    Market-Based Instruments." *Review of European Community and International
    Environmental Law* 11, no. 1 (2002): 84-95.

Goodland, R. "Sustainability: Human, Social, Economic and Environmental." In
    Encyclopedia of Global Environmental Change. John Wiley & Sons Ltd., 2002.

Hancock, T. "People, Partnerships and Human Progress: Building Community Capital."
    Health Promotion International 16, no. 3 (2001): 275-80.

Hart, S. L. "Beyond Greening: Strategies for a Sustainable World." *Harvard Business Review*
    75, no. 1 (1997): 66-77.

Imrie, R. H. Thomas and T. Marshall. "Business Organizations, Local Dependence and the Politics of Urban Renewal in Britain." *Urban Studies* 32, no. 1 (1995): 31-47.

Institute for Community Economics (ICE). *The Community Land Trust Handbook.* Emmaus, PA: Rodale Press, 1982.

Institute for Community Economics (ICE), www.iceclt.org (accessed January 2005).

International Council for Local Environmental Initiatives (ICLEI). *Accelerating Sustainable Development: Local Action Moves the World.* New York: United Nations Economic and Social Council, 2002.

International Independence Institute (III). *The Community Land Trust: A Guide to a New Model for Land Tenure in America.* Cambridge, Mass: Center for Community Economic Development, 1972.

Jacobs, M. "The New Politics of the Environment." In *Greening the Millennium*, edited by M. Jacobs. Oxford: Blackwell Publishers, 1997.

Lawless, P. and D. Robinson. "Inclusive regeneration? Integrating Social and Economic Regeneration in English Local Authorities." *Town Planning Review* 71, no. 3 (2000): 289-310.

Lowe, M. D. *Shaping Cities: The Environmental and Human Dimensions.* Worldwatch Paper 105. Washington: Worldwatch Institute, 1991.

Meadows, D.H., et al. *The Limits to Growth.* NY: Signet, 1972.

Meadows, D., et al. *Beyond the Limits.* Post Mills, VT: Chelsea Green, 1992.

National Roundtable on the Environment and the Economy (NRTEE). *Environment and Sustainable Development Indicators for Canada.* Ottawa: NRTEE, 2003.

Newman P. and J. Kenworthy, *Sustainability and Cities: Overcoming Automobile Dependence.* Washington: Island Press, 1999.

Norberg-Hodge, H. In *Small is Beautiful: Economics as if People Mattered*, edited by E. F. Schumacher, Vancouver: Hartley & Marks, 1999.

O'Holliday, C. O., S. Schmidheiny and P. Watts. *Walking the Talk: Business Case for Sustainable Development.* San Francisco: Greenleaf Publishing, 2002.

Osborne, D., and T. Gaebler. *Reinventing Government.* New York: Plume, 1993.

Ostrom, E. *Social Capital and Development Projects.* Cambridge, Mass: American Academy of Arts and Sciences. 1993.

Otto-Zimmermann, K. "Local Action 21: Motto-Mandate-Movement in the Post-Johannesburg Decade." *Local Environment* 7, no. 4 (2002): 465-69.

Rainey, D. V., K. L. Robinson, I. Allen, and R.D. Christy, "Essential Forms of Capital for Sustainable Community Development." *American Journal of Agricultural Economics* 85, no. 3 (2003): 708-15.

Roseland, M. *Eco-City Dimensions: Healthy Communities, Healthy Planet.* Gabriola Island, BC: New Society Publishers, 1997.

———. "Natural Capital and Social Capital: Implications for Sustainable Community Development." In *Communities, Development, and Sustainability Across Canada,* edited by Pierce, J. T., and A. Dale, 190-207. Vancouver: UBC Press, 1999.

———. "Sustainable Community Development: Integrating Environmental, Economic, and Social Objectives." *Progress in Planning* 54, no. 2 (2000): 73-132.

————. *Toward Sustainable Communities: Resources for Citizens and their Governments* Gabriola Island, BC: New Society Publishers, 1998, 2005.

Rybeck, R. *Tax Reform Fights Sprawl.* OECD International Conference, Vancouver, 1996.

Ryle, M. *Ecology and Socialism* London: Radius, 1988.

van Vliet, W. "Cities in a Globalizing World: From Engines of Growth to Agents of Change." *Environment and Urbanization* 14, no. 1 (2002): 31-40.

Wackernagel, M. and W. E. Rees, *Our Ecological Footprint.* Gabriola Island, BC: New Society Publishers, 1996.

Williamson, I. P. "Re-Engineering Land Administration Systems for Sustainable Development—from Rhetoric to Reality." *International Journal of Applied Earth Observation and Geoinformation* 3, no. 3 (2001): 278-89.

World Commission on Environment and Development. *Our Common Future.* New York: Oxford University Press, 1987.

Gayle Broad and Linda Savory-Gordon

Worker Ownership as a Strategy For Community Development

In the afternoon of July 31, 1990, as the final hours of the Collective Agreement with the United Steelworkers of America Local 2251 expired, Algoma Steel Corporation in Sault Ste. Marie, Ontario, notified workers scheduled for the night shift that they were not to report for work, thereby sparking a lockout/strike that continued until late September. By the time the employees returned to work, the steel company was in a financial crisis from which it could not recover. Adversarial labour relations, high environmental clean-up costs and a downward spiralling global steel market guaranteed serious difficulty in obtaining a new buyer.

Over the course of the next eighteen months, the company was put on the market, entered bankruptcy protection and proposed a restructuring plan that was unacceptable to both workers and creditors. On June 1, 1992, the United Steelworkers of America (USWA) made history as it led an employee buyout of the third-largest steel company in Canada. With the purchase of more than 50 per cent of the company's shares, the new Algoma Steel Inc. (ASI) became the largest worker-owned company in Canada.

The employee purchase of ASI contained a major proviso: that ownership by the workers would include a joint union/management decision-making structure and process. Union representatives obtained the right to participate, in equal numbers with managers, at all levels of the decision-making structure from the Board of Directors to the shop floor, including a Joint Steering Committee, Department Co-Chairs, and Self-Directed Workgroups (SDWGs).

From 1997 until 2000, Broad and Savory-Gordon in collaboration with sixteen steelworkers at ASI conducted two participatory action research inquiries into worker ownership and participation at the worker-owned company. One group of researchers explored issues related to worker ownership and participation within the workplace, while the other group explored the "spillover" effects of workplace change in the lives of the workers, their families and the community of Sault Ste. Marie.

Workers at ASI no longer control the majority of shares in the company. The first major sell-off of shares occurred in 1995 when they were required by financiers to sacrifice a portion of their control in order to obtain financing required for a new mill. Since then there has been a gradual erosion of both the ownership and the control by workers. The collaborative research conducted by steelworkers with Broad and Savory-Gordon, however, offers a number of insights into the potential of worker ownership as a community economic development strategy.

Worker Ownership as a CED Strategy

> One of the prime reasons for the union to be involved is economic
> viability ... to control what the company does here, so there's not
> somebody outside Sault Ste. Marie dangling us like puppets.

(Trade union activist at Algoma Steel Inc.)[1]

Local control of the local economy is an important goal of community economic development (CED), and Shragge points out that in the face of plant closures, an effective CED strategy is to generate local investment in the local community.[2] Worker ownership, or employee buyouts, is certainly one way of both gaining local control of the local economy and of generating investment in the local community, yet it has remained relatively unexplored terrain for CED practitioners.

Research by the authors has indicated that financial benefits are not the only reason for practitioners to consider worker ownership as a CED strategy. The participation of worker-owners in decision-making can build community capacity and social capital through the provision of a more democratic, empowering setting for workers.[3] Worker ownership can therefore provide an alternative that can raise the consciousness of, and be transformative for, the workers and their community.[4]

Critics of worker ownership have suggested concerns about both the economic and social aspects of the strategy. On the economic side, worker ownership is sometimes viewed as too high-risk, in that workers would lose both wages and investment were the company to fail.[5] This would expose workers in industrial settings to the same risks taken by small entrepreneurs in starting up a small business. On the other hand, critics have also been concerned that worker participation in decision-making would result in a form of class collaboration, whereby workers' knowledge is actually used to reduce the number of employees with little-or-no-benefit to the workers remaining nor to the working class at large.[6]

The research at ASI provides some contradictory evidence to these concerns. After two years of research with worker-owners, the authors have concluded that worker ownership is a viable strategy for CED practitioners and in certain situations may be the best strategy. Their research at ASI provides a number of reasons for practitioners to consider this alternative.

For worker ownership to be considered as a tool, CED practitioners need answers to the following questions:

1. What are the benefits of worker ownership?
2. What are the conditions necessary for its success?
3. When is worker ownership an appropriate strategy for CED practitioners?
4. What policies can be introduced to support worker ownership?

The Benefits of Worker Ownership

> *We have to think about what Algoma will look like not just for the next two or three years, we're not just looking out for* ourselves.... There's *the spin-off jobs in the community too – if everybody was only making $7 per hour we wouldn't be buying much.* (A worker-owner).[7]

Pateman has outlined three types of worker participation that illustrate various levels of power-sharing: pseudo, partial and full.[8] Authors such as Brannen and Wajcman have shown that "full" participation must include workers at all levels of the organization, and that pseudo or partial participation is unlikely to result in greater democratization.[9] Arnstein and Burns, Hambleton and Hoggett support the concept that qualitatively, participation varies significantly depending on such factors as access to high-quality information, weight accorded the opinions of participants, who selects the participants and access to resources.[10]

To ensure that the workers at ASI had the resources and developed the skills and knowledge to fully participate in the new structures, two particularly important committees were established—the Worker Training Committee and the Workplace Redesign and Technology Committee. A consensus decision-making approach was adopted at all levels of the structures.

The ASI research also demonstrated that "full" participation cannot be realized if participation is restricted to one sphere alone (i.e., that "full" participation for workers meant to participate both in owning the company and in making decisions about its future and the way it was run). Workers frequently referred to their ownership of shares as a key factor in giving them the right to participate in the joint process.

Recent research has found that worker ownership at ASI has been cut from 50 per cent to only half that, and the worker participation in management is in disarray. Despite this unfortunate decline in active ownership and participation of the workers, there is a great deal that can be gained from reviewing this case study for CED practitioners. This case illustrates that worker ownership can be a valuable tool both in controlling local assets and in building community capacity.

Economic Benefits

After Algoma Steel Corp. spent more than a year of searching for a buyer in 1990-91, it became apparent that worker ownership was the only way of securing the millions of dollars required to keep the plant from closing down. One of the major benefits of worker ownership at ASI was the continued employment of more than 7,500 workers at the plant, and another 350 at an iron ore mine in Wawa,[11] a small community located about 250 kilometres north of Sault Ste. Marie. The rescue of Algoma Steel through the worker buyout resulted in local job preservation, wealth creation and provision of a sufficient material base to sustain local public institutions.

In Sault Ste. Marie the worker buyout is largely responsible for the survival of Algoma Steel and therefore the survival of the city itself at its present size. At the time of the buyout the average age of workers was forty years, making transition to another community or type of employment difficult, both for them and for their families. Their age, together with an average length of employment at ASI of 18 years and the general downsizing in the industry at the time, compounded the challenges faced by workers in seeking other types of employment:

> I was a hard line steward for a lot of years but the writing was on the
> wall. Without doing what we did...there just wasn't going to be any jobs.
> (A worker-owner).[12]

A 1996 publication, Terri Lynn Williams and Jong You[13] found the Algoma Steel employment multiplier in Sault Ste. Marie to be two-to-one. In 1992 estimates showed that closing the plant would have resulted in the loss of 23,100 jobs—7,800 at Algoma Steel and 15,300 in Sault Ste. Marie and other parts of Ontario.[14] Municipal tax loss is another indicator of the devastating economic impact Algoma's closure would have had on Sault Ste. Marie. In 1991 Algoma Steel's "municipal taxes amounted to about 20 per cent of the overall taxes of the city, not including the property taxes paid by Algoma's employees."[15]

Another major economic benefit of a worker buyout is the determination of workers to maintain wages and benefits at former rates. Workers want to maintain their standard of living and therefore look for other cost-cutting measures. At ASI, although workers did purchase their shares through payroll deduction, thereby reducing their income for a period of time, they were able to restore wages to previous levels within five years, and they were able to maintain all benefits, including those for retirees.

While economic benefits have accrued from employee ownership, they have also accrued from the joint process of employees participating in decision-making. According to Strauss another economic benefit of worker participation is improved productivity.[16] By involving workers in problem-solving and harnessing their intimate knowledge of production issues and equipment, significant gains can be made in efficiencies of operation. The study at ASI confirmed this:

"Why aren't you pushing 75 ovens every shift?"...And you really have to stand up and say "no."...Let's analyze what's the problem with the equipment, how can we make the equipment operate faster so we can give you more? (A worker-owner).[17]

For the company, the worker buyout provided an opportunity to capitalize on the substantial knowledge of the workers, something that a previously adversarial culture and hierarchical management style prevented. The research at ASI indicated a number of areas where significant efficiencies were gained due to workers' knowledge being shared with managers as well as the exchange of knowledge between managers and workers. One particular example was in developing just-in-time delivery strategies that meet high quality requirements of the auto industry, one of the major customers of ASI. Other examples given by the co-researchers included: significant savings through recycling materials, improved worker satisfaction due to improved scheduling arrangements and many examples of improved production processes.

In the new structure, the worker-owners were more willing to share their knowledge, contributing to the company's long-term viability: in a competitive global market such as the steel industry, workers' knowledge could be the asset that maintains ASI's edge in the industry.

Paton suggests that if a worker buyout survives for five years after the purchase, the initiative has been successful because it has provided the community with an opportunity to diversify and gradually adjust to the loss of a major industry.[18] Because ASI has survived for twelve years, it must be considered an economic success. As a one-industry town in a hinterland region, Sault Ste. Marie has been provided with an opportunity to diversify its economic base over a substantial number of years, gradually absorbing the reduction of employment through attrition.

Building Social Capital and Community Capacity

Some of us are socially inept. We're socially backward and isolated from information and our neighbours.... For some of us, participating in self-directed work groups enhanced our ability in relationship-building with our families, our neighbours and so on. More people are volunteering for fundraising for local sports teams for example. (A worker-owner)[19]

When the workers became owners of ASI on June 1, 1992, they also obtained the right to participate in decision-making structures from the shop floor through to the Board of Directors' levels, an arrangement known as the "joint process." Following the initiation of the joint process many ASI employees, including shop floor workers, received varying amounts of "soft skills" training in interpersonal or communication skills, meeting skills, conflict resolution, consensus-building, problem-solving processes and how to criticize in appropriate and constructive ways. Although a cost-benefit analysis of this training has not been conducted, the total investment was $10 million spread out over a period of five years, a minuscule portion of the more than $250 million annual salary expense.

Within ASI, the workers began participating in a wide variety of committees and groups: forming Self-Directed Work Groups which strategized around improved production; developing training programmes rooted in the principles of trade union collectivism; serving as co-chairs of Department Steering Committees. This resulted in a substantial workplace democratization in some parts of the plant, and a steep learning curve for many of the participants. One worker described the transition at ASI:

> For eight hours a day there was a hierarchical tyranny and for the other sixteen hours we lived in a democracy. Then suddenly we tried to move from hierarchy to pure socialism without any steps in between. (A worker-owner)[20]

As Bronfenbrenner points out, the developmental effects resulting from experience in one setting are carried over into other settings in the form of developmental trajectories.[21] In the case of ASI, this contributed to building the community's capacity both within the ASI community and in the larger community outside the workplace and contributed as well to the building of social capital. This concept of "spillover" effects was readily apparent in research conducted in Sault Ste. Marie following the employee buyout.[22]

One of the spillover effects into the community was the evidence of attempts to develop more democratic decision-making in a number of community organizations. Some workers and managers transferred the new practices at ASI into their communities of practice in their churches, sports associations, schools and health care facilities. A First Nation community tried to use the ASI model to change their decision-making processes.

Some organizations in Sault Ste. Marie were affected by the requirement for the joint-process set for equal union/management representation in all activities undertaken by ASI. As a result, a number of community organizations which previously had only ASI management representatives on their boards were required to invite equal numbers of unionized employees, contributing to a more equitable distribution of community power. In this way, some working-class people began sitting on community boards and councils that were overwhelmingly composed of those in more powerful social locations.

Many employees displayed greater confidence, asserted themselves or felt proud of being an Algoma Steel employee as a result of having some say at work, learning to express ideas and concerns, acquiring new skills and knowledge and/ or feeling they had a stake in the company as employee owners. There was evidence of ASI employees valuing relationship-building to a greater extent in their lives outside of work. For some it took the form of spending more time with their families or making more effort to improve personal relationships. Some of the workers, having seen the value of working together as a team at work, were trying to work as a team at home. One expressed it this way:

> …we work our problems out together; I take what she has to say, instead of just saying we have to do this. It's more teamwork. So teamwork

carries on to the wife and we work together to solve our problems. (A worker-owner)[23]

In a society in which individual private ownership is the dominant form of ownership of productive property, the cooperative venture of steelworkers collectively owning more than 50 per cent of ASI flies in the face of mainstream values of competitive individualism. Some employees transferred the new values outside the plant, placing increased value on collectivist ways of meeting their needs or contributing to the common good of their communities.

A praxis approach to community development considers both egalitarian, democratic process and egalitarian, democratic values-based content to be indispensable. Some community developers contend that workplace democratization in a capitalist economic system is only a form of class collaboration that cannot contribute to social transformation. This premise ignores the role of practice or action learning. Learning to create the egalitarian, cooperative, democratic processes in the workplace can be part of the unmasking of the existing unequal, authoritarian social relations.

The research at ASI illustrated on many occasions that the participatory practices made workers even more aware of the inequalities of power relations in the workplace, and suggested that their previous security of employment and income had made them more complicit with maintaining the status quo:

> *I wanted a revolution back in 1980, '81....I said "Stu we got to have a*
> *revolution." He says "a revolution? Are you crazy? I've got two cars in*
> *the driveway, a couple of snow machines in the garage, a boat sitting out*
> *there, what the hell do we need a revolution for? I'm in heaven already."*
> (A worker-owner)[24]

In 2003, as ASI went through yet another restructuring process to avert bankruptcy, an ASI steelworker made the following comment, during an interview on CBC radio. His comment shows the value he now places on the need for non-authoritarian social relations as a result of his experience in the joint process:

> *As it stands right now we have a joint participation. I am a [departmen-*
> *tal] co-chair [representing unionized employees of the department]. I*
> *have participation with the managers at all levels and information flows*
> *back and forth. The concern is: will it go back to the old autocratic way*
> *that we have no input, no say and everything will be dictated?* (A worker-owner)[25]

This statement reflects not only an experience of empowerment for that employee but also allows that experience of empowerment to spill over into the community discourse and consciousness in the form of a commentary on a public radio broadcast. Other members of the Sault Ste. Marie and district community listening that morning were thereby exposed to an alternative vision of the form social relations at work can take. They could also have been prompted to reflect on social relations in other social institutions in their lives—introducing the idea of autocratic/

dictatorial versus participatory organizational programs. The democratization model spilled over, in that radio interview, entering the public discourse.

The new worker-ownership structure became a visible alternative economic arrangement in public discourse beyond Sault Ste. Marie. Majority employee ownership, accompanied by a significant governance role for the union, made Algoma Steel unique among large North American industrial corporations. It caught the attention of academics, researchers, business administrators, human resource professionals and unions nationally and internationally, becoming the topic of publications and presentations in several countries. As a result, ASI served as an example of the fact that alternative economic ownership arrangements are possible alternatives to the dominant corporate ownership structure.

What are the Conditions Necessary for Its Success?

> The biggest impediment [to change] is stepping outside your safety zone … we're asking people to shift their values, values that have been based on competition. We need to find ways of supporting people in a values-changing exercise…. (A worker-owner).[26]

Paton found in his study of a large number of worker buyouts that union involvement was a rarity, but Ted Jackson suggests that trade unionists and CED practitioners need to stand together in the fight for "economic justice, dignity and social peace."[27] In the ASI context, the USWA was crucial in providing the research, planning and advocacy necessary to achieve such a huge undertaking. The union also played a major role in securing the contract provisions necessary for worker participation in decision-making, and in democratizing the workplace, all of which played into the capacity-building process.

As the above quotation indicates, the cultural change necessary to move from a hierarchical workplace to a more democratic decision-making style is very difficult. Other successful initiatives show that workplaces with a few hundred workers, rather than several thousand, are more likely to be able to make the transition.[28]

The type of industry should also be considered carefully in the assessment of worker ownership for a particular situation. A few years after the buyout, in the fall of 1995, ASI was forced to decrease its worker ownership of shares and some of its democratic practices as a condition of obtaining financing of over $300 million for a new mill. Given the unlikely occurrence of finance capitalists supporting CED initiatives, worker ownership is best considered as a strategy in industries which require smaller amounts of capital than steelmaking, or where capital is more readily available from funds such as labour investment funds.

Another condition essential to the success of the worker buyout at ASI was the legitimization of the purchase through efforts of the union, the community and the provincial government. The USWA together with a Community Action Team (CAT) invested heavily in building support for the worker buyout, opening an office and recruiting small investments from the community. This initial activity and involvement of the community led to widespread community support for the buyout itself. Since the workers were faced with taking a substantial cut in wages (in order to purchase the shares) and each worker had to vote on the buyout, it was essential that they felt supported in the endeavour.

Bob Rae's NDP government also contributed by adding credibility to the concept of worker ownership through a variety of methods. The government supported worker ownership in a number of companies throughout the early 1990s and it also amended legislation and was instrumental in bringing the financial players to the table to negotiate the buyout at ASI. After the purchase at ASI, however, the CAT efforts were abandoned and, with the election loss of Rae's NDP government in 1995, much of the initial support and credibility for the concept of worker ownership was lost. Increasingly, workers were faced with criticism—both from within ASI and without—and the negative attitude affected the morale of the workers.

It is important to emphasize that only "full" participation is effective in producing positive spillover.[29] The ASI findings as well as Greenberg, Grunberg and Daniel's[30] research both support this conclusion. Both demonstrate the co-relation between (a) workers' perceptions that they were included in processes aimed at fuller participation and (b) positive spillover effects, such as enhanced feelings of efficacy and morale. In the ASI spillover research there was evidence that those workers who were transferring their new experience and skills most were those who were involved in more intense participatory opportunities (e.g., in self-directed work groups, in departmental steering committees or active committees and task forces) and had taken extensive training. The corollary was evident in the form of disinterest in spillover experiences from the New Algoma to life outside as the democratization was increasingly diluted. As the training was terminated, support for the workplace redesign efforts to set up SDWGs diminished and the joint process was side-stepped by senior management; the participants in the action research project became less and less interested in promoting spillover.

In other words, as the participation goals shifted from full participation to partial participation and pseudo participation, spillover declined.

This concept of partial participation was also found in the workers' views of the right to participate, derived from their ownership in shares. As the percentage of share ownership declined, due to pressures from financial corporations in the 1995 refinancing of the Direct Strip and Plate Complex (DSPC), so too did the workers' sense of entitlement to participate in decision-making. Once again, the ASI research illustrates the interconnectedness of economic and social participation. As one steelworker phrased it:

> I've paid $36,000 and my family gave that up too, so that I could
> participate in the decisions about how this company is run, and whether
> it keeps running. (A worker-owner)[31]

CED practitioners employing worker ownership as a tool need to ensure that there is ongoing awareness and education regarding the benefits of the strategy to ensure its success. As the ASI research indicates, awareness of the power differentials between employees and managers, and taking steps to address those through education and support, are essential for the realization of democratizing the workplace.

In Algoma Steel's case, the pressure that financial institutions were able to place on the structures of participation, combined with only a partial implementation of the training plan, and the lack of support from policy makers and others for the initiative, have resulted in a decrease in the potential benefits. There is also a need for workers to be aware that power-sharing does not occur overnight—it is a gradual, lengthy process. Workers need support for the long term to shift such entrenched power relations.

When is Worker Ownership the Appropriate Strategy for CED Practitioners?

Under particular circumstances worker ownership can be the best solution. In cases where plant closure is being considered due to insufficient profit margins, worker ownership has proven itself to be a viable alternative, both in Europe and throughout Ontario in the early 1990s.[32] In industries where unions already exist and can provide leadership, or where the investment required may be too great for a cooperative purchase, worker ownership may be the preferred choice.

The research at ASI has demonstrated that worker ownership can contribute to reducing production costs, particularly in one-industry communities where the technical skills of workers are highly specialized as in steelmaking. Many examples of improvements in production were evident throughout this research. The ASI research showed that worker ownership is much more likely to succeed when leadership can be provided by either the union or another community "champion." As CED practitioners are aware, this is often the case with CED initiatives as they run counter to mainstream or dominant beliefs and need support systems.

As well, worker ownership may be a viable alternative in succession planning, when entrepreneurs or family-owned businesses have no apparent heirs, yet are financially viable, particularly where long-time employees have acquired substantial knowledge and specialized skills in production. In small to medium-sized enterprises (SMEs) worker ownership would appear to be a preferred choice.

The research at ASI points out that at least in the short-term, worker ownership is still too innovative to receive support from major financial institutions, so in industries such as steelmaking which are highly capital-intensive, worker ownership is not often indicated as an option. In other industries, where smaller investors can finance the purchase, worker ownership should be considered.

Public Policy Issues

Public policy support for workplace ownership would be logical for the achievement of civic, economic and social goals and the ASI research provides additional support for this policy direction.

Worker ownership combined with workplace democratization improves peoples' capacity for civic participation.[33] When the new company was providing opportunities for its employees to receive training in, and to apply, skills that contribute to increased political participation and civic voluntarism, civic capacities were being developed. Workers developed skills such as the ability to participate in, organize and plan meetings, make presentations and use tools such as email for plant-wide communication.

By supporting models of worker ownership such as employee buyouts and co-operatives, government could contribute to the creation of viable places of employment. Such modes of ownership (a) have jobs, not just profit, as a goal of the enterprise, and (b) can result in the maintenance of industrial and manufacturing jobs, and therefore a higher multiplier effect (small business, public services). In these ways the alternative economic arrangements such as employee ownerships and co-operatives reduce unemployment and all of the related social health problems that accompany unemployment.

Workplace democratization also makes sense from a government social policy perspective. Skills such as communication skills, conflict resolution and problem-solving skills were used both to develop a more egalitarian workplace and to help resolve family problems. From a social policy perspective, workplace democratization can be seen as a form of social problem prevention. The adoption of government policy to support workplace democratization could improve the quality of life outside and inside the workplace and even reduce social programme expenditures for the treatment of social problems such as work-related stress and family breakdown.

Some examples of the kinds of public policies that would help to facilitate workplace ownership and democratization might include: legal supports to accommodate worker-owners, financial support for training and moral and facilitative support from civil servants and politicians. At ASI, the government provided assistance with retirement bridging, to assist in easing the transition to a smaller workforce, and loan guarantees which were never utilized. These interventions were essential in the negotiations with creditors, and should be available to other communities and workplaces.

The political support could be prescribed in policy regulations rather than leaving it to the chance circumstance of a government favourable to employee participation. The support and facilitation provided by the two local Members of Provincial Parliament, the federal Member of Parliament and the provincial Premier was to a great extent due to the fact that as New Democrats they espoused this collectivist endeavour.

Public policy that emphasizes the interrelatedness of the social and economic spheres needs to be encouraged rather than separated into distinct categories of research and development. Regional development agencies, for example, should be encouraged to assist communities in CED activities which consciously and explicitly link the two spheres. At the academic level, such linkages should be encouraged in the design of postsecondary community development programs. The newly instituted Bachelor of Arts degree in Community Economic and Social Development at Algoma University College is, at time of writing, the only undergraduate degree program in Canada which explicitly combines both economic and social development. The community development movement could lobby for community development agencies to stop separating their mandates along economic and social lines and pressure for more programs which marry the two aspects.

Worker ownership should be viewed as one of a collection of tools which support community economic development—not as a unique experiment. The research at ASI clearly illustrated the need for worker-owners to be supported in their endeavours by a broad coalition from their community, from others engaged in CED and from the government:

> … there is a need to feel that you belong….(A worker-owner).[34]

Conclusions: Implications for CED Practice

> … employee ownership is often introduced for economic reasons … [but] there are additional arguments … employee ownership may be seen as having the beneficial effect of consolidating democratic institutions [and] it can also perform a number of social functions…. [35]

The research at ASI suggests that worker ownership should be considered as a CED strategy, particularly when the circumstances are as outlined above. This research provides two major lessons for CED practitioners: first, that worker ownership combined with worker participation in decision-making can be a powerful tool for building community capacity and controlling local assets. It is this combination of the two aspects of worker participation—in the financial sphere as well as in the social relations sphere—that is most likely to lead to its success. A dilution of either will decrease the effectiveness and spillover effects of the effort. Second, structures that support full participation of workers—rather than pseudo or partial—contribute to spillover from the workplace to the home and the community of democratizing principles, relations and processes.[36] The opportunity for workers to fully engage in new structures and processes results in transformative change.

People involved in community development tend to be divided in their focus—working exclusively in relation to either economic or social concerns. The research at ASI points to the shortcomings of such a division. Those working in the economic field are mainly concerned with creating employment, while those in social development are dealing with the fallout from unemployment, or from stressors resulting from workplaces where the focus is solely on financial efficiency. Rarely do community development people work on both aspects and maximize the benefits of the reinforcing relationship between the two.

The research at ASI demonstrates the value which community economic development, if based on collectivist values and processes, can have for community social development and vice versa. While community economic development workers are cognizant of the social benefits to community in terms of the social effects of increased employment, the mutually reinforcing effects of human and social development in the "social" and "economic" or workplace settings need to be more consciously used in development work. Those involved in democratization and empowerment efforts in the workplace sphere could find ways to converge their cultural transformation approaches and action with those involved in democratization and empowerment efforts in the community and domestic spheres. The two-way character of spillover shows the potentiality when development in one sphere is used as a starting point for the enhancement of development in other spheres. This calls for further attention to overcoming not just the economic/social divide, but also the gender divide: Workplace democratization tends to be the purview of primarily male trade unionists while community social development tends to focus on women's issues and involve more female participants (though many of the paid organizers are men).

The research at ASI demonstrated that participation encompassing both the social *and* economic relations of the workplace and which provided processes and structures for workers to participate at all levels of decision-making—from the shop floor to the Board of Directors—offered workers an opportunity for transformative learning and experience. Full participation—where workers were provided with the resources to participate on an equal footing with managers and senior executive members—was necessary for the engagement and willingness of workers to take the experiences into other spheres of their lives. Community developers who are content with consultation with stakeholders, rather than finding practices which create opportunities for full engagement, are likely to obtain unsatisfactory results, or at least are unaware of the potential.

Gaventa eloquently summarizes the multi-dimensional approach to community development that the ASI research supports:

> [T]he approach must be "both-and" rather than "either-or." The critical challenge for building participatory democracy is to understand and develop the dynamic interrelationships among the differing aspects of overcoming powerlessness, to develop a unified approach that educates for consciousness, mobilizes for action, and advocates on the issues simultaneously. Such an approach requires developing new networks and constellations of organizations in differing sectors that can work together for common goals. Such a capacity for collaboration could greatly deepen our work for a more participatory and democratic society.[37]

Worker ownership and participation could become part of a leadership role in developing a broadly based working class social movement.

Notes

1.   Quoted in Broad, "Stepping Outside the Safety Zone," (PhD diss.), 167.
2.   Shragge. *Community Economic Development*; Nozick, *No Place Like Home*.
3.   Strauss. "Participation works," in *Organizational Participation*.
4.   Mathiesen, *The Politics of Abolition*; Andrew and Klodawsky, "Women's Safety," *Women and Environments*.
5.   Burawoy, *The Politics of Production*.
6.   Parker and Slaughter, "Unions and Management by Stress," in *Lean Work, Empowerment and Exploitation*.
7.   Worker-owner, quoted in Broad, 167.
8.   Pateman, *Participation and Democratic Theory*.
9.   Brannen, *Authority and Participation in Industry*; Judy Wajcman, *Women in Control* 193.
10. Arnstein, "A Ladder of Participation," *Journal of the American Institute of Planners*; Burns, Hambleton and Hoggett, *The Politics of Decentralization*.
11. These numbers have been gradually reduced through attrition at the main plant in Sault Ste. Marie and through closure in 1996 of the iron ore mine in Wawa. Currently, there are approximately 2800 hourly workers employed by ASI.
12. Worker-owner, quoted in Broad, 117.
13. Williams and You, *Employment Multipliers in Northern Ontario Cities*.
14. McCartney, "Algoma Steel Inc: A Successful Restructuring." In *Case Studies in Recent Canadian Insolvency Reorganizations*, 238.
15. Quarter, *Crossing the Line*, 122.
16. Strauss.
17. Worker-owner quoted in Broad, 164.
18. Paton, *Reluctant Entrepreneurs*.
19. Worker-owner, quoted in Savory-Gordon, "Spillover Effects of Increased Workplace Democracy." (PhD diss.).
20. Broad, 146.
21. Bronfenbrenner, *The Ecology of Human Development*.
22. Savory-Gordon. Most of the spillover effects that were identified had occurred spontaneously. There was *very* little encouragement of the workers to transfer their new experiences into their lives outside the plant. In spite of the lack of official promotion of spillover it was clearly occurring during the period of "fuller" participation. One of the goals of the action research on spillover was to promote spillover and assess whether conscious promotion of spillover would increase it. The conclusion was that promotion of spillover did increase and enhance it.
23. Quoted in Savory-Gordon.
24. Quoted in Broad, 159.
25. Quoted in Savory-Gordon.
26. Quoted in Broad, 164.
27. Paton, *Reluctant Entrepreneurs*; Ted Jackson, "Unions Matter to CED, and CED Matters to Unions," *Making Waves*.
28. Paton.

29. Pateman.
30. Greenberg, Grunberg and Daniel, "Industrial Work and Political Participation, *Political Research Quarterly*.
31. Quoted in Broad, 157.
32. Paton.
33. Verba, Schlozman and Brady, *Voice and Equality*.
34. Quoted in Broad, 152.
35. ILO, *Employee Ownership in Privatization*.
36. Pateman.
37. Gaventa, "Citizen Knowledge." In *Citizen Competence and Democratic Institutions,* 63.

Bibliography

Andrew, Caroline and Fran Klodawsky. "Women's Safety and the Politics of Transformation." *Women & Environments* 14.1 (1994).

Arnstein, Sherry R. "A Ladder of Participation." *Journal of the American Institute of Planners* 35.4 (1969): 216-24.

Brannen, Peter. *Authority & Participation in Industry.* Great Britain: Billings Ltd, 1983.

Broad, Gayle. "Stepping Outside the Safety Zone: Worker Ownership and Participation at Algoma Steel Inc." Ph.D. diss., University of Bristol, 2000.

Bronfenbrenner, Urie. *The Ecology of Human Development: Experiments by Nature and Design.* Cambridge, MA: Harvard University Press, 1996 [1979].

Burawoy, Michael. *The Politics of Production: Factory Regimes under Capitalism and Socialism.* London: Verso Press, 1985.

Burns, Danny, Robin Hambleton, and Paul Hoggett. *The Politics of Decentralization: Revitalizing Local Democracy,* Basingstoke: Macmillan, 1994.

Gaventa, John. "Citizen Knowledge, Citizen Competence, and Democracy Building." In *Citizen Competence and Democratic Institutions,* edited by S. Elkin and K. Soltan. University Park, PA: Pennsylvania State University Press, 1999.

Greenberg, Edward, Leon Grunberg, and Kelly Daniel. "Industrial Work and Political Participation: Beyond 'Simple Spillover'." *Political Research Quarterly* 49.2 (1996).

Jackson, Ted. "Unions Matter to CED, and CED Matters to Unions." *Making Waves* 7. 2 (1999).

ILO *Employee Ownership in Privatization: Lessons from Central and Eastern Europe, Experts' Policy Report.* Hungary: ILO, 1998.

Mathieson, Thomas. *The Politics of Abolition.* New York: John Wiley & Sons, 1974.

McCartney, James C. "Algoma Steel Inc: A Successful Restructuring." In *Case Studies in Recent Canadian Insolvency Reorganizations,* edited by J. S. Zeigel, 238. Canada: Carswell, 1996.

Nozick, Marcia. *No Place Like Home: Building Sustainable Communities.* Ottawa: Canadian Council on Social Development, 1992.

Parker, Mike and Jane Slaughter. "Unions and Management by Stress." In *Lean Work, Empowerment and Exploitation in the Global Auto Industry,* edited by S. Babson. Detroit: Wayne State University, 1995.

Pateman, Carole. *Participation and Democratic Theory.* Cambridge: Cambridge University Press, 1970.

Paton, Rob. *Reluctant Entrepreneurs.* Milton Keynes: Open University Press, 1989.

Quarter, Jack. *Crossing the Line.* Toronto: James Lorimer & Company, 1995.

Savory-Gordon, Linda. "Spillover Effects of Increased Workplace Democracy at Algoma Steel on Personal, Family and Community Life." Ph.D. diss., University of Bristol, 2003.

Schragge, Eric. *Community Economic Development: In Search of Empowerment.* Montreal: Black Rose Books, 1997.

Strauss, George. "Participation Works – If Conditions are Appropriate." In *Organizational Participation: Myth and Reality,* edited by F. Heller, Eugene Pusic, George Strauss, and Bernhard Wilpert. Oxford: Oxford University Press, 1998.

Verba, Sidney, Kay Schlozman and Henry Brady. *Voice and Equality: Civic Voluntarism in American Politics.* Cambridge, Mass: Harvard University Press, 1995.

Wacjman, Judy. *Women in Control.* Milton Keynes: Open University Press, 1983.

Williams, Terri Lynn and Jong You. *Employment Multipliers in Northern Ontario Cities: Sault Ste. Marie, Sudbury and Thunder Bay.* Research Report 96-2 (December), Sault Ste. Marie, ON: Algoma University College, 1996.

Gertrude Anne MacIntyre and Jim Lotz

State of the Art: The Third Option

> *"Everything in war is simple, but the simplest thing is difficult."*
> Karl von Clausewitz, On War.

What the German military strategist wrote of war applies with equal force to all forms of community-based development and especially to community economic development (CED). The principles of CED are simple and easy to grasp, rooted in the belief that people in communities, working together, can organize collective ventures to create employment and generate and distribute new wealth.

The practice of CED is incredibly complex and difficult.

There is no "one-size-method-process-model-approach-fits-all" way to do CED. Every community is unique, as are the people who live in it. With the collapse of communism and the steady withdrawal of governments from providing the necessities of life for their people, coupled with the recent exposure of the excesses of capitalist greed, there is a danger that CED may be seen as an instant solution to the complex problems of creating democratic, egalitarian, efficient and humane societies.

In 1990, the Economic Council of Canada issued *From The Bottom-Up: The Community-Economic Development Approach.*[1] This "statement" promoted CED as a way of revitalizing depressed and single-industry communities. It claimed that, despite decades of government interventions, disparities in Canada between rich and poor areas, urban centres and marginal regions persisted. The Council concluded that: "[T] op down bureaucratic-driven plans for regional development have fallen into disrepute and policy-makers know they need to consider new approaches."[2]

The Council commissioned several case studies on CED. When the Bank of Montreal closed its branch at L'Anse au Loup on the south coast of Labrador, local residents created a credit union. The bank manager stayed in the community to pass on his knowledge and a Caisse populaire, across the provincial boundary in

Québec, provided services to the new venture.[3] This example reveals the ability of community residents to come together, draw resources from inside and outside their boundaries and bring into being a new way of pooling capital for collective ventures.

Other case studies show how CED relied on dynamic individuals, rather than on collective initiatives, for the revitalization of ailing communities. The credit union at L'Anse au Loup arose from a crisis. In West Prince County, Prince Edward Island, a man with business experience brought energy and direction to a local development agency mired in inertia.[4] Here, organizational development preceded CED—and then the key person moved elsewhere. A burnt-out American veteran of the Vietnam War with some knowledge of CED went to Northern Saskatchewan in search of peace and quiet. Members of a First Nation sought his help and advice on generating employment and he became the director of their economic development agency. Separating the band's political processes from those associated with business development, he helped create Kitsaki Development Corporation.[5] This new body formed joint ventures with non-Aboriginal business people, creating employment and income for the Kitsaki. Here again, organizational development directed by an outsider preceded CED. And the prime mover, in time, moved on to other opportunities.

All successful CED ventures involve individuals who transcend and seek new ways of meeting human needs. They operate with one foot in the traditional business world and the other in the wild and uncertain arena of human emotions, wants, desires and visions about the best way to create a more open, responsive and abundant society. The Economic Council, however, simply saw CED as another instrument for generating jobs and wealth in regions where the traditional approaches to doing so had failed. Its statement offered no insights into the kinds of people who make CED work among marginalized and deprived individuals and collectivities. The Council did not examine why neither the state nor the private sector had been effective in meeting the needs of these people. By treating CED as it did, as just another way of creating employment, the Council depoliticized the process.

Looking Back

This quasi-government body, The Economic Council—which was abolished shortly after it promoted CED as a new way to solve development problems of poor regions and people—paid no attention to the history of past efforts in community-based development. In Eastern Nova Scotia, in the depths of the Great Depression, was the site of a pioneering enterprise in what today would be labelled CED. Residents pooled their nickels and dimes, formed credit unions and co-operatives and gained a considerable measure of control over their social and economic destinies. Father Moses Coady, the charismatic leader of what became known as the Antigonish Movement, working with a group of clergy and lay people, urged rural residents to: "Listen! Study! Discuss! Act!" Based at the Extension Department of St. Francis

Xavier University, these "noble souls," as Coady called them, took knowledge to the people. They showed how, through collective action, they could learn their way out of poverty and dependency and become *Masters of Their Own Destiny*, the title Coady chose for his book on the movement.[6]

As Western societies became more affluent after the Second World War, governments became increasingly aware of the poverty within their own nations. Community development emerged as a way of eliminating it and integrating people into the mainstream life of the nation.

In July 1966, Prime Minister Lester Pearson promoted community development as a panacea for all the ills of Canada:

> As a philosophy and a method, community development offers a way of involving people more fully in the life of their communities. It generates scope and initiative which enables people to participate creatively in the economic, social and cultural life of the nation. It provides, above all, effective use of the democratic processes. These are the essential elements in Canada's social policy. These principles underlie our current and social programmes which, in essence, are designed to make it possible for people to overcome low income, poor education, geographic isolation, bad housing, and other limitations on their environment.[7]

At the time this statement appeared, Canada lacked a trained corps of community developers. As money flowed into this new field, turf wars began. Social workers and adult educators each claimed the field as their own. And almost any outsider intervening in a community or among the poor claimed to be doing "community development." Conferences, committees (including several set up by the Special Planning Secretariat of the Privy Council, the federal coordinating body for Canada's War on Poverty), task forces and others discussed exactly what constituted community development. Members of the Company of Young Canadians, a federally funded body, saw community development as a way of fighting the system, of radically changing Canadian society, seizing power, and running the revolution on government money. The CYC became a seedbed for radicals. Established agencies used community development as a way of maintaining the status quo and ensuring their continued existence.

The story of community development in Canada has yet to be told.[8] In one western province, the director of the government program led a protest march to the legislature. Manitoba pioneered CED in effective ways, but the program became encapsulated by the bureaucracy when the first director left. In this province, a community development worker ran against his minister in an election—and won. One conclusion that emerged from these experiences was that governments, for a variety of reasons, could nurture community-based development, but they could not do it through the traditional bureaucratic structures.

New nations adopted community development with great enthusiasm and attempted to implement top-down programs to eliminate poverty—with little success. During the 1970s, these programs faded away, replaced by attempts at large-scale planning and ad hoc efforts to improve the living standards of the poor. In the 1980s, neoliberalism and reliance on market forces, linked to structural adjustment of national economies, appeared to offer a way of generating enterprise, initiative and economic expansion. Bayat notes the ambiguity implicit in community development which "has had the double effect of maintaining the status quo and engendering social change." He claims that the programs of community development were aimed at "counter-insurgency against communism in the colonies, containing discontent among blacks in the United States and managing the poor in Britain."[9] Reviewing social change in the Middle East, Bayat notes that it is the initiative of individuals through their everyday actions—the prevalence of "quiet encroachment." He describes it as "the silent, protracted and pervasive advancement of ordinary people on those who are propertied and powerful in a quest for survival and improvement of their lives."[10]

Appropriating Community Development

This may well be what community economic development is about. It became popular in Canada as the recessions of the early 1980s and 1990s revealed the inability of governments and the private sector to generate jobs and wealth during times of rapid economic and social change. By inserting "economic" in the middle of the term, the concept of community development—and the clichés associated with it—took on new life. In 1980, Employment and Immigration Canada launched Canada Community Economic Development Projects to create jobs that had value for the unemployed and their communities. In 1991, the Department of Health and Welfare commissioned studies to determine how social goals could be linked to economic ones through CED projects.

A familiar pattern emerged as a wide variety of ventures were labelled "community economic development" to secure government funding. This strategy, focusing on poor people and marginal areas, diverted attention from the ideological biases of government and their performances in creating a more open, egalitarian and democratic society. Was CED being used as a way to keep people quiet, to control dissent, to hobble revolutionary or reformist impulses by invoking the concept of community? This feeling permeated the earlier community development movement.

Retaking CED: New Dawns

In Cape Breton, federal and provincial governments poured millions of dollars into the coal and steel industries when their foreign owners found them no longer profitable. They also launched programs to hire displaced workers by offering grants to offshore companies and individuals. The nationalized industries lost massive amounts of money while employing fewer and fewer workers and many of the subsidized industries failed—or moved to more tax-friendly countries. As the 20th century ended, the last coalmine on the island closed, as did the steel mill.

These old industries left a huge legacy of environmental pollution: the Sydney Tar Ponds have become the largest environmental blight in Canada. Attempts to clean it up have resulted in conflict and failed efforts in the choice of technology to eliminate this residue of hundreds of years of a capitalism that did not include pollution on its balance sheet.

The controversy over the tar ponds has received local and national media coverage. The work of CED ventures in Cape Breton has received less publicity as the island emerges as the centre of this grassroots approach to economic development. CED has arisen here, as elsewhere, in response to the failure of top-down efforts to generate employment and viable business ventures. In 1974, a small group of local citizens, many of whom worked at Xavier College (now Cape Breton University), came together to create New Dawn (now New Dawn Enterprises) which was incorporated as Canada's first community economic development corporation. Led by Father Greg MacLeod, who was inspired by the work of the priest who helped to found the Mondragon business complex in the Basque region of Spain, the venture arose out of an effort to help a craft project that needed new quarters. Seed money from the Department of Health and Welfare provided the core funding for New Dawn in its first five years.

The leaders of this CED corporation sought to go beyond the bottom line in individual and community revitalization, to offer a third option to the traditional ones using government or private sector methods to provide goods and services. They were not obsessed with globalization and its impact. This word was not part of the discourse about world development as it is today. The pioneers of CED on Cape Breton and elsewhere saw it as a countervailing force to the increasing control by governments and large domestic corporations over the lives of Canadians. A concern with human dignity and social and economic justice, a respect for the ability of ordinary people to work together for the collective good, a belief that individuals could become participants in their development and that of their communities—all these values underlay early efforts at CED. Coupled with these values was an understanding of the importance of the bottom line, of running businesses efficiently and effectively to meet consumer needs. CED does not fit neatly into bureaucratic and academic boxes. So politicians and civil servants— and most academics—have trouble with it. In the 1970s, no Canadian learning institutions offered opportunities for learning how to do CED. If politics is the art of the possible, CED soon began to be seen as the art of the impossible, an arena where new ways of meeting human needs could be tested and implemented.

CED has moved from being seen as a panacea for all the problems of poor people and peripheral regions to acceptance as a place for innovations and creativity in individual and human development, where economic democracy can flourish while offering employment opportunities for those who find work in government and the private sector unrewarding in the spiritual sense. Like community development, CED sometimes suffered from messianism—over-reliance on saviours to assuage the ills of communities.

While governments and the private sector pay lip service to the importance of innovation and creativity, they like to keep it under control. Even the New Democratic Party, which promotes patrician socialism, prefers to do things *for* people rather than *with* them. The experiences with the ill-fated CED programme by the NDP government in Ontario in 1990-95 bears this out.

Among other things, CED ventures in Canada have created a new language which avoids the rhetoric of politicians and bureaucrats and the boosterism and hucksterism that marks talk about development in the private sector. New Dawn learned how to manage internal tensions while coping with the forces from outside their community over which they had little or no control. As MacLeod put it: "We adapted, we became 'sea lawyers' clever at finding loopholes ... like other community groups ... and that's how we kept going. Several times we almost went bankrupt."[11]

By 1985, New Dawn had $10 million in assets, a volunteer board of directors and a staff of thirty. Everyone learned on the job as governments struggled to understand this new kind of economic development. As MacLeod pointed out, when a group built up equity and became independent, "government officials don't like dealing with local groups that have any kind of independence."[12]

In the 1980s, after extensive public discussions about the future of Nova Scotia, the provincial government set up a Community Development section in its Department of Development. It hired a skilled and experienced individual who did not set out to sell CED to the public or the politicians. Instead he sought to spread an understanding of its potential and limitations. Money has often been seen as the main problem in community-based development. Through the establishment of Community Investment Funds, investors can put their money into local economic ventures. New Dawn was supportive of BCA Holdings, a community economic development investment fund in Sydney that gathers community investment for community ventures. The provincial government limits losses that might be incurred by failed ventures. The results of the CIF approach has been mixed, with some successes, some short-term success and, of course, some failures. In Meteghan, Nova Scotia, the West Nova Investment Co-op-funded Eagle Timber folded after three years' operation because of poor market conditions.[13]

CED in Prince Edward Island has also flourished. Here too a key official in the provincial government served as an enabler, supporting local initiatives while explaining their rationale and style of operation to politicians and civil servants who are unfamiliar with them.[14] On the Island, despite all the rhetoric in the private sector about free enterprise, market forces and the value of competition, organizers of funeral co-ops were harassed by large funeral corporations as they struggled to set up locally-controlled ventures. The National Film Board film, *We're The Boss*, promoted CED,[15] but two of the ventures it examined, a potato chip plant and a children's clothing enterprise, ceased operation as collective efforts after the film was made. CED initiatives, like enterprises in the private sector, operate in a competitive marketplace. Initially, New Dawn played it safe, investing in real estate ventures. In 1990, misreading the market, the corporation lost $150,000 on a cloth diaper service. New Dawn also had to cope with tensions between the volunteer board of directors and the paid staff—something that pervades all community-based ventures. By 1993, however, the corporation had built more than 230 apartments and assisted in the development of two co-ops and eight business or non-profit ventures.

Risk-taking in CED has to be more sophisticated than in the private sector. Those who do it are accountable to the community—not to shareholders who recognize that their investments might not bear the expected fruit. When a military base near Sydney went up for sale, New Dawn developed an innovative proposal for turning it into a senior's community. Two welders laid off by a learning institution asked the CED venture for help in setting up a training school, which has been very successful. New Dawn also attracted dentists to Sydney by building and equipping a clinic.

CED ventures operate in areas that suffer from dependency. Residents in such areas fall prey to the Western version of cargo cults, believing that all good things come from elsewhere without any effort on their part, they are prone to substituting magic for rational planning in seeking to determine their future.[16] Hence the overblown rhetoric of hucksters and boosters who claim they can generate jobs and income in depressed communities and regions. Among their number are academics who believe that if their theory is implemented, all will be well. The cargo cult approach weakens self-reliance and local initiative, the essential underpinnings of community economic development. New Dawn Enterprises has been effective in generating local initiative and developing ways of stimulating self-help. It has also sponsored joint ventures with other community groups. In June 2003, the corporation joined with local business people, a First Nations organization, and BCA Holdings to build a $3.5 million steel fabricating plant on Sydney harbour. The provincial government provided a matching loan of half this amount.

The principles underlying any form of community development—self-help, mutual aid, collective action—are as old as humanity. They are difficult to put into practise in highly individualized, fractured societies undergoing rapid change. The Antigonish Movement showed that it is possible for deprived individuals and communities to learn their way out of poverty and dependency in hard times. Discussions about CED often focus on concerns like infrastructure, strategic planning and capacity building, ignoring the fact that the process is about doing things for and with people. The rising interest in CED, a field in which practice is well ahead of policy—and politicians—increases the risk of it being seen as an ideology. The dangers of this appeared in a study of 150 local organizations throughout the world:

> Some of the most successful training efforts have been found among co-operatives, where there has been a great deal of emphasis on the philosophy and goals of co-operation, but not enough on the mechanics of

making co-operatives operate efficiently. This emphasis may derive from the fact that it is easier to impart abstract ideas than to explain organizational dynamics, financial management or legal issues.[17]

Building Training and CED Education

Our own experiences with the MBA program in CED at Cape Breton University bear out this conclusion. The courses focus on both "hard" skills (principles of accounting, marketing, finance, venture analysis, organizational behaviour, etc.) and "soft" ones (history and theory of community development, community organization, leadership training, etc.) which are difficult to quantify. Options are offered that focus on First Nations, Middle East (where CBU offers the program in Cairo), and other areas of concern. The leading process in the CED program mirrors that in the field. Students take responsibility for their own learning—and that of their classmates. They are urged to take control of the processes involved, while at the same time sharing their knowledge, experience and street smarts, to create a learning community and to support and encourage each other.

Canada, and especially Nova Scotia, is uniquely positioned to become a world centre for learning the theory and practice of CED. We have accumulated a great deal of knowledge and experience in understanding both. Our experience with the MBA program in Egypt reveals that our learners have much in common with those in developing nations:

> A lot of the [students'] previous education has been acquired through the memorization process. Although they were knowledgeable of the subject matter, it was readily apparent that they had not been encouraged to think independently—an essential component of graduate study.[18]

The business literature, especially in North America, now stresses the need for innovation, creativity and new thinking in ensuring the survival and growth of private companies. They are of even more importance in the formation and development of CED ventures.

Our focus on learning CED—it is very hard to teach it in the traditional manner of academe—is on the following:

> • Determining ways whereby individuals, groups and communities can make better decisions to inform their actions. This involves learning how to sort out the signals (relevant information) from the noise of the many information systems that impinge upon our everyday consciousness. Students learn how to identify reliable sources of knowledge, information and experience.

> • Encouraging resourcefulness. This involves newer and more cost effective ways of meeting human needs, and ties in with notions of sustainability.

> • Learning how to motivate and organize people, starting with the student herself or himself. A high level of awareness is required by individuals in CED so that they do not mislead or confuse themselves—

and others. Learners carry out personal SWOT (Strengths, Weaknesses, Opportunities, Threats) analyses over time, and come to terms with their demons—and their angels. Saviours pop up in times of change and confusion and can be helpful or harmful to communities. Our experience has been that messiahs do not make good managers and that saviours only too often become scapegoats.

CED is no longer an arena for inspired amateurs or rebels, with or without causes, or saviours seeking to create economic utopias. It is a fertile field of human endeavour that can transform individuals and communities. It offers a third option to statism and capitalism for those willing to take responsibility for their own social and economic destinies rather than relying on others.

New ideas always emerge from the margins of society, away from the complexities, distractions, infighting and other features of the centres of power and the interminable struggles for ascendancy there.

And so it is with Community Economic Development.

Rankin MacSween, president of New Dawn Enterprises, summed up the essence of this intriguing, frustrating approach to bettering the human condition:

> It's not what you know that's important. It is what you try to remember. The key to innovative ventures like New Dawn lies in identifying the gifts that people possess and determining what each person has to offer to the collective good.[19]

Notes

1. The Economic Council of Canada, *From The Bottom Up.*
2. Ibid. pp 2-3.
3. Wickham and Miller-Pitt, *Where Credit is Due.*
4. MacKinnon, *The West Prince Industrial Commission*, Ottawa, Economic Council of Canada, October, 1989.
5. Decter and Kowall, *A Case Study of the Kitsaki Development Corporation.*
6. Coady, *Masters of Their Own Destiny.*
7. In *The Journal of the International Society for Community Development*, July 1966 devoted to "Community Development in Canada."
8. Lotz, *Understanding Canada* and *The Lichen Factor* include surveys of community development in Canada and elsewhere in the world.
9. Bayat, Social Movements, Activism and Social Development; United Nations Research Institute for Social Development, Civil Society and Social Movements.
10. Ibid., 24
11. Quoted in Commission of Inquiry on Unemployment Insurance, 70-71.
12. Ibid.
13. Milson, *Voices of Nova Scotia Community*, 20-24.
14. Wilkinson and Quarter, *Building a Community-Controlled Economy.*

15. Subtitled "Making the Connections Between Culture and Community Economic Development," the film was released in 1990.
16. On cargo cults, see Worsley, *The Trumpet Shall Sound*.
17. Esman and Uphoff, *Local Organizations*, 229.
18. Goth, quoted in "Global MBA promotes community development," *Atlantic Co-operator*, May 2003. College students at elite institutions in Cairo study Dickens and 19th-century Russian authors, but not the works of Naghib Mahfouz, the Egyptian Nobel Prize winner.
19. MacSween, "A CED Corporation's Contribution to the Cultural and Economic Development of the Cape Breton Economy," address to the North Atlantic Forum 2003, Sydney, October 13, 2003.

Bibliography

Bayat, Asef, "Social Movements, Activism and Social Development in The Middle East." United Nations Research Institute for Social Development, Civil Society and Social Movements, Programme Paper Number 3, November 2000.

Coady, M. M. *Masters of Their Own Destiny: The Story of the Antigonish Movement of Adult Education Through Economic Cooperation.* New York, Harper and Brothers, 1939.

Commission of Inquiry on Unemployment Insurance. Ottawa, 1986.

Decter, Michael B. and Jeffrey A. Kowall. *A Case Study of the Kitsaki Development Corporation.* Ottawa, Economic Council of Canada, October, 1989.

The Economic Council of Canada. *From The Bottom Up: The Community-Economic Development Approach.* Ottawa, 1990.

Esman, Milton J. and Norman T. Uphoff. *Local Organizations.* Ithaca, Cornell University Press, 1984.

"Global MBA promotes community development." *Atlantic Co-operator*, May 2003.

Lotz, Jim, *Understanding Canada: Regional and Community Development in Canada*, Toronto, NC Press, 1977.

———. *The Lichen Factor: The Quest for Community Development in Canada.* Sydney, UCCB Press, 1998.

MacKinnon, Wayne, *The West Prince Industrial Commission.* Ottawa, Economic Council of Canada, October, 1989.

MacSween, Rankin. "A CED Corporation's contribution to the Cultural and Economic Development of the Cape Breton Economy." Address to the North Atlantic Forum 2003, Sydney, October 13, 2003.

Milson, Scott, *Voices of Nova Scotia Community: A Written Democracy.* Halifax, Fernwood Publishing, 2003.

Pearson, Lester B. In *The Journal of the International Society for Community Development.* July 1966 devoted to "Community Development in Canada."

We're the Boss: Making Connections Between Culture and Community Economic Development. National Film Board, 1990.

Wickham, John, Richard Fuchs, and Janet Miller-Pitt, *Where Credit is Due: A Case Study of the Eagle River Credit Union*. Ottawa, Economic Council of Canada. October, 1989.

Wilkinson, Paul and Jack Quarter, *Building a Community-Controlled Economy*, University of Toronto Press, 1966.

Worsley, Peter, *The Trumpet Shall Sound*. London, Paladin, 1970.

Margaret Wilder, Jocelyn D. Taliaferro,
Raheemah Jabbar-Bey and Bahira Sherif-Trask

CED Practice in the United States

Although most U.S. citizens enjoy a standard of living which exceeds that of much of the world population, poverty and inequality have been persistent elements in the American social and economic landscape. For decades, efforts to address disparities have been promoted through community economic development (CED). As a field of practice, CED has an explicit goal to improve the quality of life and life chances for economically and socially disadvantaged individuals, families and neighbourhoods. This goal is sought through a number of strategies aimed at reducing poverty and giving those in need a greater voice in planning and implementing positive economic, physical and social change in their own communities. Moreover, CED in its most aggressive form seeks to promote social justice by attacking barriers to economic and social equality.

This chapter provides an overview of the conceptual and practice landscape of CED in the United States. We describe the basic historical context in which CED evolved, major models of practice, achievements within the field and critical assessments of its strengths and weaknesses.

Historical Overview

After several decades of severe economic and social disparities, the crisis of America's cities and neighbourhoods became evident in the context of the 1960s as the frustration of poor and minority residents spilled out onto the streets of urban centres. Political and economic leaders could no longer afford to ignore the problems and needs of the urban poor and disenfranchised. Community development was catapulted into the national policy arena with the 1960s Ford Foundation Grey Areas program. The program created initiatives in five cities (Boston, Oakland, New Haven, Philadelphia and Washington, DC) with the specific purpose of addressing the ineffectiveness and unresponsiveness of urban schools and local government.[1] It attempted to coordinate youth-oriented service programs among local bureaucracies in each city, but did not include residents in the visioning and planning processes, an omission that led to its demise.

The next major CED national initiative was enacted through the 1964 Economic Opportunity Act, a major component of the Johnson administration's War on Poverty. The Act brought about innovative social programs such as Head Start and Community Action Programs (CAP). The CAPs were distinguished by the primary goal of promoting "maximum feasible participation" of local residents in the regeneration of communities.[2]

The CAP created community action agencies (CAAs) to pursue its goal of promoting a self-help methodology for addressing neighbourhood and community concerns. The emphasis of CAAs was on the direct engagement of community residents in planning, program development and political advocacy. Federal funding to support CAP projects were given directly to CAAs, bypassing local government and creating a form of community empowerment. This fiscal independence, as well as internal squabbles, created a significant backlash against CAAs and led to the dismantling of the program.[3] Nevertheless, the CAA program proved significant in providing residents the opportunity to engage in local governance processes, and produced new local leaders in the political arena.

In the late 1960s and early 1970s, Community Development Corporations (CDCs) began to emerge at the grassroots level. The first wave of CDCs, characterized as activist organizations, were supported by the federally-funded Special Impact Program (SIP) under the Economic Opportunity Act. SIP provided significant funding for these community agencies with more than $75 million in federal support between 1968 and 1986.[4] As non-profit 501(c)3 organizations with volunteer boards, CDCs focused on bottom-up comprehensive community reinvestment strategies, particularly physical development.[5] These first-generation CDCs undertook a broad comprehensive approach as a means of addressing issues of capitalist market failures, physical infrastructure deterioration and a myriad of social problems affecting impoverished neighbourhoods.

In the mid- and late 1970s, a second generation of CDCs evolved. As the numbers grew, federal funding cuts, as well as the promotion of Nixon's "Black Capitalism" (which focused on African-American self-help through business development) undermined the original comprehensive model of community economic development. Many CDCs began to emphasize entrepreneurship and "brick and mortar" projects. Community empowerment became secondary to sustaining CDC projects and programs.[6] The third generation of CDCs, developed in the 1980s and 1990s, adopted a highly professionalized and specialized approach to community development. Much of their efforts focused on housing and physical development and related issues, such as unfair lending practices and housing discrimination.[7]

Despite of the work of CDCs, the 1970s and 1980s brought highly concentrated levels of poverty in central cities as well as an ideological shift toward conservatism.[8] The trends of social disorganization that emerged in urban neighbourhoods in the 1960s and 1970s intensified under the federal cuts of social programs and record-high unemployment rates of the 1980s. A more targeted strategy was advocated for an urban community development policy, one which would appeal to the new conservative federalism of the time. In 1980 the Reagan administration proposed the idea of "enterprise zones" for distressed communities. After several failed attempts in Congress, the Clinton administration succeeded in getting the passage of the 1993 Empowerment Zones and Enterprise Communities (EZ/EC) Act. The Act provided tax incentives and other enticements for businesses to locate to depressed urban areas with the goal of job creation and economic development.[9] Community-based development organizations are expected to play key roles in the program implementation. To date, however, many of these organizations have experienced difficulty implementing the program and attracting the types of economic activities that would yield positive benefits for local residents.[10]

More recently the Bush administration launched the White House Office on Faith-based and Community Initiatives to promote the involvement of religious organizations and groups in "meeting the needs of the poor." The Compassionate Care component of the 1996 welfare reform legislation gave churches and other charitable organizations an increased role in assisting impoverished families, but modest funding has limited the scope of these initiatives.

The Role of Philanthropy and Intermediaries

Private non-profit and corporate-based foundations have been financial supporters of CED since the late 1960s. Several national private foundations, such as Ford, Pew Charitable Trusts, Annie E. Casey, Rockefeller, James D. and Catherine T. MacArthur, Lilly Endowment and W. K. Kellogg, have provided grants and loans, particularly to CDCs. Corporate philanthropic institutions of the Prudential Insurance Company, Citigroup, J. P. Morgan-Chase, and Bank of America have been consistent financial supporters as well. Local philanthropic foundations in many major urban centres (e.g., the Boston Foundation) and rural communities (e.g., Babcock Reynolds Foundation) provide significant income support to CDCs and other CED organizations.

After federal government budgets for housing and urban development were deeply cut in the 1980s, a number of national and local financial intermediaries emerged to provide financing for CDC projects and capacity-building efforts. There are three national intermediaries—Neighbourhood Reinvestment Corporation (NRC), the Enterprise Foundation and the Local Initiatives Support Corporation (LISC). Each organization has distinct characteristics and areas of focus.

NRC, founded in 1978 by Congress, brings together neighbourhood residents, community-based organizations, private lenders, and local government to revitalize deteriorated areas primarily through the rehabilitation of housing by residents. In 1998, the 184 NRC affiliates received a total of $819.3 million to support their housing rehabilitation initiatives.[11] The Enterprise Foundation was founded in 1981, by real estate developer James Rouse and his wife Patricia.[12] Enterprise supports the efforts of more than 1500 non-profit community-based organizations through two subsidiaries: the Enterprise Social Investment Corporation and the Enterprise Housing financial services. In 1999, Enterprise committed more than $30 million in short-term loans, and its equity subsidiary raised $390 million to finance development of approximately 14,000 dwelling units in 16 cities. In addition to major housing efforts, Enterprise runs programs for crime prevention, collaborative problem-solving, job training/placement and child care.[13]

LISC was founded in 1980 as a result of a grant of $9.3 million from the Ford Foundation and six major corporations. LISC does its work through a national network of CDCs that raise their own funds from local corporate and philanthropic sources, which LISC then matches from its general capital fund.[14] LISC has also created a number of subsidiaries to support CDC housing and economic development projects through loan programs and tax credits. In 1997, LISC expanded its scope through the Community Building Initiatives that supports block clubs, youth development programs, anti-drug efforts and health care plans.

In addition to the establishment of national intermediaries, major foundations have also launched their own community development initiatives. Two major initiatives emerged in the early 1990s: the National Community Development Initiative (NCDI) and the Comprehensive Community Initiatives (CCI).

In 1991, several major foundations (e.g. Casey, Lilly, MacArthur), three corporations (Metropolitan Life, J. P. Morgan and Prudential Life) and the U.S. Department of Housing and Urban Development pooled resources to create a series of capacity-building and project initiatives aimed at strengthening CDCs.[15] To promote CDC leadership and staff development training, the NCDI provided $8 million to the National Congress for Community Economic Development (NCCED), the national professional organization for CDCs. The NCDI also provided grants and loans to CDCs in 23 cities through LISC and Enterprise. NCDI ended in 2000, having provided over $253 million to CDC capacity building.[16]

During this same period, several foundations and private corporations seized upon the idea of multi-year funding for "comprehensive community initiatives" (CCIs) to encourage comprehensive planning and collaboration between community residents, and public and private organizations and leaders. The Ford Foundation enacted its Neighbourhood and Family Initiative (NFI) in 1990 in four cities— Detroit, Memphis, Milwaukee and Hartford.[17] Ford invested about $6 million in community foundations over a six-year period to establish collaboration between neighbourhood residents and civic-oriented professionals.[18] The SURDNA Foundation initiated its CCI in 1991 with $9.4 million given to its Comprehensive Community Revitalization Program (CCRP) in the South Bronx neighbourhood of New York City.[19] At the end of the CCRP in 1998, CCRP Inc. was formed which acts as an intermediary at the neighbourhood level. Lastly, the Annie E. Casey Foundation (AECF) launched its CCI in 1993, as the Rebuilding Communities

Initiative (RCI) in Boston, Denver, Detroit, Philadelphia and Washington, DC.[20] The RCI consisted of a seven-year, $15 million dollar initiative.[21]

As this review suggests, CED has changed and responded to community needs while effectively garnering the resources of a broad spectrum of the stakeholders. CED organizations are consistently seeking to address the wide range of needs found in distressed communities. Therefore, they have proven quite flexible and malleable, which has contributed to their ability to flourish in the U.S. CED-oriented organizations have adopted a variety of strategies to respond to the continuing needs of disadvantaged communities.

Models of Community Economic Development Practice

Community Economic Development has impressive goals that include alleviating poverty, identifying and responding to local needs, being accountable to the community, investing in human capacity, utilizing democratic processes, engaging in wealth redistribution, improving working conditions and advancing local autonomy.[22] Ultimately, CED seeks to empower community residents based on the premise that empowerment is generated through control of resources. For low-income communities this must be promoted through economic redistribution.[23]

During the last forty years, the application of theoretical concepts within community economic development has generated two prevailing models of practice: community-based economic development (CBED), and community organizing (CO). Community-based economic development advocates sought to promote CED through the establishment of formal community-based organizations that encompassed community representation and promoted the development of human and physical resources. Community organizers with the same goal focused their efforts on mobilizing community members to identify systemic inequities, target public and private institutions of power and effect changes in the distribution of resources. Today there is considerable overlap in the activities of CBED and CO entities. While each model has its own distinctive strategies, both seek to improve the quality of life of economically and socially distressed community residents and their environments.

Community-based economic development (CBED)

The focus of CBED is on developing strategies to address resource mismatches in the areas of housing, capital access and business development.[24] CBED strategies focus on community-controlled development that provides goods, services and opportunities relevant to the needs of residents. This approach promotes the development of assets and the retention of financial capital within the community.[25] Two current conceptualizations of CBED are particularly relevant to this discussion: comprehensive and faith-based community development.

Comprehensive community development

Comprehensive community development is a relatively new term for the traditional concept of community-based economic development. As CED evolved throughout the 1970s and 1980s, a growing concern with fragmented practices led to a call for renewed emphasis on integrated and comprehensive approaches. In the early 1990s, comprehensive community development became the conceptual catchphrase for this renewed focus: the interdependencies of people and place. The basic premise of this approach is that social problems are interrelated and concentrated in certain communities; therefore, targeted community-focused initiatives are necessary. Criticism of community deficit based service-delivery models led to an increased focus on identifying strengths and resources, resulting in a new "assets-based" development orientation. From this perspective, comprehensive community development begins with an assessment of the social and human capital that resides within communities. As currently practised, this approach seeks to integrate human, social, cultural, economic and political capital for the improvement of communities. In response to this orientation, various strategies have emerged which attempt to address the multiple problems faced by individuals, families and communities. These strategies run the gamut from housing and economic development to service provision and policy advocacy.

Case example: Centers for New Horizons was founded in 1971 by Dr. Sokoni Karanja with the aim of reducing poverty and rebuilding Chicago's African-American Bronzeville community. Its mission emphasizes family self-reliance and resident involvement in community redevelopment. New Horizons has a broad array of programs that range from early childhood care and education, youth development (e.g., after-school programs), child welfare services (e.g., foster care family support) and senior outreach (e.g., senior day care), to job training, and building and maintaining over 300 housing units. Through its 19 centres, approximately 2000 services are provided on a daily basis. New Horizons implements the philosophy that residents bring strengths and capacities to their communities: of a staff of approximately 210 individuals, more than 60 per cent are community residents. New Horizons plays a significant role in citywide, statewide and nationwide advocacy around issues of early childhood education, affordable housing and community building.

Faith-based community development (FBCD)

Faith-based community development (FBCD) is predicated on theological principles related to stewardship—the notion that people of faith have a moral obligation to help those in need. "Faith-based" is a term used to describe any religious organization and may encompass local congregations, denominations, a collaboration of religious groups or religiously affiliated organizations. Faith-based entities, particularly African-American churches, have long been considered an anchor and a seat of leadership in distressed neighbourhoods.[26] Faith-based community development brings a mixture of organizational and spiritual resources to the community with initiatives that range from social service ministries to economic development and policy advocacy.

Case example: Established in 1992, FAME Renaissance is a faith-based community economic development subsidiary of the First African Methodist Episcopal Church (the oldest African-American congregation in Los Angeles). The church's ministry includes about 40 task forces engaged in activities that include a prison ministry, tutoring, college preparation classes and an adoption/foster care program. FAME Renaissance is committed to community-based business development. The FAME Renaissance Business Incubator launched in 2001, is a collaborative effort between various state and private-sector entities to provide mentoring, networking opportunities, marketing support and training to fledgling new media companies in the communities served by church. The basic strategy is to help develop new multimedia and entertainment-related firms that can benefit from the local media industry, and simultaneously bring technologically advanced skills and resources to low wealth neighbourhoods in South Central Los Angeles.

As this review suggests, the emphasis of community-based economic development strategies is the mobilization of economic resources for community well-being. The counterpart of CBED is community organizing which is primarily concerned with the mobilization of human and social capital resources to attain power over political and economic institutions, and decision processes.

Community organizing

In the context of the late 1930s and early 1940s Depression era, Saul Alinsky pioneered a new approach to affecting community change. Working with the "Back of the Yards" organization of community residents, churches and stockyard workers, Alinsky utilized confrontational tactics to pressure stockyard owners, legislators, landlords and others to make positive changes in housing, wages, health and safety conditions.[27] These efforts signalled the tremendous power of collective action and gave birth to the community organizing model of social change. While community-based economic development is concerned with advocacy, asset building and collaboration, community organizing focuses on restructuring institutions of power and creating more equitable distribution of resources.

The central premise of community organizing is that change can only be brought about through direct action of mobilized community members. The application of direct action has yielded at least three approaches to community organizing in the U.S. context: conflict-based, institution-based and consensus. Conflict-based organizing engages individual community members affected by economic and social problems in strategies of direct action, such as protests, sit-ins, petitions and media campaigns. Institution-based organizing mobilizes organizations (e.g., labour unions and churches) rather than individuals to effect social change.[28] The strategies and tactics used by institutionally-based organizing include demonstrations as well as large-scale public meetings that increase accountability and pressure.[29] Consensus organizing emphasizes collaboration and partnership building as opposed to confrontation and more conflictual methods.[30] The goal of consensus organizing is to build new partnerships across traditional institutional boundaries and community groups.[31]

Case example: The Association of Community Organizations for Reform Now (ACORN) is the nation's largest community organization of low and moderate-income families (with 750 chapters and 150,000 members). ACORN campaigns address issues that are central to the lives of its members and the viability of low-and-moderate-income neighbourhoods. The Philadelphia neighbourhood chapter of ACORN has addressed better housing for first-time homebuyers and tenants, living wages for low-wage workers, better public schools and more investment in neighbourhoods through the Community Reinvestment Act (i.e., a national program whereby lending institutions reinvest in poor neighbourhoods) and the Community Development Block Grant (a federal program that supports local housing and community development). In 2001, ACORN Philadelphia campaigned to establish an Anti-Predatory Lending Ordinance in the city that is the strongest piece of local anti-predatory lending legislation in the country. ACORN Philadelphia uses the national organization's methods to bring about social change: direct action, negotiation, legislation and voter participation. Members, not staff or lawyers, speak for and lead the organization. ACORN views non-partisan voter participation as an essential part of its strategy for empowering poor people.

Case example: Action in Montgomery (AIM) is a congregation-based, non-ideological and non-partisan non-profit organization that builds a political base among voluntary institutions in several communities in Montgomery County, Maryland. Founded in 1996, AIM includes 18 congregations of various faiths and is an affiliate of the Industrial Areas Foundation (IAF), a national community-organizing network. AIM uses the IAF methodology of using power—organized people (of all races, ethnicities, religions and political persuasions) and organized money—to affect decision-making in a community to produce social change in that community, particularly for its most vulnerable. IAF staff act as consultants to, rather than directors of, the social change process. AIM member organizations choose delegates who participate in delegate assembly meetings where issues or common agendas are chosen to address and develop strategies and solutions, and action steps are determined to have those solutions carried out. AIM has engaged in action campaigns on predatory lending, healthcare, public education and housing for working families.

Case example: In the late 1970s, the Mon Valley Pennslyvania, economy was collapsing due to the failing U.S. steel industry. In 1985, a group of Pittsburgh corporate leaders engaged Michael Eichler and his team of consultants to use consensus organizing to develop a strategy for addressing the area's economic woes.[32] The team found that the steel unions and company owners each blamed the other for the industry's problems. As a result of the area's overwhelming focus on steel production, local leaders had limited knowledge and experience with other business sectors. The area lacked community-based organizations, and residents were not politically mobilized. Eichler's team enlisted the assistance of LISC to form CDCs in fourteen Mon Valley cities. A coalition was built among "downtown interests," local unions, churches, businesses, social groups and the new CDCs. These efforts resulted in the establishment, in December 1988, of the Mon Valley Initiative (MVI) whose mission is to unite communities and restore economic vitality to the area. MVI acts as a regional community development umbrella organization that provides planning and coordination, as well as staff and funding support to its CDC members. MVI has fostered the development of affordable housing, a business incubator centre, a recycling company, a regional arts school, playgrounds, a façade loan program and district beautification programs. Equally important, the MVI has engaged hundreds of residents in the planning and decision-making process of community development.[33]

Outcomes and Limitations of CED in the U.S. Context

As the previous section suggests, CED has evolved into a diverse array of practices, all aimed at a common goal of improving the well-being of disadvantaged communities. Given the importance of CED and the resources that have been devoted to its programs and projects, it is not surprising that it is continually being assessed and evaluated for effectiveness. The overall assessment of CED practice and outcomes in the U.S. context is a mixed one. While some commentators point to myriad examples of successful community projects and programs, others argue that these accomplishments are too limited in scope and that CED as an overall model has serious inherent limitations. A brief overview of these perspectives reveals the tensions that exist within the CED field.

Successful outcomes of CED

Community economic development has had several accomplishments. The numbers of organizations doing the work of community economic development has increased from a few hundred in the 1970's to more than three thousand. These organizations have provided yeomen service, considering the magnitude and depth of the problems they seek to address.

Provision of diverse services

A 1998 survey by the NCCED (National Congress for Community Economic Development) reported that the population of CDCs had reached 3,600. This number represented a 64 per cent increase since 1994, and a 200 per cent growth rate since 1988.[34] In a 1992 study, Vidal found that the median total annual budget of a sample of larger CDCs was just over $700,000, and the average was about $2.4 million.[35]

While CDCs are not the only organizations engaged in community development activities, their number and scope of work is highly indicative of the level of achievements in the field. CDCs are committed to improving the social, economic and physical conditions of low-income and disenfranchised neighbourhoods by engaging in a myriad of activities including residential and commercial development, credit unions, loan funds, job creation and training, placement, lobbying, advocacy, counselling, education and other social services.[36]

Provision of space for leadership development and citizen participation
Since the development of the 1960s Community Action Agencies in particular, CED has provided the training ground for the emergence and grooming of political and civic leadership among indigenous populations. Further, CED, particularly its organizing arm, has served to educate individuals about issues of power and rights. The illumination of inequality, abuse and oppression that is inherent in the efforts of community organizing in that part of the mobilization process, brings individuals to a state of praxis.

One of many good examples of this process can be found in the Pico-Union neighbourhood in Los Angeles. The area is home to a number of community-based organizations who are engaged in CED and advocacy work. Unfortunately, the four-square-mile neighbourhood is also home to more than 500 liquor outlets. One group, Pico Union in Action has organized residents to push for change by pressuring local government officials to enforce zoning and other restrictions, and to encourage police officials to stem related drug activities. The process of organizing around these issues has galvanized residents, many of whom have become outspoken neighbourhood advocates and leaders. Some of the targeted stores have closed and police have increased their interactions with residents. Problems persist, but residents are more engaged in fighting for solutions.

Through the process of heightened awareness and group mobilization, citizens are given an opportunity to participate in political action and advocacy, and thereby gain a greater understanding of political and policy processes. Such experiences encourage the development of self-confidence and leadership skills. Most important, they are given a chance to see their own potential role in social action and systems change. CED has been particularly instrumental in providing this enlightenment and empowerment of community residents.

At the same time that CED has created opportunities for engagement of residents, it has also promoted the development of leadership within community-based organizations. CDCs and other community organizations are fertile environments for the nurturing of new leadership. An excellent example of this dynamic is found in the Mexican-American Community Services Agency (MACSA), a San Jose-based CDC. Through an innovative organizational strategy, MACSA incubates indigenous leaders by hiring residents as staff members, facilitating their educational training and encouraging them to take leadership roles. One former staff member has successfully gained public office, while others have assumed key decision-making roles within the non-profit and public sectors.

Production of significant physical development

One of the most notable achievements of CED is its contribution to affordable housing and other physical development within urban communities. In one recent NCCED (1999) survey, over 80 per cent of CDCs reported that they engaged in housing development. Annual production of housing units has increased from over 20,000 in the late 1980s to approximately 40,000 by the early 1990s. Significantly, between 1994 and 1997, over 245,000 housing units were developed by CDCs. [37] In addition to housing rehabilitation and construction, approximately 31 per cent of CDCs engage in commercial or industrial development. This is a substantial increase over the 18 per cent level reported in 1995. These organizations have developed more than 71 million square feet of retail space, offices and other industrial complexes, compared with 23 million in 1995.[38]

These levels of development are considerable, especially in relation to that of private, for-profit development in distressed communities. CDCs are often the only entities willing to risk the investment and cultivation of these areas, making CDCs primary development forces in low-income areas.

Federal policy response

In its young tenure, CED has fostered and been the catalyst for important pieces of urban policy. Several major pieces of federal legislation have emerged from the efforts and campaigns of CED organizations. These policies include the creation of the Community Services Block Grant (CSBG), the Community Reinvestment Act (CRA), the Home Mortgage Disclosure Act (HMDA), the New Markets Tax Credit (NMTC) and, most recently, the proposed Community Economic Development Expertise Enhancement Act. Although U.S. public policy has made some attempts to respond to the needs of poor, disenfranchised neighbourhoods, these efforts have been fragmented and subject to shifting political environments. Still, CED advocates have played a central role in keeping the interests of poor communities on the public agenda.

Limitations of CED

While CED has had many accomplishments, it is no panacea. As a strategy, CED has limitations. Community economic development has largely been unable to articulate its contributions to the less tangible aspects of social capital development and other non-investment neighbourhood activities. Scholars have long criticized the field for its inability to capture its successes beyond anecdotal descriptions.[39] The analysis of impacts has been scarce with much of the emphasis placed on community development corporations. There is considerable confusion about how to identify and measure the impacts of CDCs.[40] Where evaluation has lagged, criticism of community economic development has been in abundance. The primary condemnations of CED are: the inability to make systemic change, vulnerability to co-optation and inadequate capacity to carry out goals.

Inability to make systemic change

Many evaluations, particularly of CDCs have measured CED impacts by counting the number of houses rehabilitated or built, new jobs created or businesses begun, but beyond those quantitative measures, there is very little qualitative analysis. The evidence that CED makes an impact on the quality of life for its community members is less than conclusive. Most of the problems CED seeks to address are imposed on the community from external sources. Yet the limited amount of change that occurs has little effect on the larger systems (economic, political, educational, power, etc.) that affect communities. CED has produced rather modest gains and even some of those have been temporary; the social problems that CED seeks to address are still in abundance in urban communities.

Risk of co-optation

Community development organizations are consistently under-funded and government funds provide a significant part of community development resources. Once an organization accepts money from "political" sources, they are reticent to "bite the hand that feeds them." Dangers of co-optation arise when CBOs take government funds because as a result they are often prohibited from engaging in the radical, confrontational, political activities that served so well in the 1960s and 1970s.[41]

Although community development organizations espouse community control, often it is not a reality, but instead a mechanism reduced to a formality. Rarely are community residents in decision-making positions that directly affect the workings of the organization. Often this disconnect is a result of the need to professionalize services due to programmatic and reporting requirements from funders, specifically the federal government, and other market forces.

Inadequate capacity

Capacity is the ability of organizations to garner the resources and skills (internal and external) necessary to achieve their goals. CED organizations tend to have capacity deficiency in three major areas: funding, technical expertise and organizational structure. Organizations rarely have enough funding or financial capital to be effective. Researchers have found significant variability in the size and budgets of CDCs, but most were small and under-funded. The average CDC had a budget of $705,000 and a staff of seven. [42]

Of particular interest is the lack of operating support. Many organizations have program-specific funding and lack the resources to pay non-program-related expenses. Minimal financial resources also affect the organizations' ability to attract well-trained, experienced staff. Staff limitations directly affect the ability of the organizations to engage in certain types of community development initiatives. Therefore, organizations tend to have weak infrastructure, often held together by the strong personality of the leadership. This clearly places these organizations in a tenuous position that is subject to instability over time as funding shifts occur.

Conclusion

Despite its limitations, the CED field plays a unique role in addressing the inequities and gaps of the traditional U.S. economic, social and political systems. While concepts and strategies continue to evolve and change, the basic mission of CED has remained the same: to empower residents of disenfranchised, low-income communities to achieve their own goals. As CED evolves, it must retain its traditional core values, its commitment to social justice and the establishment of an equitable society.

Notes

1.   Halpern, *Rebuilding the Inner City.*
2.   Day, *A New History of Social Welfare.*
3.   Quadagno, *The Color of Welfare.*
4.   Vidal, *Rebuilding Communities.*
5.   See Stoecker, "The CDC Model of Urban Redevelopment," *Journal of Urban Affairs*, 1-22; and Vidal (1992).
6.   See Fisher, *Let The People* Decide; Glickman and Servon, "More Than Bricks and Sticks," *Housing Policy Debate*, 497-539; Stoecker; and Vidal.
7.   Vidal.
8.   Day.
9.   Rubin, *Can Reorchestration of Historical Themes Reinvent Government?*
10.   Whitt, "Few mourn end of flawed urban renewal program," *The Atlanta Journal-Constitution*, 1A.
11.   Neighbourhood Reinvestment Corporation, *Neighbourhood Reinvestment Corporation 1998 Annual Report.*
12.   Enterprise Foundation, *Enterprise Foundation Annual Report, 1993.*
13.   See Enterprise Foundation (1994), and *Enterprise Foundation Annual Report, 1999.* (Baltimore: Enterprise Foundation, 2000).
14.   Vidal, Howitt and Foster, *Stimulating Community Development.*
15.   Walker, and Weinheimer, *Community Development in the 1990s.*
16.   National Community Development Initiative. *NCDI Press Release.*
17.   Aspen Institute Roundtable on Comprehensive Community Initiatives, www.commbuild.org.
18.   Ibid.
19.   Spilka and Burns, *Final Assessment Report.*
20.   Annie E. Casey Foundation, "Comprehensive Community Initiatives," *Shelterforce.*

21. Pitcoff, "Redefining Community Development."
22. See Chekki, *Community Development Theory*; Marquez, " Mexican-American Community Development Corporations," *Economic Development Quarterly*, 287-95; Swack and Mason, "Community Economic Development as a Strategy for Social Intervention," in *Social Intervention: Theory and Practice,* edited by Bennett; Shragge, *Community Economic Development In Search of Empowerment*; Gittell and Wilder, "Community Development Corporations, *Journal of Urban Affairs*, 341-61.
23. Church, "Business (Not Quite) as Usual," Shragge (ed.).
24. Cary, "The Present State of Community Development," Chekki (ed.).
25. Swack and Mason.
26. Warren, *Dry Bones Rattling*.
27. Alinsky, *Reveille for Radical*.
28. Warren.
29. Delgado, *Beyond The Politics of Place*.
30. Eichler, "Community Organizing Partnership," *National Civic Review*, 256-61.
31. Gittell and Vidal, *Community Organizing*.
32. See Eichler, 1995, and Eichler, *The Consensus Organizing Model*.
33. Eichler, 1995, 1996.
34. National Congress for Community Economic Development, *Trends and Achievements*.
35. Vidal.
36. Cowan, Rohe and Baku, *Factors Influencing the Performance of Community Development Corporations*; and Vidal.
37. National Congress for Community Economic Development, 1999.
38. See National Congress for Community Economic Development, *Tying It All Together*; and National Congress for Community Economic Development, 1999.
39. See Stoecker; Rohe, *Do Community Development Corporations Live Up to Their Billing?*
40. Glickman and Servon.
41. Shragge.
42. See Trulear, *Faith-Based Institutions and High-Risk Youth*; Glickman and Servon; Vidal.

Bibliography

Alinsky, S. D. *Reveille for A Radical*. (New York: Vintage Books, 1946).

Annie E. Casey Foundation. "Comprehensive Community Initiatives: Rebuilding Communities Initiative." *Shelterforce*, National Housing Institute, January/February, 1998.

Aspen Institute Roundtable on Comprehensive Community Initiatives, 1999. www.commbuild.org,

Cary, L. J. "The Present State of Community Development —Theory and Practice." In D. A. Chekki, ed., 1979.

Chekki, D. A., *Community Development Theory and Method of Planned Change*. New Delhi: Vikas, 1979.

Church, K. "Business (Not Quite) as Usual: Psychiatric Survivors and Community Economic Development in Ontario." In E. Shragge, ed., 1997

Cowan, S. M., W. Rohe, and E. Baku. *Factors Influencing the Performance of Community Development Corporations*. Fort Worth: Center for Urban and Regional Studies, 1998.

Day, P. J. *A New History of Social Welfare,* Third ed. Boston, Massachusetts: Allyn and Bacon, 2000.

Delgado, G. *Beyond The Politics of Place: New Directions in Community Organizing in the 1990's*. Oakland: Applied Research Center, 1994.

Eichler, M. "Community Organizing Partnership." *National Civic Review*, Summer/Fall, 256-61. National Civic League Press, 1995.

———. *The Consensus Organizing Model*. Consensus Organizing Institute. San Diego, California, 1996.

Enterprise Foundation. *Enterprise Foundation Annual Report, 1993*. Baltimore: Enterprise Foundation, 1994.

Enterprise Foundation. *Enterprise Foundation Annual Report, 1999*. Baltimore: Enterprise Foundation, 2000.

Fisher, R. *Let The People Decide*. New York: Twayne Publishers, 1994.

Gittell, R. and A. Vidal. *Community Organizing: Building Social Capital as a Development Strategy*. Thousand Oaks: Sage Publications, 1998.

——— and M. Wilder. "Community Development Corporations: Critical Factors That Influence Success." *Journal of Urban Affairs*, 21 no. 3, 1999: 341-361.

Glickman, N. J. and L. J. Servon. "More Than Bricks and Sticks: Five Components of Community Development Corporation Capacity." *Housing Policy Debate*, 9, no. 3, 1998: 497 – 539.

Halpern, R. *Rebuilding the Inner City*. New York: Columbia University Press, 1995.

Marquez, B. " Mexican-American Community Development Corporations and the Limits of Directed Capitalism." *Economic Development Quarterly*, 7 no. 3, 1993: 287-95.

National Community Development Initiative. *NCDI Press Release*. 1999

National Congress for Community Economic Development. *Trends and Achievements of Community-Based Development Organizations*. Census report of member organization. Washington, DC: NCCED, 1999.

———. *Tying It All Together: The Comprehensive Achievements of Community-Based Development Organizations*. Washington, D.C.: NCCED, 1995

Neighbourhood Reinvestment Corporation. *Neighbourhood Reinvestment Corporation 1998 Annual Report*. Washingon, DC: NRC, 1999.

Pitcoff, Winston. "Redefining Community Development: Part 1: New Partnerships," *Shelterforce,* National Housing Institute, November/December 1997.

Quadagno, J. *The Color of Welfare: How Racism Undermined the War on Poverty*. New York: Oxford University Press, 1994.

Rohe, W. *Do Community Development Corporations Live Up to Their Billing? A Review and Critique of the Research Findings.* Working paper S95-16. Chapel Hill, NC: Center for Urban and Regional Studies, The University of North Carolina at Chapel Hill, 1995.

Rubin, M. M. *Can Reorchestration of Historical Themes Reinvent Government? A Case Study of the Empowerment Zones and Enterprise Communities Act of 1993.* New York: John Jay College, The City University of New York, 1994.

Shragge, E., ed. *Community Economic Development In Search of Empowerment.* Montreal: Black Rose Books, 1997.

Spilka, G. and T. Burns. *Final Assessment Report: Comprehensive Community Revitalization Program.* The OMG Center for Collaborative Learning, OMG Center, Philadelphia, 1998.

Stoecker, R. "The CDC Model of Urban Redevelopment: A Critique and an Alternative." *Journal of Urban Affairs*, 19 no. 1, 1997: 1-22.

Swack, M. and D. Mason. "Community Economic Development as a Strategy for Social Intervention," In *Social Intervention: Theory and Practice*, edited by E. M. Bennett. Lewiston: The Edwin Mellen Press, 1987.

Trulear, H. D. *Faith-Based Institutions and High-Risk Youth.* Philadelphia: Public/ Private Ventures, 2000.

Vidal, A., A. M. Howitt and K. P. Foster. *Stimulating Community Development: An Assessment of the Local Initiatives Support Corporation.* Cambridge, MA: The State, Local and Intergovernmental Center, Harvard University, 1986.

Vidal, A. *Rebuilding Communities: A National Study of Urban Community Development Corporations.* New York: Community Development Research Center, Graduate School of Management and Urban Policy, New School for Social Research, 1992.

Walker, C. and M. Weinheimer, *Community Development in the 1990s.* Washington, DC: Urban Institute, 1998.

Warren, M., *Dry Bones Rattling.* Princeton: Princeton University Press, 2001.

Whitt, R. "Few mourn end of flawed urban renewal program." *The Atlanta Journal-Constitution* 1A, September 25, 2002.

Michael Lyons, Michael Majale, Paul Chege

Creating Sustainable Local Economic Development Through Sustainable Partnerships: The BIP-PUP Process in Kitale, Kenya

This chapter reports on Building in Partnership: Participatory Urban Planning (BIP-PUP), an action research project developed and implemented by the Intermediate Technology Development Group (ITDG) with funding from the U.K. Department for International Development. An innovative approach to local development, it brings together three methodologies: participatory planning, neighbourhood development and partnerships. It aims to achieve locally-appropriate development—which is economically, socially and environmentally sustainable—momentum and institutional infrastructure for development that will continue to function in the long term. An analysis of the context in which it was developed and applied, its achievements and the lessons learned, are the focus of this chapter.

LED, Sustainability and Public Participation in the North and in the South

In sub-Saharan Africa, as in many developing regions, globalization, trade liberalization and institutional restructuring have been concomitant with rapid urbanization. Urban expansion has not, however, been accompanied by economic growth,[1] and the growth in informal employment and economic inequality noted in OECD* countries over the past twenty years, have been matched by far more rapid expansion of poverty and inequality in sub-Saharan African cities.[2] Thus, local economic development, viewed in the developed world as a response to

---

*Organization for Economic Co-operation and Development.

pockets of deprivation and stagnation, is a key feature of development work in Third World cities in general, and in sub-Saharan Africa in particular.

The framework within which local development has been carried out in developing regions has changed and adapted throughout the post-colonial period. The Vancouver Declaration prompted a range of participative settlement upgrading and development projects and programs in several Southern countries. Most were undertaken with backing from large international funding agencies such as the World Bank and GTZ,* and these developments were extensively assessed.[3]

Since then, participative planning has become widely accepted. Funders and development professionals have become increasingly conscious of the importance of public participation in engendering local commitment to the successful completion of economic and other development projects. Increasingly this is seen as important in reaching marginalized populations,[4] in planning appropriate developments,[5] enabling public facilities to be better maintained after completion, empowering marginalized groups,[6] and in rare cases allowing a continuing momentum to develop.[7] While some have argued that participation has become too widespread,[8] others have emphasized its power to achieve transformation,[9] arguing that to be transformative, participation must be institutionalized in local government processes.

Evidence has mounted that even projects following participative methods often flounder or decline following completion with the withdrawal of a funding or development agency.[10] As in the North, three main strands of criticism have dogged participative development. These have included: (a) failures of engagement and representation, or limitation of levels of participation, which on one hand render it less effective in terms of project design and specification and on the other hand community ownership and empowerment; (b) failure to develop sustainable institutional structures which can continue to support further community-initiated development after project completion; and, (c) problems of scale, where program are designed at too large a scale for the local level, or are too singularly adapted to a particular local context to be scaled up or replicated.

One interpretation places the reason for these failures with the lack of vertical integration in project structure between local, neighbourhood-level institutions at the project or community level and various institutions and processes of the state. By extension, this analysis suggests that a weakness of traditional participative projects in both the North and the South, has been a failure to establish an effective partnership among all stakeholders for the longer term. It has been argued that the responsibility for institutional change lies with the state.

> For example, in their analysis of integrated local social and economic policy in England during the 1990s, Valler and Bettley argued that "the process of integrated strategy making is critically mediated by pre-existing institutional and political forms in localities, producing distinc-

---

*Technische Zusammenarbeit GmbH—German technical cooperation

tive institutional responses and policy processes, which in turn suggest
the limits of policy integration in contemporary local government." [11]

They identify the fractious nature of local government, as well as other government
tiers, as a barrier to formulation of a "state" policy, and the willingness of local
authorities to adapt, as a crucial element of successful integrated development.

Another example of the importance of adaptation by formal institutions, as
well as by local citizen groups, is found in the Social Funds and Works program
developed in sub-Saharan Africa for local-level infrastructure works. Evaluation
suggested that they were only sustainable because of a dual focus on local-level
participation and ownership, on one hand, and changes to procurement and
management systems at an institutional level, on the other. [12] Similarly, Narayan
and Ebbe [13] contend that public participation at a local level, essential for ownership
and sustainability of developments, may by itself be unsustainable, unless state
and donor institutions change to accommodate the needs of collaboration with
participating communities.

Attempting to design an institutional structure and process which responds
to these needs and addresses the three critiques identified above, is: "Building in
Partnerships—Participatory Urban Planning," or BIP-PUP, proposed by
Intermediate Technology Development Group and funded by the U.K. Department
for International Development over the past three years in the municipality of
Kitale, a secondary town in Kenya with an estimated population of 100,000. The
process aimed to overcome the three critiques of participatory development practice,
identified above, by bringing together three methodologies: participatory planning,
neighbourhood development and partnerships.

The BIP-PUP project's goal was to enhance the effectiveness of city and
municipal planning and management. The goal was to be met through the
development and dissemination (national and international) of a partnership
approach to the planning of urban space with men, women and children living in
poverty and community-based, public and private organizations. At the heart of
this approach lay the understanding that, to be sustainable, development
interventions must resolve human, social, political and economic dimensions, and
that these need to be self-sustaining and mutually sustaining beyond the initial
development phase. Some background is necessary in order to better understand
the project itself.

Planning in the South and in Kenya

The institutional context for participatory planning in the South has been
transformed far more radically than in the North. It is revealing of the breadth of
acceptance of these principles in sub-Saharan Africa, that at the Johannesburg
World Summit on Sustainable Development in 2002, the declaration issued by the
African Mayors' Forum undertook to address poverty and development
sustainability primarily through empowerment, democratic governance and
participatory processes. [14]

In the North, participative and strategic preparation of planning has become increasingly accepted as a substitute for earlier technocratic approaches.[15] A broader institutional change has been initiated in a number of countries in the South, which includes strategic planning, budgeting and implementation at a municipal level. Begun in isolated cities (with Porto Allegre the archetypical example), this has become a central building block of local government reform in a number of developing countries. Widely supported by the World Bank and International Monetary Fund (IMF), these reforms were first legislated in South Africa's Local Government Bill in 2000. The movement has now spread to other sub-Saharan African countries.[16]

Kenya has adopted and adapted these principles in its own legislation. Since the mid-1990s, there has been an attempt, under the Kenya Local Government Reform Programme (KLGRP), to strengthen the local government system so as to transfer financial resources to local authorities (LAs), enable them to deliver services and to increase local accountability. A key element in this is the Local Authorities Transfer Fund (LATF) initiated in 1999/2000. Under LATF conditions, LAs have been required since 2001 to prepare Local Authority Service Delivery Plans (LASDAPs). A structured annual cycle of participative budgeting and planning, the LASDAP process aims to govern the strategic prioritization and deployment of an increasing proportion of the municipal allocations from central government.[17] It also aims to create partnerships by matching this budget with funds from other ministries, as well as with private sector investments and other donor or development partner aid. The new legislation builds on a strong tradition, promoted since independence, of a widespread community participation movement called "Harambee," for mobilizing and supporting development and funding of public facilities such as school buildings and health facilities.[18]

Ranked 148 of 177 countries in the 2004 Human Development Report,[19] Kenya is among the poorest countries in the world, although not the poorest country in sub-Saharan Africa. Its economic growth was strong in the first two decades after independence in 1963, but has been weak or negative thereafter.[20] Unemployment levels have been estimated at 40 per cent. While overall 50 per cent of the population live below the poverty line, there are pockets of poverty throughout Kenya where this is true of more than 70 per cent of the population. Socio-economic inequality is high and growing. The lowest-earning decile of population account for 2 per cent of consumption, and the highest, for 37 per cent, while the Gini coefficient for family income was 44.7 in 1997, and is estimated to have risen.[21]

Nairobi serves as the financial and trading hub for the East African region, and Kenya has urbanized rapidly over the past twenty years. Between 1985 and 1995 the urban population grew by seven per cent per year, on average, slowing to six per cent per annum over the following decade, with growth expected to continue, albeit at a somewhat slower rate, to 2025.[22]

However, urbanization does not only take place in major national centres. Kitale is the administrative headquarters of Trans-Nzoia district, as well as a market town for a relatively wealthy agricultural area of some 800,000 inhabitants. It is a destination for rural-urban migrants, as well as migrant pastoralists fleeing political strife and drought in the northern territories. It is the fastest growing town in the district, with average growth rates of 12 per cent per annum. Migration is expected to rise, in the next few years, with greater numbers of people turning to the informal sector for employment and swelling outlying slum populations.

The BIP-PUP project objectives were to help Kitale develop an institutional structure that could respond to local development needs and develop sustainable and locally adapted solutions to address them. The process aims at developing a long-term institutional capacity at the municipal level linked with the "grassroots," to sustain the development momentum in Kitale.[23]

How BIP-PUP worked

Preliminary activities[24]

In 2001, a partnership was established between Intermediate Technology Development Group—Eastern Africa (ITDG-EA) and the Kitale Municipal Council (KMC). With strategic assistance from ITDG-EA, the Council, in particular the Department of Housing and Social Services (DHSS), drew on its resources and local knowledge to carry out a preliminary "scan" survey. This used a stratified sampling technique to identify a base-line of socio-economic conditions, and to map them by ward.

The survey identified and mapped concerns over land tenure, housing conditions, infrastructure, services and amenities (including water, sanitation, roads, recreation facilities, education and medical services), governance (corruption in particular) and funds for development. It was used to prioritize Kitale's ten electoral wards by need in those areas and to identify priority concerns among their residents. Wards were ranked, and one informal settlement in each of the top three rated wards was selected for active intervention through integrative, participatory planning and implementation. The settlements identified were Kipsongo, Shimo La Tewa and Tuwan.

A second city-wide survey mapped locally-active churches, community-based organizations (CBOs) and non-governmental organizations (NGOs) operating in each ward or settlement, and these were invited to join the participatory development partnership initially established between KMC and ITDG-EA—thus KMC and ITDG-EA took a proactive role in drawing in members of civil society. Approaches to members of the business community were made at a later stage.

Development Priorities

In March 2003, intensive one-week consultations with communities drawn from each of the three settlements drew heavily on local knowledge. These consultations resulted in re-evaluation of up to ten priority development needs in each settlement, identification of locally-appropriate methods of implementation, of individually feasible contributions of each partnership member to costs, materials and labour, and of social and human development necessary to enable the developments to be sustained in the long run. This culminated in the development of a Strategic Action Plan (SAP) for each settlement.

Kipsongo[25]

Kipsongo, on the eastern outskirts of Kitale, suffers many of the archetypal problems of the peri-urban environment. The residents are primarily from the Turkana community, a traditionally pastoralist group, and migrated to Kitale to escape environmental disasters such as drought and human conflicts over contested grazing lands and cattle rustling. They have no previous experience of urban life. The area was previously semi-rural and housed a large slaughterhouse.

This community settled on the dumping ground for the slaughterhouse. Water in the local stream, from which most residents drew water for domestic use, is polluted by activities upstream, and there were neither sanitary facilities available nor the tradition of allocating particular spaces to sanitary activities. Disease vectors thus multiplied and infectious diseases spread. Literacy rates and school attendance rates are low, and unemployment very high.

Through a community-driven, participatory planning process, with technical support from project staff and the municipal council, Kipsongo residents were to draw up the Kipsongo Neighbourhood Plan, spelling out a Strategic Action Plan (SAP), which included immediate measures but was still sufficiently flexible to allow for various growth options (e.g., setting up a women's community centre, police station and a health clinic).

The plan is being implemented through a joint effort between the Community Council, ITDG and other partners. Five sanitation blocks have been constructed, each serving a cluster of households. Since residents cannot afford to pay for use and maintenance of the facilities, each group of households contributes the labour and cleaning materials necessary. Two springs have been constructed and protected. They are managed by a women-led Water and Sanitation Committee, who are developing a seedling nursery and hoping to develop a laundry block to cover the costs of maintenance and create income. The group plans to start a commercial vegetable garden to support them in protecting the stream's catchment area.

The development of income generating activities (IGAs) to support the maintenance of infrastructure developments directly is critical to their long-term sustainability. In addition, however, other local economic development initiatives have been undertaken on a group basis, and are at various stages of development. There is a daily savings scheme for women who plan to establish a handicraft workshop; another has been developed with men. Youth group members in all three settlements were trained in the production of stabilized soil blocks (SSBs) and each group given a brick press. Notably, the Kipsongo Youth Group has been the most active and successful at disseminating training, undertaking contracts and earning money.

The provision of health clinic services has been agreed upon in principle by the council, but the premises have not yet been built. The project and the Council are exploring the availability of land. A number of initiatives are under way with regard to education, which involve public-sector schools, a non-profit-sector training centre and a school-based feeding programme.

Shimo La Tewa [26]

The action plan for Shimo La Tewa, a larger and slightly more prosperous settlement, was prioritized differently, with larger infrastructure works on one hand and more emphasis on individual ownership and individual business initiatives, on the other.

A grant acquired from another British donor has been used to establish a revolving loan fund managed by the Catholic Diocese of Kitale and a board of trustees comprising local partnership members. This is presently being used for individual plot owners to secure personal loans for the construction of latrines on their private plots, which will serve not only the owners, but also their tenants and neighbours, generating income for the owners. Improvement of public infrastructure focused on the rehabilitation of roads, and on the construction of a footbridge, which spans 130 metres across a ravine that divided the settlement and was a major obstacle to communication.

Training in appropriate building technologies (ABTs) has taken place among women and youth (mainly young men) and been disseminated, and various construction projects are under way.

Development of two protected springs and a women-managed water kiosk, which allows people who do not want to walk down to the spring to pay for piped municipal water, have combined to radically improve access to safe water. Both initiatives are self-sustaining in the sense that IGAs and community-donated labour contribute to long-term maintenance. Protection of Shimo La Tewa's water springs also means that when the municipal water supply fails, non-residents come to the spring where a charge for the water can be levied, supporting maintenance costs.

Protection of riparian areas is of course not entirely a settlement problem—pollution can come from elsewhere upstream or can enter the aquifers well beyond the boundaries of the settlement. Pressure and environmental education by the Green Town Group (see below) has been instrumental in promoting environmental activities here. Within the settlement, improvements to sanitation and the collection and disposal of solid waste, have also contributed to general health and to cleanliness of the local section of the river basin.

Tuwan[27]

Tuwan is the largest of the three settlements, with 5,000 plots, and the most populous in Kitale, with an estimated 100,000 residents. It is also somewhat more prosperous than the others. Priority actions identified included access to clean water, reduction of water-borne diseases, income improvement through water-kiosk management and other IGAs, and construction of sanitary facilities.

Tuwan chose to address its sanitation problems centrally through the construction of a communal, gender-segregated ablution block, comprising running-water latrines, showers with provision for hot water, laundry facilities and a multi-purpose room, which will serve as a clinic and an HIV voluntary counselling and testing centre.

Income generation was addressed on both a collective and individual basis. During the construction of the sanitation facilities, stabilized soil blocks were produced by the youth groups from Kipsongo and Tuwan settlements. Beams and concrete floor slabs were manufactured by a local women's group. The latrines, showers and laundry facilities will be used by settlement residents for a fee. Thus, the sanitation block will continue to provide income, which will ensure continued maintenance by the women's group that will run it. The block utilizes a closed-loop water recycling system and methane-generating waste-treatment method. The decomposed waste will be used as manure in an income-generating, vegetable-growing project for the women's group. The methane will be used in heating water for showers, keeping down maintenance costs. A merry-go-round in the playground for children's use will operate a pump that will also supply water to the facility.

The settlement has developed two protected water springs, similar to those developed in the other two settlements. At the sanitation block, it has also developed a water kiosk. Tuwan's proximity to the town centre, and the proximity of the kiosk to the main road, mean that the kiosk will provide the women's group with income from selling water to non-residents as well as when municipal water supplies in the town are low. A nearby plot has been identified for a nursery and the possibility of establishing an organized market. The block has been the focal point for realization of most of the settlement's development objectives.

Social Development

Social structures have evolved to support planning and development, serving numerous needs of maintenance and sustainability. In all three settlements, partnership funds for micro-credit have been widely supplemented by fast-growing daily savings groups with rapidly increasing funds, expanding loan portfolios and rising expectations.

Daily-savings associations provide services at two levels. For example, Tuwan Daily Savings and Development Group, launched in August 2003, had within six months disbursed "soft" loans for school fees for 48 secondary-school children (Kshs 500,000), given loans to micro-businesses and for emergencies (Kshs 400,000), and there are plans to provide loans within two years for land purchase and housing construction. These associations were not part of the original project, but were introduced to strengthen sustainability and local resource mobilization. The idea was well supported by the partnership, with exchange visits and education on daily savings experiences by groups from Nairobi and Nakuru that had formed in 1996.

Some CBOs have responsibilities at settlement level. The construction of communal water and sanitation facilities has been associated with the development of groups specializing in construction skills, targeting both men and women artisans. Training began with a small core, and gradually spread throughout the group. There were no evident barriers to women joining. Any money earned is shared between those directly involved in block production and some goes to the group fund. In conducting the initial shelter technology training, the project brought in community artisans previously trained in other ITDG projects in Nakuru and Nairobi to train their Kitale colleagues.

The success of these groups has varied. Although Kipsongo is the poorest and least urbanized of the three settlements, the Kipsongo Youth Group has been more successful than any other youth group in getting outside work. In contrast, the machine at Shimo la Tewa was first put to commercial use only two years after initial training. Whatever their success level, young people appear to consider their membership in these groups to be important. Women's groups are responsible for operating and maintaining water kiosks, and will earn income for their households from associated activities, such as the sale of water, the development of a vegetable garden and a charge for using laundry or sanitation facilities.

The Voluntary Health Committees (VHCs), formed mainly from an initial core of people identified by the partnership and trained in Participatory Hygiene and Sanitation Transformation (PHAST), are very active in spreading this hygiene behaviour campaign. This has led to impressive transformation in levels of cleanliness in public places and in personal hygiene. The genuine appreciation with which these activities and the CBOs which promote them are received was expressed clearly by one community member in Kipsongo, who said: "We were in the dark, but now we have seen the light."

The next tier of CBOs formed through partnership activities is "KITUSH." This is an association of the three settlements which were the main focus of partnership activities in Kipsongo, Tuwan and Shimo La Tewa. According to community activists, the formation of this association is a response to the void they fear will be left when ITD-EA withdraws from Kitale and its active role in the partnership. "KITUSH will be the next ITDG," said Mr. Kibe of Shimo La Tewa.

Community representatives drawn from each settlement also participate in the sanitation revolving loan fund as trustees. At the group level the members have organized themselves into small loan groups, where they use peer pressure and influence to ensure loan repayment.

Impact and Ties Outside the Settlements and Beyond Kitale

Some activities are citywide. Kitale Green Towns Environmental Group, for example, engages directly with the municipality in planning and executing cleaning and greening activities in the major public spaces and public institutions in the town. Many of the CBOs have met with counterpart CBOs in Nairobi and Nakuru slums. This has had the effect of creating informal links beyond Kitale, with people hundreds of kilometres away. Although these links are not formalized in organizations, they have a strong cultural impact.

To give some idea of the strength of community identity, and of communal purpose in escaping poverty, it is striking that in all three settlements, communal meetings at a number of levels open and close each presentation with the International Slum Dwellers Association slogan: "Umoja Haki Silaha Yetu, Uwonga Umasikini Milele!" (Unity our strength, fear Poverty forever).

Human Development

The partnership has engaged a large number of community members in training and capacity building in provision of water and sanitation services on a sustainable basis: a wide range of building skills, health promotion and community management. In each case, a core group of people has been trained directly, and others have benefited from training by members of this core. There have been substantial gains on four important fronts.

Technical Training

Health and sanitation: In each of the three identified settlements a core group of 65 volunteers (40 women and 25 men) were identified for training in personal hygiene and environmental sanitation. These have now trained other members of the communities, and there is widespread consciousness of practices which avoid the spread of infectious diseases and of their importance and value to the community.

Appropriate building technologies: Youth groups in all three settlements (four groups in all) have benefited from training in SSB production and have been given a machine so that they can undertake IGAs. Women and men in Tuwan have been taught to manufacture pre-cast concrete floor elements using a technology imported from India. Proper techniques for planning and building wells, protecting springs and constructing different latrine types are now widely understood. A large number of people have participated in construction work and 23 of them are now building latrines on their own account.

Impact: Both forms of training are widely appreciated in the communities and are particularly critical in Kipsongo, where residents are poorest, as well as being more recent rural-urban migrants. In Kipsongo there is anecdotal evidence of a drop in mortality from infectious disease, and in Shimo la Tewa, of a lower incidence of infectious diseases among children and elderly people, as explained by a community nurse during the evaluation.

Sustainability: Social structures have been established to support a continuation of this work, for example, the Voluntary Health Committee in each settlement, whose membership is very committed. However, they are under pressure, and members at Shimo La Tewa pointed out that although the training is spreading, the process would be more sustainable if IGAs could be devised to support it.

There has also been training in environmental management and sustainability, covering solid waste disposal and appropriate urban greening and plant care. This training has supported the development of a volunteer core (Green Towns Group) and is widely supported and endorsed. The project conducted a one-week environmental planning workshop and prepared the Kitale Environmental Development Plan, jointly with the Ministry of Lands and Settlement Physical Planning Department, CBOS, NGOs, other key government departments and the Council. The plan provides a framework for various environmental actions (e.g., springs and riparian protection, greening, sanitation, solid waste management and urban agriculture practices).

Citizenship

Training and capacity building has included not only technical matters, but training in rights and responsibilities. Groups have been taken to see conditions and solutions in Nakuru and Nairobi, thereby increasing awareness of the problems facing slum dwellers in other parts of Kenya and the ways in which they are being addressed. Residents' view of themselves as isolated and without rights has given way to a view of themselves as people and communities with rights: the right to secure tenure, the right to a clean and sanitary environment, the right to adequate housing and the right to earn a living.

Another component of education has been the insistence of partnership leaders on a contribution from community members. Thus, although the bulk of the funding has come from donors such as DfID (Department for International Development) and ITDG, and a considerable contribution has come from the Council, no developmental interventions have been implemented without a significant contribution from the direct beneficiaries. Details of these arrangements are varied and depend on needs and skills. They include, among others, community labour (site clearance, digging the foundations and the contribution of timber for decking to the construction of the Shimo La Tewa footbridge, production by the Tuwan youth groups of SSBs for the public sanitation block and the labour contributed by their elders in the production of floor modules).

One important impact has been the widespread acceptance in community circles that they are responsible for their fate, that as a group they are more powerful, and that they can expand the boundaries of what has been initiated by the partnership already. The project to develop latrines on individual plots in Tuwan is a case in point. The establishment of five savings and loans associations, not originally part of the partnership plan, based as it was on early consultations, is another.

This change in attitude by community members is well exemplified by the Tuwan Daily Savings Association, which has developed a vision of "Tuwan without slums by 2010." Its philosophy was summed up by Mr. Maina, the chairman, with a quote from the Book of Hosea (Old Testament of the Bible): "A nation without vision shall perish."

Summary and Conclusions

Overall, the BIP-PUP process in Kitale has shown itself able to plan and implement a remarkable amount of development in terms of physical infrastructure and amenities, social infrastructure and personal attitudes.

Physical development priorities differed among the three informal settlements but everywhere have had a substantial impact on peoples' lives. Each development has been planned, located and developed with its long-term management and sustainability in mind. Progress in water and sanitation technology, management and behaviour has produced a radical change in the cleanliness of the settlements. The ground is clean of solid and human waste; insects and other infection carriers have been sharply reduced; and new cases of infectious diseases appear to have dropped sharply. There is enormous pride and relief on the part of residents in these achievements.

It is apparent that there is a great deal of enthusiasm for the formation and maintenance of CBOs. The long-term sustainability of voluntary membership is seen as dependent on the success of planned income generation activities, in addition to the evident improvements in sanitation and welfare. Savings and loans associations have been popular and successful at an individual and community level, as well as providing a forum in which ambitions for the future are developed. The success of income generation groups has been more uneven. For example, the Shimo La Tewa youth group has not been as successful as the youth groups elsewhere at mobilizing itself, looking for opportunities and taking on work. This reluctance is now the focus of further study.

Enhanced consciousness of rights and responsibilities and of the potential for individual and collective action has also been a notable success of the project. It is clear that the procedural "tool kit" developed with BIP-PUP presented an opportunity for thorough analysis of problems and proposed solutions, as well as a medium for comparative analysis between projects and among settlements. Those community members who were more actively involved in the planning process have a good appreciation of its value to their community. Involvement of business enterprises is still at a formative stage, but it is clear that there is genuine interest. Municipal officials have also become increasingly conscious of the effectiveness of this approach and have increasingly lent it support. Awareness has also been raised within central government, which has likewise demonstrated its support.

As a result, the BIP-PUP institutions and process have largely been embraced at all levels and by all sectors in Kitale. Recognition has also developed among all parties to the project, that its long term transformative capacity depends on its institutionalization within the annual cycle of local authority budgeting, management and development work. In Kenya, this necessitates tying in future developments of BIP-PUP to the LASDAP (Local Authority Service Delivery Plans) cycle.

Nevertheless, the long-term sustainability of this approach to development in the town depends also on the emergence of a lead member of the partnership who will take over leadership once ITDG, the initiating NGO, has withdrawn. There is widespread awareness among partners of the importance of this role in bringing together partners and in drawing involvement from outside the town, activities which require time and skill. The nature and demands of this role are becoming clearer following three years of project work in the town, and it is expected to be undertaken by the Town Clerk. The tragic death on the roads of both Kitale's senior officials, the Mayor and the Town Clerk, in November, 2004, will test the depth of transformation in the town's ability to initiate and manage the processes of its own development.

Notes

1. Cohen, "Urban Growth in Developing Countries," *World Development,* 23.
2. ILO Employment Sector, *Women and men in the Informal Economy.*
3. Sheng, *Community Participation in the Execution of Low-income Housing Projects*; Skinner and Rodell, *People Poverty and Shelter*; Paul, *Community Participation in World Bank Projects*; Syagga, Gatabaki-Kamau and Ondiege, *Access by Women and the Urban Poor to Urban Land and Credit.*
4. African National Congress, *Reconstruction and Development Plan.*
5. Hamdi, *Housing without Houses.*
6. Lyons and Smuts, "Community Agency in the New South Africa," *Urban Studies,* 2151.
7. Sheng, *The Urban Poor as Agents of Development.*
8. Cooke and Kothari, *Participation: The New Tyranny?*
9. Hickey and Mohan, *From Tyranny to Transformation?*
10. Lyons, Smuts and Stephens, "Participation, Empowerment and Sustainability," *Urban Studies,* 1233.
11. Valler and Betteley, "The Politics of 'Integrated' Local Policy in England," *Urban Studies,* 2393.
12. Frigenti, Harth and Huque, *Local Solutions to Regional Problems.*
13. Narayan and Ebbe, *Design of Social Funds.*
14. African Mayors' Forum, *Declaration on Sustainable Development,* 2.
15. Healey, "Planning Through Debate," *Town Planning Review,* 143.
16. Halla, *Participatory Approaches to Urban Planning in Tanzania.*
17. IDD (International Development Department) *Building Municipal Accountability.*
18. Yahya, *The Origins of Participatory Planning in Kenya.*
19. UNDP, *Human Development Report.*

20. Legovini, *Kenya: Macro Economic Evolution Since Independence.*
21. UNDP, *Human Development Report 2004.*
22. Nabutola, *Upgrading Informal Settlements.*
23. Majale, "Towards Pro-poor Regulatory Guidelines for Urban Upgrading."
24. Chege and BIP-PUP Project, *Kitale Community Based Planning Tool Kit.*
25. BIP-PUP Project, *Kipsongo Neighbourhood Plan.*
26. BIP-PUP Project, *Shimo La Tewa Neighbourhood Plan.*
27. BIP-PUP Project, *Tuwan Neighbourhood Plan.*

Bibliography

African Mayors' Forum. *Declaration on Sustainable Development.* Johannesburg World Summit on Sustainable Development, Johannesburg, June, 2002.

African National Congress. *Reconstruction and Development Plan.* Pretoria: African National Congress, 1994.

BIP-PUP Project. *Kipsongo Neighbourhood Plan.* Nairobi: ITDG-EA and KMC, 2002.

BIP-PUP Project. *Shimo La Tewa Neighbourhood Plan.* Nairobi: ITDG-EA and KMC, 2002.

BIP-PUP Project. *Tuwan Neighbourhood Plan.* Nairobi: ITDG-EA and KMC, 2002.

Chege, Paul, and BIP-PUP Project, *Kitale Community Based Planning Tool Kit,* Nairobi: ITDG- EA and KMC, 2002.

Cohen, Barney. "Urban Growth in Developing Countries: A Review of Current Trends and a Caution Regarding Existing Forecasts." *World Development* vol. 1 no.1 (2004) : 23.

Cooke, Bill and Uma Kothari. *Participation: The New Tyranny?* London & NY, Zed Books, 2001.

Frigenti, Laura, Alberto Harth and Rromana Huque. *Local Solutions to Regional Problems: The Growth of Social Funds and Public Works and Employment Projects in Sub-Saharan Africa.* Washington, DC: World Bank, 1998.

Halla, Francos. "Participatory Approaches to Urban Planning in Tanzania." Unpublished working paper. Dar es Salaam, University College of Lands and Architectural Studies, 2002.

Hamdi, Nabeel. *Housing without Houses.* New York: Van Nostrand Reinhold, 1990.

Healey, Patricia. "Planning Through Debate: The Communicative Turn in Planning Theory, *Town Planning Review* vol. 63 no. 2 (1994) :143.

Hickey, Samuel and Giles Mohan. *From Tyranny to Transformation? Exploring New Approaches to Participation in Development.* London and NY: Zed Books, 2001.

International Development Department (IDD). *Building Municipal Accountability: Local Government Decision-Makin: Citizen Participation and Local Accountability in Kenya and Uganda 2001-2002* University of Birmingham, 2002. www.idd.bham.ac.uk/research/Projects/municpal_accountability/accountability.htm

ILO Employment Sector. *Women and Men in the Informal Economy: A Statistical Picture.* Geneva: International Labour Office, 2002.

Legovini, Arianna. "Kenya: Macro Economic Evolution Since Independence," (2002). www.ke.undp.org/KENYA%20MACRO%20ECONOMIC%20EVOLUTION% 20SINCE%20INDEPENDENCE.doc

Lyons, Michal and Carin Smuts. "Community Agency in the New South Africa." *Urban Studies* vol. 36, no. 12 (1999): 2151.

Lyons, Michal, Carin Smuts and Anthea Stephens. "Participation, Empowerment and Sustainability: (How) Do the Links Work?" *Urban Studies* vol. 38 no.8 (2001): 1233.

Majale, Mike. "Towards Pro-poor Regulatory Guidelines for Urban Upgrading: A Review of Papers Presented at the International Workshop on Regulatory Guidelines for Urban Upgrading," held at Bourton-on-Dunsmore, 17-18 May 2001, paper presented at the International Workshop on Regulatory Guidelines for Urban Upgrading, Fairview Hotel, Nairobi, 14-16 January 2002.

Nabutola, Wafula. *Upgrading Informal Settlements—Kenya: Rural and Urban*, 2004. www.fig.net/pub/athens/papers/ts24

Narayan, Deepa and Katrinka Ebbe. *Design of Social Funds: Participation, Demand Orientation and Local Organization Capacity*. Washington, DC: World Bank Discussion Paper No. 375, 1997.

Paul, Samuel. *Community Participation in World Bank Projects – the World Bank Experience*. World Bank Discussion Papers 6. Washington, DC: The World Bank, 1987.

Sheng, Yap Kioe. *Community Participation in the Execution of Low-income Housing Projects*. Nairobi: UNCHS-Habitat, 1984.

Sheng, Yap Kioe. *The Urban Poor as Agents of Development: Community action planning in Sri-Lanka*. Nairobi: UNHCS, 1993.

Skinner Reinhard J. and Michael J. Rodell. *People Poverty and Shelter: Problems of Self-help Housing in the Third World*. London: Methuen and Co., 1983.

Syagga, Paul, Rose Gatabaki-Kamau, and P.O. Ondiege. *Access by Women and the Urban Poor to Urban Land and Credit: A Socio-Economic Evaluation of the Third Urban Project in Kenya*. Nairobi: Housing Research and Development Unit, University of Nairobi, 1989.

UNDP. *Human Development Report 2004*, (2004). http://hdr.undp.org/reports/global/2004

Valler, David and David Betteley. "The Politics of 'Integrated' local Policy in England," *Urban Studies* vol. 38 no.13 (2001): 2393.

Yahya, Saad. "The Origins of Participatory Planning in Kenya." Unpublished working paper, ITDG-EA.

David Welch

A Time of Globalization and Neoliberalism: The Franco-Ontarian Community, Community Economic Development and the Social Economy

Frequently, in discussions around the social economy, the references turn around specific examples without situating them in the larger context of globalism and neoliberalism. An example of this would be the Franco-Ontarian community that is often presented as a dynamic entity unto itself but not situated into the larger social debates. As will be shown, though often marginalized socially and economically, Franco-Ontarians have been active participants in many of these wider events that are affecting us all globally. In this chapter I would like to discuss a number of issues. First, I want to situate a community such as that of the Franco-Ontarians into the larger context of neoliberalism and globalization where excluded societies are seeking new socio-economic alternatives. Then I present the notions of community economic development and the social economy as social and economic alternatives that carry elements of greater democracy, especially at the local level.[1] Next some of the historical examples of the Franco-Ontarian social economy will be examined in the context that despite their limits they have allowed the community to survive and develop. Finally, I propose to demonstrate how certain contemporary projects are allowing the community to develop greater socio-economic autonomy and how in turn to open new doors for greater democracy within the Franco-Ontarian community.

New Ways of Understanding Democracy, the Role of the State in an Era of Globalization

There are different ways in which the at times overused word of *globalization* can be defined. One definition might be:

> the confluence of economic, political, social, and cultural factors interacting on a world scale thanks to expansion of knowledge, information, trade, and technology beyond geographical borders and poles of economic activity. Thus, the impacts triggered by globalization express themselves in a myriad of changes in the social, economic cultural, and political organizations, and in the policy and governance systems of the nation states interacting on the global scale.[2]

Instead of seeing globalization as part of an historical process, writers, politicians and others often speak of it as something that is overwhelmingly beyond our ability to grasp, let alone be able to control. For them, globalization leads to a feeling of powerlessness.Unfortunately the concept of globalization is often mixed up with that of neoliberalism.[3]

Globalization is not a negative process in itself. Rather what is negative is the neoliberal agenda that is calling the shots about the forms that globalization should take. A global agenda with greater solidarity, equality and collaboration between oppressed peoples could be a very positive process. It becomes a question of introducing global relationships based on a valuing of diversity, a respect for the democratic decisions of individual countries and a privileging of equality over dominance.[4] It has been pointed out that the international women's movement can take advantage of globalization, by challenging the negative economic forces unleashed by globalization, by transforming international organizations and states to make them more accountable, and by creating the institutions of civil society.[5]

As people have been struggling against the excesses of neoliberalism, they have begun to look again at democracy. During this process of rethinking democracy, one can see the positive evidence of a renewal of "a certain culture of the excluded: horizontal relations of power, an economy of solidarity, and self-education."[6] It is an attempt to go beyond a situation of hopelessness and apathy, pessimism and fatalism that is often found in the excluded sectors of society. It is the realization that every time some people somewhere are going hungry, there is in fact a decrease in the collective well-being (*bien commun mondial*), even if the overall collective wealth of the world continues to increase.[7]

Just as neoliberalism has led to a certain displacement of many of the cultural values, beliefs and customs that once were specific to particular countries, regions or cultural groupings, there is also occurring a resurgence of traditional identities, values and communities. "[It] has provoked the active resistance of many previously passive ethnic and religious groups who now see the survival of their distinct identities and values increasingly threatened."[8] This has often been linked to the possibility of belonging to a larger entity where people are accepted as being important for who and what they are and as participants in the democratic process.

However, something different seems to be emerging in regard to the more recent mobilizations. By the size and degree, it leads one to believe that some of these present-day social movements (to avoid the overused term new social movements) are undertaking actions that fundamentally question some of the most cherished beliefs of the world order of neoliberalism. They reject the "old, centralized, elite-based vision of modernization for the small minority—which has brought mass poverty, slow growth and wide inequalities to many Southern societies" and advance the idea "that democratization opens up ... gender-balanced, rural-centred, green, bottom-up spread of broad-based opportunities and action against poverty."[9] Gender issues have not only become far more visible but are central to many of the emerging struggles in developing countries as well as the more developed world.[10] These movements do not so much question technological change, as the forms this new technology is taking while asking how the benefits from these changes will be shared among the peoples, regions and countries of the world. It is a concerted effort to reclaim what minority communities consider their public space or commons.

Communities are by no means linear, for they remain social constructions. Thus, in an age where the tendency is toward atomization and individualism, they continue to form and reform with probably even more diversity in terms of their focus of attention than was the case with groups thirty years ago. Whether it is by theme—poverty, human rights, the environment—or by social groupings such as youth, women, ethnic and racial minorities, gays and lesbians or specific ethno-cultural communities such as the Franco-Ontarians, communities continue to be,

> on one hand, collective systems of reciprocal recognition, expressing old and new collective identities, with important cultural and symbolic components. On the other hand, they are non partisan political intermediaries who bring the needs and demands of unarticulated voices to the public sphere, linking them to state institutions.[11]

In their attempts to be more democratic and anti-authoritarian in their functioning, they are often opposed to multinational capital and much of their activity comes from the grass roots. The goal of these social movements is not simply power, but the alteration of values at the level of civil society.[12] This process can become

> an interaction between national-level democratization and community-based efforts for change by these civil society movements, aiming at different aspects of poverty reduction. The community-based efforts become not only learning experiences at the micro-level, helping to identify specific policies and tactics that are more effective in countering poverty, gender inequalities, and the environmental degradation, but also political initiatives, highlighting the importance of these concerns on the national policy agenda of society.[13]

This process is long and full of zigzags, at times moving quickly and at other times leaving people wondering if there is any movement at all.

The Third Sector or Social Economy as Social and Economic Alternatives

As groups of citizens within minority communities and elsewhere have begun mobilizing against neoliberalism, they have also been seeking new solutions to the on-going problems of poverty, lack of citizen participation and other social exclusions. These new movements are both political and socio-economic in that they are seeking social solidarity and social citizenship in everyday life, but at the same time financial autonomy.

Some of this new social and economic activity is coming out of that part of civil society that we refer to as the social economy. As will be shown, the social economy can become an alternative to the historic either/or of the private sector and the state as the only roads for human progress.[14] It has its own particular logic and set of values. In turn, these values and actions have the potential of better utilization of resources—both human and natural. They can allow a more concerted struggle against poverty, can provide a means to create new employment, can revitalize the economy from the bottom-up and, finally, can nurture new forms of social integration of the various sectors of society.[15]

What is meant by the social economy?

By social economy we refer to the formally constituted, self-governing, democratically structured organizations established for the social and economic benefit of the collectivity or the mutual benefit of its members or the larger community. The notion of profit-making is secondary and is seen as a means to reach the established goal of greater social development. Frequently the term social economy is used interchangeably with third sector, non-profit sector, community economic development and community development. It is often closely linked to social movements and to the broader civil society. Much like community economic development and sustainable development, it is an attempt to erase the boundaries between the economic and the social.[16] Though the social economy is often associated with services to people, such as daycare co-operatives or homecare services, to name only two, it has the potential of developing into other areas such as culture, new technologies, natural resources, housing and environmental protection.[17]

It is important to keep in mind that the third sector frequently overlaps with the areas of the state and even the private sector, making clear-cut distinctions more difficult to make do. Many see it as playing the role of the more human counterpart to the private sector. The latter is more concerned with private profits than actual citizen participation and will tend to avoid areas of production that it sees as not being profitable. It is felt that the third sector, through building on the positive aspects of the welfare state, can better mobilize volunteer efforts, all the while providing job opportunities for those unemployed people who have few or no job skills. Thus it is possible to have a situation where the state continues to have a regulating and financial role, but at the same time allow a far greater role for the social economy in the provision of services.[18]

The Changing Welfare State and the Social Economy

All discussion about the social economy needs to be placed in a broader historical context. One should remember that

> the rise of the welfare state and the pluralistic nature of liberal-demo-
> cratic politics in the 1960s, 1970s and 1980s, gave a considerable
> impetus to the expansion of the third sector…. Historically, the nature,
> structure and evolution of the social economy has been a function of state
> formation.[19]

The state has played the role of supplanting or absorbing some of the activities done previously by minority communities and, at the same time, through its policies and financial support it has supported the formation of many others.[20] It is in studying the changing role of the state that we can better grasp the place of the third sector. It is important then, to keep in mind that as neoliberalism attacks the state, the third sector also is affected, as funding is cut and as the responsibility for social programs is downloaded to the lower levels of government, to the private sector and to the family.[21]

However, at the same time it is important to keep in mind that much of the criticism of the welfare state has come from what many perceive as its ever-greater bureaucratization, its top-down tendencies and its being too far removed from the basic needs of the population. The universalism of the welfare state has been

> challenged by particularism arising out of the replacement of classed-
> based social inequality by a plethora of social movements, all concerned
> with the recognition of their identity and attendant rights. The resulting
> Welfare rights paradigm has challenged the paternalism of the Welfare
> State and exposed its weaknesses and limitations.[22]

As mentioned earlier, it is important to see the social economy as interacting with the state and not as something operating on its own, independent of the state and even the private sector. This means that one must have a clear notion of where the state is situated in the overall scheme of things. To recognize that the state has an important place in society is to accept that to be effective it must play a role on a number of levels. The state must strive to continue to reorganize its own institutions so that it can continue to carry out the tasks that are essential to the society as a whole and in turn to make them more responsive to citizen needs and to assure that state functions become more transparent and effective.[23] It must assure basic public rights such as education, health, transportation and communications as well as the protection of the most vulnerable.[24] It means interacting with the institutions of civil society, mediating conflicting social and class interests in order to reach what many might consider to be the common good, all the while assuring respect for the less powerful, including those of minority communities.

This implies that the state must accept the idea that the development of space for new institutions independent of political parties is not only vital but absolutely necessary. It must not just see the social economy as simply a sub-contractor providing local services, but seek to develop solidarity with communities, in the more flexible creation of jobs and the development of services. It must respect their autonomy so that organizations of civil society or the third sector (especially those at the local level who frequently have a strong sense of their own identity), can continue to be strengthened, with a diversified presence and with a recognized legitimacy to participate in problem solving. In the end, the social economy can become a means of strengthening both citizenship and democracy.[25]

The Social Economy Understood at the Local Level

The trend toward globalization has led to a belief by some that because of the greater internationalization of the world economy, minority communities no longer have much control over their own situation and are basically dependant on external economic factors, such as the mobility of capital. This means that any local attempts at redistribution of wealth would be counter-productive. On the contrary, a better sharing of wealth, created from economic development, helps to prevent increased social tensions, in part stemming from social polarization.

This means that even in the new economic world, one cannot look only at the economic aspects of a minority community cut off from the social aspects. Greater decentralization to the local level leads to new responsibilities for the social sector.[26] For minority communities to prosper they must develop alliances between the different actors and develop new social projects, including those linked to sustainable development and the environment, alongside and in liaison with those of the economic sector, including the social economy.

By looking to minority communities such as that of Franco-Ontarians we are better able to understand that the "small-scale alternative is just not more appropriate in social and antipoverty terms but also carries important economic advantages in efficiency of production and lower-cost provision of basic needs to the poor."[27] By their importance, both numerically and economically, it is important not to see these groups only as "survival strategies" but rather as important means to create jobs and revenues.[28] Local popular organizations within minority communities can have important socio-political effects for

> they situate impoverished groups such as women and the unemployed in the public view. To ensure that the benefits of national growth are channelled to the local level for the benefit of the majority, a number of elements become essential and new values as to the importance of people participating in the 'social construction of their daily lives' need to become accepted.[29]

As a result, activities such as food preparation and childcare—traditionally considered of a private nature and resolved in the private sector—constitute material for discussion and rethinking.[30]

The acceptance of the organizations of the third sector and the social economy as being part of the democratic process and not just "special interest groups" could, over time, lead to creation of greater social capital or trust between citizens and in turn to a reinforcement of local democracy. Strong local democracy, consisting of real citizen participation, is essential to the building and reinforcing of democracy at other levels. It becomes in essence an interaction of elected and non-elected officials of different levels of the state, with the various actors and organizations of civil society, assuring their direct participation. It is the recognition that in today's world of increased globalization, the local has more and more a vital role to play. It is in the interaction of the state and its various components with the organizations of civil society, including the minority communities that new forms of democracy are born.

Many new social and economic projects of the third sector are already taking place as people strive for the basic rights of sufficient food, work, transportation and housing. People struggle over who will control these rights: Will it be the private sector, the state or the local community, made up of the local citizens? New alliances are formed, since problems such as air and noise pollution as well as security tend to cross geographic barriers, even if usually the popular classes are more affected. What we are beginning to realize and better appreciate, more than ever before, is that the potential for trust and the desire for greater democracy tends to be far stronger at the local level, due to the immediacy of so many local problems.[31]

Franco-Ontarians and the Social Economy in a Historical Perspective

When studying the history and development of the Franco-Ontarian community, one realizes how the different forms of the social economy, both past and present, have played an essential role in survival and development. Soon after initial settlement in the 18th century, French-speaking settlers created social practices and resources built around self-help and social solidarity.

One of the earliest examples of the social economy within the Franco-Ontarian community was the volunteer work done by women, both in the cities and the rural areas. Women worked as midwives or healers, organizing communities' services. As well, the community established various charitable institutions—hospitals, orphanages and shelters for the aged, usually under the direction of female religious congregations.

By the beginning of the 20th century, women began to set up their own autonomous organizations, in order to better deliver social services to the community. One of the most important organizations was without a doubt the

Fédération des femmes canadiennes françaises, (FFCF) founded in 1914 by Almanda Walker-Marchand.[32] Though its initial mission was to assist in the war effort, very quickly the FFCF expanded to the various parishes across French Canada outside of Québec and began to diversify its works to the larger social service field.[33] For instance, in 1916 and in 1921, the FFCF took charge of many of the victims of the devastating forest fires that raged across northeastern Ontario.

There were also volunteer organizations that had both social and economic objectives. The Saint-Vincent-de-Paul Society, founded in Ottawa by French Canadians in 1860, was responsible for giving help to the poorest families in Lower Town, a neighbourhood of Ottawa. For instance, in 1874, members of the Society asked for meat from the local butchers as well as heating wood from the local saw mills and farmers to assure that the poorest survived winter.[34] During the economic crisis of 1875-1880, along with the Soeurs de la Charité, they organized a community kitchen for the poor.

During the Depression of the 1930s, the Franco-Ontarian elite and its main umbrella organization, the Association canadienne-française d'éducation de l'Ontario (ACFEO), founded the Oeuvre des Chômeurs. It was founded as an early form of unemployment centre for young men. The centre offered direct financial aide, housing for those most in need and counselling to help the unemployed to find work. It was hoped that its activities within the Franco-Ontarian working class would counterbalance whatever influence the Communist Party might have with the younger unemployed men.[35] It was at this point that ACFEO began looking at ways to create a youth centre for young Franco-Ontarians to counterbalance the YM-YWCA, seen as a Protestant and Anglophone organization. In 1957, the Patro-St. Vincent was founded as a sport/recreation organization for young boys.

In the mid-19th century, under the leadership of the lay and religious elite, Franco-Ontarians began setting up their first co-operatives. One of the first was a mutual-aid society, called the Union St. Joseph (now Union du Canada), initially founded by French Canadian workers in 1863 in Ottawa. In its early years the society had only about 700 members. However, by 1910 its membership had increased to around 8,000 members in Ontario, divided into 145 local councils. The policies covered from 50,000 to 60,000 persons out of a total Franco-Ontarian population of about 203,000.[36] The Union St. Joseph, in spite of its cooperative spirit and its aim to furnish non-profit services, rejected all social and economic practices that might be seen as promoting state intervention. Though it was ready to defend the identity interests of Franco-Ontarians, the Union rejected any state intervention on social issues as being too socialistic or communistic.[37] This narrow social and economic vision could best be summed up in a book published in 1939, in which the author, Charles Leclerc, wrote that:

> ... la Saint Joseph s'inscrit en faux contre les doctrines entachées de
> socialisme, qui demandent à l'État de se constituer en une sorte de
> providence, qui veulent faire peser sur tous les citoyens indifféremment

le poids de la subsistance d'un certain nombre, qui veulent tuer
l'initiative individuelle, et entraver la compétition. Plutôt que de verser,
même modérément, dans les théories à saveur socialiste, elle rappelle que le
Christ a dit qu'il y aurait toujours des pauvres et que c'est eux qu'il a aimés.[38]

The same vision was present in the founding of the first Caisses populaires, a form of parish credit union. They were established on much the same model as those in Quebec—Alphonse Desjardins who had founded the first Caisses populaires in Québec, resided in Ottawa for many years. The Caisses that grew quickly in numbers after the Second World War (a period when Franco-Ontarians were able to save, after seeing prosperity for the first time) allowed community members to save and borrow, thereby assuring that money stayed in the community. Today the various *caisses populaires* in French-speaking Ontario have more than four billion dollars in deposits.

Many of these organizations, under the leadership of the emerging middle class had a very conservative moral vision. Their aim was to help the less fortunate without questioning the underlying social and economic inequalities that existed. Despite the limits of their actions, their strategies built on a belief in social solidarity, assuring their survival as a distinct community in a larger society that was undergoing very rapid change.

New Visions, New Social Practices Since the 1960s

Out of the many reforms that directly affected the Franco-Ontarian community since the 1960s, new social practices emerged. As the state was pushed to allow greater recognition and space for the Franco-Ontarian community, many Franco-Ontarians turned away from the more traditional model above to a more "modern" one advocating the importance of working with the government to bring about what was perceived as needed reforms. Others went even further and sought parallel French language services (based in part on the New Brunswick model of services), rather than spending huge amounts of energy on attempting to "bilingualize" existing English language services.

Out of these various mobilizations, some social advocates went beyond the historic demands for French language services. They began pressing for the establishment of totally new services that were not simply translations of English language services with all their "professionalism" and lack of citizen participation. Rather, they proposed original, more democratic social practices that reflected the culture and needs of the community, especially its more vulnerable members.[39] This process reinforced a break with the traditional leadership that frequently remained preoccupied with increasing the number of educational institutions and tended to ignore the importance of developing social services.[40] It was as if they were perceived as services for "the less fortunate" or "those with problems," an attitude that demonstrated a difficulty in understanding that new daycare centres and support centres for women victims of violence were real community needs that touched all sectors of the community.

Some of the most dynamic alternative projects have come out of the various women's organizations, around the need for better daycare, shelters for women victims of violence and immigrant information services for women. In some cases these were new organizations, such as les Ontaroises de l'Est, Franco-femmes in the North and le Réseau des femmes du Sud de l'Ontario in the South.[41] In other cases some of the more traditional women's organizations reorganized their activities with new perspectives and objectives.[42]

Other community practitioners became directly involved in economic as well as social issues. This led to actively supporting striking forestry workers during the Elk Lake mill strike of 1980 in North-eastern Ontario and the AMOCO textile strike of 1981 in Eastern Ontario.[43] They even went as far as supporting striking Union du Canada office workers, going against the tradition of not striking against the co-operative movement. These actions were new attempts to link up social issues with the basic economic realities of many community members, even when it meant coming into conflict with the more traditional leadership.

The eight-year period of the Harris/Eves Conservative governments, from June 1995 until their defeat in October 2003, was a time of massive cutbacks in social programs and a transfer of formerly government programs to the private sector. These cutbacks had an extremely negative effect on Franco-Ontarian social and educational institutions as well as community-based projects. People were put on the defensive in an attempt both to retain what had already been won and to achieve further reforms. The notion that success or failure depends upon one's ability, hard-work, risk-taking and personal initiative,[44] or that there is no civil society but only individual enterprise and self-reliance, were attitudes that went against much of the historical understanding of many Franco-Ontarians—that the "social" does indeed exist and that society cannot be reduced to one of simple self-interest. Franco-Ontarians had learned over the years that the state's actions attempting to better distribute the national wealth and assuring a greater respect for minorities had generally benefited the community. People had discovered by trial and error that civil society, in spite of its limitations, had benefited the majority within the community and that the private sector had little interest in the limited benefits to be won from the social or educational needs of the Franco-Ontarian community.

On a number of levels, Franco-Ontarians during that period of cutbacks remained vulnerable. For instance, the functional illiteracy rate within the community was still about 30 per cent and many families remained poor.[45] Though the vast majority of Franco-Ontarians are urbanized, many live isolated and dispersed in small towns, far from the main networks of services. Any cuts in government funding potentially can be very harmful.[46]

Franco-Ontarian Alternatives: A Return to Community Economic Development and the Social Economy

Those who have been seeking new alternatives in social practices base their thinking on two premises. On one hand, many have criticized the tendency of government to become too paternalistic, overly bureaucratic and too top-down in its dealings with the social sector. The welfare state has been shown to have important weaknesses and limitations. On the other hand, some believe that though the state has played a role in supplanting or absorbing some of the activities done previously by the third sector, through its policies and financial support, it has led to the formation of many new social practices.[47]

At least since the 1970s, some Franco-Ontarian social activists have been critical of the welfare state, not limiting their criticisms to issues of weaknesses in the provision of French language schooling and services. However, while criticizing government as being too rigid, hierarchal and impersonal, they have continued to defend the notion that the state has an important role, by means of the tax system, of providing the financial means for organizations to provide services as defined democratically by the community.

In recent years, they have been supporting the struggle for reduced government, but at the same time rejecting the transfers of service provision to the private sector. Many Franco-Ontarians have realized that the private sector, with its notions of profit, makes many of the vital services needed in the community simply uneconomical except to the wealthiest. Rather, they have defended the idea that though funding and overall regulation should be provided by the state, these funds should be transferred to community-based groups that can better mobilize volunteer efforts while providing the necessary services. In practice, this can lead to a greater number of options, as community-based groups would be alternatives to state agencies, thereby providing "the advantage of the qualitative (flexibility, proximity to clients, capacity for innovation, etc.) and quantitative (expected lower costs)..." delivery of services.[48] As pointed out previously, Franco-Ontarian community service providers would also give a service that better respects both the language and culture of the community. It is not a question of "better managing poverty and social exclusion,"[49] but rather an attempt to link present-day practices with those of the past, urban practices with those of the rural areas and finally social issues with those that are more economic in nature. The Franco-Ontarian social economy means that the state must respect the autonomy of organizations within civil society, so that they can continue to be strengthened with a diversified presence and with a recognized legitimacy to participate in problem solving. In the end it becomes a means of strengthening both citizenship and democracy.[50]

In these times of rapid social change and cutbacks in many social sectors, for some Franco-Ontarians, the social economy has been seen as one means by which they can win back the social, economic and even political power that they have lost or not yet obtained.

At the same time, it is important to keep in mind that any discussion around the place and role of the social economy reflects the various struggles around debates of what some perceive as undemocratic power relations with their own forms of exclusion. Franco-Ontarians have at times lived the contradiction where different people within the community with opposing interests can all sing in praise of the social economy, without recognizing these unequal power relationships. Many strong advocates of the social economy can also be defenders of the status quo or with quite conservative views on any notion of bottom-up democracy.

In Hearst, a women's co-operative tree nursery called the Maison Verte was founded in 1981, under the direction of a local women's group called Parmi-elles. Originating with some federal government funding, the project has provided eight full-time jobs and about thirty-five part-time jobs. The participants in the project are now growing millions of tree seedlings, garden plants and building new green houses to begin growing tomatoes for the local market.[51] On a larger scale there was the participation of Franco-Ontarian women in the organization of the International Women's March that was held throughout the world in October 2000. In collaboration with Anglophone groups, Franco-Ontarian women's groups sought to unite their struggles with others across the world against poverty and violence against women.[52] Previous to the October demonstration, Franco-Ontarian women in the province organized many activities.

These few examples show that Franco-Ontarians, not unlike many other communities living in Ontario, are up to the challenge of assuring new forms of the social economy.[53] Starting from grass-roots initiatives, as they have sought and recognized the importance of government funding, they have attempted to avoid the over-professionalization of state agencies. At the same time, they have remained confronted by the challenge of avoiding within their own organizations these same tendencies and becoming bureaucratic, too professionalized and, in the end, anti-democratic. The social economy has permitted reaching populations that have often been neglected notably francophone immigrants (especially women) and those with less schooling.

Alternatives have helped to rekindle self-confidence in communities that have over the years suffered losses in population, (especially the younger population) and have reinforced sentiments of social solidarity. As had often happened in the past, new practices have helped reinforce existing French-language institutions and have helped to create new ones often better adapted to new needs in the communities.[54]

A final challenge has been the need to avoid becoming inward-looking, thereby developing other forms of intolerance and exclusion and of finding new ways of uniting their actions with those in other communities who have common interests. It has become a "struggle between very different values; the logic of competition versus the logic of community; the logic of machines and machine efficiency versus the logic of people trying to make a life for themselves and participate meaningfully in their society." [55] In the end it becomes a question of whether "the local [will] be an extension of global uniformity, or the global [will] be an extension of local diversity."[56]

Conclusion

In this chapter I have sought to demonstrate that as global capitalism under neoliberalism continues to dominate, new economic and social crises will continue to occur leading to more people becoming excluded. However, as civil society develops, and people continue to rethink democracy, people will be better positioned to win back social, economic and political power. Democracy will permit the gradual growth of civil society and in turn civil society can facilitate the development of greater democracy. One cannot really have one without the other.

Without putting our ability to continue criticizing the state and its institutions on the shelf of history, we realize that new ways of reading and understanding the state are necessary. It is the continuing realization that the disadvantaged are capable of understanding their world and "drawing on their own intelligence and sensitivity that the people themselves have the ability to transform not only themselves, but the whole of society."[57] In turn, it is a realization that they are directly affected by specific and overall state policies.[58]

The variety of political settings or places for political exchange[59] can in the end have a multiplier effect, creating greater social trust between people and thereby social capital. It is a form of socially-added value that can lead people to new projects and initiatives. People have realized that the

> third sector or civil society is not a replacement for the state but a
> mechanism to influence the form of the state and the market [and that
> indeed] there is no evidence that the third sector exists separately from
> the state and the market or that this separation is to be preferred.[60]

It is important to keep in mind that these many forms of social interactions have not just occurred, but have been given a certain space by the openness of a state for greater citizen involvement. Thus people are looking for the state to play a different role, not its disengagement, a theme so dear to neoliberals.

Out of theses struggles for greater democracy and rethinking the place of the state, has come a social and economic strategy often referred to as the social economy. It has come out of the desire for people to try to find other ways for economic and social development. Action, both of a political and economic nature, has resulted from efforts to respond to basic issues such as the kind and availability of work, the adequacy of income and basic living conditions. Questions of cultural identity in the case of projects linked to specific ethno-cultural communities, such as the Franco-Ontarians, are also closely linked to the seeking of means for a better livelihood.

This discussion raises the issue of how to unite the democratic impulses and practices of particular struggles that are occurring locally to other ones elsewhere.

Out of this strengthening of civil society, and in turn democracy, people are working to ensure that new alliances are formed between social movements, social classes and social and ethnic minorities in order to win control of the state away from the wealthy minority and their allies in the free market world. It is the latter that control an ever-greater part of the world's wealth and whose greed is leading humanity to environmental and human destruction. Those who refuse the status quo will have to build on the existing strengths of what exists and what is continually being created, and in turn mobilize other social actors. There is a need to develop concrete programs of action that support the creation of alternative centres of power at the grassroots level where, with time, enough people become mobilized to democratically win power. This action program must have as its centrepiece the struggle against poverty, greater gender equality and a concern with the environment that permits the long-term sustainability of local communities and an active participation in decision-making by local communities.[61] It must clearly show how neoliberalism is fundamentally undemocratic and leads to greater underdevelopment, the destruction of the eco-system, the further marginalization of indigenous peoples and, in the end, casting off industries, peoples and even countries that it has no use for.[62]

Notes

I would like to thank Éthel Côté, researcher and community organizer from Eastern Ontario for her very helpful comments on an earlier draft of this chapter. Also thanks to Josette Kodsi of l'École de service social of the University of Ottawa for her help in the editing and technical processes.

1. The terms community economic development and the social economy are often used together. More recently, attempts have been made to define the terms a bit differently. Community economic development refers to isolated or marginalized communities taking in hand their local economy on a territorial basis. The aim is to revitalize communities economically and socially. The social economy refers more to local economic and social enterprises that seek by means of specific activities to improve the social as well as economic situation of a particular group of people (Lewis, 2004). In this chapter both terms will at times be used somewhat interchangeably as they are not contradictory but, rather, complementary. Thus a broader understanding of what the social economy is will be used.

2. Morales-Gómez, *Transnational Social Policies*, 3.

3. For those who defend neo-liberalism, capitalism as an an economic form provides greater individual freedom from the state than any other. It subjects all people to the forces of the market, thus allowing them to succeed or fail on their own abilities, hard-work, risk-taking and personal initiative (Browne, 2000). Neoliberals make no real mention of how, in reality, uncontrolled free markets also lead to negative results such as environmental degregation and to lower wages, to name only two. Believing that what is important is individual enterprise and self-

reliance, neoliberals reject the notion of social solidarity and indeed deny the existance of the "social"; Powell and Guerin, 1997. This could be summed up in the famous statement of Margaret Thatcher that "there is no such thing as society, there are only individuals," and that the family should be the basis on which people construct their policies for education and social welfare.

It is important to remember that neoliberalism goes beyond economics, for it provides a political and cultural world view, in which the highest value is economic freedom in the sense of the freedom to make choices, both as a producer and consumer, without government interference. Any government intervention to regulate the market denies individual liberty and "thwarts the development of a prosperous economy by undercutting the creative capacity of individual entrepreneurs and enthroning bungling bureaucrats"; Collins and Lear. Thus government interventions to control markets, ensure greater distribution of the national wealth, or to impose regulations are considered wrong. One of the effects of the neoliberal discourse is that the "private interests are now so integrated into the functioning of the public good that our practical sense of the latter has been erased"; Saul.

4.   Rebick, *Imagine Democracy*, 53

5.   Ibid., 55.

6.   Barrera, "Political Participation and Social Exclusion," in *Markets and Democracy in Latin America.*

7.   Petrella, *Le bien commun.*

8.   Harris, "The Global Context of Contemporary Latin American Affairs," in *Capital, Power and Inequality in Latin* America, 299-300.

9.   Langdon, *Global Poverty; Democracy and North-South Change*, 197.

10.   Ibid.

11.   Jelin, "Toward a Culture of Participation and Citizenship," in *Cultures of Politics / Politics of Culture*, 413.

12.   Burbach, Nunez and Kagarlitsky, *Globalization and its Discontents*, 158.

13.   Langdon, 198

14.   Petrella, *Le bien commun.*

15.   Larraechea and Nyssens, "L'économie solidaire, un autre regard sur l'économie populaire au Chili," in *L'économie solidaire, une perspective internationale.*

16.   Ninacs, *A Practitioner's Perspective on the Social Economy in Québec.*

17.   Ibid.

18.   Vaillancourt et al. *L'Économie sociale, santé et bien-être* (2000) ; Vaillaincourt et Labesse (1997) : 1 dans Vaillancourt et al. (2000).

19.   Browne, "The Neo-liberal Uses of the Social Economy," in *Social Economy, International Debates and Perspectives*, 66.

20.   Ibid.

21.   Ibid.

22.   Powell and Guerin, *Civil Society and Social Policy*, 45.

23.   Quiróz and Palma, "Chili," in *Community Development Around the World.*

24.   Langdon, 1999.

25.   Ninacs, 1998.

26. Quesnel, "Les nouveaux rôles des villes dans le contexte de la mondialisation," in *Les villes mondiales*, 132, 137.

27. Langdon, 196.

28. Larraechea and Nyssens, "L'économie solidaire, un autre regard sur l'économie populaire au Chili," in *L'économie solidaire, une perspective internationale*.

29. Quiróz and Palma, 398.

30. Ibid., 409.

31. Langdon.

32. Desjardins, "Les femmes de la diaspora canadienne-française."

33. Brunet, *Amanda Walker-Marchand (1868-1949)*.

34. Brault, *Ottawa, capitale du Canada de son origine à nos jours*.

35. Gravel, *Quelques aspects de la vie des Franco-Ontariens durant les années de la Grande Dépression (1930-1939)*.

36. Comeau, *The Role of the Unioin Saint Joseph du Canada*.

37. Grimard et Vallières, *Travailleurs et gens d'affaires canadiens-français en Ontario*.

38. English translation: "... the (Union) St. Joseph is opposed to all doctrines that are stained with socialism, that demand that the state become some sort of providence, which forces all citizens to carry the weight of a few, that wants to kill all individual initiative and is opposed to competition. Rather than, even in a moderate way, fall into theories with a socialist flavour, we must remember that Christ stated that there would always be the poor amongst us and that it was them whom he loved." (Leclerc cited in Grimard & Vallières, 195).

39. Tissot, "L'auto-détermination." *Revue du Nouvel-Ontario*, 95.

40. Coderre, "Femmes et santé, en français s'il vous-plaît." *Reflets: Revue ontaroise d'intervention sociale et communautaire*, 38-71.

41. Cardinal and Coderre, "Les francophones telles qu'elles sont: les Ontaroises et l'économie," *Revue du Nouvel-Ontario*, 151-181.

42. For more in-depth analysis of the transformations in the Franco-Ontarian women's movement see: Bouchard and Cardinal (1999), Cardinal (1992a, 1992b), Cardinal and Coderre (1990, 1991), Coderre (1995), Garceau (1996), Gérome (2000), Juteau-Lee (1983), Juteau-Lee and Robarts (1981), Mianda (1998), Michaud (1999), Pelletier (1980,1987), Proulx (1982).

43. Andrew et al., *Une communauté en colère*.

44. Browne and Landry, unpub. paper. "The 'Third Sector' and Employment."

45. Coderre and Dubois, "Solidarité et citoyenneté,"*Reflets: Revue ontaroise d'intervention sociale et communautaire*, 61-86.

46. For the effects of the programs of obligatory workfare for welfare recipients in the Franco-Ontarian community, see Michaud (2000).

47. Browne, "The Neo-Liberal Uses of the Social Economy," in *Social Economy. International Debates and Perspectives*.

48. Browne and Landry, 370.

49. Ninacs, *A Practitioner's Perspective on the Social Economy in Québec*, 31.

50. Ibid.

51. Kihumbi, "La Maison Verte: un cas réussi de développement économique communautaire," *Reflets: Revue ontaroise d'intervention sociale et communautaire*, 176-83.

52. Gérome, "La Marche mondiale des femmes en l'an 2000 en Ontario français," 192-96.

53. Besides the historical examples of cooperatives, such as the Caisses populaires and the Union des cultivateurs franco-ontariens, founded in 1945 as a farmers' union, and the projects mentioned above, in recent years other community economic development projects have begun. The Conseil de la Coopération de l'Ontario (CCO) was established in 1964 to encourage the development of the co-operative movement in French-speaking Ontario. Founded in 1995, the Centre d'avancement et de leadership en développement économique communautaire de la Huronie (CALDECH) is a CED project with the aim of integrating the Franco-Ontarians of Simcoe County into the regional economy. In Ottawa, since 1998, the Centre d'intégration, de formation et de développement économique (CIFODE) exists to facilitate the social and economic integration of ethnic and racial minorities, especially women, into the local economy. This organization aims to help integrate immigrants, to develop CED projects, as well as training for job seekers. See also Bagaoui and Dennie (2002) for an anlysis of CED projects in North Eastern Ontario, both French and English language.

54. Though there are many new social practices being developed in French-speaking Ontario, in the past they have often not been documented. Since 1995, a journal called *Reflets, revue ontaroise d'intervention sociale et communautaire* has been produced jointly by the schools of social work at Laurentian University and the University of Ottawa. By encouraging researchers and social activists to write articles, more of these new practices are being documented and studied. For instance, one article (Coderre and Dubois, 2000) documented a number of creative projects in low-income neighbourhoods of Ottawa (Coderre and Dubois, 2000; Bagaoui and Dennie, 1999; Welch, 1999).

55. Menzies, *Whose Brave New World?* xv.

56. Ibid., 19.

57. McGrath et al., "Community Capacity: The Emperor's New Clothes," *Canadian Journal of Social Policy*, 14.

58. Barker, *Street-Level Democracy*.

59. Ibid.

60. McGrath et al., 18

61. Langdon, *Global Poverty*.

62. Burbach, *Socialism is Dead*, 18.

Bibliography

Andrew, C., C. Archibald, F. Caloren and D. Serge. *Une communauté en colère. La grève contre Amoco Fabrics à Hawkesbury.* Hull: Éditions Asticou, 1986.

Bagaoui, R. and D. Dennie. "Le développement économique communautaire: nouveau départ pour le mouvement associatif Franco-Ontarien?" *Reflets: Revue ontaroise d'intervention sociale et communautaire* 1, (1999): 75-94.

————. "Les facteurs de réussite des organisations du développement économique communautaire du nord-est de l'Ontario." *Revue du Nouvel-Ontario, 27,* (2002): 123-50.

Barker, J. *Street-Level Democracy.* Toronto: Between the Lines, 1999.

Barrera, M. "Political Participation and Social Exclusion of the Popular Sectors in Chile." In *Markets and Democracy in Latin America: Conflict or Convergence?*edited by P. Oxhorn and P. Starr. Lynne Rienner Publishers, 1999.

Bouchard, L. et L. Cardinal. "Conditions de possibilités des services en français en Ontario dans les domaines de la santé et de services sociaux: un enjeu pour les femmes." *Reflets, Revue ontaroise d'intervention sociale et communautaire* 5, no. 2 (1999): 111-122.

Brault, L. *Ottawa, capitale du Canada de son origine à nos jours.* Ottawa: Éditions de l'Université d'Ottawa, 1942.

Brunet, L. *Amanda Walker-Marchand (1868-1949): Une féministe.* 1992.

Browne, P. L. and P. Landry. "The 'Third Sector' and Employment." Unpublished paper. Ottawa: Canadian Centre for Policy Alternatives, 1995.

Browne, P. L. "The Neo-Liberal Uses of the Social Economy: Non-Profit Organizations and Workfare in Ontario." In *Social Economy: International Debates and Perspectives,* edited by Eric Shragge and Jean-Marc Fontan. Montréal: Black Rose Books, 2000.

Burbach, R. "Socialism is Dead, Long Live Socialism." *NACLA Report on the Americas* 31, no. 3 (1997).

Burbach, R., O. Nunez and B. Kagarlitsky. *Globalization and its Discontents: The Rise of Postmodern Socialisms.* London: Pluto Press, 1997.

C'est le 'temps, groupe. "Se prendre en main." *Revue du Nouvel-Ontario,* no. 3 (1981) : 110-14.

Cardinal, L. "Théoriser la double spécificité des Franco-Ontariennes." In *Relevons le défi! Actes du colloque sur l'intervention féministe dans le nord-est de l'Ontario,* 177-88, edited by M-L. Garceau. Sudbury, ON, 1992a.

Cardinal, L. "La recherche sur les femmes francophones vivant en milieu minoritaire: un questionnement sur le féminisme." *Recherches féministes* 5, no. 1 (1992b) : 5-29.

Cardinal, L. et C. Coderre. "Les francophones telles qu'elles sont: les Ontaroises et l'économie." *La revue du Nouvel-Ontario* no. 12, (1990a) : 151-81.

Coderre, C. et M. Dubois. "Solidarité et citoyenneté : initiatives pour contrer la pauvreté chez les francophones dans Ottawa-Carleton." *Reflets: Revue ontaroise d'intervention sociale et communautaire 6,* no. 2 (2000) : 61-86.

Coderre, C. "Femmes et santé, en français s'il vous-plaît." *Reflets: Revue ontaroise d'intervention sociale et communautaire* 1 no. 2 (1995) : 38-71.

Collins, J. and J. Lear. *Chile's Free Market Miracle: A Second Look.* Oakland, CA: Food First Books, 1995.

Comeau, G. "The role of the Unioin Saint Joseph du Canada in the Organization of the Association canadienne-française d'Ontario." MA Thesis, University of Montreal, 1982.

Dennie, D. "Entrevue avec Éthel Côté, Directrice générale du Conseil de la coopération de l'Ontario." *Reflets: Revue ontaroise d'intervention sociale et communautaire* 5, no. 1 (1999a) : 18-25.

Dennie, D. "Je refuse de laisser mourir mon village." *Reflets: Revue ontaroise d'intervention sociale et communautaire* 5, no. 1 (1999b) : 15-28.

Desjardins, M. *Les femmes de la diaspora canadienne-française. Brève histoire de la FNFCF de 1914 à 1991.* Ottawa: Fédération nationale des femmes canadiennes-françaises 1991.

Garceau, M. "Bénévolat des femmes vieillissantes à l'aube de l'an 2000." *Reflets: Revue ontaroise d'intervention sociale et communautaire* 2, no. 2 (1996) : 58-81.

Gérome, M. "La Marche mondiale des femmes en l'an 2000 en Ontario français." *Reflets: Revue ontaroise d'intervention sociale et communautaire* 6, no. 1 (2000) : 192-96.

Gravel, J. *Quelques aspects de la vie des Franco-Ontariens durant les années de la Grande Dépression (1930-1939).* Thèse de maîtrise, Toronto, Université York, 1980.

Grimard, J. et G. Vallières. *Travailleurs et gens d'affaires canadiens-français en Ontario,* Montréal: Éditions Études Vivantes, 1986.

Harris, R. "The Global Context of Contemporary Latin American Affairs." In *Capital, Power and Inequality in Latin America*, edited by S. Halebsky and R. Harris, 299-300. Boulder: Westview Press, 1995.

Jelin, E. "Toward a Culture of Participation and Citizenship: Challenges for a More Equitable World." In *Cultures of Politics / Politics of Culture: Re-visioning Latin American Social Movements*, edited by S. Alvarez, E. Dagnino and A. Escobar. Boulder: Westview Press, 1998.

Juteau-Lee, D. "Ontarois et Québécois: Relations hors-frontières?" In *Du continent perdu à l'archipel retrouvé: le Québec et l'Amerique francaise*, edited by D. R. Louder and E. Waddel. Québec: Les presses de l'Université Laval, 1983.

Juteau-Lee, D. et B. Roberts. "Ethnicity and Femininity: (d') après nos expériences." *Revue canadienne des études ethniques* 8, no. 1 (1981) : 1-23.

Kihumbi, M. "La Maison Verte: un cas réussi de développement économique communautaire." *Reflets: Revue ontaroise d'intervention sociale et communautaire* 5, no. 1 (1999) : 176-183.

Langdon, S. *Global Poverty; Democracy and North-South Change.* Toronto: Garamond Press, 1999.

Larraechea, I. et M. Nyssens. "L'économie solidaire, un autre regard sur l'économie populaire au Chili." In *L'économie solidaire, une perspective internationale*, edited by J-L. Laville. Paris: Declée de Brouwer, 1994.

Lewis, Mike. "Front Commun. DEC et économie sociale: tri des notions fondamentales." *Making Waves* 15, no. 1 (2004).

McGrath, S., K. Moffatt, U. George and B. Lee. "Community Capacity: The Emperor's New Clothes." *Canadian Journal of Social Policy* 44 (1999) : 9-23.

Menzies, Heather. *Whose Brave New World?* Toronto: Between the Lines, 1996.

Mianda, G. "Etre une immigrante noire africaine francophone à Toronto: vécu et perception des rapports de genre." *Reflets: Revue ontaroise d'intervention sociale et communautaire* 4, no. 1 (1998) : 34-52.

Michaud, J. "Les femmes francophones et le travail obligatoire: un enjeu pour l'économie sociale." *Reflets: Revue ontaroise d'intervention sociale et communautaire* 5, no. 1 95-113.

Morales-Gómez, D., ed. *Transnational Social Policies. The New Development Challenges of Globalization.* Ottawa: International Development Research Centre, 1999.

Ninacs, William A. *A Practitioner's Perspective on the Social Economy in Québec.* Victoriaville: Human Resources Development Canada, 1998.

Petrella, R. *Le bien commun.* Bruxelles: Éditions Labour, 1995.

Powell, F. and D. Guerin. *Civil Society and Social Policy. Voluntarism in Ireland.* Dublin: A and A Farmer, 1997.

Proulx, P. *La part des femmes il faut le dire.* Ottawa: La Fédération des femmes canadiennes-françaises, 1982.

Quesnel, L. "Les nouveaux rôles des villes dans le contexte de la mondialisation." In *Les villes mondiales, Y a-t-il une place pour le Canada?* edited by A. Caroline et al., 131-40. Ottawa: Presses de l'Universite d'Ottawa, 1999.

Quiróz, T. and D. Palma. "Chili." In *Community Development Around the World: Practice, Theory, Research, Training,* edited by C. Hubert. Toronto: University of Toronto Press, 1997.

Rebick, Judy. *Imagine Democracy.* Toronto: Stoddart, 2000.

Roberts, W. and S. Brandum. *Get A Life.* Toronto: Get A Life Publishing, 1995.

Saul, John Ralston. *Reflections of a Siamese Twin. Canada at the End of the Twentieth Century.* Penguin, 1997.

Tissot, G. "L'auto-détermination." *Revue du Nouvel-Ontario* no. 3 (1981) : 91-96.

Vaillancourt, Y. and D. Labesse. "Projet d'équipe de recherche Économie social, santé et bien-être." Présenté au Conseil québécois de la recherche sociale (CQRS). Programmation 1997-2000, Cahiers du LAREPPS, 97-10. Montréal: UQAM, 1997.

Vaillancourt, Y., F. Aubry, M. D'Amours, C. Jetté, L. Thériault et Tremblay. *L'Économie sociale, santé et bien-être: la spécificité du modèle québécois au Canada.* Montréal: Cahiers du Labouratoire de recherche sur les pratiques et les politiques sociales, 2000.

Notes on Contributors

Gayle Broad led a participatory action research project with eight steelworkers from Algoma Steel Inc. in 1997-99 while completing her PhD at the School for Policy Studies at the University of Bristol, U.K. She is currently an Assistant Professor of Community Economic and Social Development at Algoma University College in Sault Ste. Marie.

Nicole Chaland has been working in community economic development, the women's movement and co-operative organizing for almost ten years. She is the founding member of Roofs and Roots Housing Co-op which is a model for urban sustainability and inclusive housing in her home town of Victoria, BC. She works at the Canadian CED Network and leads a project that provides peer learning support and resources to immigrant and refugee community leaders.

Paul Chege is Program Manager, Urban Planning and Development Program with Practical Action- Eastern African (formally Intermediate Technology Development Group). Main areas of work are focused on action research and implementing technology-focused approaches and processes to address pro-poor challenges in urban development.

Kathryn Church is Assistant Professor in the School of Disability at Ryerson where she teaches courses in community organizing and research methods. She also directs the research program for the Ryerson-RBC Institute for Disability Studies Research and Education. A strong ally of the survivor movement, Dr. Church spent ten years as an independent researcher doing projects with psychiatric survivor organizations engaged in knowledge development.

Melanie Conn is a long-time community activist who has been working in community economic development since the early 70s in Vancouver, British Columbia. Her experience in the women's movement and with co-operatives continues to ground her CED work in practice and with a focus on social change. Melanie is a program director and instructor at the Centre for Sustainable Community Development at Simon Fraser University as well as a certified co-op developer.

Jocelyn DeVance Taliaferro, is a professor of Social Work at the North Carolina State University. She has a PhD in Urban Affairs and Public Policy from University of Delaware. Her research focuses on welfare reform, community development, and the nonprofit sector. She has more than years practice experience in nonprofit organizations as volunteer, staff, consultant, executive director, and board member and chair. Dr. Taliaferro has also published in *Journal of Human Behaviour and the Social Environment* and *Journal of Family Social Work.*

Jean-Marc Fontan is a Professor in the Department of Sociology at Université du Québec à Montreal. He is a member of the Research Centre on Social Innovations (Centre de recherche sur les innovations sociales-CRISES) and he co-directs two large research networks: Community University Research Alliance on the Social Economy and Réseau québécois de recherche partenariale en économie sociale.

Pierre Hamel is Professor of Sociology at the Université de Montréal. He has written extensively on social movements, urban politics and local democracy. His current research includes a comparative analysis of city-regions in Canada.

Jill Hanley is a Montreal-based researcher and community organizer. Her work has concentrated on housing, immigration and labour rights, with an emphasis on migrants and multicultural neighbourhoods. She is currently completing a post-doctoral project with the Université Libre de Bruxelles

Raheemah Jabbar-Bey, MS, is a professor of Urban Affairs and Public Policy, University of Delaware, and Director of the Community-Based Development Training Program in the Center for Community Research and Service. She has a Masters Degree in Community Economic Development (CED) from Southern New Hampshire University. She is a nationally recognized practitioner and expert in community economic development with over 25 years field experience in Washington, DC, Columbus, Ohio and Kansas City, Missouri. Ms. Jabbar-Bey is a co-founder and the board chair of the CED Association of Delaware. She has been twice elected to the board of the National Congress for Community Economic Development as a Northeast region director.

Laura Lamb is a doctoral student of economics at the University of Manitoba. She is a researcher for the Manitoba Research Alliance on Community Economic Development in the New Economy. Her fields include community economic development, applied microeconomic theory, and industrial organization.

Andrea Levy holds a PhD in History from Concordia University in Montréal. In 2004, she completed a two-year post-doctoral fellowship in the sociology department at the Université de Montréal. A politically engaged independent scholar, she has published essays on a variety of subjects, including the New Left, the peace movement, the ecology movement, the work of French social theorist André Gorz, municipal politics and the social economy.

Jim Lotz was born in Liverpool, England. He came to Canada in 1954 after serving in the RAF and working as a trader in West Africa. Jim learned has learned about Canada by living in its urban centres as well as its hinterland. He began his research in community development in 1960 and his writing has appeared in a wide range of publications. He has taught courses on community development in several

Canadian universities and published several books on the subject, including *The Lichen Factor: The Quest for Community Development in Canada* and, with Gertrude Anne MacIntyre, *Sustainable People: A New Approach to Community Development*, both from CBU Press.

John Loxley is a Professor of Economics and Research Coordinator, Global Political Economy Program at the University of Manitoba. He specializes in International Money and Finance, International Development and Community Economic Development and has published extensively in these areas. He chaired the board of SEED Winnipeg, a micro financing and community economic development agency working mainly in the inner-city of Winnipeg. He was also Chair of the board of the North-South Institute, Ottawa. Since 2002, he has been Principal Investigator of the Manitoba Research Alliance into Community Economic Development and the New Economy.

Michael Lyons, architect, planner and geographer, is now Professor of Urban Development and coordinator of developing country research at London South Bank University. Her research interests and consultancy work focus on urban poverty and governance, in particular migration, participatory development and the informal sector.

Gertrude Anne MacIntyre is the Founding Director of the Community Economic Development Institute, and the Master of Business Administration [MBA(CED)] program at Cape Breton University. In her research and writing she has sought to reinterpret the politics of education and community economic development, searching for ways to link the two solitudes. Her publications include *Active Partners: Education and Local Development*, 1995, *Perspectives on Communities: A Community Economic Development Roundtable*, 1998, and co-author with Jim Lotz of *Sustainable People: A New Approach to Community Development*, 2003, all from CBU Press, along with several papers and journal articles on CED.

Michael Majale, formerly with Intermediate Technology Development Group (now Practical Action), is a lecturer in the School of Architecture, Planning and Landscape, University of Newcastle upon Tyne. His research interests and consultancy work focus on improving the lives and livelihoods of slum dwellers in the developing world.

Richard Morin is a professor in the urban studies department of the Université du Québec à Montréal. His teaching and his research concerns social aspects of cities as well as community and local development. For twenty years, he has carried out many studies about community economic development particularly in Montreal.

David Newhouse is Chair and Associate Professor, Department of Indigenous Studies, Trent University, Peterborough, Ontario, Canada. He is Onondaga from the Six Nations of the Grand River Territory in Ontario.

Mark Roseland is Director of the Centre for Sustainable Community Development at Simon Fraser University in Vancouver, Canada, and a professor in SFU's Department of Geography. His publications include *Toward Sustainable Communities: Resources for Citizens and Their Governments* (New Society Publishers, 2005).

Linda Savory-Gordon conducted participatory action research with eight steelworkers from Algoma Steel Inc. from 1997 to 1999 to investigate spillover effects of worker ownership, while working toward her PhD at the School for Policy Studies at the University of Bristol. She is an Associate Professor in Social Welfare teaching courses, which are part of the Community Economic and Social Development program at Algoma University College in Sault Ste. Marie.

Luba Serge, PhD, is a Montreal based researcher and consultant. Luba has performed and has published extensive research focused on supportive housing, homelessness, affordable housing and neighbourhood revitalization.

Bahira Sherif-Trask, PhD, is a professor of Individual and Family Studies, University of Delaware and is a Policy Scientist in the Center for Community Research and Service. She has a PhD in Cultural Anthropology from the University of Pennsylvania. Her research focuses on the relationship between gender, work, economics and family, as well as issues of cultural diversity. She recently co-edited *The Greenwood Encyclopedia of Women's Issues Worldwide* and has published in numerous journals including *Journal of Family Issues, Qualitative Inquiry, Anthropology Today* and *Journal of Teaching About Families and Marriage: Innovations in Family Science*.

Eric Shragge teaches in the School of Community and Public Affairs at Concordia University, Montreal, where he directs the Graduate Diploma Program in Community Economic Development. His most recent books include *Activism and Social Change- Lessons for Community and Local Organizing* (Broadview Press, 2003), which will be published in French in 2006 by Ecosociété. His areas of interest include community organizing and issues related to the rights of immigrant workers. He is active in several organizations in Montreal including La Cooperative Maison Verte and the Immigrant Workers Centre.

Michael Toye is Community Learning Program Director with the Canadian CED Network. Prior to CCEDNet, he was a member of and helped develop two worker co-operatives that provide research, consulting and training in fields related to community economic development and the social economy. He lives in Warwick, Québec.

David Welch is presently an Associate Professor at the School of Social Work of the University of Ottawa. Until 2002, he was President of the Social Planning Council of Ottawa, an organization active in doing social research on the most excluded sectors of society in Ottawa. Since July 2001 he is one of the Ontario representatives on the National Council of Welfare, a federal government advisory board on issues of poverty. He continues to write on the social development of his own community, that of the Franco-Ontarians, with special emphasis on the third sector. More recently he has been studying the place of civil society food security and democracy in the urban context.

Margaret Wilder, PhD, is a professor of Social Policy in Urban Affairs and Public Policy at the University of Delaware. She also serves as the Executive Director of the Urban Affairs Association, an international, interdisciplinary organization focused on urban issues. She received her PhD in urban geography and planning from the University of Michigan. Dr. Wilder has a long and distinguished record of research on urban development, housing and community development. Her research projects have been funded by the Annie E. Casey Foundation, the Ford Foundation and the Lilly Endowment.

Wanda Wuttunee, acting head of Native Studies, University of Manitoba, focuses on effective economic governance in all its many forms. CED is one strategy in which Aboriginal peoples are engaged. Other economic activities cover a range of strategies from working with the land to information technology.